Food Security: Theory, Policy, and Perspectives from Asia and the Pacific Rim

Food Security: Theory, Policy, and Perspectives from Asia and the Pacific Rim

Edited by
Anthony H. Chisholm
Rodney Tyers
Australian National University

LexingtonBooks
D.C. Heath and Company
Lexington, Massachusetts
Toronto

Library of Congress Cataloging in Publication Data
Main entry under title:

Food security: Theory, policy, and perspectives from Asia and the Pacific rim.

Papers from the East-West Resource Systems Institute's research program on food security in Asia and the Pacific.
Includes index.
1. Food supply—Asia. 2. Agriculture and state—Asia. I. Chisholm, Anthony H. II. Tyers, Rodney. III. East-West Resource Systems Institute.
HD9016.A2F66 338.1'9'5 81-48396
ISBN 0-669-05356-2 AACR2

Published simultaneously in Canada

Printed in the United States of America

International Standard Book Number: 0-669-05356-2

Library of Congress Catalog Card Number: 81-48396

Contents

List of Figures

List of Tables

Foreword

The problem of sustaining adequate food supplies in countries dependent on fluctuating domestic production and volatile international commodity markets has long been a focus for policy analysis in Asia and the Pacific. The maintenance of a stable domestic food supply through secure access to international markets is not sufficient, however, to provide food security to all consumers, especially those in developing countries. A complex set of interactions determines the degree to which policies are able either to stabilize national food supplies or improve access to food by vulnerable groups. Thus an improved understanding of the behavioral patterns of national and international food systems is needed so that governments may realize the potential benefits from increased international cooperation and so that those countries most vulnerable to food scarcity might be protected through effective policies.

The East-West Resource Systems Institute engages in research on problems—regarding, in particular, food, energy, and raw materials—that are of mutual interest to a wide variety of scholars and practitioners in Asia and the Pacific. Interaction occurs through direct investments in research output by international groups of academics and policy administrators and by cooperation and communication between researchers in interested countries throughout the region. As part of a larger Food Systems Project, the institute has established a research program on food security in Asia and the Pacific, designed to contribute to the formulation of more effective international and domestic policies to achieve food security. As a result, a series of research papers by authors from a number of Asian and Pacific nations has been completed. The chapters in this book are a selection from that series, and they treat the major aspects of food-security theory and policy.

The work of the program on food security has been financed in part through Cooperative Agreement No. 58-3J22-0-0026 with the International Economics Division, Economics and Statistics Service, U.S. Department of Agriculture. The contributions of participants, as well as the interest of cooperating institutions in Asian and Pacific countries, in facilitating participation by their staff members are greatly appreciated. It is hoped that the results of their efforts in this important field will help in the achievement of real improvements in security of access to food supplies throughout the Asia-Pacific region.

Harrison Brown
Director
East-West Resource Systems Institute

Preface

This book has its origin in a program of cooperative research on food security in Asia and the Pacific organized at the East-West Resource Systems Institute in Hawaii. The program has centered on research activities carried out at the East-West Center by staff, visiting Fellows, research interns, and graduate students sponsored by the Resource Systems Institute. The work discussed by Anthony Chisholm in chapter 4, James Roumasset in chapter 6, John Dixon and Rodney Tyers in chapter 9, John Dixon in chapter 11, and Rodney Tyers and Anthony Chisholm in chapter 14 has been carried out in Hawaii as part of this cooperative research program.

An additional important element of the program has been the participation of eminent scholars and policy analysts from Asian and Pacific Rim countries whose work has focused on food security and commodity-market-stability issues. To facilitate this cooperation, two international conferences were held at the East-West Center. The first—the Working Group Meeting on Food Security in Asia and the Pacific, held June 18–30, 1979—brought to Hawaii fifty participants from eighteen Asian and Pacific Rim countries. The chapters by Shlomo Reutlinger, Ralph Lattimore, Alexander Sarris, Soegeng Amat, Neville Edirisinghe, Howarth Bouis and Robert Herdt, and Somporn Hanpongpandh, all began as draft papers presented at this meeting. All chapters have been substantially revised and updated prior to their inclusion, and the chapters by Shlomo Reutlinger and Alexander Sarris were prepared, more recently, specifically for this book.

The second meeting—the Workshop on Trans-Pacific Food Commodity Trade held in Hawaii July 21–25, 1980—was organized to review the international and national policy components of the food-security research being carried out at the Resource Systems Institute, to chart the closing phase of the program, and to promote further exchange between food-policy analysts in Pacific Rim countries. On the recommendation of Professor Kenzo Hemmi, who participated in the 1979 Working Group Meeting, Japan was represented in the 1980 workshop by Professor Saburo Yamada, who subsequently agreed to assist with the translation of his earlier paper on Japan's food security. The translation appears with the kind permission of Nihon Keizai Chosa Kyogikai (the Japan Economic Research Institute), as chapter 10 of this book.

We are grateful to the East-West Resource Systems Institute for the extensive support provided in Hawaii to both the research and the conference components of the food-security program. Without the enthusiastic participation of Harrison Brown, the institute director, and Bruce Koppel, the Food Systems Project leader, a successful program would not have been possible. Thanks are also due to the U.S. Department of Agriculture for its financial support of the program and, in particular, to Charles Hanrahan, assistant director for research, and Carmen Nohre, chief of the Asia branch, both of the Department of Agriculture, International Economics Division, Economics and Statistics Service.

Thanks are also due to the following individuals who participated in the 1979 Working Group Meeting and the 1980 workshop and who provided valuable comments on the work described in the chapters of this book: Mohiuddin Alamgir, Mohammed Amin, Kym Anderson, Alfredo Gutierrez, Kenzo Hemmi, Alex McCalla, Gil Rodriguez, Young Kun Shim, Soe Lin, Jesus Tanchanco, Pranee Tinakorn, Robert Thompson, and Anthony Zwart. Others who have read individual chapters and provided valuable comments and suggestions are cited, where applicable, in each chapter.

We are especially grateful to John Dixon for his support and major contributions during the latter stages of the project to the preparation of Part II.

Finally, no international cooperative research program could be successful without the research assistance of graduate students and the contributions of support staff. Valuable research assistance was provided by Jan Hiranaka, Thammanun Pongsrikul, Suthad Setboonsarng, Hideki Uehara, Ik Soon Im, Ann Miyashiro, Peter Kuhbach, and Ray Yamate. Kajorn Howard assisted in the planning and management of the 1979 Working Group Meeting and the 1980 workshop. Our special thanks go to Barbara Yount for valuable editorial assistance and to Lorna Emdy, who worked so hard and competently in typing and assembling the manuscript.

1 Food Security: An Introduction and Overview

Anthony H. Chisholm and
Rodney Tyers

This chapter provides an introduction and overview of the subject matter of the book. First, trends in international food markets and Asian and Pacific Rim trade and economic interdependence are reviewed. Second, the nature and causes of food insecurity are discussed and the major international and national policy instruments for its alleviation are outlined. Third, each of the chapters in the book is briefly described so the reader may quickly obtain an overview of the general framework of the book and some appreciation of the major results and conclusions.

Trends in International Food Markets and Trade among Asian and Pacific Rim Countries

International markets in staple foods have changed markedly over the past twenty years. Dependence on food trade has increased. The volume of the world grain trade has grown at an average annual rate of 5.5 percent, compared with a 3.5 percent annual growth rate in world grain production (table 1–1). While population growth has been a significant determinant of increased demand for food exports, rising incomes have played a more important role. In particular, rising incomes in the industrialized, centrally planned, and middle-income developing countries have led to a large increase in the demand for livestock products from grain-fed animals. This has had a profound effect on international trade and food security. Since the 1950s the share of global grain production fed to livestock has doubled, to 40 percent. Livestock now consume more grain than is consumed by the 1.4 billion people living in the world's low-income countries.[1]

While the share of world grain trade between industrialized countries has remained constant at about 40 percent, the dependence of developing and centrally planned countries on imports from the Western industrialized world has markedly increased. In 1976 the developing countries' cereal imports from the industrialized countries represented 28 percent of world cereal trade, compared with 18 percent in the late 1950s.[2] Cereal exports from the United States alone to the developing countries accounted for 19

Table 1–1
International Trade in Cereals: Net Imports to Regions and Selected Countries, 1951–1979

Region/Country	*1951–1956*	*1957–1962*	*1963–1968*	*1969–1974*	*1975–1979*
Africa	.04	1.4	3.3	4.9	11.3
Americas	−25.7	−36.6	−57.9	−66.2	−100.4
Central	−.2	1.5	1.0	3.4	6.4
North	−23.1	−35.6	−55.5	−65.4	−102.0
Canada	−9.5	−9.5	−13.0	−14.3	−16.7
United States	−13.6	−26.1	−41.5	−51.1	−85.3
South	−2.4	−2.5	−4.4	−4.2	−4.8
Asia	6.3	12.9	28.1	38.2	50.6
East	3.8	4.2	15.7	23.3	33.4
China	−.6	−.8	4.6	4.5	8.2
Japan	4.0	4.5	10.2	15.9	21.6
South Korea[a]	.4	.5	.9	2.9	3.6
South	3.3	5.7	9.9	5.9	5.7
Bangladesh	—	—	.9	1.7	1.4
India	2.3	3.9	7.5	3.3	2.8
Nepal	—	—	−.3	−.2	−.1
Pakistan	.3	1.0	.8	.2	.4
Sri Lanka	.7	.8	1.0	.9	1.1
Southeast	−1.1	−.9	−1.4	−.2	−.2
Burma	−1.4	−1.6	−1.1	−.5	−.5
Indonesia	.6	1.0	.8	1.4	2.5
Malaysia	.7	.9	.8	.9	1.1
Philippines	.3	.4	.8	.9	.8
Thailand	−1.3	−1.6	−2.6	−3.0	−4.1
Europe	23.2	30.3	30.6	27.4	32.4
Oceania	−3.2	−3.9	−6.9	−8.6	−11.2
Australia	−3.5	−4.6	−7.2	−8.9	−11.5
USSR	—	—	.1	2.1	16.5
Total world imports	46.8	67.7	100.5	127.6	208.0
Total world production	665.7	909.1	1074.8	1285.3	1495.0

Note: Net imports are annual five-year averages measured in million metric tons. Net exports are listed as negative. All data are drawn from FAO Trade Year Book: 1953–1979. The category "cereals" includes wheat and wheat flour, rye, barley, oats, maize, rice, sorghum, and millet.

[a]The statistics for South Korea in 1951–1958 include North Korea.

percent of world cereal trade in 1976. These trends have continued, with Organization of Petroleum Exporting Countries (OPEC) absorbing about 60 percent of incremental world wheat exports between 1976 and 1979. Grain imports have also continued to rise in a number of Asian countries, especially in Indonesia, China, Japan, and South Korea (see table 1–1).

Further important changes in the world food market became evident in the 1970s. Of these, perhaps the most important is the increase in the volatility of international cereal prices.[3] Johnson (1975) argues that the fluctuations in global cereal production in the early 1970s were no greater in magnitude than those of the mid-1960s, yet their impact on prices was vastly greater. This is partly attributable to the lower grain stockpiles held by the major exporters at the beginning of the decade. But Johnson (1975, p. 825) gives as the principal reason that "a much larger percentage of the world's grain production and consumption in the 1970s than in the 1960s occurred within the framework of policies to achieve internal price stability through the control of imports and/or exports." In the 1970s approximately one half the world's grain use occurred in the Soviet Union, the rest of Europe, and China.

It is now well known that countries that seek to achieve a high degree of price stability for their own consumers and producers by varying net trade exacerbate world price variability. Johnson argues effectively that the stronger commitment in the 1970s by the Soviet Union and China to domestic stabilization contributed significantly to the greater instability of international grain prices. However, as shown by Tyers and Chisholm in chapter 14, the coefficients of variation of domestic prices for a number of countries reveal that only the United States and Canada have permitted domestic grain prices to fluctuate to the same degree as international trading prices. Most other countries—developed and developing alike—have generally maintained more stable domestic prices, either through variable import or export levies, other nontariff trade policies, or complete government monopolies on trade.[4]

The combination of increased world cereal-market volatility, increased dependence of developing countries on grain imports, and a strong commitment by governments in the developing countries to stabilize domestic prices and consumption, raises important issues with respect, for example, to fluctuating foreign exchange requirements and high costs of domestic food policies. As Donaldson and Lewis (1981) indicate, this is particularly true of the rapidly growing middle-income developing countries, since the poorest of countries are relatively self-sufficient at prevailing levels of effective demand, and most of their food-grain imports are still obtained on concessional terms. Many of the world's rapidly growing developing countries are to be found in the western Pacific, especially those dependent on imports from the relatively volatile international rice market.

In the light of some general trends toward economic interdependence among Asian and Pacific Rim countries and proposals for more formal relationships, it is pertinent to consider the corresponding trend in interdependency with respect to trade in food.[5] An analysis of the international trade matrices for food commodities in the years 1970 and 1976 by Tyers (1982) shows that, while the degree of interdependence among Asian and

Pacific Rim countries declined slightly between these years, the contribution toward this interdependence due to trade in the principal food and feed grains declined markedly. The share of rice, wheat, and coarse-grain exports from Pacific Rim countries that were directed to other countries within the Pacific Rim fell from 51, 39, and 49 percent to 34, 28, and 24 percent, respectively, between 1970 and 1976. At the same time, the share of all food exports from these countries to others within the Pacific Rim fell from 52 percent to 43 percent.[6]

The centers of growth in world demand for the staple foods were outside Asia and the Pacific Rim. Only the Association of Southeast Asian Nations (ASEAN) increased their cereal interdependence, principally as a result of growth in demand within the group for Thai rice. There has, however, been a significant increase in trans-Pacific trade in livestock products and processed foods and feeds, which has limited the decline in the overall level of ASEAN, Pacific Rim, and Asia-Pacific Rim interdependence in total food production and trade.

While trends toward overall Pacific region economic interdependence may lead to formal agreements enhancing the security of access to some food markets—particularly livestock products and processed foods—important market forces affecting the prices of the staple cereals will probably continue to stem from growth and fluctuations in excess demand outside the region. It is important, therefore, to evaluate the effects future trends and fluctuations in cereal prices are likely to have on food policies in Asian developing countries and the extent to which adverse effects on economic welfare can be traced to their food policies or to the policies adopted by industrialized countries within and outside the region.

On the Concept and Causes of Food Insecurity and Policy Alternatives

Food security has become a clearly enunciated and central policy goal for most developing countries only within the last decade, although the problem of attaining an adequate food supply is as old as mankind. This now-widespread concern was kindled by the 1972–1974 world food crisis, which saw unprecedented increases in the international trading prices of staple foods. In response to this crisis, the World Food Conference was convened in Rome in 1974 under the auspices of the United Nations, and the issue of food security was the dominant theme of the conference. The concept of food security and the means of its attainment have many interpretations.[7] Some analysts put emphasis on the role of national and international stockpiles of grain. Others advocate that each country should strive toward self-sufficiency in food production, while still others see the dismantling of barriers to food trade as leading to improved food-market stability and efficiency.

The broadest interpretation and ultimate goal of food security can be summarized as the provision of "an adequate supply of food for all people at all times." The complete attainment of this goal would require major changes in the structure of the world economy, not the least of which would be the elimination of poverty.[8] For the purposes of this book, a less ambitious concept for food security is adopted. *Food security* may be defined as the ability of countries to meet target consumption levels.[9] The choice of the target consumption levels is perhaps the most important aspect of a developing country's food policy, and it can be viewed under two time frames. First, there is the problem of chronic and persistent malnutrition that is caused by low productive capacity and secular problems of poverty. This constitutes a long-term problem that can be overcome only by a steady continuing rise in productive capacity and the real income levels of the poor. Selected aspects of this problem are analyzed and discussed in later chapters,[10] but we do not attempt to comprehensively address the problem of chronic malnutrition caused by persistent poverty.

The second problem—and one that is a major focus of this book—is that of short-term variability of entitlements of consumers to food. Food insecurity in this sense is ultimately a problem that stems from real income fluctuations that affect the ability of people to command adequate food through legal means. The basic causes of real income fluctuations and individuals' consequent entitlements to food are production and price fluctuations in both the food and nonfood sectors.[11] For the urban population, fluctuations in staple food prices are usually the major cause of a food-security problem. These price fluctuations arise from year-to-year fluctuations in the domestic or world harvest or from more irregular natural disasters such as floods, chronic droughts, earthquakes, wars as well as from changes in government food policies.

In rural areas, there is an additional important dimension to the food-security problem. Farm household incomes are directly affected as a result of fluctuations in their own production that stem from climatic uncertainty. Further, nonfarm rural households (landless rural laborers, for example) are indirectly affected as a result of fluctuations in farm production and incomes. Rural people will, on occasion, suffer simultaneously from high food prices and low incomes. Historically, food-security policy has been framed in terms of meeting urban food demands. Governments in developing countries appear to have been powerless to provide rural households with adequate income supplements, or purchasing power, at times of crop failure.

Food-security problems and policies to combat them can be viewed from a world, regional, national, village, and even household perspective. The focus of this book is on food-security problems at the international and national levels, with particular reference to Asian and Pacific Rim countries. The major international and national approaches to alleviating the food insecurity problem are as follows: (1) grain stockpiles, (2) trade policies, (3) financial approaches to alleviate the foreign-exchange constraint, (4) consumption adjustment in the developed countries, and (5) interventions in the capital market and in the pricing and distribution of food for vulnerable groups.

The first two policy approaches—grain stockpiles and trade policies—are comprehensively dealt with later in the text and will not be discussed here. The use of financial approaches to alleviate the foreign-exchange constraint has been treated in depth by researchers elsewhere, and we do not analyze these policy instruments. Historically, the variability of import *volume*—and not import prices—explains most of the variability of the food-import bill for most developing countries. Typically, only one-fourth of the variability of the import bill is explained by world price movements (Valdes and Siamwalla 1981a). Two main approaches to alleviating the foreign-exchange constraint have been proposed. First are variable food-aid programs like the grain-insurance scheme proposed by Gale Johnson (1977). One possible drawback of this scheme is that it requires precise and promptly available information on the size of domestic harvest, which is the main parameter in triggering the release of reserve grain. But in many developing countries, there are acute problems in collating accurate information on the state of the harvest. Second is the financial food-facility approach. One approach would be to enlarge the scope of existing compensatory financing schemes such as those adopted by the International Monetary Fund (IMF) or the European Community's STABEX scheme so as to include the cost of cereal imports. Alternatively, a quite separate new facility could be established.

Since the natural shortfalls of food supplies relative to trends in one region of the world tend to be offset by surpluses in other regions, equal adjustment throughout the world to changes in aggregate food supply would spread food risk and minimize hardship. The unwillingness of governments in some industrialized and centrally planned countries to permit their consumers to share in this adjustment imposes an undue burden on other countries. Perhaps the most important potential means by which consumption adjustment could be made in developed countries in years of poor world cereal harvests would be to directly divert grain as an input to livestock, or meat production, to grain for direct human consumption. The safety valve is the capital inventory tied up in livestock that could be run down a little in years of poor world cereal harvests.

To the extent that food insecurity is ultimately a problem that stems from real income fluctuations, it can be argued that the first-best solution is a reliance on the capital market. There are differing views on the degree of imperfection of the capital market facing households in developing countries.[12] But most analysts claim that the capital market would be a costly means of attaining food security. A number of low-income countries have subsidized and attempted to stabilize retail food prices to provide food security for urban consumers. While such programs have had some success in benefiting urban consumers, they appear to have been relatively costly to governments and to have imposed implicit costs on rural households (Valdes and Siamwalla 1981b).

Organization

The chapters comprising this book fall into three broad groups. Part I analyzes various aspects of general theory and policy issues relating to food security. Part II presents case studies and perspectives on food security in four Asian countries. In part III, the four chapters each describe the approach taken in empirical research work on a food-security problem and present results from quantitative analysis.

Part I: Food Security—General Theory and Policy Issues

The chapter by Shlomo Reutlinger challenges the conventional wisdom that the best way to eliminate periodically recurring shortfalls in food consumption in developing countries is through extensive national and international stockpiling of grain. A stochastic simulation model of the grain sector of a hypothetical small, normally importing country is developed and used to investigate the consequences of a country pursuing alternative trade and stockpiling policies. The use of appropriate trade policies that would permit more flexible volumes of food trade is found to be a considerably more efficient means of attaining food security than is the accumulation of large buffer stocks. The resulting less-restrictive trade policies to achieve food security place the burden of adjustment on the foreign-exchange market. But even when the food-import bill becomes highly unstable, Reutlinger concludes that only modest levels of domestic buffer stocks are justified. In essence, it is cheaper for a food-importing developing country to store money, in the form of foreign-exchange reserves, than to store food.

The chapter by Ralph Lattimore examines the problem of world grain-market instability and food security from the view point of Canada, a major grain exporter. Instability in the world grain market is seen, in large part, as being caused by trade-policy interventions that most countries have made to insulate their domestic market from the supply and demand forces of the world grain market. In attaining greater domestic-price stability, the protective policies of the acting countries greatly increase instability in the world grain market. So long as these protective policies persist, larger grain stockpiles will be needed so as to overcome not only the world grain market instability caused by nature but also the man-made instability. As compared with an international reserve-stock scheme that would require a multilateral agreement, Lattimore points out that a supply-insurance program between one or two exporters and a number of grain-deficit countries, which would guarantee the availability of grain in times of crop shortfalls in importing countries, has the strength that it could be implemented on a bilateral basis. The implementation of such contracts is seen as being clearly superior to food-deficit countries striving to become self-sufficient in food production when this goal is quite inconsistent with comparative advantage and gains from trade.

In chapter 4, Anthony Chisholm surveys and critically evaluates the large body of theoretical research on the economic effects of price stabilization with a particular emphasis on the microeconomic foundations of the theory and the implications for real-world buffer-stock schemes. The practical experience with various government-controlled stockpiling schemes is then surveyed and found not to be encouraging for supporters of public storage programs who believe that a public authority can attain greater price stability than the private storage sector while earning normal profits on its operation.

A major shortcoming of most of the research on price stabilization is that the case for public-stockpiling operations is not based on the identification of specific sources of market failure in the private storage sector. Chisholm identifies two potential areas of market failure that may lead to excessive price instability. The first area of market failure relates to a possible divergence between social and private aversion to the risks inherent in holding large commodity stockpiles. The main conclusion is that in industrialized countries like the United States with highly developed capital markets and mature futures markets, the case for public stockpiling or subsidizing private stockpiling is weak on efficiency grounds. There is a stronger case for some public intervention in developing countries where capital markets are more imperfect, and futures markets usually do not exist. This conclusion lends theoretical support to the thrust of the simulation results presented by Reutlinger in chapter 2 that indicate that public stockpiling in excess of levels prevailing in a competitive storage market is a costly and inefficient means of attaining food security.

The second potential area of market failure relates to the complex question of whether or not speculative commodity markets collect, process, and disseminate information efficiently. A large section of the chapter is devoted to analyzing and discussing this issue. The main conclusion that emerges is that although some areas of market failure are found to exist, at least from a microeconomic perspective, there is no compelling evidence of excessive price instability as a result of major agricultural commodity markets in developed countries being poorly informed. To the extent that some areas of information market failure can be identified, the first-best course of government action is to ensure an optimal supply of information and not to attempt to take corrective action through public stockpiling.

In chapter 5, Alexander Sarris provides a rigorous theoretical analysis of public stockpiling in the presence of a private storage sector. Most of the voluminous theoretical literature on price stabilization completely ignores the existence of a private storage sector, thereby leaving unresolved the major issue of the reaction of the private trade to public intervention in grain markets through stockpiling. A striking result of Sarris's research, which has important implications for public policy, is that a private storage industry with many traders will carry a socially optimal level of stocks. In the presence of such private-storage trade, there is precisely one-to-one substitution between private and public stockpiling, and in this environment public stockpiling will be completely ineffective. If there is a less than one-to-one trade-off between private and public stocks, caused by, perhaps, a divergence between private and public discount rates or a public authority having superior information to that possessed by private traders, a case for public intervention can be made. Sarris interprets the existing scanty empirical findings as suggesting that the trade-off between public and private stockpiling is significantly smaller than one-to-one and that this implies that the private-storage sector does not behave as an ideal many-trader market. In our view, however, it is difficult to be confident about the latter conclusion since the empirical findings relate to periods when public storage was often at levels substantially above the many-trader competitive optimum. If a one-to-one substitution between private and public stockpiling does exist, it would be found only when aggregate stocks (that is, private plus public) did not exceed the competitive optimum level.

Chapter 6 by James Roumasset, represents a departure from other chapters in that it addresses the problem of food security primarily from the micro perspective of the rural household. This is an important problem, not least because it appears that famines are largely a rural phenomenon. Roumasset suggests that food insecurity more generally is also largely a rural phenomenon. In particular, the vagaries of nature will occasionally cause rural households to be exposed both to high food prices and to low incomes or entitlements. Sources of rural food insecurity are classified in the chapter according to whether they affect the price, the household's production, or the household's purchasing power.

Roumasset analyzes both short- and long-run rural food-security issues since he believes that from a policy perspective problems of food security rooted in short-term fluctuations cannot be separated from the problems of rural poverty and the possibility of a stagnation or secular decline in real wages in some countries. A part of the chapter is therefore devoted to an examination of the impact of institutions and institutional change on real wages in the rural sector. An additional focus is on some of the costs of stabilization and the potential conflict that scarce government revenue that is used for stabilizing short-term fluctuations may replace investments in long-term poverty reduction. Roumasset provides examples, however, of some stabilization policies that may also contribute to the reduction of poverty in the long run.

Part II: Perspectives on Food Security in Asian Countries

In chapter 7 Soegeng Amat reviews the experience of Indonesia in promoting national food security. The central plank of Indonesia's food-security policy has been the Rice Stabilization Program administered through its National Logistics Agency (BULOG). Rice is the single most important commodity in the economy of Indonesia, having been given a weight of 30 percent in the overall cost of living index. Although rice production occupies one-third of the total cropped area of Indonesia, annual rice imports have varied between 1.2 and 2.0 million tons, making Indonesia the largest rice-importing country in the world. This chapter provides a detailed account of all facets of the Rice Stabilization Program, including the procedures for setting floor and ceiling prices, the domestic procurement scheme, and the operation of the National Stock.

The historical record of food security in Sri Lanka is analyzed in chapter 8 by Neville Edirisinghe. Beginning with wartime rationing requirements, post-independence governments in Sri Lanka continued to administer rice and wheat imports and supply rice rations as part of a comprehensive social-welfare program. The results have been impressive. Average nutritional levels are higher than in most other countries with similar low levels of per-capita income, and, most importantly, a very equitable distribution of consumption has been achieved. While the historical record of Sri Lanka shows that a government-implemented food-security system can have major impacts on food consumption, the costs of such a program are very high. Recent changes in government food policy have in part been in response to the rising costs of food subsidies. The post-1977 changes in Sri Lanka's food policy are discussed by John Dixon in the Postscript. With the change of government in 1977 and the movement to a more market-oriented economy, the rice-ration system was phased out and replaced by a food-stamp program. As inflation erodes the purchasing power of the food stamps, some deterioration in consumption levels by poor consumers is expected. The issue, therefore, is whether new policies will create enough broad-based economic growth to maintain or improve on previous nutritional levels.

The problem of food security in India is analyzed and discussed in chapter 9 by John Dixon and Rodney Tyers. The dependence of three-quarters of India's population on agricultural income, the relatively low labor productivity in Indian agriculture, and the random effects of weather on agricultural production and income all give rise to widespread rural poverty and undernourishment in normal years. This problem is considerably exacerbated in years of unfavorable weather. Food security can be approached from the following two perspectives: (1) assuring that adequate supplies of food grains are available, and (2) assuring that incomes are sufficient to ensure effective demand. In the past five years, India has made dramatic progress on the supply side; total food-grain production has reached record levels in recent years, and government stocks are large. In the short run, therefore, the best avenue for improving food security is to combine effective management of the total supply of grain—through domestic procurement, stocks, and imports when necessary—with more efficient distribution to food-deficient areas.

Creating effective demand has been a greater problem than increasing total food-grain production. Poverty and malnutrition coexist with record grain stocks and rice and wheat exports. Manufacturing employment creation in rural and urban areas is part of the solution as is increased agricultural productivity. While wheat has led the growth in agriculture, sizable gains remain to be realized for rice and the coarse cereals. A combination of increasing agricultural productivity and broad-based employment creation is essential to meeting India's food-security needs.

In chapter 10, Saburo Yamada examines the problem of food security from the viewpoint of a major industrialized food importer, Japan. The vigorous debate on food security in Japan is, in large part, a result of the U.S. soybean embargo of 1973 and the increasing public awareness of the continuing decline in the level of food self-sufficiency in Japan. Yamada outlines trends in Japan's food production and imports and examines Japan's vulnerability to disturbances in international food markets and markets for factors of production essential to Japan's food production, particularly the world petroleum market. The chapter then proceeds to a consideration of policy measures Japan should take to attempt to prevent a food crisis and policies to ameliorate the effects of a food crisis should one occur.

Yamada concludes that food security in Japan can best be obtained through an internationalist approach of maintaining and strengthening economic and political ties with major trading partners, especially the large Pacific Rim food exporters: the United States, Canada, and Australia. It is interesting to note that this policy parallels the policy for food security advanced by Ralph Lattimore in chapter 3 from the viewpoint of Canada, a major grain exporter. As a supplementary insurance strategy, Yamada argues for the continued maintenance by Japan of emergency stocks of rice, soybeans, and petroleum.

Part III: Results from Empirical Analysis

In chapter 11, John Dixon gives an overview of staple-food consumption patterns in Indonesia and then uses the National Socio-Economic Surveys (*Susenas*) to make a detailed examination of the consumption patterns of different segments of the population. The financial burden of Indonesia's large imports of rice has led to increased interest by policymakers in stimulating the consumption of nonrice staples, notably corn and cassava. A major focus of the chapter is on these nonrice staples. Techniques of consumption analysis based on disaggregated data are discussed, and then empirical results based on the National Socioeconomic Survey (Susenas) data set are presented and carefully interpreted. Problems that are inherent in the use of the survey data are identified. For example, the bias toward higher estimates of expenditure and price elasticities due to the consumption by farm households of own-produced corn, cassava, and rice is examined. If expenditure and price elasticities for corn and cassava are overestimated, the estimated responsiveness to a price policy that switches consumption away from rice by raising its relative price will be exaggerated.

The use of only aggregate, national-level data does not supply sufficient information on which to base efficient food-security policies. John Dixon argues persuasively that, at the very least, consumption differences between urban and rural areas have to be considered, and further disaggregation by rural-income subsets is desirable. While the country studied is Indonesia, the problems discussed and the framework of analysis used are applicable to other developing countries.

The focus of chapter 12 by Howarth Bouis and Robert Herdt is on the trade-off between the basic long-term policy objective of increased growth in rice production in many Asian countries and the short-run governmental concern with the stabilization of retail rice prices at sufficiently low levels to ensure consumer food security. In land-scarce Asia, increasing rice productivity provides the only means of meeting both consumers' and producers' needs. Bouis and Herdt develop models for evaluating the trade-offs between short-run food security and long-run food and agricultural policy objectives. Rice output is linked both to short-run price expectations and to the more gradual effects of investments in production technology. In order to determine the short-run pattern of consumption and storage over time (by month) that would occur under given trade and domestic policies, the authors use an anticipatory price model. The long-run production model recognizes that yields depend on the degree of control of water supply, fertilizer use, and the breeding and introduction of newer varieties. These inputs are in turn dependent on the amount of government expenditures on agricultural research, irrigation projects, or extension and credit programs. A preliminary version of the supply model is applied to study long-run production policies, independently of the short-run price effects, for the case of the Philippines. The results show, for example, the types and amounts of long-run investments needed in the next decade to maintain the real price of rice at its present level.

In chapter 13 Somporn Hanpongpandh presents a simulation model of ASEAN rice production and trade that is then used to examine the ASEAN Emergency Rice Reserve. Rice is the main staple food in the ASEAN countries, and the governments of these countries have identified the stability of domestic rice supplies and prices as being an important condition for economic stability and development. The international rice market is extremely volatile, largely because only a very small percentage (less than 5 percent) of the total value of world rice production enters world trade. The ASEAN Emergency Rice Reserve (initially 50,000 metric tons) is an integral part of the ASEAN Food Security Reserve Agreement that was signed in 1979.[13] This international agreement is the only one of its type presently in existence. Although the 50,000-ton Emergency Rice Reserve seems small, results from the simulation model indicate that its implementation will cause the incidence of a shortfall by more than 10 percent in the imports needed by ASEAN rice deficit countries to decline from once in five years to about once in ten years. The role of Thailand in the agreement is found to be a crucial factor in improving the rice-import security of ASEAN governments.

Chapter 14, by Rodney Tyers and Anthony Chisholm, explores the interdependence of countries engaged in trade in foods. The authors present and test the general hypothesis that with appropriate multilateral changes in food and agricultural policies, nonzero-sum improvements in economic welfare can be realized that would be widely distributed internationally. Tyers and Chisholm introduce an innovative stochastic simulation model that is global in coverage, distinguishing eighteen countries and country groups in Asia and the Pacific Rim and dividing the rest of the world into five-country aggregates. The model's primary aim is to measure the international distribution of welfare costs and benefits from the pure protection, pure stabilization, and stockpiling components of agricultural and food policies in industrialized and developing countries.

The quantitative analysis conducted by the authors bears out the theoretical result that the cost to consumers of protectionist policies in the industrialized food-importing countries exceeds the corresponding gain to their producers and governments. Although these policies significantly affect the level and stability of international food-trading prices, their impact on Asian developing countries is shown to be mixed. The lower, yet more unstable, prices that result appear to benefit the net food importers among them while imposing a welfare cost on the net food exporters. The provisionist (that is, domestic prices below border prices) and stabilizing policies of Asian developing countries are also found to impose a net welfare cost domestically as measured in expected welfare terms. These policies, however, are shown to provide considerable protection against food insecurity to consumers in relatively poor countries. Their effect on international markets results in higher and less stable grain prices, imposing a net welfare cost on industrialized food importers such as Japan and benefiting the major food exporters such as Australia, Canada, and the United States.

Market intervention by governments of developing countries to reduce and stabilize domestic food prices tends to suppress producer incentives, especially where governments do not have the resources to compensate producers at higher-than-consumer prices. The authors propose that part of the gains from trade liberalization in the industrialized food-importing countries might be employed for the restoration of production incentives in developing countries, while low and stable retail food prices are retained in developing countries. The adoption of policies of this type is estimated to result in an annual net welfare gain (as measured in terms of expected economic surplus) to producers, consumers, and stockholders of U.S. $ (1970) 47 billion by 1985, two-thirds of which would accrue in Organization for Economic Cooperation and Development (OECD) countries. There would be a net increase in the burden on governments, however, of U.S. $ (1970) 25 billion, 70 percent of which would need to be borne by governments of developing countries. Thus, should a means be found to redistribute the welfare gains and the cost burden so that the net gain would be more equitably distributed internationally, consumers in poor countries would face no greater food insecurity while the outcome would be Pareto superior in expected welfare terms.

Notes

1. See Donaldson and Lewis (1981). These authors base their analysis on U.S. Department of Agriculture data and define low-income countries as those having per-capita incomes below U.S. $250.

2. Over the same period, Schmidt et al. (1978) estimate that the centrally planned countries increased their cereal imports from the industrialized West from 2 percent of world grain trade to over 11 percent, of which 6 percent was from the United States.

3. Other changes in cereal markets include a dramatic decline in concessional food sales to developing countries. Donaldson and Lewis (1981) estimate that concessional grain sales in 1960–1963 had characterized more than 90 percent of the trade, whereas in 1976–1979 only 16 percent of global grain trade was on concessional terms, and this was largely confined to the poorest food-grain-importing countries.

4. State trading authorities monopolize trade in the rice-importing developing countries: Indonesia, South Korea, Bangladesh, Malaysia, the Philippines, and Sri Lanka.

5. See the study by Hickman et al. (1977) for evidence of increasing economic interdependence among Pacific Rim countries. Kojima (1980) and Drysdale and Patrick (1979) are among those authors proposing a formalization of these economic ties.

6. The region entitled "Pacific Rim" is defined by Tyers (1982) to include Oceania (Australia, New Zealand, Papua New Guinea, and the Pacific Island Nations), East Asia (Japan, China, North and South Korea, Indonesia, and the ASEAN countries), Canada, and the United States. Total food exports are defined according to the U.N. Commodity Trade Statistics category SITC:0 (food), for 1970 and 1976.

7. This section seeks to highlight selected aspects of food security that are particularly relevant to the subject matter of this book. For a more detailed and comprehensive treatment of the topic of food security, see Valdes and Siamwalla (1981a and 1981b).

8. Without a major reallocation of income internationally, some significant improvements would still be possible. In principle, most developing countries could divert sufficient resources from the nonfood sectors to adequately feed all their people. But large segments of the population might then remain for a longer period in a state of poverty with respect to consumption of other goods and services.

9. This is similar to the definition of food security adopted by Valdes and Siamwalla (1981a) and James Roumasset in chapter 6 of this book.

10. See chapter 6 by James Roumasset and chapter 12 by Howarth Bouis and Robert Herdt.

11. Sen (1981) provides an excellent description of the entitlement approach to food security and contrasts it with the more traditional food-availability-decline approach. A sharp reduction in food supply (availability) can be a cause of some people not having enough food to eat to stave off malnutrition or starvation, but it is only one of a number of possible causes. Sen points out that it is even possible for famines in some areas to be caused by *boom* conditions when the output of goods in general, including a country's aggregate food production, is increasing. If the boom takes the form of uneven expansion between sectors, substantial declines in real incomes of some groups within society (some rural groups, for example) may ensue.

12. Morris (1974) claims that most analysts do not appreciate the extent to which resources like gold and silver are accumulated as stores of value to be drawn on in bad years by households in developing countries.

13. The text of the ASEAN Food Security Reserve Agreement is reprinted in Appendix 13A.

Bibliography

Donaldson, G., and Lewis, C. 1981. "Food Security in Developing Countries—The Story of the 1970's," mimeo., World Bank, June.

Drysdale, P., and Patrick, H. 1979. "An Asia-Pacific Regional Economic Organization: An Expository Concept Paper." Prepared for the Committee on Foreign Relations, U.S. Senate, 96th Congress, First Session, Committee Print, July.

Hickman, B.G., Kuroda, Y., and Lau, L.J. 1977. "The Pacific Basin in World Trade." Working Papers Nos. 190, 191, and 192, National Bureau of Economic Research, Inc.

Johnson, D.G. 1975. "World Agriculture, Commodity Policy and Price Variability." *American Journal of Agricultural Economics* 57:823–828.

Johnson, D.G. 1977. "Increased Stability of Grain Supplies in Developing Countries: Optimal Carryovers and Insurance." In *The New International Economic Order: The North South Debate* ed. J.N. Bhagwati. Cambridge, Mass.: MIT Press.

Kojima, K. 1980. "Economic Cooperation in a Pacific Community," Project 80s: Foreign Policy Guidelines of Japan Series No. 1. Tokyo: Japan Institute of International Affairs.

Morris, D.M. 1974. "What is Famine?" *Economic and Political Weekly* 9, no. 44 (India: November 2).

Schmidt, S.C., Guither, H.D., and Mackie, A.B. 1978. "Quantitive Dimensions of Agricultural Trade." In *Speaking of Trade: Its Effect on Agriculture,* National Public Policy Education Committee Publication

No. 6, Agricultural Extension Service, University of Minnesota, Special Report No. 72.

Sen, A. 1981. "Ingredients of Famine Analysis: Availability and Entitlements." *Quarterly Journal of Economics* 46:433–464.

Tyers, R. 1982. "ASEAN Food Security: Effects of Improved Pacific Economic Cooperation." Paper prepared for the ASEAN and Pacific Economic Cooperation Project, Development Planning Division, Economic and Social Commission for Asia and the Pacific. Bangkok.

Valdes, A., and Siamwalla, A. 1981a. "Assessing Food Insecurity in LDCs—Roles of International Schemes in Relation to LDCs." In *Proceedings of the Seventeenth International Conference of Agricultural Economists* ed. G. Johnson and W. Maunder. Westmead, England: Gower Publishing Co.

Valdes, A., and Siamwalla, A. 1981b. "Introduction." In *Food Security, for Developing Countries* ed. A. Valdes. Boulder, Colo. Westview Press, Inc., 1981.

Part I
Food Security: General Theory and Policy Issues

2 Policies for Food Security in Food-Importing Developing Countries

Shlomo Reutlinger

The ultimate goal of food security might be described as the freedom from food deprivation for all of the world's people all of the time. Lack of food security in developing countries has been widely deplored in recent years. Depending on how food deprivation is defined, approximately 400 to 1,000 million people experience food insecurity in a year characterized by normal food supplies. It has been said repeatedly that the basic cause of food deprivation is poverty. Short of eliminating poverty, countries can institute a number of specialized food and nutrition-education programs supported by international-aid efforts. These plans all require enormous resources as well as political will and time for implementation.

Given this broad context, it becomes important to examine closely some manifestations of food insecurity that can be brought under control realistically at a cost that does not jeopardize other development efforts, particularly those required to eliminate food deprivation. One such manifestation is food insecurity caused by periodically recurring shortfalls from accustomed average or trend food supply levels. This kind of food insecurity causes deprivation even among people consuming an adequate amount of food in normal years and further aggravates food insecurity for the chronically deprived. In light of this broad view of food security, the relevant questions are as follows:

How much instability from one year to the next can be expected in the domestic food supply and in the price at which food can be imported?

How stable or unstable will consumption be in a particular environment under different sets of policies?

What are the long-run costs or gains of the different policies for the economy, the government, producers, and consumers?

And finally, to the extent that high levels of stabilization are costly, how valuable is protection against future undesirable supply contingencies?

Views expressed are those of the author and should not be attributed to the World Bank. Research on which this paper is based is part of a study undertaken by the World Bank (RPO 671-24) on various aspects of food stabilization in developing countries. The author wishes to express his gratitude to D. Bigman, D. Eaton, Y. Levy, and K. Knapp, who participated in various stages of the development of the model and computer programs.

Surprisingly, little substantive analysis of these questions has yet been undertaken in spite of a high level of awareness in developing countries and in international forums about the importance of reducing food-consumption instability in populations subsisting at the margin of minimal food consumption. One objective of this chapter is to outline an approach that countries might use to analyze alternative policies in terms of their effectiveness for reducing periodic reductions in food consumption in unstable supply environments. Another objective is to challenge some perceptions about the problem and some policy recommendations, widely advocated both in the developing countries and in international forums.

First I will present a brief discussion of commonly held perceptions and preferred policies with regard to the supply-stability dimensions of food security. A simple model and analytical approach that, though crude and incomplete in several respects, represent an advance over other methods of analysis are then recommended for coping with certain supply and policy scenarios. Next are reports on policy-simulation experiments with parameters believed to represent a wide range of supply-instability conditions and illustrate the effectiveness and costs of instituting alternative policies. Finally, I present a brief summary of tentative policy recommendations and recommendations for directions of further research.

Conventional Wisdom and Some Alternative Perceptions about the Causes of and Remedies for Food Insecurity

The food crisis of the early–middle 1970s can be credited for having drawn renewed attention to a long-standing problem: the periodic shortfalls from barely adequate levels of food consumption in many developing countries. Indeed, recent studies have confirmed that the probability of consumption falling below 95 percent of "normal" is high. Based on a review of twenty-four representative developing countries during 1961–1976, these probabilities ranged from 6 percent to 42 percent. In twenty of these countries, the probability of such a shortfall was in excess of 15 percent (Valdes and Konandreas 1980).

It is readily understandable that the phenomenon of instability should surface for attention at a time of crisis—and indeed a crisis occurred in the early–middle 1970s when many countries suffered from poor harvests, and global stocks reached a low point in recent history. Crises rarely, however, provide the appropriate perspective for conceptualizing the true nature of risk-related events and suitable remedial policies.

The conventional wisdom that has gained wide currency in the wake of the food crisis in the 1970s might be briefly summarized as follows:

1. Instability in the price of internationally traded grain is a major source of food insecurity in developing countries.
2. International food-grain prices are likely to become very unstable unless international agreements can be signed for instituting large buffer-stock operations.
3. The primary source of international price instability is instability in global supplies, and hence price stabilization requires a high level of global (internationally agreed-on) buffer-stock operations.
4. A stable food-grain supply and a stable price are highly desirable for all countries, and therefore all countries are willing to share in the high cost of operating buffer-stock operations.
5. For developing countries, it is also advantageous to operate large buffer stocks in order to insulate themselves from the unstable international market.

There is ample evidence, however, that appropriate measures to enhance food security will not be initiated unless much of this conventional wisdom is replaced with insight that more appropriately describes the true nature and sources of food insecurity.

Food-grain consumption in developing countries has been unstable during the 1950s and 1960s in spite of relatively stable world-market prices. Annual per-capita consumption and production for developing countries by major regions for the period 1961–1972 are shown graphically in figure 2–1, and table 2–1 provides some summary statistics based on the same data. For Africa and East Asia, annual consumption was about as unstable as production. For the remaining regions, the coefficient of variation of annual consumption was a little over half the coefficient of variation of production.

Clearly, a stable world price provided little insurance against food insecurity. We can only surmise that in the absence of food aid, consumption in several developing countries would have been even more unstable. The major cause of consumption instability was instability of production in the developing countries and *not* unstable external supplies or prices. Imports were not used more aggressively to compensate for the inherent instability in production of individual countries probably for the following good reasons: balance-of-payments problems, instability in demand caused by instability in consumers' incomes, inadequately flexible distribution channels and transportation and port handling facilities. But unstable world supplies and prices were not an important factor.

All of this does not suggest, of course, that unstable world supplies and prices cannot aggravate, on some occasions, food insecurity in a developing country. Recent history shows that perhaps one out of four or five sharp

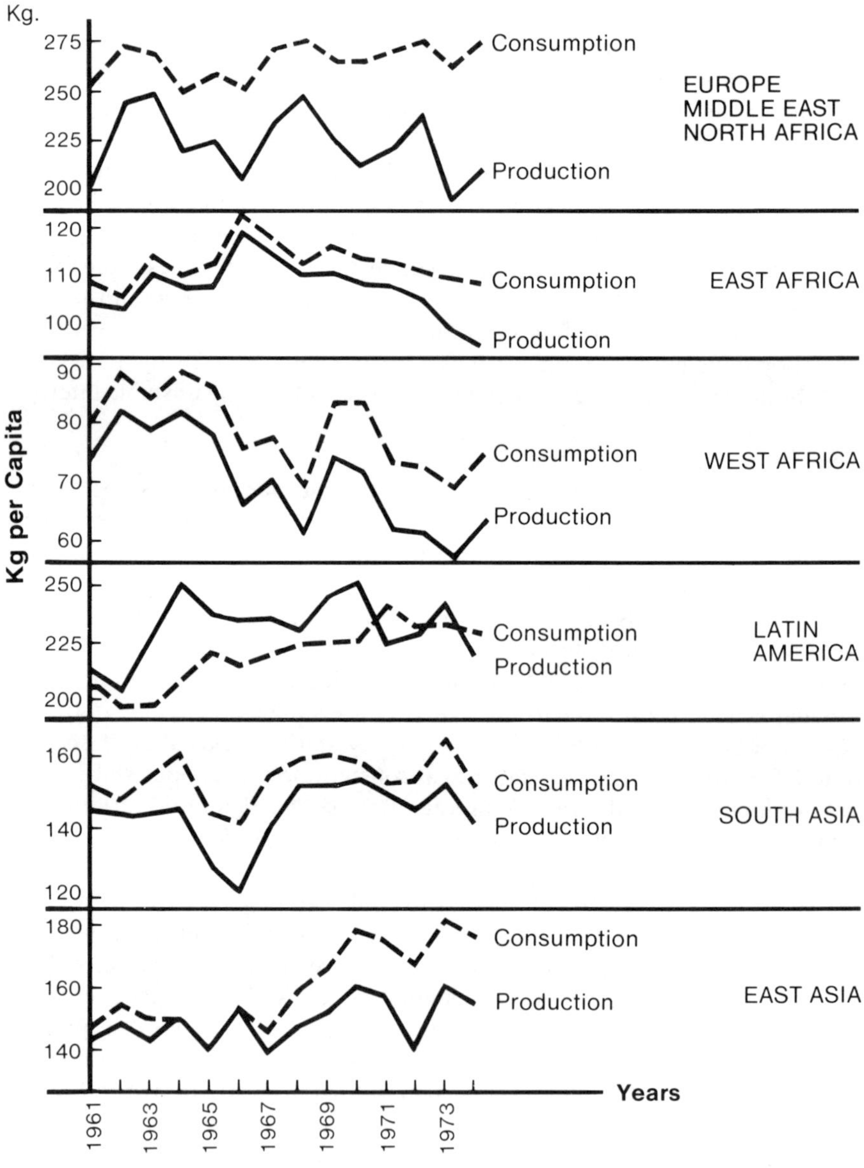

Figure 2–1. Total Grains: Production and Consumption per Capita, 1961–1974

Source: Sandra Hadler, "Developing Country Foodgrain Projections for 1985," World Bank Staff Working Paper No. 247, November 1976.

Table 2–1
Regressions of Annual per Capita Consumption on Production, 1961–1972

	Regression Coefficients			
Region	*Constant*	*Production*	*Time*	R^2
EMENA	.154	.45* (4.8)	.001* (2.8)	.78
East Africa	.009	.94* (11.9)	.0002* (1.96)	.95
West Africa	.003	1.01* (15.7)	.0006* (4.04)	.98
South America (excluding Argentina)	.126	.29 (1.6)	.002* (4.4)	.80
South Asia	.069	.58* (4.7)	.00007 (.2)	.74
East Asia and the Pacific	.007	.91* (3.52)	.002* (3.94)	.83

Note: Numbers in parentheses are t-statistics.
*Indicates significance at the 95 percent level.

declines in consumption below trend occurred as a result of or was aggravated by abnormally high world prices. In this limited context, it is relevant to ask whether the price of internationally traded food grains can be expected to be more unstable in the future than in the past. A related question is whether an international agreement on global stock operations would significantly enhance price stability of internationally traded grains. Answers to these questions are complex, but there is good reason to challenge the current conventional wisdom.

The stability of prices of internationally traded grains depends most importantly on the following elements:

1. the stability of world production
2. the level and nature of buffer stocks operations
3. the elasticity of excess demand (or supply) by major trading countries

Let us briefly discuss these elements in turn, and consider the likelihood of instability becoming more pronounced in the future.

Production Instability

Barring major changes in weather patterns (such as have been hypothesized by some individuals but on which there is little consensus among meteorologists), there is little reason to expect global production to become more unstable in the future. Widely scattered production among ecological regions will continue to remain the major stabilizing factor for total world production. If anything, global production will become more stable in the future since increases in the real cost of energy, and hence shipping costs, are likely to lead to more dispersed production. In addition, improvements in irrigation and flood control will further reduce instability in production in those regions of the world with low and unstable rainfall conditions.

National Buffer Stocks

As recent evidence bears out, incentives for nations to engage in buffer-stock operations have not drastically changed from what they were in the past. Major producing countries continue to stabilize farmers' incomes by defending a floor price through withdrawals of grains from the market into buffer stocks. In the short run, there are few alternatives. Supply controls are a poor substitute for stocks, given the long lead time involved in passing legislation and implementing controls. Similarly, there is growing concern with assuring supply stability and simultaneously reducing dependence on imports in many major developed countries, including the USSR. Consequently, importing countries are likely to hold larger rather than smaller stocks in the future.

The Elasticity of Excess Demand

There is extensive documentation that the sharp increase in the world price of grains in the early–middle 1970s was in no small measure the consequence of many developed countries maintaining stable levels of consumption (and domestic prices) rather than adjusting to world market conditions. In the interim, the United States has negotiated an agreement with the USSR to hold trade within bounds. Furthermore, the less favorable balance-of-payment conditions, partly as a consequence of higher energy-import bills, are likely to make it more difficult in the future for countries to afford the "luxury" of maintaining consumption and internal-price stability, irrespective of global supply conditions.

In view of these considerations—production stability, the size of national buffer-stock operations, and import and export policies of major grain-trading countries—it is highly questionable to postulate growing price instability in internationally traded food grains. But in any case, to make food security in developing countries conditional upon stabilization of world supplies through extensive buffer-stock operations is a dubious proposition. A large proportion of the world's grain is consumed in countries that feed large amounts of grain to livestock. The demand for feed is quite elastic, which means that consumers place a low value on price stabilization. It is not surprising, therefore, that governments of the major grain-producing and consuming countries have been slow to accept the high cost that large buffer-stock operations entail.

Finally, the argument that food security justifies a high level of buffer-stock operations also requires reexamination since it ignores options of trade.

Alternative propositions about the source of food insecurity in many countries that might prove more useful than the conventional wisdom in seeking remedies may be stated as follows:

1. The observed instability in food consumption in the developing countries is sometimes caused by unstable world prices but more frequently reflects the inability or unwillingness of countries to permit the highly flexible volumes of trade required to offset unstable domestic harvests.
2. In this context, arrangements to permit more flexible volumes of trade are a distinct alternative to buffer-stock operations for achieving greater food security. The alternatives should be examined in terms of cost-effectiveness.
3. Food security might require more stable consumption than would be obtained under free trade when international prices are unstable. The domestic price could then be stabilized further to any desired degree by implementing a stabilizing trade policy.
4. Price stability will not assure consumption stability if demand is unstable. In this case, the achievement of food security requires either stabilization of demand and price or unstable prices to offset the unstable demand.

The model covered in the following discussion and the subsequent illustrative calculations are presented to evaluate the first three propositions. Extension of the model to evaluate the consequences of unstable demand by different segments of a country's population for food security and examination of the relevant parameters and appropriate remedial policies are desirable but have not yet been accomplished.

Analytical Model

The model used to analyze food security under alternative policies is a partial equilibrium model of the grain sector in a small, normally importing country. Although only a single grain commodity is assumed, this may be interpreted as being some aggregation of the various food grains actually consumed. Time is discrete in this model, with the length of each period being the time between successive harvests.

Domestic production is assumed to be a normal random variable with identical, independent distributions in each year. There is no supply response to annual price variations. Mean production, however, is responsive to the expected price prevailing under different trade-policy scenarios. World prices are generated from a normal distribution of world production and a kinked world demand.

Policies pursued by the government are of two general types: (1) *grain reserves* and (2) *trade policies*. The grain reserve is of fixed capacity and is operated by the government with public knowledge of its operating rules.[1] The rules are food-security oriented. The trade policies are of four types as follows:

1. *Free trade*. The government imports grain so that domestic prices and border prices are equalized.
2. *Restricted trade*. A tariff is added to the border price, and grain is imported so that domestic price equals the border price plus the tariff.
3. *Stabilizing trade*. The government stabilizes the domestic price and hence, consumption, by the use of variable import taxes or subsidies.
4. *Constrained trade*. Grain is imported as under free or stabilizing trade, with the exception that the total import bill can be no larger than a specified amount.

Operation of the model is straightforward. By sampling procedures, a large number of supply events are generated in accordance with predetermined probabilities. For each world-supply level, the model determines a world price. Similarly, for each level of the country's supply and world price and given carryover levels of stocks the model determines the following: (1) the amount of grain imported, stored (positive or negative), and consumed in the country, and (2) the country's internal grain price and the economic and financial gains (or losses) to various sectors, generally calculated on the basis of the incremental consumer and/or producer surplus from a particular policy. Summary statistics and frequency distributions of many variables are obtained on the basis of nine thousand observations (three hundred replications of thirty-year time horizons).

Trade Policies

Trade policies may be viewed as different perceptions, on the part of the government, of either the marginal cost of importing additional food or the desirability of using the market-demand curve to determine consumption levels. In each case, however, consumption in a particular year is fixed at the level at which the marginal cost of imports intersects the relevant "demand" function. Imports make up any difference between the consumption level so determined and production in that year.

1. Under *free trade*, demand is the market demand (DM), and the marginal cost of imports is the import price (p_m), that is, the world price plus import costs. (Consumption, domestic production, and imports corresponding to free trade are designated as c, q, and m in figure 2–2.)
2. Under *restricted trade*, demand is the same as under free trade, but the marginal cost of imports is the import price plus a tariff, p_m^*. (Consumption and imports corresponding to restricted trade are designated as c^* and m^* in figure 2–2.)
3. Under *stabilizing trade*, the government imposes its demand schedule (DG), which implies import subsidies when the import price is high and import tariffs when the import price is low. (Consumption and imports corresponding with stabilizing trade are designated as c^{**} and m^{**} in figure 2–2.)

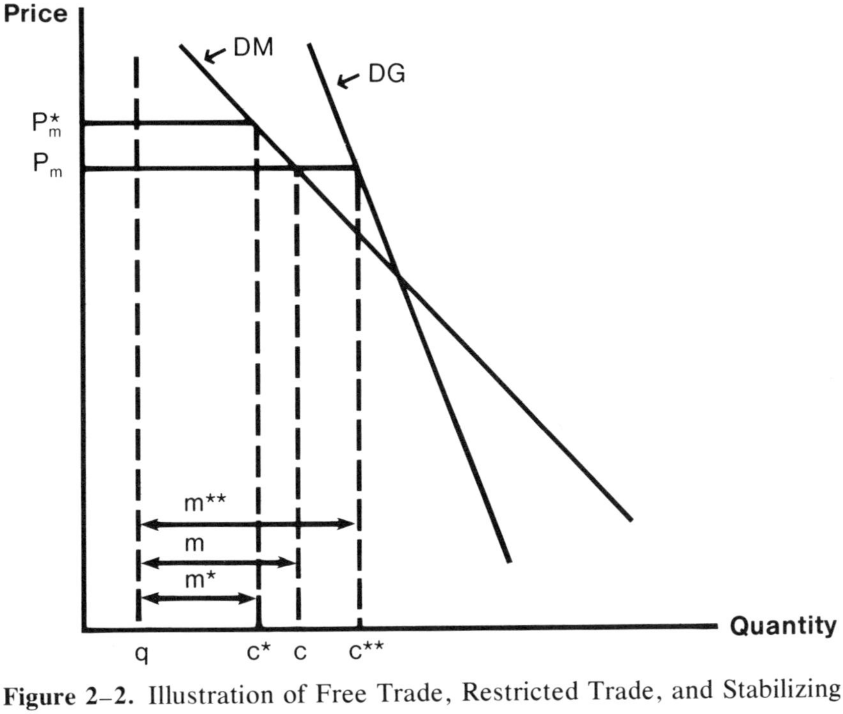

Figure 2–2. Illustration of Free Trade, Restricted Trade, and Stabilizing Trade Policies

4. Under *constrained trade*, there is an upper limit on the food-import bill. This implies that the marginal import price is either the import price or the intersection of the domestic demand and the inelastic production plus the maximum allowable import level, depending on the level of production in the particular year and the import price. If production is high, consumption and imports are likely to be the same as under unconstrained trade; however, when production is low, consumption and imports could be less. (In figure 2–3, note that when production (q_2) is high, imports and consumption (m_2 and c_2) are the same under both unconstrained and constrained trade. When production (q_1) is low, however, imports and consumption are m_1 and c_1 under unconstrained trade, whereas imports and consumption are m_1' and c_1' under constrained trade.)

Stock Policy

In the present model, the effects on food security of buffer stocks and the costs of operating such stocks are investigated for different maximum-

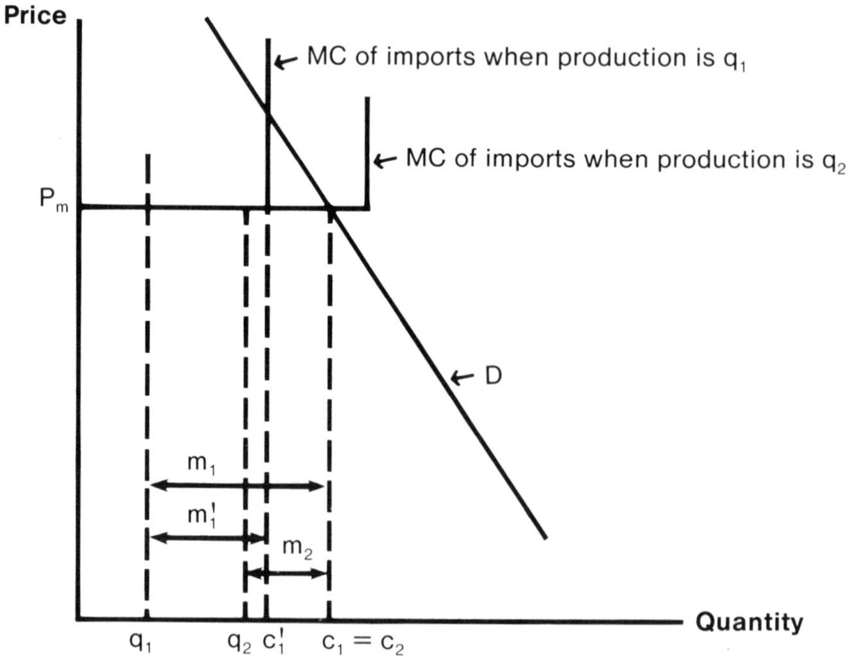

Figure 2–3. Illustration of Constrained Trade Policy

storage capacities and for one particular storage-operating rule. The operating rule chosen is one that offers a high chance of preventing a shortfall in consumption below a predetermined critical level.

As illustrated in in figure 2–4, the level of annual storage activity is determined on the basis of a carry-over-demand function. Under the adopted food-security rule, the carry-over-demand function (D^K) is infinitely elastic at a "critical" price, which is the price at which consumption is at the desired food-security level. Carry-over demand is zero above the critical price and can, of course, not exceed the maximum storage capacity. Total demand (D^T) is the demand for current consumption (D^C) plus carry-over demand (D^K). If the import price is above P^{crit}, stocks will be used to increase consumption up to the critical level, C^{crit}. Any excess stocks will remain in storage to cover future shortfalls of supply (that is, when the import price will be again above P^{crit}). Under free, unconstrained trade, consumption will be in excess of C^{crit}, and carry-overs will be at maximum storage capacity when the import price is below P^{crit}. Under constrained trade, if the choice is between importing for current consumption in excess of C^{crit} or securing higher carry-overs, higher carry-overs will take precedence. (As illustrated in figure 2–3, the intersecton of the marginal cost of imports, *MC*, and the total demand occurs at P^{crit}.) The total amount of imports and current demand for stock accumulation is always dependent on current production and the size of the inventory carried over from prior years. A higher carry-over from previous years would tend to shift the constraint on imports to the right and thereby enhance the chances of consumption being in excess of C^{crit}.

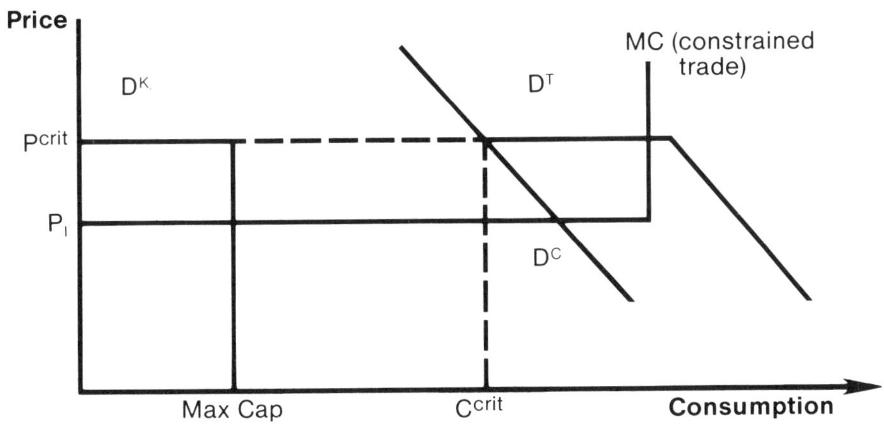

Figure 2–4. Illustration of Carry-Over Demand that Minimizes the Probability of Consumption Being Less than C^{crit}

Policy Simulations

Here, application of the model is illustrated with some hypothetical, but plausible, parameters. Specifically, the purpose of the simulation experiments is to investigate the consequences of a country's pursuing alternative trade and stocks policies for food security and the stability of grain consumption, prices, and external food trade. A related purpose is to determine the long-run expected gains or losses by consumers, producers, the government, and the economy at large.

The initial parameters were assumed to be as follows:

1. World price is a random variable generated from transforming a normal distribution of world production with mean 350 and standard deviation of 14 with a kinked linear-demand function. At the vicinity of $Q = 350$, the elasticity of demand of the segment corresponding with $Q < 350$ is -0.1, and the elasticity of the segment corresponding with $Q > 350$ is -0.3. The derived price has a skewed distribution with a mean of approximately U.S. \$140, a median of \$125, and a standard deviation of approximately \$33. Ninety-five percent of the time, the world price is in the range of \$92 and \$223.
2. The import price is assumed to be U.S. \$25 above the world price; hence, the average import price is approximately \$165. The country's imports are assumed not to affect the world price.
3. Domestic demand is linear with an elasticity of -0.2 when the price is \$165, and consumption per capita is 130 kg.
4. Expected domestic per-capita production Q^* is a function of the expected domestic price P^* under a given trade policy as follows: $ln\ Q^* = 3.0734 + 0.3\ ln\ P^*$. Annual domestic production is $Q_t = Q^* + e_t$ where e_t is distributed normally with mean zero and standard deviation of 7 kg. Under free trade, expected per-capita production is 100 kg. For restricted and constrained trade, P^* and Q^* were derived through successive iterations of the model.
5. The restricted-trade policy is assumed to be implemented through a constant import tax of \$25.
6. Under the stabilizing-trade policy, the country's demand is assumed to be linear with an elasticity of -0.1 when the price is \$165 and per-capita consumption is 130 kg. At the mean import price, no tax or subsidy is required. The marginal subsidy (tax rate) above (below) \$165 is 0.5. When the import price is \$30 above the mean price, for instance, the subsidy to the domestic market is \$15. The total cost of the subsidy is about 8 percent of the import bill. Similarly, the tax collected when the import price is \$30 below the mean is \$15. The tax revenue is then about 12 percent of the food-import bill.

7. Under the constrained-trade policy, the maximum allowable food-import bill is approximately the mean-import bill, that is, \$5 per capita (30 kg × \$0.165/kg).
8. The carry-over-demand function is horizontal at P=195. This price corresponds with a critical per-capita consumption level of 125 kg.
9. The assumed storage cost is 8 percent of the value of grain held in storage, a \$5 per-ton loading charge and a fixed amortization charge of \$9.36 per ton of storage capacity (that is, an investment of \$100 per ton amortized at 8 percent over thirty years).

Simulated Results: National Trade Policies

Table 2–2 shows the consequences of different trade policies for food security and the stability of related indexes, given the just-specified parameters. A primary concern for food security is the probability of consumption falling below a critical level and the extent of such shortfalls when they occur.

Since the import price is postulated to be unstable—either as a consequence of instability in the dollar price of imported grain and/or as a consequence of an unstable foreign-exchange rate—it is not surprising that per-capita food consumption is unstable, and food security is low under free trade. Free trade is also seen to result in a high probability of encountering a large import bill.[2]

Both the constrained free-trade and the constrained stabilizing-trade policies further reduce food security. It is noteworthy, however, that a financial constraint decreases food security only slightly when imposed on an otherwise free trade policy, whereas financial constraints on imports practically defeat the intent of the stabilizing-trade policy. The category of constrained trade probably best represents the actual food-import policies pursued in many developing countries.

The consequences of restricted trade for food security are, as expected, negative. What is interesting is the magnitude of the effect on food security from a relatively low tax on imports (about 15 percent). Protection of agriculture is increasingly advocated in some quarters in order to provide an incentive to increase production. There can be no question, however, that for a food-deficit country, protection reduces consumption and hence could be detrimental to food security.

At the other end of the spectrum, food security can be significantly enhanced by the kind of intervention subsumed under a stabilizing-trade policy. This policy, which is effectively pursued by some of the wealthier food-deficit and food-surplus countries, can be used to stabilize the food supply to any desired degree, but implementation of an unconstrained

Table 2–2
Policy Simulations: Indexes of Stability with Different Trade Policies

	Food Security Consumption below 125 kg/cap		*Import Bill: Probability of Being in Excess of $5/cap (%)*	*Coefficient of Variation of: (%)*			
Policy	*Probability of Occurrence (%)*	*Expected Shortfall[a] (kg/cap)*		*Consumption*	*Farm Income*	*Import Bill*	*Government Revenue*
Free trade	18	4.3	41	4.2	22.4	24.9	0
Constrained free trade	26	5.3	0	5.0	21.6	20.0	196
Stabilizing trade	6	1.9	41	2.1	12.7	26.1	696
Constrained stabilizing trade	20	4.8	0	3.8	14.9	19.1	167
Restricted trade	33	5.2	7	4.2	19.3	35.5	40

[a] Average amount by which consumption is below 125 kg when shortfall occurs.

stabilizing-trade policy requires measures to cope not only with unstable foreign-exchange requirements but also with unstable demands on the fiscal resources of the government. Removing restrictions on imports will occasionally make the difference between adequate food security and inadequate consumption. Imports also would need to be subsidized more frequently to attain adequate consumption levels for food security.

Table 2–3 reports some selected long-run consequences that might also explain why one policy is preferred over another. For instance, the restricted-trade policy is shown to reduce the average food-import bill by about 25 percent because of both reduced average consumption and increased production. It is also noteworthy that, in general, deviations from free trade are not extremely costly to the overall economy. For instance, a cost of $0.02 per capita (for example, $200,000 for a country with a population of 10 million people) incurred with the stabilizing-trade policy, which has a large positive effect on food security, may be quite tolerable. Some policies, however, are seen to result in very sizable gains for some and losses for other groups in the population or for the government account. These distributional consequences of different policies may well explain why some policies have greater political support than others.[3]

How robust are the previously reported conclusions when the basic parameters are varied? Tables 2–4 and 2–5 report results from simulation experiments based on three variations from the scenario assumed in the base case. Under the scenario of a Higher Demand Elasticity, the assumed demand elasticity (at the expected price) is 0.4 instead of 0.2. Similarly, under the Higher Supply Elasticity scenario, the supply is increased from 0.3 in the base case to 0.6. Under the More Stable World Price scenario, the coefficient of variation of world supply is half as much as in the base case, that is, about 2 percent rather than 4.

With a higher demand elasticity, the case for a stabilizing trade policy and for reducing constraints on the maximum import bill becomes even stronger. While in the base case free trade has been noted to provide a reasonable degree of food security by comparison with constrained or restricted trade, a higher demand elasticity implies highly unstable consumption under free trade.

With the higher supply elasticity, the decline in food security associated with restricted or constrained trade policies is only slightly less than in the base case. This is so because, in spite of the increased domestic supply, the country's consumption level essentially remains dependent on the ability or willingness to import.

With a more stable world price, the decline of food security associated with restrictions on trade becomes substantially more pronounced. Two observations are particularly noteworthy. As expected, a relatively stable world price translates into a high level of consumption stability under free

Table 2–3
Policy Simulation: Expected Values of Price, Consumption, Production, and Import Bill and Gains (Losses) Caused by Deviating from Free Trade

	Expected Annual Value of:				*Expected Annual Gain (Loss) Caused by Deviation from Free Trade ($/cap)*			
Policy[a]	*Consumption (kg/cap)*	*Production (kg/cap)*	*Import Bill ($/cap)*	*Government Revenue ($/cap)*	*Consumers' Surplus*	*Producers' Surplus*	*Government Revenue*	*Economy*
Free trade	130	100	4.75	—	—	—	—	—
Constrained free trade	129	101	4.27	0.31	(1.28)	0.92	0.31	(0.05)
Stabilizing trade	130	100	4.82	−0.07	(0.15)	0.06	0.07	(0.02)
Constrained stabilizing trade	128	102	4.25	−0.38	(1.47)	1.03	0.38	(0.06)
Restricted trade	126	105	3.38	0.55	(3.18)	2.53	0.54	(0.11)

[a]The respective expected prices with the different policies are U.S. $164, $174, $164, $175, and $188.
[b]Net farm income divided by the total population.

Table 2–4
Food Security: Probability (Percentage) of Consumption below 125 kg/cap and Expected Shortfall
(kg/cap)

	Scenario Percent (kg/cap)			
Policy	*Base Case*	*Higher Demand Elasticity*	*Higher Supply Elasticity*	*More Stable World Price*
Free trade	18 (4.3)	27 (9.1)	18 (4.3)	3 (1.7)
Constrained free trade	26 (5.3)	46 (10.2)	25 (5.0)	19 (2.4)
Stabilizing trade	6 (1.9)	6 (1.9)	6 (1.9)	0 (1.2)
Constrained stabilizing trade	20 (4.8)	24 (5.3)	18 (4.6)	15 (4.1)
Restricted trade	33 (5.2)	34 (8.4)	33 (5.0)	17 (4.0)

Table 2–5
Expected Annual Loss to Economy Caused by Deviation from Free Trade

	Scenario ($/cap)			
Policy	*Base Case*	*Higher Demand Elasticity*	*Higher Supply Elasticity*	*More Stable World Price*
Constrained free trade	0.04	0.04	0.04	0.07
Stabilizing trade	0.02	0.11	0.12	0.10
Constrained stabilizing trade	0.06	0.11	0.05	0.07
Restricted trade	0.11	0.15	0.15	0.11

trade. But more important, it should be noted that a more stable world food price will not significantly increase food security if trade is severely constrained by a maximum foreign-exchange allotment. Thus food-deficit countries would see little improvement in food security from international stabilization schemes unless they are able and willing to change their food-import policies.

Table 2–5 shows that the expected annual cost of deviating from free trade (as measured by changes in the combined consumer and producer surplus) is generally not very sensitive to the various scenarios. The only exception is the significant increase in the cost of engaging in stabilizing trade when the demand elasticity is high. In other words, with a higher demand elasticity, both the stabilizing effect and the cost of the stabilizing trade policy are more pronounced.

Simulation Results: The Relative Importance for Food Security of Removing Constraints on Imports, Modifying Domestic Market Demand, and Increasing International Price Stability

The illustrative results derived from the model can be usefully re-stated in terms of the contribution of different factors to food insecurity. The major constraints on food security in a food-deficit country, defined as the probability of consumption falling below a desired level, consist of all or some of the following conditions:

1. constraints on imports or on the maximum import bill
2. a less than perfectly inelastic market demand
3. instability in the import price

The question addressed here is what contribution can be expected from a partial but quite radical removal of any one or a combination of these constraints on food security.

The results are summarized in table 2–6. The parameters assumed for the hypothetical country were described earlier. Specifically, the food security constrained case assumes that the food-import bill is not allowed to exceed the average food-import bill, that the market demand is linear with an elasticity of 0.2 at the mean price, and that the import price is highly unstable. The unconstrained case analyzes scenarios with the import-bill constraint completely removed, the market demand replaced by a linear-demand function (obtained through government intervention) with an elas-

Table 2–6
Food Insecurity under Different Policy Scenarios

Policy Scenario			*Food Insecurity (%)*
Restrictions on Imports	*Market Demand Constraint*	*Import Price Instability*	*Probability of Consumption Falling below 125 kg/cap*
X	X	X	26
0	X	X	18
X	0	X	20
X	X	0	19
X	0	0	15
0	0	X	6
0	X	0	3
0	0	0	0

Note: X denotes full constraint in force; 0 denotes constraint substantially reduced.

ticity of 0.1 at the mean price, and world price instability reduced by approximately 50 percent.

The main conclusion is that the removal of any single constraint alone would not significantly improve food security. The most "stubborn" constraint is an inability or unwillingness to allow the food-import bill to exceed an upper limit.

Simulation Results: Buffer Stocks

In contrast to the high sensitivity of food security to trade policies, as seen in the previous discussion, the simulation results of different stock scenarios reported in table 2–7 show that stocks are relatively ineffective and/or costly.

Under free trade, stocks are completely ineffective with respect to the food-security objective explored in the study unless the storage capacity is very high. Following food-security-oriented stock rules, whereby stocks are accumulated to the full extent of the storage capacity whenever the import price is below U.S. $195 per ton, and stocks are released in whatever quantity needed to prevent consumption from falling below 125 kg per capita (that is, to prevent the price from rising above $195 per ton), the

Table 2–7
Food Security and Economic Costs of Buffer Stocks under Free Trade and Constrained Free Trade

	Free Trade		*Constrained Free Trade*	
Storage Capacity (kg/cap)	*Food Security (%)*	*Cost ($/cap)*	*Food Security (%)*	*Cost ($/cap)*
0	17.6	—	26.9	—
4	17.6	0.03	23.0	0.03
8	17.6	0.07	21.0	0.06
12	17.3	0.11	20.1	0.11
16	16.2	0.16	18.8	0.15
20	14.4	0.20	17.4	0.20
24	11.1	0.26	—	—
28	8.2	0.32	—	—
32	6.0	0.39	—	—
36	4.6	0.46	—	—
40	3.8	0.54	—	—

Note: *Food security* is defined as the probability of per capita consumption falling below 125 kg. *Cost* refers to the expected annual overall economic cost (consumer plus producer surplus plus government cost).

minimum storage capacity having any perceptible food-security impact is seen to be on the order of 15 kg per capita, or approximately 50 percent of average imports. To reduce the probability of consumption falling below 125 kg per capita to a level of 6 percent would require a stock that approximately equals the average level of imports. The cost of \$0.35 per capita would be far in excess of the \$0.02 per capita that it would cost to achieve an equal level of food security through the stabilizing trade policy described earlier. Moreover, the operation of such a large stock, while slightly reducing the average import bill, would imply extremely unstable imports. The coefficients of variation of both the quantity of imports and the food-import bill under free trade plus a 30 kg per capita stock operation are nearly 0.60, whereas the coefficients of variation of imports and the food-import bill under stabilizing trade are approximately 0.25.

Food security can be slightly improved with a modest buffer stock and at a reasonable cost under constrained free trade. Stocks are used in this case to augment consumption whenever imports are restricted for lack of foreign exchange. Large improvements in food security are not possible because the financial constraint that limits imports for consumption in the current year also prevents large accumulation of stocks irrespective of available storage capacity.

Summary

The main theme of this chapter has been to challenge the proposition that the best and perhaps only way to eliminate temporary, periodically recurring shortfalls in food consumption from normal levels in developing countries is through extensive buffer-stock operations at the international and national level. Instead, I suggest that far more attention be given to the opportunities of providing for food security through appropriate trade policies. Empirical evidence about food insecurity in developing countries persisting during long periods of relative stability in international food-grain prices and a stochastic simulation analysis with a simple country food-grain market model were presented to support the hypothesis that the removal of trade and market-demand constraints are likely to be more effective and less costly than buffer stocks for eliminating temporary and periodic shortfalls in consumption.

While the model and the illustrative applications presented in this chapter were not intended to be comprehensive, they do suggest the following opportunities and dilemmas different policies hold for countries wishing to attain food security:

1. If the supply of food imports to a normally importing country is infinitely elastic and the import price is stable, food security in the

sense of stabilizing per-capita food consumption can be achieved by resorting to free trade. The dilemma is how to cope with a highly unstable food-import bill. To a limited extent, a buffer-stock buildup from imports in years of good harvests can be substituted for imports in later years. As has been illustrated, however, the scope of substituting stocks for flexible financial arrangements is limited in terms of achieving food security and the cost of stocks in terms of resources that might be used otherwise for general and agricultural development is high. To put it very simply, it is cheaper to store money than to store food.

2. If import prices are unstable, either because the dollar price of the food grain is unstable or because the shadow exchange rate of the country's currency is unstable, food security requires that imports be subsidized and that constraints on imports be removed. Import subsidies during years of high import prices can be offset by import tariffs during years of low prices. The dilemma becomes one of unstable foreign-exchange requirements and unstable fiscal budgets, however. Under these circumstances, a buffer stock can play a somewhat greater, though still only limited, role in attaining food security.
3. Constant levels of protection are inimical to food security. If a developing country, for whatever reason, is bound on protecting its food-production sector, it ought to imitate the stabilizing-trade policies (variable levies, and so forth) successfully pursued by developed countries.

These conclusions are robust with respect to a wide range of parameters applicable to the hypothesized model. Needless to say, the model and the analysis presented in this chapter do not confront all types and causes of periodic food insecurity and all relevant environments. Some fruitful directions for further research and extensions of the model and analysis lie in the following directions:

1. *Instability of Demand Caused by Instability of Income.* Periodic declines in food consumption may be caused by periodic reductions in demand resulting from declines in personal income as well as by higher-than-normal food prices. For people whose level of income is not derived directly or indirectly from agriculture, food security could then be achieved only by supplying them with food at lower-than-normal prices. On the other hand, agriculture-related incomes may further deteriorate if, as a consequence of a poor harvests, a large amount of food is imported, and the price of food is depressed. Possibly, the optimal solution for this case lies in a combination of income- and supply-stabilization policies.
2. *Highly Segmented or Fractured Markets.* Particularly in large countries with underdeveloped marketing infrastructures and transportation

facilities, the incidence of a bad drought in the interior may turn a normally food-exporting region into a food-deficit region. In such a case, (decentralized) stocks may hold much greater promise than suggested by the existing, spatially undifferentiated model.

3. *Inelastic Supply of Imports.* The model used in this paper assumes that the supply of the imported food to the country is infinitely elastic at a constant price unrelated to the country's volume of imports. This is certainly an unrealistic assumption for some countries that import a substantial share of the internationally traded supply in a commodity (for example, the case of Indonesia with respect to rice). Moreover, limited capacity for handling grain imports may cause the import price to rise with the quantity of imports.
4. *Substitutability in Demand of Different Foods.* In assessing food insecurity, food-security targets, and the costs of meeting them through different policies, it is important to know to what extent one food can be substituted for another. The extreme cases of either perfect or zero substitutability can be analyzed with the existing model, but intermediate cases require substantial modifications.

Finally, it should be noted that the country focus for analysis and initiation of remedial policies proposed in this chapter does not deny the validity of an international dimension to the food-security problem of developing countries. As has been shown, instability in the price of internationally traded food grains does aggravate the problem. The analysis does suggest, however, that negotiations to achieve a high degree of price stabilization through costly buffer-stock operations should be evaluated in the context of their limited benefit for food security in developing countries. Instead, international efforts might well be more effectively invested, with more direct benefits for food security, in financial-insurance schemes that would assist countries to incur the highly unstable food-import bills needed for securing stable consumption at current, barely adequate average levels.

The basic proposition advocated in this chapter has been that the periodic, as well as the chronic, food-security problem at both the national and the subnational level is a poverty rather than a food-supply problem. Effective solutions must therefore be addressed to providing opportunities and incentives for reallocating existing and growing food supplies through active national and international intervention in markets as well as to investment for increasing and stabilizing the aggregate food supply. An article in *The New York Times* (1979), "A Bounty of Rice in Asia, Stubborn Poverty in Laos," provides an excellent exposition of this point of view. The article describes the irony in the current rice situation.

> . . . The granaries of India, once a major importer, are bulging with surplus rice. Sri Lanka, a traditional importer, reduced its imports last year to the lowest level in 30 years . . . and
>
> Many poor nations still unable to feed themselves, are the least able to afford rice imports even at current low prices. . . .

The article goes on to outline a particular remedy.

> As a result, President Marcos, along with delegates from 60 nations at a Food and Agriculture Organization meeting here last week, called on developed countries to help food-poor countries to import rice from third world nations with surpluses. The group suggested using more triangular transactions in which rich nations extend loans or credits to poor countries, allowing them to buy rice from developing nations with surpluses. . . .[4]

I do not know about this particular solution, but the underlying perception is correct—as far as it addresses the needs of poor *nations*. Perhaps we should only remind ourselves that there is also an irony in the coexistence of surpluses and poor *people* unable to feed themselves within developing countries. Perhaps if the same kind of solution advocated by President Marcos for augmenting consumption by poor nations were carried forward also to augment poor people's consumption of food, there would be no surplus problem and food security would be immensely improved.

Notes

1. A somewhat more elaborate model that includes the analysis of buffer stocks under optimal rules derived separately with a dynamic programming routine, is presented in Reutlinger and Knapp (1980). A similar model and analysis applicable to normally self-sufficient countries is reported in Bigman and Reutlinger (1979). The detailed features of the model are described in *Grain Stabilization Model (GRAST): Features, Fortran Program and Users' Manual* (available on request from the author).

2. Parenthetically, we should note the consequences of a trade policy that would insulate the country entirely from instability in world market prices. This could be achieved by holding imports at a constant rate of 30 kg per capita. The probability of per capita food consumption falling below 125 kg would then be approximately 25 percent, and the coefficient of variations of food consumption and the food-import bill would be 5.3 percent and 38 percent, respectively. In this case, free trade provides for more food security and for a more stable food-import bill than would insulation from free trade.

3. The actual magnitude and even whether some group gains or loses is very sensitive to the particular specification of the demand and supply function. For instance, with a linear demand function, it is a foregone conclusion that consumers lose, and producers gain from stabilization (Turnovsky 1978). With a constant elasticity function and certainly with a demand function by which elasticity increases with the quantity supplied, the distribution of gains and losses between consumers and producers from stabilization would be reversed.

4. James P. Sterba, "A Bounty of Rice in Asia, Stubborn Poverty in Laos," *The New York Times.* © 1979 by The New York Times Company. Reprinted by permission.

Bibliography

Bigman, D., and Reutlinger, S. 1979. "National and International Policies Toward Food Security and Price Stabilization." *American Economic Review* 69:159–163.

Hadler, S. 1976. "Developing Country Foodgrain Projections for 1985." World Bank Staff Working Paper No. 247, Washington, D.C.

Reutlinger, S., and Knapp, K. 1980. "Food Security in Food Deficient Countries." World Bank Staff Working Paper No. 374, Washington, D.C.

Sterba, J.P. 1979. "A Bounty of Rice in Asia, Stubborn Poverty in Laos." *The New York Times,* April 4.

Turnovsky, S. 1978. "The Distribution of Welfare Gains from Price Stabilization: A Survey of Some Theoretical Issues." In *Stabilizing World Commodity Markets* ed F.G. Adams and S.A. Klein. Lexington, Mass.: Lexington Books, D.C. Heath and Company.

Valdes, A., and Konandreas, P. 1980. "Assessing Food Security in Developing Countries." In *Food Security for Developing Countries.* Washington, D.C.: International Food Policy Research Institute (IFPRI).

3 World-Grain-Market Instability and Food Security: An Exporter's Perspective

Ralph G. Lattimore

This chapter examines selected aspects of the world-grain-market instability and food-security issues from the viewpoint of a major exporter, Canada. Many comparisons can be made, however, between the experience of Canada and that of other major grain exporters, that is, Argentina, Australia, France, and the United States.

Later in the chapter, I scrutinize the stake that Canada, and to a greater or lesser extent, other major exporters have in increased world-grain-market stability and food security. In addition, I summarize the effects that current unilateral policy actions have on grain-market stability. Then I investigate the issue of apparent changes in the structure of world-grain-market power. I conclude with a discussion of the implications these views have for possible future multilateral grains agreements.

It seems to be generally accepted that the degree of price variation in world-grain markets is unacceptable from both the producers' and consumers' (exporters' and importers') viewpoints. This phenomenon of grain-price volatility is closely tied to the surety-of-supply question for importing countries. Hence, in international discussions on grains, there tends to be a close relationship between price stability and food-security concerns.

This market instability has two sources. The first is a set of natural or market forces including climatic variation, the incidence of crop diseases and pests affecting the supply side, and consumer tastes and preferences for grain and products derived from grain (directly and indirectly) on the demand side. The supply factors cause rather considerable short-term variation in the production of grains worldwide. The consumption characteristics tend to induce relatively inelastic responses in the demand for grains. The combination of these two factors results in wide year-to-year variations in international grain prices. The second source of grain-market instability stems from policy interventions (mainly unilateral) that virtually all countries have made to insulate or buffer the effects of instability —whatever its source—on their own economies.

The considerable amount of theoretical and empirical work in the area of grain-market stability has addressed the problems created by both sources of instability but with much more emphasis on the first. From this work, it is possible to make two generalizations relating to the distribution of benefits from improved market stability. The first is that there is no "free lunch" simultaneously available to both consumers and producers (importers and exporters) in market stabilization programs (Samuelson 1972). There will be losers and gainers, and contributions have to be tailored—implicitly or explicitly—to compensate the losers if a mutually acceptable solution is to be achieved.

The second generalization, as Gray (1974) argues, is that the demand for grains has tended over time to become more inelastic at high prices. This can be explained by changing consumer preferences toward livestock products based on grain. The more inelastic the demand schedule for grain becomes at higher prices, the greater are the benefits that accrue to consumers (importers) from stabilization.

Since all countries are producers and consumers of grains and contribute in some way, however small, to world-market instability, it would be ideal if a solution to the instability/food-security issue could be formed on a multilateral basis. It is obvious that, for a number of reasons, this is difficult to achieve in practice. Countries do not contribute to world-grain-market instability equally nor necessarily simply in proportion to grain production and trade or economic size. Moreover, instability effects arising from unilateral policy intervention are more difficult to ascribe and even more difficult to admit to. In addition, the sizes of grain economies vary tremendously in relation to the overall sizes of the economies of countries. This affects the feasible fiscal scope for insulating unilateral action as a substitute for a multilateral program.

Exporters' Stake in Increased Grain-Market Stability

In order to set the stage for this section, consider the representation of the world market for grain in figure 3–1. The world market is represented by the excess demand (*ED*) and excess supply (*ES*) for grain derived from the supply and demand curves (*S, D*) in the importing and exporting regions under free-trade conditions and zero-transportation costs. In this environment, the world price (*PW*) is determined by the intersection of *ES* and *ED* and *PW,* and imports will equal exports at a level *I*.

If the importing region sets its domestic price (*PD*) by fiat at *PD,* above the level that would have occurred in the free-trade environment (PD^{1}), two major effects would follow. First, import requirements would become inelastic with respect to the world price. Imports would fall, and excess demand would become more inelastic, as represented by ED^{1}. This would cause the world price to drop to PW^{1} and the domestic price in the exporting

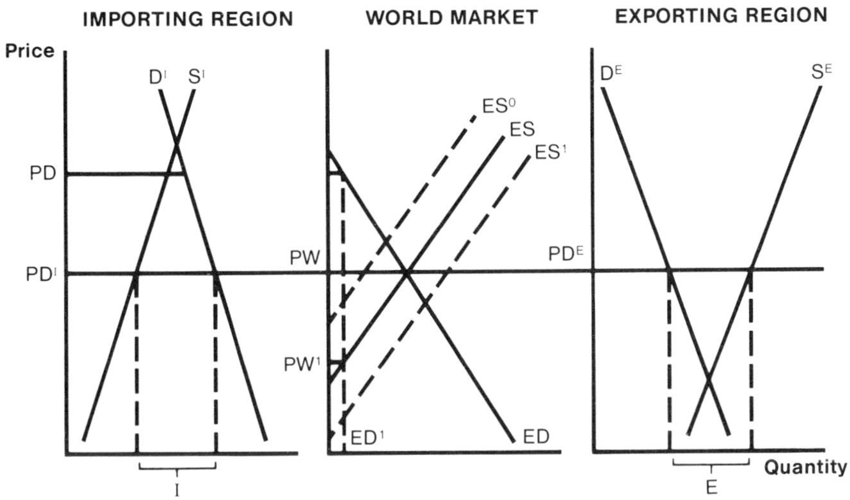

Figure 3–1. Representation of World Grain Market

region to fall similarly. Grain production would fall in the exporting region as producers move to relatively more profitable ventures on or off the farm, leaving grain-producing resources idle in those regions that are best able to produce grain.

The other major effect of the insulating domestic-pricing policy in the importing region would be to increase the instability of the world price. The excess supply of grain onto the world market is subject to considerable stochastic variation, largely due to weather. The coefficient of variation of grain yields is between 10 and 15 percent in major producing countries like Argentina, Australia, Canada, and the USSR and over 7 percent in most other major grain-producing countries. Such variations cause movements in the excess supply schedule from year to year, as represented by the movement from ES^0 to ES^1. As can be seen from figure 3–1, this results in a wider variation in world-grain prices if the excess demand schedule is inelastic as in ED^1. Hence, when regions insulate themselves from the price adjustments required in the world market, additional market instability is transmitted to other market participants, thereby destabilizing domestic grain prices, producer incomes, and consumer prices of grain products including livestock-product prices. Thus in attempting to stabilize grain prices, a trade-off exists internationally between (1) adjusting insulating domestic policies and (2) grain-reserve schemes.

The degree to which these effects on price levels and stability impinge on the world market is an empirical question. We can gauge the degree of distortion by examining producer and consumer grain prices for various countries. Tables 3–1 and 3–2 present producer and consumer prices for wheat and corn, respectively, for 60 countries as of October 1978. A number of factors need to be taken into account when directly comparing these prices as a measure of distortions,[1] but they do nevertheless indicate the direction of these distortions. Since policies affecting wheat and corn markets on a world scale are similar, both tables are discussed together.

It is possible to distinguish a number of policy regimes among the countries. Those in the first group, (which includes Japan and Switzerland), have adopted highly protective policies, with wheat support prices of U.S. $844 and $655 per metric ton, respectively. A second group, which includes the European Economic Community (E.E.C.), other Western European countries, and some developing countries, offers moderate to high levels of protection to producers. Producer support prices for this group are in the range of $160 to $300 per metric ton. A third group is composed of the major exporters and other countries that have no significant barriers to trade in grain. In these countries, producer prices range from $110 to $150 per metric ton. Finally, there is a group of developing countries that keep the price of grain below international levels as part of a cheap-food policy. The only obvious examples of these policies shown in the tables are Egypt and Pakistan. Other countries, however, not identifiable from the price data in the tables, have adopted instruments that overvalue the exchange rate to achieve cheap internal grain and other food prices. Domestic prices in such countries are overestimated when expressed in U.S. dollars, as in tables 3–1 and 3–2.

The prices in tables 3–1 and 3–2 have been used to calculate average producer and consumer prices for major groups of countries (table 3–3).

A number of points emerge from observing these average prices. First, a wide margin exists between grain prices in major exporting countries and in other countries. For example, the average price of wheat in all countries, excluding major exporters, is around 30 percent higher than in the exporting countries. For corn, other countries are over 75 percent higher, mainly as a result of the policies mentioned. Furthermore, the regions with the most protective policies and hence the highest domestic prices are Western Europe and Japan, where current producer prices average U.S. $219 per metric ton for wheat and $213 per metric ton for corn.

Second, it is possible to gain an appreciation for the cost of distortions imposed on exporting countries (see table 3–3). If all barriers to trade in grain were removed, then it could be expected that world-market prices would rise to around U.S. $150 for wheat and around $106 per metric ton for corn.[2] For wheat, this is very close to average prices ruling in other countries, with the obvious exception of Western Europe and Japan. The result would be a significant rise in export prices and income, as well as

Table 3–1
Wheat: Support, Producer, and Mill Prices for October 1978, unless Otherwise Specified
(U.S. $/metric ton)

Country	Producer Prices		Mill Purchase Prices		Description
	A. Support or Guaranteed	*B. Selling or Total Return*	*C. Domestic Wheat*	*D. Imported Wheat*	
Argentina	100	130	130	NA	A. Minimum support price at port. B. and C. Buenos Aires FAS port price.
Australia	87/94	116	135	NA	A. Initial payment for 1978/79 estimated guaranteed stabilization price for 1977/78. B. Estimated pool return for 1977/78. C. Home consumption price for 1978/79.
Austria	240	244	261	—	A. Base price for soft wheat. B. Total exfarm price, July/August.
Belgium	211	231	248	303	A. Intervention price for feed-quality wheat. D. U.S. wheat levy included.
Brazil	275	NA	80	80	A. Guaranteed producer price. C. and D. Government resale price.
Canada	111	120	127	NA	A. Initial payment for No. 1 CWRS 13.5%. B. Total return for No. 1 CWRS 13.5%. C. Minimum mill price for No. 1 CWRS 13.5%.
Chile	150	146	177	183	A. Approximate support price. B. Approximate government purchase price. C. Government resale price. D. U.S. wheat delivered to Santiago.
Colombia	219	192	225	248	A. Support price. B. Indicator producer price. D. Delivered to Bogota.
Costa Rica	NA	NA	NA	—	
Czechoslovakia	170	NA	—	—	
Denmark	233	224	224	270	A. Reference price for bread-quality wheat. D. Threshold price.

Table 3–1 continued

Country	Producer Prices		Mill Purchase Prices		Description
	A. Support or Guaranteed	*B. Selling or Total Return*	*C. Domestic Wheat*	*D. Imported Wheat*	
Dominican Republic	NA	NA	NA	—	
Ecuador	220	NA	—	138	A. Producer support, including bonuses. D. Fixed price.
Egypt	67	NA	42	42	A. Nonhigh-yielding variety support price. C. and D. Government resale price.
El Salvador	NA	NA	NA	—	
European Economic Community (EEC)	199/244	NA	NA	225	A. Intervention/reference price for feed/baking-quality wheat. D. Threshold price for feed wheat.
France	185	211	211	—	A. Intervention price for feed-quality wheat. B. and C. Market price for soft wheat.
German Democratic Republic	112	NA	—	168	D. U.S. wheat, CIF Rostock.
Germany, Federal Republic	258	239	258	331	A. Reference price for baking-quality wheat. B. Producer selling price. C. Wholesale price. D. U.S. wheat, levy included.
Greece	198	NA	167	NA	A. Support price for soft wheat. C. Government resale price.
Guatemala	261	253	261	180	C. Government set price.
Hong Kong	NA	NA	NA	—	
Hungary	161	NA	209	—	A. Approximate producer return.
India	141	NA	156	156	A. Producer support/guaranteed price. C. and D. Government resale price.
Indonesia	NA	NA	NA	140	D. Basic resale price for imported wheat.
Iran	198	—	106	106	A. Support price. C. and D. Government resale price.
Ireland	181	181	—	222	A. Intervention price for baking-quality wheat. B. Approximate producer price. D. Includes levy.
Israel	138	NA	132	132	
Italy	203	221	226	289	A. Intervention price for feed-quality wheat. D. Canadian soft wheat, levy included.

Japan	844	NA	228	339	A. Guaranteed basic producer price. C. and D. Government resale price to mills.
Kenya	182	—	—	—	
Korea, Republic of	385	—	NA	151	D. Government set price for western white or hard red winter.
Lebanon	164	160	—	92	A. Average support price for soft wheat. D. Government delivery price.
Malaysia	NA	NA	NA	163	D. U.S. wheat.
Mexico	115	158	92	—	A. Producer guaranteed price. B. Average September market price. C. Government set price.
Morocco	213	213	219	142	A. All bread-wheat prices.
Netherlands	202	212	212	241	A. Intervention price for feed-quality wheat. B. and C. Approximate producer price. D. French baking-quality wheat.
New Zealand	142	NA	150	NA	C. Wheat Board resale price to mills.
Nicaragua	NA	NA	NA	—	
Nigeria	367	NA	367	—	C. Selling price to mills.
Norway	352	358	NA	131	D. January–June average.
Pakistan	100	NA	87	87	C. and D. Government resale price.
Peru	146	—	—	142	A. Minimum guaranteed price. D. Government set price.
Philippines	NA	NA	NA	232	D. Government resale price.
Poland	181	170	—	—	A. Guaranteed initial price. B. Average selling price to state in June.
Portugal	168	NA	134	134	A. Minimum support price. C. and D. Government minimum resale price.
South Africa	—	153	160	NA	B. Net producer price for grade B1. C. Board selling price of grade B1.
Spain	181	NA	—	NA	A. Minimum support price.

Table 3–1 continued

Country	Producer Prices		Mill Purchase Prices		Description
	A. Support or Guaranteed	*B. Selling or Total Return*	*C. Domestic Wheat*	*D. Imported Wheat*	
Sweden	167	NA	167	—	A. August minimum guaranteed price, average-quality wheat.
Switzerland	644	NA	491	437	A. Guaranteed producer price. C. Resale price to mills. D. U.S. wheat levy and duty included.
Syria	155	187	218	180	A. Minimum support price. B. Average 1978 producer price. C. Government flour mills purchase price. D. Approximate import cost.
Taiwan	278	NA	NA	140	D. February 1978 price for U.S. western white.
Thailand	NA	NA	NA	—	
Turkey	115	115	105	NA	A. Minimum support price. C. Government resale price to mills.
United Kingdom	150/169	157/165	165	240	A. August intervention price for feed-quality/baking wheat. B. Feed-quality/milling. C. Average selling price for baking wheat, August. D. August price for U.S. DNS.
United States	86	112	126	NA	A. Loan rate. B. National average farm price on October 15 of all wheat. C. HRW wheat average wholesale price, Kansas City, October 13.
Uruguay	176	NA	—	187	A. Minimum support price, May 1978. D. U.S. wheat.
USSR	143	NA	—	—	A. Base procurement price.
Venezuela	NA	NA	NA	—	
Yugoslavia	146	NA	146	—	A. Producer guaranteed price for soft wheat. C. Resale price.

Source: U.S. Department of Agriculture, *Foreign Agriculture Circular FG-6-79,* Washington, D.C., 1979.
Note: NA denotes not applicable to specified country; — denotes not available.

Table 3–2
Corn: Support, Producer, and Feed Manufacturer Prices for October 1978, unless Otherwise Specified
(U.S. $/metric ton)

	Producer Prices		*Compounder Purchase Price*		
Country	*A. Support or Guaranteed*	*B. Selling or Total Return*	*C. Domestic Corn*	*D. Imported Corn*	*Description*
Argentina	NA	92	92	NA	B. and C. FAS port price.
Australia	NA	121	121	NA	B. and C. Approximate price, Sydney market.
Austria	NA	239	255	NA	B. Minimum exfarm price for feed corn. C. Wholesale price.
Belgium	211	—	—	253	A. Intervention price. D. U.S. corn, levy included.
Brazil	67	111	111	111	A. Guaranteed minimum price. B., C., and D. Official price.
Canada	NA	90	90	—	B. and C. Bid price for No. 2 corn, Ontario shipping points.
Chile	NA	—	—	152	D. Argentine flint corn price, September.
Colombia	186	171	199	NA	A. Support price for flint yellow corn. B. Approximate producer indicator price. C. Approximate processor price in July.
Costa Rica	209	—	—	—	A. Support price.
Czechoslovakia	152	NA	—	—	B. Approximate producer price.
Denmark	NA	NA	NA	245	D. Threshold price.
Dominican Republic	148	121	143	—	A. Support price. B. Approximate producer selling price. C. Approximate feed-mill price.
Ecuador	155	—	255	255	A. Minimum support price. C. and D. Official resale price.
Egypt	NA	NA	NA	47	D. Government resale price.
El Salvador	203	165	NA	NA	A. Guaranteed price for small and medium producers.
European Economic Community (EEC)	199	NA	NA	230	A. Intervention price. D. Threshold price.

Table 3–2 continued

Country	*Producer Prices*		*Compounder Purchase Price*		Description
	A. Support or Guaranteed	*B. Selling or Total Return*	*C. Domestic Corn*	*D. Imported Corn*	
France	185	210	210	—	A. Intervention price. C. and D. Market price.
German Democratic Republic	NA	NA	NA	—	
Germany, Federal Republic	230	251	257	270	A. Intervention price. B. Producer selling price. C. Wholesale price. D. U.S. corn, levy included.
Greece	195	—	125	125	A. Support price. C. and D. Government resale price.
Guatemala	186	157	159	119	C. Wholesale price.
Hong Kong	NA	NA	NA	—	
Hungary	147	NA	206	NA	A. Approximate producer price.
India	106	NA	NA	NA	A. Support price.
Indonesia	108	—	—	—	A. Floor price.
Iran	170	—	135	135	A. Producer support. C. and D. Government resale price.
Ireland	NA	NA	NA	224	D. Levy included.
Israel	NA	NA	NA	—	
Italy	180	205	210	223	A. Intervention price. D. U.S. corn, levy included.
Japan	NA	NA	NA	125	D. August price.
Kenya	132	—	—	—	
Korea, Republic of	350	—	NA	135	D. Government set price.
Lebanon	NA	144	144	—	
Malaysia	NA	—	NA	127	D. U.S. corn.
Mexico	128	159	103	—	A. Guaranteed producer price. B. Average September market price.
Morocco	163	205	210	149	C. Government set price.
Netherlands	202	NA	NA	238	A. Intervention price. D. U.S. corn, levy included.
New Zealand	112	NA	126	NA	

Nicaragua	124	124	124	—	All prices for yellow corn.
Nigeria	233	NA	NA	—	
Norway	NA	NA	NA	320	D. Government resale price to feed compounders.
Pakistan	87	—	—	NA	A. "Guideline" or target price.
Peru	109	—	156	156	C. and D. Government resale price.
Philippines	122	NA	155	155	C. and D. Government resale price.
Poland	190	—	—	—	A. Guaranteed initial price.
Portugal	131	NA	131	131	A. Support price for yellow corn. C. and D. Government resale price.
South Africa	—	92	96	NA	B. Net producer price. C. Board selling price for best grades.
Spain	—	—	—	179	D. Threshold price.
Sweden	NA	NA	NA	—	
Switzerland	416	523	523	396	A. Target price. B. and C. Average domestic price, June–August. D. U.S. corn, levy and duty included.
Syria	205	212	—	206	A. Support price. B. Approximate market price. D. Government resale price.
Taiwan	222	NA	156	119	D. U.S. No. 2 yellow corn, July.
Thailand	NA	79	98	NA	B. Inland producer price.
Turkey	NA	178	178	NA	
United Kingdom	NA	NA	NA	190	D. U.S. corn, levy included.
United States	79	76	87	NA	A. Loan rate. B. National average farm price on October 13. C. Average wholesale price, Chicago, No. 2 yellow, on October 13.
Uruguay	79	96	96	NA	A. Minimum guaranteed price. B. and C. Market price, November.
USSR	106	NA	—	—	A. Base procurement price.
Venezuela	214	214	149	149	A. and B. Yellow corn. C. and D. Resale price.
Yugoslavia	114	205	205	135	A. Guaranteed price. B. and C. August prices. D. Resale price.

Source: U.S. Department of Agriculture, *Foreign Agriculture Circular FG-6-79,* Washington, D.C., 1979.

Note: NA denotes not applicable to specified countries; — denotes not available.

Table 3–3
Average Producer and Consumer Prices for Wheat and Corn, October 1978
(U.S. $/metric ton)

	Weighted Average Price[a]			
	Producer[b]		Consumer[c]	
	Wheat	Corn	Wheat	Corn
Major exporters[d]	124	86	124	90
Eastern Europe (including USSR)	145	150	173	205
Western Europe and Japan	219	213	220	198
All countries (except major exporters)	159	149	162	164
All countries[e]	150	106	155	122

Source: Adpated from U.S. Department of Agriculture, *Foreign Agriculture Circular FG-6-79,* Washington, D.C., 1979.

[a]The weights used are the proportion of total production and consumption for the producer and consumer price, respectively.

[b]The producer price is (whenever possible) the producer selling price or total return per unit. When this was not available, the support or guaranteed producer price was used.

[c]When available, the consumer price is the wholesale or resale price to millers or feed manufacturers. Otherwise, it is the CIF import price.

[d]In the case of wheat, the major exporters are taken as the United States, Canada, Australia, and Argentina; for corn, the United States, Brazil, and South Africa are the major exporters.

[e]The producer price of grain in the United States was taken as a target price in this table rather than the loan rate used in tables 3–1 and 3–2.

greater price stability to world markets. The major point here is that protective policies not only insulate and raise domestic prices of the acting country; they also lower the prices on world markets and increase price instability.

The stake of any exporter in increasing world-grain security and improved international-grain-price stability is related to the absolute and relative importance of the following: (1) grain exports to the country, (2) grains for domestic human consumption, (3) livestock production based on grain, and (4) the country's food-aid program.

The degree to which an exporter will act alone to alleviate grain price instability and security depends on an additional set of factors. The scope for unilateral action depends on the relative size of the grain sector in the economy as a whole, which affects the fiscal burden of domestic intervention. It is also dependent on the share of the world-grain market of the country that affects the degree to which the burden of domestic intervention can be passed on to the world market. An exporter's actions are also related to the absolute importance of the country in world affairs, which affects the leverage that can be brought to bear in multilateral negotiations and hence in expectations regarding the probability of achieving a shared solution, rather than incurring the higher costs associated with unilateral action.

Canada's broad objectives relating to world food security and grain-market stability relate to all four areas: production, consumption, commercial trade, and aid in grain.

1. As a middle-rank power and a grain-producing country, Canada is committed—both publicly and privately—to assisting food-deficit countries to meet their national dietary and production objectives through research and development and food-aid programs.
2. As a country with a comparative advantage in grain production, Canada is keen to expand export opportunities for grains and grain products.
3. As a consumer of grains and livestock products derived from grain, Canada is concerned with stabilizing producers' incomes and consumer prices of grain and livestock products.

These considerations temper Canadian grain policy and are manifest in the array of unilateral policy actions that the government has taken over the years. Grain production in Canada, as in Australia, is highly variable due to climatic and other naturally occurring phenomena. To compensate, Canada has supported the largest storage capacity in the world in terms of population, grain production, or aid and trade in grain. This capacity has been used extensively to buffer the impact of Canadian production variation on the international market and the domestic market. This is achieved through a variety of programs. Grain producers pay directly to maintain stocks through the buffering policies of the Canadian Wheat Board, with assistance from the government (that is, taxpayers) through a number of grain-industry stabilization and other assistance programs.

As a result of these actions, Josling (1980) shows that Canada contributes relatively more to international-grain-market stability than does any other country. Australia and the United States also make some contribution to stability through offsetting stocking actions, but as Josling demonstrates, some other developed countries (for example, members of the E.E.C. and Japan) tend to contribute to instability.

The inventory policies also ensure that adequate domestic food grain and feedgrain supplies are available throughout the country at all times of the year. The sheer physical size, regional separation of major grain producing and consuming areas, and climatic considerations all mean that considerable resources must be devoted to this task.

The stocking actions also ensure that Canada's food-aid commitments are available in the right place at the right time. These programs are administered through the Canadian International Development Agency (CIDA) and other organizations.

Canada's position as a middle-rank power in geopolitical and grain-trade terms and the relative importance of the grain industry also temper the approach. To use an economic analogy, it places Canada in that middle ground between a "price-maker" and a "price-taker." It means that multilateral solutions are relatively more attractive due to the high fiscal burden of unilateral stabilization programs. Countries occupying this middle ground, like Australia and Canada, do intervene directly to stabilize the domestic price of milling wheat. This policy protects domestic consumers of bakery and cereal products. Since these programs only cover a small proportion of total grain production (20 to 25 percent of wheat production in the case of Canada's two-price wheat policy), however, treasury costs are tolerable. The cost of intervening to completely insulate domestic feed grains from world-market fluctuations, along the lines of the E.E.C. common agricultural policy, would involve fiscal outlays many times higher than the milling-wheat programs. As with insulation-type policies in other countries, the two-price wheat programs have a negative stabilization impact on the world market. This effect is not large, however, because the price elasticity of demand for wheat for human consumption is still quite low (less than 0.1 in absolute value). The main impact is to stabilize consumer expenditures on wheat products and domestic prices. That is, the artificial consumption raising effect during times of high prices tends to zero as the absolute value of the elasticity of demand tends to zero.

The other major set of unilateral stabilization policies are, among others, the Western Grain Stabilization Act (WGSA) for western grain producers, related Agricultural Stabilization Act (ASA) programs for grains in other areas and for livestock producers, and the crop-insurance program. These tend to stabilize net returns to grain and livestock producers and hence to stabilize grain production and the domestic demand for feed grains. The grain programs tend to stabilize production available for domestic and export utilization, whereas the livestock programs can be expected to increase the inelasticity of domestic feed-grain demand. Since the livestock programs remove only part of the effect of variation in feed-grain prices, however, livestock production remains sensitive to international-price variation.

In summary, a large grain exporter like Canada has a major stake in action leading to improved grain-market stability. This remains true in spite of significant unilateral policy actions taken to buffer the effect of instability on the domestic market and on recipients of Canadian grain through both aid and trade. Some of these policies have a negative impact on world-market stability, but the net impact of all unilateral actions taken together is likely to be highly positive.

World-Grain-Market Power

It is generally assumed that the major exporters have considerable market power in influencing world-grain prices. Such views have been popularized in work by McCalla (1966) and more recently by Alaouze et al. (1978). If we consider the market processes involved in figure 3–1 and the way in which domestic grain price and trade policies have been set over the last fifteen years, it is possible to arrive at a quite different conclusion.

Producer wheat prices in Japan and the E.E.C. (six-country grouping) have shown almost no tendency to move in relation to world prices.[3] Given the importance of these two factors, it might well be suspected that world-grain prices are primarily set by policies in the major importing regions rather than in the exporting regions. Evidence on this point is provided by Carter and Schmitz (1979), who show that there is a reasonable basis to conclude that major importers have more market power than the exporters, and indeed may be approaching the application of an optimal import tax, at least in effect, if not by design. In welfare terms, such importers' policies appear to transfer income from grain producers in noninsulated exporting countries to the government treasuries of the importers.

Multilateral Grain-Market Stabilization

A large number of studies in recent years have addressed the issue of stabilization of world-grain markets, and a major attempt has been made to negotiate a new International Wheat Agreement incorporating a grain-reserve convention. Furthermore, both the breakdown of the United Nations Conference on Trade and Development (UNCTAD) wheat talks and the generally firming trend in grain markets have led to public discussion about the possibility of an exporter/cooperative arrangement (or in the extreme, an exporter cartel) as a means of stabilizing the world market. In the context of continuing discussions and research, it might be worth reiterating the central contentious issues.

First, there is a basic desire on the part of exporting and importing countries to stabilize the international grain market. This objective has many functions that may be in conflict, however. Exporters are interested in export revenue stabilization for grain producers and grain-price stabilization for consumers, especially in countries where the grain-livestock economies are highly interrelated.[4] Importers may also be concerned with stabilizing grain-consumption levels and assuring access to foreign supplies.

The price-stabilization objective can be attained in two main ways as follows: (1) by decreased protection[5] and/or (2) by a grain-reserve scheme. If domestic-policy adjustments are not forthcoming, any grain-reserve policy must be more comprehensive so as to overcome the "natural" instability resulting from climate, disease, and other factors, as well as the instability induced by domestic-policy interference.

The second factor that needs to be considered concerns the level around which the market is to be stabilized. This aspect is most important but seldom addressed. In price terms, two possibilities are usually discussed. First, one would attempt to impose a price-enhancing scheme. By its nature, such a scheme must involve a cartel to enforce supply restrictions and hence raise prices, on the average, above what they would otherwise be. In view of the coordination difficulties involved, however, and in the light of the earlier discussion on world-price determination, the best that could probably be achieved is the elimination of the current income transfer implicit in the present market structure. More often, discussions center on attempts to stabilize prices around the long-term trend dictated by production costs in the major trading regions. This is an easy statement to make in the context of the certain world described in most texts, but it is very difficult to assess just where the trend is in relation to current prices, especially in an international negotiation context. There appear to be four major areas of uncertainty.

1. The extent to which rising energy-related production costs are altering patterns of comparative advantage among major grain-producing countries.
2. The grain supply potential of the developing countries at competitive prices as advances in production and distribution technology come on stream in those countries.
3. Exchange-rate fluctuations between major exporting and importing countries.
4. The real supply price of grain in the developing countries that pursue cheap-food policies and maintain consumption levels with a high proportion of food aid.

Figures 3–2, 3–3, and 3–4 show the trends in world wheat, coarse grain, and rice production compared with a set of naive forecasts. I derived naive forecasts from a relatively simple econometric model of the world supply and demand for wheat, coarse grains, and rice at Agriculture Canada. These forecasts are used in an attempt to "adjust" the trend in world production for changes in the world price of grain and a proxy for

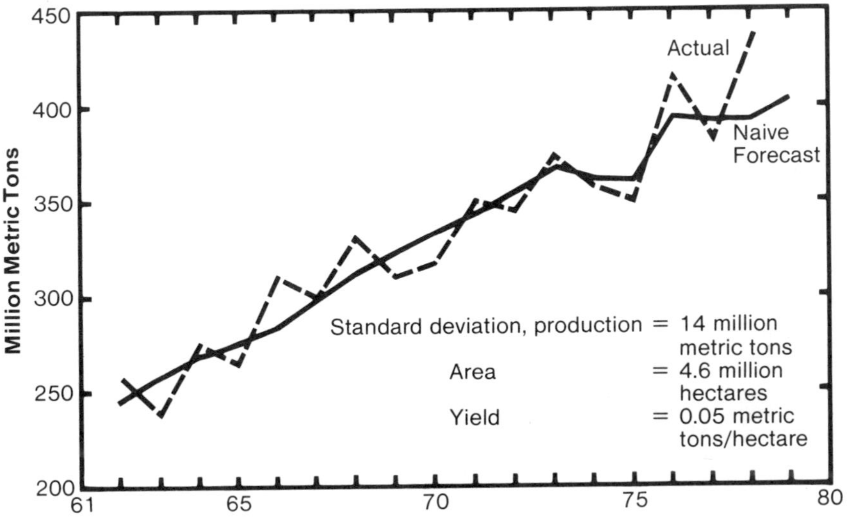

Figure 3–2. World Wheat Production

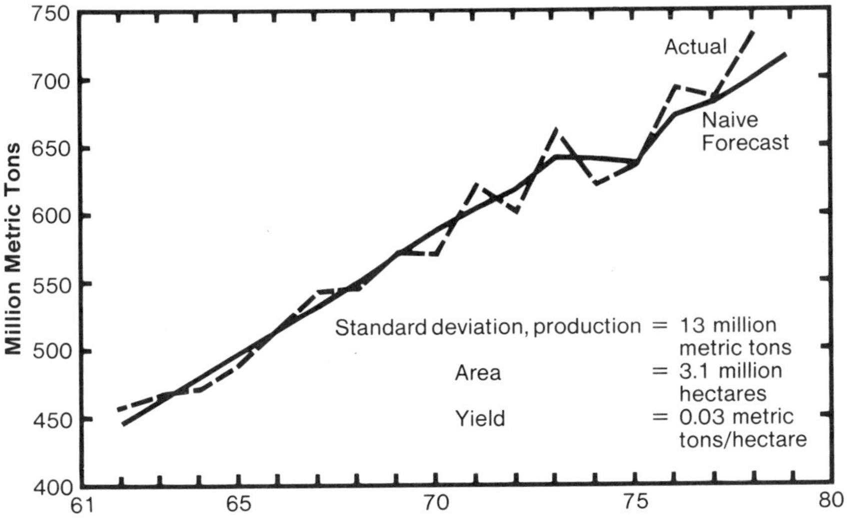

Figure 3–3. World Coarse-Grain Production

input costs (price of fertilizer). If recent production trends are compared with world grain-price movements,[6] aspects of this current uncertainty become apparent. During the period 1974/75 to 1976/77, the indicator price declined from U.S. $189 per metric ton to $161 per metric ton as a result of

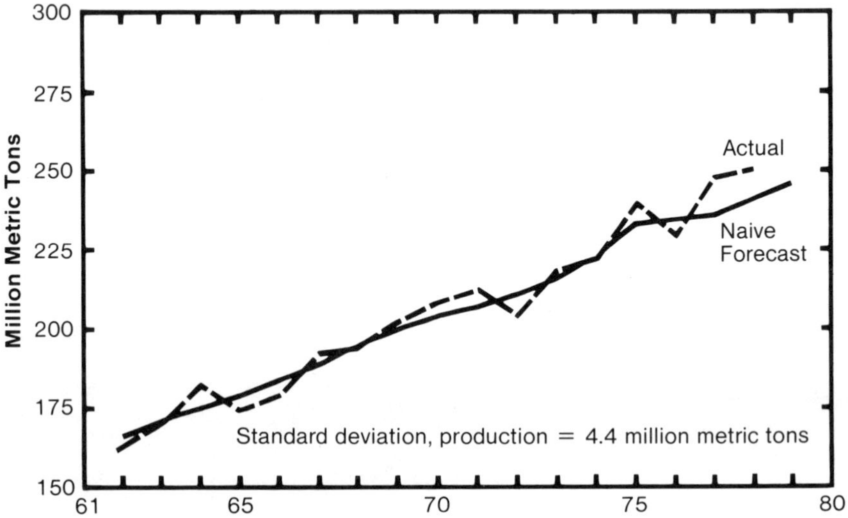

Figure 3–4. World Rice Production

large crops in 1976/77. The main impact of this crop was not felt until the following year as a result of the inventory buildup, and the indicator price fell to $121 per metric ton in 1977/78.

Following the lower-than-expected crop in 1977/78, prices began to increase in the last quarter of 1977 and have continued to rise ever since. The indicator price rose from a low of U.S. $102 per metric ton in August 1977 to $141 per metric ton in December 1979. It is surprising that prices remained firm in spite of the huge crop expected for the 1978/79 crop year. This crop was approximately two standard deviations above the naive forecast. The U.S. grain-reserve scheme sterilized one-third of this deviation, and the weakness of the U.S. dollar tended to support prices. Nevertheless, the underlying strength of demand is thought to have had a major impact. This inherent instability continues to be reflected in prices through 1980/81, especially when these are expressed in real terms. During the partial grain embargo of the USSR, the indicator price fell to U.S. $168 per metric ton and rose to $207 per metric ton at the end of 1980. By June 1981, the price had fallen again to $175 per metric ton as a result of a large U.S. crop, exchange-rate fluctuations, and other factors. The key question that must be faced in designing an international grain price-stabilization scheme at the present time is: Where can the trend in prices reasonably be expected to go over the next five years in light of the uncertainties given earlier?

The third set of economic decisions to be faced concerns the technical aspects of the reserve stock itself. Three interrelated decisions have to be made for a price-triggered reserve stock scheme as follows: (1) the width of the price band between the trend and the upper and lower trigger points, (2) the desired degree of confidence that the scheme will cope with future outcomes, and (3) the size of the buffer stock. If the price triggers are set, perhaps, one standard deviation around the mean value, and it is agreed that the reserve scheme would meet 90 percent of the outcomes (in terms of production variability), then the size of the required buffer stock is determined. In short, if any two instruments are set, the third is determined automatically.

Only the major decision points relating to a price-triggered reserve-stock scheme have been discussed. There are many other schemes that are more applicable on a bilateral basis and other configurations that are worthy of consideration. For example, Hathaway (1976) has suggested a supply insurance program between exporters and importers to guarantee (for an insurance premium) the availability of grain to make up crop shortfalls in importing countries. This suggestion has a number of strengths. First, it does not have to be implemented on a multilateral basis and hence avoids the time and effort associated with reaching a consensus with a large number of countries. It is quite likely that Canada or Australia and perhaps other exporters could organize such a scheme independently, with a group of grain-deficit countries who suffer from wide variability in domestic-grain production. Second, the scheme addresses the key objective of stabilizing grain supplies, particularly in the developing countries. Third, the premiums associated with the scheme could be covered under existing or extended-aid programs in the exporting country, in the case of the poorer developing countries.

It is often assumed that the trigger points of an international-stabilization scheme must be explicitly set and then, presumably, become public knowledge. It is well known in other commodity markets,[7] however, that such action invited adverse private behavior. As Zwart (1977) points out, a flexible unannounced price-trigger mechanism has certain advantages, especially in the uncertain market outlook discussed earlier.

Conclusions

This chapter has argued that, in large part, world-food insecurity arises from unstable world-grain markets. This instability is due both to "natural" and policy-induced factors. Almost all grain-producing and trading countries are partly responsible; the importing nations do not have a monopoly on such policy-induced distortions.

Second, there is wide acceptance of the principle that self-sufficiency in food production should be a major objective for food-deficit countries. It may be seriously questioned whether this goal is consistent with comparative advantage and gains from trade arguments. If it is not, what are the welfare costs involved in disregarding such potential gains? Furthermore, where increased self-sufficiency can only be achieved with increased production, what will be the reactions of exporting countries to an increasingly unstable world market? In addition, will traditional exporters tend to deemphasize grain production and hence become less able to meet the world-grain shortfalls that will certainly arise in the future?

A range of potential food insurance programs exists between food exporters and importers that deserves greater consideration within the context of both aid programs and commercial food trade.

Notes

1. These included transportation costs, quality differentials, distorted exchange rates, and so forth.

2. Market conditions similar to those ruling in the fall of 1978 are assumed. Strictly speaking, the new world price under free trade needs to be calculated on the basis of a weighting of supply and demand quantities and elasticities. As a rough approximation, however, this price can be expected to be close to the current weighted average price.

3. For evidence of this, see Lattimore and Zwart (1978), table 9, p. 98.

4. In North America the volatility of the food component of the consumer price index over the past six years has been largely a result of grain prices having an impact on the livestock sector.

5. Decreased protection would make national grain markets more responsive to international events.

6. The IWA basket of indicator wheat prices is used as a representative grain price.

7. Examples of such markets are: the foreign-exchange stabilization procedures of central banks, the wool-price-stabilization schemes of Australia and New Zealand, and the price-stabilization scheme operated under the International Tin Agreement.

Bibliography

Alaouze, C.M., Watson, A.S., and Sturgess, N.H. 1978. "Oligopoly Pricing in the World Wheat Markets." *American Journal of Agricultural Economics* 60:173–185.

Carter, C., and Schmitz, A. 1979. "Improve Tariffs and Price Formulation in the World Wheat Market." mimeo, Giannini Foundation of Agricultural Economics, University of California, Berkeley, January.

Gray, R. 1974. "Grain Reserves Issues." Paper presented at the 1974 National Agricultural Outlook Conference, Washington, D.C., December 9.

Hathaway, D.E. 1976. "Grain Stocks and Economic Stability." In *Analyses of Grain Reserves,* Washington, D.C.: E.R.S., U.S. Department of Agriculture, August.

Josling, T. 1980. "Developed-Country Agricultural Policies and Developing-Country Supplies: The Case of Wheat." Research Report No. 14, Washington, D.C.: International Food Policy Research Institute (IFPRI), March.

Lattimore, R.G., and Zwart, A.C. 1978. "Medium Term World Wheat Forecasting Model." In *Commodity Forecasting Models for Canadian Agriculture,* Vol. 2. Ottawa: Agriculture Canada.

McCalla, A. 1966. "A Duopoly Model of World Wheat Pricing." *Journal of Farm Economics* 48:711–727.

Samuelson, P.A. 1972. "The Consumer Does Benefit from Feasible Price Stability." *Quarterly Journal of Economics,* August, 476–503.

Zwart, A.C. 1977. *An Empirical Analysis of Alternative Stabilization Policies for the World Wheat Sector.* Unpublished Ph.D. dissertation, University of Guelph, Canada.

4 Commodity-Price Stabilization: Microeconomic Theory and Policy Issues

Anthony H. Chisholm

The world food crisis of 1972–1974 has spawned a large body of economics literature on the role of grain buffer stocks in stabilizing prices and providing food security. A major conclusion of this theoretical literature is that price stabilization will always improve the economic welfare of consumers and producers in aggregate. The purposes of this chapter are basically twofold. First, it seeks to survey and critically evaluate the microeconomic theoretical literature on price stabilization with the particular aim of drawing out the implications for empirical and policy-oriented problems. Second, it attempts to identify potential areas of market failure that may cause excessive price instability and to consider the consequent implications for alternative forms of government intervention. Two possible areas of market failure are identified, the first relating to risk and stockpiling and the second to the issue of the informational efficiency of agricultural-commodity markets.

Some important issues relating to instability of commodity prices are not discussed in this chapter. It is now widely recognized that major causes of world-market price variability are the national and regional restrictive trade policies adopted in both food-importing and food-exporting countries that prevent world-price signals from being reflected across their borders into the domestic market. Johnson (1975, 1976) in particular has argued strongly that man and not nature is responsible for a large part of world-market-price variability, including the substantial rise in international grain prices that occurred after mid-1972. The optimal level of stockpiling is clearly influenced by the existing pattern of trade policies and also by the degree of risk-aversion of food-importing countries (Feder et al. 1977). Various aspects of the impact of trade policies on domestic and world-market-price variability are analyzed in chapter 2 by Shlomo Reutlinger, chapter 3 by Ralph Lattimore, and in chapter 14 by Rodney Tyers and Anthony Chisholm. A further issue that is beyond the scope of this chapter

This chapter was developed from a paper I presented to the Working Group Meeting on Food Security Issues held at the East-West Resource Systems Institute in June 1979. I would like to thank Kym Anderson, Alex McCalla, Larry Miller, Mark Powers, James Roumasset, Rod Tyers, and Brian Wright for helpful discussion and comments.

is that of the largely income-distribution questions pertaining to the New International Economic Order and the North-South Debate (Corden 1979; Sarris and Taylor 1976; and Solow 1977). The international distribution of welfare impacts from food and agricultural policies in developed countries is examined empirically by Tyers and Chisholm in chapter 14.

First, the theoretical literature on commodity-price stabilization is critically evaluated, with particular emphasis on the microeconomic foundations of the theory and the implications for real-world buffer-stock schemes. Second, the practical experience with various government-controlled (public) buffer-stock schemes is surveyed. Third, the first potential area of market failure—namely, the supposed divergence between private and social risk-aversion inherent in the holding of large commodity stockpiles—is dealt with. Fourth, the complex issue of whether or not speculative agricultural commodity markets collect, process, and disseminate information efficiently is addressed.

Section four is the largest in the chapter. If—as some writers claim—underproduction and underutilization of information exist in agricultural commodity markets, decisions relating to production, storage, and international trade will be made inefficiently. Consequently, price uncertainty and instability will be excessive. The traditional view that in a market economy there will be underinvestment in the production of commodity outlook information because of its public good characteristics is reviewed, and consideration is then given to a more recent view that when opportunities for speculation are taken into account, there can be no a priori presumption that the provision of information in a pure market economy will be socially insufficient. The analysis of speculation and the supply of information in agricultural commodity markets leads to a discussion of conceptual and empirical issues relating to futures markets.

Theory of Commodity-Price Stabilization

The theoretical framework of price stabilization developed by Waugh (1944), Oi (1961), and Massell (1969) forms the basis for the flood of subsequent theoretical research. One of the most striking conclusions to emerge from the theoretical stabilization studies that have followed in the tradition of Waugh-Oi-Massell is that price stabilization will always improve the economic welfare of consumers and producers, taken together. The aggregate welfare gain persists as changes are made in one or more of the following specifications of the model:

1. Linear or nonlinear supply and demand functions.

2. Additive or multiplicative disturbances (parallel shifts in supply and demand functions, or changing slopes).
3. Closed economy or "whole world" model.
4. Producers' supply decisions based on actual selling prices or on expected prices formed on the basis of either adaptive expectations or rational expectations.
5. Complete or partial price stabilization.

Importantly, while the net gains persist as the model variations are made, the distribution of the welfare gains among various groups in society is typically very sensitive to the model specification. These studies brought into sharp focus the potential conflict of interest in price stabilization between producers and consumers and exporting and importing countries. The detailed results are presented in a survey paper by Turnovsky (1978), who is a major contributor to this literature, and will not be repeated here.[1]

The major implication for empirical research on stabilization to be drawn from the just-described theoretical work is the need to adequately investigate the forms of supply and demand functions and the forms of the random disturbances. Just (1977) points out that the results of some empirical studies hinge critically on specifications and assumptions relating to functional forms and the nature of disturbances that often have been made quite arbitrarily.

The significance of functional form was recognized by Hillman, Johnson, and Gray (1975, p. 8) in their study on food-reserve policies.

> A demand curve grown steeper at higher prices and shallower at lower prices enhances the consumer stake while diminishing the producer stake in reserves.

This observation is supported by the results derived from a model developed by Just et al. (1977) that shows that with strong nonlinearity in the demand function, consumers and importing countries gain from price stabilization while producers and exporting countries as a whole lose. The authors show, however, that if the nonlinearity is sufficiently weak, these results can be reversed.

The qualitative results obtained in the described theoretical work are given some quantitative content in an empirical simulation study undertaken by Reutlinger (1976). The results from this study indicate that the impact of a worldwide buffer-stock scheme for wheat, in terms of gains and losses to consumers and producers and wheat-importing and wheat-exporting countries, is particularly sensitive to the assumed shape of the demand curve. Reutlinger's results, which show that producers tend to lose and consumers to gain from stabilization of world wheat prices, are supported by the results of a separate study by Sarris and Taylor (1978).[2] In an empirical study of the United States, Konandreas and Schmitz (1978) conclude that U.S. producers and consumers taken together probably benefit from instability of wheat prices,[3] although they would likely gain from feed-grain price stabilization.

Earlier, I pointed out that the major conclusion reached by Massell (1969)—namely, that price stabilization results in a *net* welfare gain—continues to hold when the assumptions are modified to incorporate nonlinear demand and supply curves, multiplicative disturbances, and alternative forms of producer price expectations. In principle, the gainers always could compensate the losers with an overall increase in economic welfare from price stabilization.

This result is perhaps not surprising when the assumptions underlying the traditional theoretical stabilization work are made apparent. The most crucial assumptions that have usually been made (implicitly or explicitly) are that there is no stockpiling by the private sector, the public stabilization authority has perfect knowledge of future prices, and it operates a costless buffer-stock scheme. The public stabilization authority through its buffer-stock operations can then, in effect, completely "iron out" random fluctuations in supply.[4]

It is remarkable how the role of stockholding by the private sector has generally been assumed away without explanation or apology in most theoretical and empirical stabilization studies.[5] The natural benchmark for evaluating the performance of a public stabilization authority is surely a competitive private-storage market. In this respect, this literature overlooks the important study undertaken nearly twenth-five years ago by Gustafson (1958). This study showed that a competitive market in which risk-neutral private-storage operators and producers respond to rational expectations of future prices will attain a Pareto-efficient level of storage. The marginal value of grain in current consumption is equated with the discounted expected value of the grain (net of storage costs) in future consumption.[6] Roughly speaking, the optimal storage rule is to carry forward a little more than one-half of the excess of current production plus carry-over stocks from the previous year over the size of the average harvest. A buffer-stock scheme that utilizes the optimal storage rule will maximize the discounted present value of consumers' and producers' surpluses net of storage costs.[7] Acquisition of stocks beyond this level will result in a loss of economic efficiency.

At the same time—because of significant differences between rationally expected prices and realized prices—competitive storage levels are consistent with wide price fluctuations, attributable mainly to weather and other nature-induced random disturbances. This important point is obscured in the theoretical stabilization investigations that have followed in the Waugh-Oi-Massell tradition. As has been well stated by Wright (1979), by focusing on complete and costless price stabilization, these studies have confounded the analysis of the economic consequences of the disturbances themselves with the much more complicated problem of the economic benefits of public or private commodity storage.[8] Any worthwhile analysis of public storage must first consider the supply of storage by the private sector in the absence of government action, and second, the response of the private storage sector to public-storage activities. The importance of private storage has been recognized by Helmberger and Weaver (1977), Johnson and Sumner (1976), Stein and Smith (1977), Peck (1977–1978), Gardner (1979), and Peck and Gray (1980). A detailed analysis of the interrelationship between private and public storage is presented by Alexander Sarris in chapter 5.

In my view, the most meaningful interpretation that can be placed on the results obtained in the theoretical stabilization literature in the Massell tradition is that they give some insight into the "potential" gains and losses to various groups from reducing the stochastic disturbances. These disturbances—arising mainly from rainfall and temperature fluctuations (sometimes resulting in severe droughts and floods) and to a lesser extent from insect attacks and plant and livestock diseases—are inherent in agricultural production processes, and their effects can never be completely removed by private or public storage or by any other means.[9]

Before proceeding to a discussion of the practical experience with public-authority buffer stocks, several conceptual problems need to be addressed with regard to the traditional stabilization literature, which contrasts no stabilization with perfect costless stabilization.

First, Townsend (1977) shows that any attempt to completely stabilize price through a government buffer-stock program so that consumption is always equal to long-run average supply must eventually fail.[10] The proof of this proposition turns on the well-known properties of random walks. The essential point is that a sufficiently long run of low-harvest years will occur (in finite time) to exhaust any finite level of buffer stocks. Thus perfect price stability would require an infinite buffer stock. It would therefore be infinitely costly.

Second, the traditional literature overlooks the fact that a commodity can only be stored forward in time and that a sensible theoretical treatment of price stabilization must therefore prohibit negative stocks. This is not just a matter of quibbling over finer points of mathematical refinement; it is critical to the analysis of the problem (Aiyagari et al. 1980).

Third, the focus of the traditional literature is on a single commodity, partial equilibrium analysis. In the context of a very simple general equilibrium model, Burmeister (1978) shows how the results from a partial equilibrium analysis can be quite misleading.

Fourth, consumer and producer surplus are used as the measure of economic welfare. This has long been a contentious issue within the economics profession. In recent years, however, criticism of the concept has been tempered in light of studies (for example, Willig 1976) that show that in many situations, consumer surplus provides a good quantitative approximation of true economic welfare or utility. The most serious limitation of the consumer-surplus measure is that it does not adequately account for attitudes toward risk. Hanock (1974) clearly recognized this deficiency; he analyzed the benefits to consumers from price stabilization under a variety of assumptions using a more general utility approach.

In a study that in some respects parallels that of Hanock, Turnovsky, et al. (1980) show that when a more general utility approach is employed, the Arrow-Pratt coefficient of relative risk aversion assumes a critical role. A major result of their study is that the desirability of price stability increases with the degree of risk aversion and also with the degree of inelasticity of demand for the commodity with respect to income and price. If the income elasticity of the marginal utility of income is used as a measure of risk aversion (that is, the Arrow-Pratt measure of relative risk aversion), a necessary condition for consumers to prefer price stability is that the coefficient of relative risk aversion exceeds twice the income elasticity of demand.

In developed countries, the consumer-surplus measure seems to provide a reasonably good approximation of the "true" utility derived from fluctuating or stable staple-food prices. In developing countries, however, the use of a consumer-surplus measure based on demand functions that do not reflect the coefficient of relative risk aversion is likely to result in a significant underestimation of the benefits from price stabilization, especially for the lower-income groups in those countries.

Fifth, producers' surplus (profits) have typically been measured as the area bounded from below by the supply schedule and from above by the price line. This is unsatisfactory, because it requires the costs, as measured by the area below the supply schedule, to vary with the stochastic disturbances (weather), thus shifting the supply schedule from year to year and not distinguishing between ex-ante and ex-poste supply curves. But most of the inputs and costs of producing a crop are, in practice, incurred before the weather and other random disturbance effects are known. Thus, at the time of harvest, the supply curve is almost vertical, with its position being determined by the level of inputs already applied and by the weather. The appropriate supply schedule for measuring producers' costs of production is an average supply function in which producers choose the level of inputs on the basis of *expected* returns per hectare.

Sixth, the conventional stabilization theory assumes that producers are risk-neutral.[11] If producers are risk-averse, price stabilization that leads to reduced income variability—with no change in mean income—will increase producer welfare. Whether or not *price* stabilization leads to lower income variability depends on, however, the price elasticity of demand of the particular commodity. For example, if the price elasticity of demand is unitary, producers have complete income stability with fluctuating prices, and the introduction of a price-stabilization scheme in those circumstances would induce income variability.

Finally, any impact of price stabilization on either income variability or expected average returns will induce a longer-run supply response. The importance of these supply responses is not recognized in the conventional stabilization theory but has recently been analyzed in some innovative theoretical studies by Newbery and Stiglitz (1979) and Wright (1979). Also, while the supply response to reduced income variability or increased average returns will usually be positive, in some circumstances it may be negative. In this regard, the elasticity of work response is an important parameter. For instance, in the absence of a price-stabilization scheme, farmers in developing countries who are highly risk-averse may work very hard to ensure themselves a sufficient level of income for survival in the worst years (low prices combined with weather-induced low yields in their region). The introduction of a price-stabilization scheme that reduces income variability would cause a reduction in work effort and a corresponding smaller supply.

The studies by Newbery and Stiglitz (1979 and 1981)[12] and Wright (1979) are the first to truly critically examine the Waugh-Oi-Massell theoretical framework and to identify its major weaknesses. These studies, in particular, have done much to provide a theoretical framework for an analysis of commodity stabilization schemes that is based on more secure microeconomic foundations.

Practical Experience with Public Buffer-Stock Schemes

The longest-standing buffer-stock scheme is the one that operates as part of the International Tin Agreement (ITA). The major economic analysis of the ITA is the study by Smith and Schink (1976). The ITA has from its inception operated in the shadow of the United States' "strategic stockpile" of tin. The conclusions, in full, of the Smith and Schink (p. 726) study were as follows:

> We conclude that supporters of commodity agreements can take small encouragement from the experience with tin. The longevity of the ITA may stem in good part from its relative powerlessness, while the major factor stabilising the market since 1960, the U.S. strategic stockpile, owes its existence to *miscalculation*.

They also suggest that, in the absence of the GSA,[13] an effective tin agreement would have been very unlikely to have been forthcoming.

The United States and Canada played a similar role in the 1960s and early 1970s when large public stockpiles of wheat were held to support prices and producer incomes. During this period, the United States sold from its stockpile at a very low margin; with such large grain stocks, the world-market price was held within a narrow band, even though there was very significant variability in production over this period. This policy had the effect of "crowding out" any significant interyear stockpiling by the private sector over this period. When full account is taken of storage interest costs, the net operating loss to the United States during this period was no doubt very considerable.[14] In a related context, Gislason (1960) concluded that the Candian Wheat Board had in an earlier period incurred substantial speculative losses in its stockpiling operations.

In 1972/73, the Soviet Union suffered a major domestic production shortfall and made an unexpected decision to import rather than reduce its consumption or stocks. The Soviet decision to maintain consumption, together with efforts by major exporters to reduce their stockpiles, led to a cut in world carry-over wheat stocks from 81.7 million metric tons in 1968/69 to 26.3 million metric tons in 1972/73.[15] World wheat stocks remained at these low levels until 1976/77. In 1976/77 and 1978/79, the world wheat harvests were very large, and world carry-over wheat stocks increased to approximately 63 million tons in 1978/79. Importantly, however, private stockholding in the United States substantially increased. At the end of 1977/78, for instance, the total U.S. ending stocks were 32 million tons, of which nearly 31 million were held by the private sector. In part, the substantial increase in private storage can be attributed to the Farmer-Owned Reserve Program, introduced under the Food and Agricultural Act of 1977, which involves a subsidy to private storage.

In Australia, various forms of buffer-stock schemes for wool have existed since 1970. In a recent analysis of Australia's experience, Campbell et al. (1980) estimate that during the period 1970 to 1978, the Australian buffer-stock operations have reduced the variability of wool prices by 44 percent. The operation of the public buffer stock scheme is estimated, however, to have lowered the revenue from Australian wool sales by A. $139 million in the period up to 1978.[16] This result hinges on empirical estimates of the own-price elasticity of demand for wool that are higher for periods of low demand (low prices) than for periods of high demand (high prices). In addition to these "hidden" revenue losses to wool producers, Campbell et al. estimate that the price-stabilization activities have resulted in a net operating loss to the buffer-stock authority of A. $91 million over the period 1975 to 1978. In other words, operating costs—mainly storage costs and interest foregone on the capital tied up in the stocks[17]—have significantly outweighed any gross trading surpluses.

The general conclusion to be drawn from the experience with government-controlled buffer stocks is that their existence can certainly lead to greater price stability. But to my knowledge, there is no clear case of a government-controlled buffer-stock scheme that has achieved, over a sustained period of time, greater price stability than that generated by a free market with private storage as well as earning normal profits on its storage activities. This is not to say that persons who speculate on behalf of public authorities are any less (or more) skilled than private speculators. In the absence of any clearly identified area of market failure, it is to be expected that a government-controlled buffer-stock scheme that seeks to provide greater price stability than that attained by the market will make operating losses. If, on the other hand, a government-controlled buffer-stock scheme is operated on a conservative basis, it seems likely the introduction of publicly controlled buffer stocks will replace a roughly similar quantity of privately controlled stocks. The addition of some public speculators to private speculators may in the end make little difference to the level of price stability.

If the private-storage sector were truly perfectly competitive, there would be precisely a one-to-one correspondence between displacement of private stockholding by public stockholding. Peck and Gray (1980) conclude from their study that in the United States the private- and public-controlled wheat stocks are generally alternatives that do not complement each other. Moreover, on the basis of the stocks data they analyzed, they were unable to empirically verify the hypothesis put forward by Brennan (1958) that the horizontal portion of the supply of storage curve must eventually turn upward as private storage approaches full capacity. More empirical and theoretical work needs to be done on the precise relationship between private and public stockpiling. This issue is examined in detail in chapter 5 by Alexander Sarris.

Finally, there are two important issues that should be noted. First, the rules by which a stabilization authority builds up and releases stocks are critical to the success of the scheme. If not properly designed, they will invite counterspeculation by private stockpilers who will then be the main beneficiaries of the scheme. Second, a publicly controlled stockpile that cannot be justified on microeconomic grounds may be justifiable on macroeconomic grounds. The macroeconomic considerations are very complicated and have not yet been satisfactorily resolved. It is likely, however, that there may be significant macroeconomic benefits from public stockpiling, especially for some developing countries where the imports or exports of a commodity loom large in the overall economy and when there are price or wage rigidities elsewhere in that country's economy.

Next, the issue of potential areas of market failure in commodity markets is examined in detail.

Risk and Stockpiling

A number of advocates of government-controlled (or government-subsidized) buffer stocks including Keynes (1938 and 1947),[18] Houthakker (1967), and Gardner (1979) have based their cases primarily on the supposed divergence between social and private aversion to the risks inherent in holding commodity stockpiles. From society's viewpoint, if private stockpilers require excessive risk premiums, stocks will be too small and price instability too great. The implied policy recommendation is either publicly held buffer stocks or a subsidy to private storage.

I am not aware of any empirical work that has attempted to measure average rates of return earned by private stockpilers and to estimate the associated size of the risk premium. Futures markets provide a market-determined price for intrayear and interyear storage; especially if the stocks are hedged, the quoted price of storage is a measure of the expected returns from storage. Hence, one approach to estimating the size of the risk premium would be by analysis of futures-market data.

The position taken by Keynes, Houthakker, and Gardner on the appropriate discount rate for public storage would appear to be supported by a proposition advanced by Arrow and Lind (1970): The total risk carried by the public sector is spread over such a large population that each individual's risk burden becomes negligible. This implies that the marginal return from public investment as a whole is virtually risk-free and should be equated to the market rate on riskless bonds.

An opposing view, however, has been advanced by Hirshleifer (1966) and Hirshleifer and Shapiro (1970). These researchers propose that when discounting the costs and benefits of a particular type of public investment, the government should take as its discount rate the rate of return on capital for a private investment (activity) of similar riskiness. Sandmo (1974) claims that the two sets of arguments are based on quite different assumptions concerning the relationship between private and public investment with respect to risk. For the Arrow-Lind result to hold, a crucial assumption is that the returns on private and public investment are uncorrelated. The Hirshleifer view, on the other hand, is clearly based on the assumption that for each type of public investment it is possible to find a private investment such that the returns are highly correlated. With respect to publicly held buffer stocks, it is my view that the Hirshleifer-Shapiro assumption is the relevant one, since a clear counterpart private investment exists in the form of private storage.

In a mature stock-market economy, in which firms are organized as corporations, there are near-perfect opportunities for the pooling of financial risk within the private sector. Firms finance their investments by issuing either bonds or shares. And the financial risk to the shareholder is not, as is commonly thought, measured by the expected variance of the return on a share in a particular corporation but rather by the *covariance* between the return to that share and the expected return on the full portfolio of investments held by the investor. For shareholders with large diversified investment portfolios, the covariance (and associated risk) will be very small. In such an economy, the efficiency rule governing public investment in storage should be to "imitate" the private storage sector.[19] Thus the appropriate discount rate for use by authorities in charge of publicly owned buffer stocks is that used by the private-storage sector.

It is important to note that while opportunities exist in the outlined economy for full pooling of *financial* risk, *real* (true) risks remain to society as well as to individuals that are inherent in stockpiling, regardless of whether it is undertaken by the public or private sector. This is because at the time of decision-making, the value of the output stemming from the storage activity is known only in an ex-ante probabilistic sense. The actual ex-poste benefits are dependent on the future state of nature (for example, weather conditions) that eventuates. The risks to society, as well as to individuals, are true risks in the sense that at any point in time—with the benefit of hindsight—society will usually find itself in the position of having undertaken too little or too much storage. The incorporation of this risk margin into the discount rate adopted by the private sector represents an evaluation of the real social risk inherent in stockpiling; the same risk margin should also be incorporated in the discount rate used by public-storage authorities.

The discussion just given assumed that perfect opportunities exist for pooling of financial risks in the private sector. If capital markets for pooling financial risks are significantly imperfect, Sandmo shows that the government discount rate should contain a risk premium, but the risk premium will now be smaller than that required by the private sector. If capital markets are imperfect, there is thus some justification for using a lower discount rate for publicly held buffer stocks than that employed by private storage firms, since government is now a more efficient pooler of risk. Alternatively, the government could subsidize private storage and all other "risky" investments. Of course, the first-best solution, if attainable, is for government to correct the source of market failure: the imperfect capital market.

The justification for using a lower discount rate for publicly held stocks or subsidizing private stockpiling will be stronger in developing than in developed countries, since capital markets are generally more imperfect in developing countries. Given the highly developed capital market in the United States and the existence of mature futures markets on which stocks can be hedged, the case for subsidizing private stockpiling or for using a lower discount rate for public stockpiling on pure efficiency grounds seems weak.

Informational Efficiency in Commodity Markets

The issue of whether or not freely operating markets optimally provide and utilize the information potentially available to them will now be addressed.[20] In recent years, some concern has been expressed that excessive price uncertainty and instability exist in agricultural commodity markets partly attributable to underproduction and underutilization of information in a market economy. If this is true, the major areas in which an improvement in the information system would lead to a more efficient allocation of resources are production, storage, and trade decisions. The public-good characteristics of information are identified, and their effect on the production and utilization of information by the private market is analyzed in the following discussion.

The study of information and agricultural commodity markets inevitably leads to a study of futures markets. Increasingly, a primary role of futures markets is being seen as one of collecting, processing, and disseminating information. A widely held view is that futures markets are the dominant institution for price discovery and formation in U.S. agricultural-commodity markets. And it is claimed that virtually all grain traded internationally throughout the world is priced in direct relationship to values competitively determined on U.S. futures markets and that in this sense, the international grain market is a direct extension of the U.S. market. Recent research has noted that in the presence of speculative markets, some types of information are likely to have high private value but low social value, with a consequent possibility of overinvestment in information collection in a market economy. This issue, in the context of commodity futures markets, is considered later in this chapter. The empirical research that has used various statistical and other tests for informational efficiency in commodity futures markets is also discussed further in the chapter.

Information as a Public Good

There is a traditional view that in the absence of government intervention, there will be underinvestment in the production of information by the market because of its public-good characteristics. That is to say, the good information has characteristics both of Samuelsonian jointness in supply (or nonrivalness in consumption) and of difficulty of exclusion of those who do not offer payment. Consequently, private firms will be able to appropriate only a small part of the full social value of the information they produce, and the supply will be socially suboptimal.

This view is apparently based on the premise that in order to profit from the provision of, say, meteorological or commodity-outlook information, firms must sell the information to each individual agent with an effective demand. In order to identify the source of market failure in this situation, it is helpful to initially assume that information is a perfectly excludable public good, characterized by jointness but not by nonexcludability. One individual's utilization of a commodity-price forecast (or a weather forecast) does not reduce the supply of identical-quality information that can be made available to others, but the individual will be excluded if he does not pay. On the other hand, the additional impossibility of exclusion characteristic of a "pure" public good, which will be considered subsequently, implies that once a unit of information is produced for any one agent it will be accessible for utilization by all, regardless of whether payment is offered.

It is important to recognize that while the degree of excludability has a major influence on market behavior, it is the degree of jointness exhibited by a public good alone that determines the necessary efficiency conditions for its provision. These efficiency conditions are as follows:

1. Efficiency in *production* requires that the level of output be set such that the sum of individual marginal valuations is equated to marginal cost (or ΣMRS = MRT)
2. Efficiency in *consumption* requires that all units produced be utilized fully by all potential consumers so that none are rationed by price.

Following the excludable public-good analytical structure recently developed by Oakland (1974), Head (1977), and others, perhaps the most surprising result to emerge for an excludable public good—as compared with a private good—is that consuming agents will face a step function of prices. An identical price is charged to all agents purchasing the same unit of information. But stepwise, higher prices will be charged for successive units of information. For example, each additional unit of information purchased may be conceived as progressively lowering the forecasting error associated with an estimate of the future spot price of a commodity or a forecast of the size of a grain crop.

Under conditions wherein large numbers of agents have an effective demand for information (as will usually be the case in agricultural commodity markets), the competitive-market supply of information will be lower than the efficient output level but will usually closely approximate it. It is important, however, for excludable public goods to make a clear distinction between units in *production* and units in *consumption*. Although in this setting, production inefficiency may be small, significant consumption inefficiency may prevail insofar as some agents will be price-excluded from consuming the higher priced units of information that are actually produced and that they could utilize at no additional cost to society.

Some markets for excludable public goods have monopoly elements. Very little work considers questions of the likely degree of monopoly and economies of scale in markets for information. Wilson (1975) proposes that economies of scale, both in the production and the utilization of information, are likely to be significant. Recent work by Brito and Oakland (1980) indicates that output of an excludable public good will be generally less under monopoly than under perfect competition, and consumption will be more severely price-rationed.

If information is assumed to be a pure public good, exhibiting both the joint supply and the impossibility of price-exclusion characteristics, then the equilibrium level of information output will be established at the point where the demand schedule of the highest-demand agent intersects marginal cost. The high-demand agent will purchase the information, and it will then be fully accessible for utilization by all others. To add the impossibility of price exclusion would appear to significantly worsen production inefficiency when the numbers of potential users of information are large and when no single user has a demand that is large in relation to aggregate demand. Consumption inefficiency will be zero but will be dominated by production inefficiency. In these circumstances, the nonexcludability characteristic appears to be the major potential force for market failure.

How important is price excludability likely to be in practice in the provision of commodity-outlook information? When it is considered that individual sales of information are made to large numbers of agents, the free-rider problem looms large. Information firms cannot easily prevent initial purchasers of information from retrading or simply disseminating the information free to other parties. Yet the existence of commercial agencies selling a wide range of quantitative and qualitative agricultural commodity-outlook information through "outlook letters," agricultural journals, and other means indicates that a significant amount of effective price-exclusion exists. The most sophisticated and costly commercial agricultural forecasting services in the United States are those based on large econometric models. Chase Econometrics, Data Resources Inc., Doanes Agricultural Service, Inc., and Wharton Econometric Forecasting Associates are four such organizations that provide agricultural commodity forecasting services for a price per client in the range of U.S. $20,000 to

$40,000. Apart from quantitative quarterly price forecasts, these firms also provide other services such as personal access to experts who monitor markets. Thus a significant component of the package of these services may be of a private-good nature.

Firms specializing in producing information for sale have options other than selling it directly to individual agents. Commodity-outlook information could be sold to the media (newspapers, radio, and television). Even in the absence of the price-exclusion problem, in situations in which there are very large numbers of individuals for whom the information is valuable, the media provide very efficient means of disseminating the information. Indeed, it would seem that only radio and television can disseminate information at a truly zero marginal cost over consumption units and thus perfectly fulfill the jointness characteristic. Furthermore, if costs are incurred by buyers in assessing the authenticity and quality of information supplied by private firms, these costs are lowered if the media rather than large numbers of individuals are the buyers.

It is difficult to judge what the commercial media would be prepared to pay for commodity-outlook information. In part, it would be determined by an estimate of the number of readers, listeners, or viewers who would value the information and the advertising revenue it could be linked with. In any event, in the absence of pay television, it is likely the information output would be below the efficient level.

A final observation is that in the provision of a joint good, the power of taxation allows government to provide the good at zero price and thus avoid the problem of consumption inefficiency. Government could itself produce commodity-outlook information or offer to purchase it from private firms and either disseminate it through its own media outlets or subsidize the commercial media. Dissuaders may argue that if no price is charged to users, the government is faced with the problem of estimating the demand for information and the efficient output it should produce or purchase from private suppliers. The difficulties of estimating the demand for a good in the absence of a market for it by considering survey responses or the market demand for private goods that are complements or substitutes are well known. Consequently, a somewhat intractible trade-off exists between production and consumption inefficiency in the provision of a good like information, regardless of the mix of private and public (government) institutions used to produce and disseminate it. While it is true that commodity-outlook information has public-good characteristics, the degree of market failure attributed to this has typically been exaggerated.

It is of interest at this point to note that under the present Freedom of Information Act, the U.S. Department of Agriculture (USDA) is obliged to provide free access to its commodity data. Firms with commercial econometric models are particularly heavy users of this free service, and over time it is likely they will exert a significant influence on the type and amount of data collected by the USDA. To the extent that some part of the information packages sold by these firms has private-good characteristics, consideration should be given to charging these firms a fee for the raw information input supplied by the USDA. Certainly, inefficiency is induced by the policy claimed to have been adopted by the U.S. National Weather Service of expanding or altering its services in the provision of raw weather data (at taxpayers' expense) so as to maximize the sales revenue of private weather-forecasting firms. In adopting this strategy, the National Weather Service has found the private-sector weather firms to be a powerful ally in making joint representations to expand the budget of the National Weather Service.[21]

It is now well known that the demonstration of market failure provides no guarantee that the use of the political mechanism will result in a more efficient allocation of resources. Because many public agencies wish to maximize the size of their budget, a problem of overinvestment in some information activities may arise in the public sector. However, the USDA appears to have a comparative advantage in the provision of raw-quantity data and domestic-crop forecasts, though in my judgment, the significance of the public good and economies of scale attributes in justifying the public production of information have been exaggerated. The provision of crop size forecasts by the USDA is, in a sense, a "joint good" with other information activities it undertakes. For reasons of national security and other political considerations, it seems likely a government would be loathe to have to depend solely on private agencies for its supply of such information.

Finally, if there is a significant degree of informational market failure and consequent excessive price instability in agricultural-commodity markets, the first-best course of government action is to assume responsibility for ensuring an optimal information supply. The traditional theoretical literature that contrasts no stabilization with perfect stabilization through a costless public buffer stock, completely obscures the crucial issue of information and the fact that the first-best course of government action is to correct market failure at its source.

Speculation, Futures Markets, and the Private and Social Value of Information

In a seminal paper, Hirshleifer (1971) contends that, contrary to the traditional view that there will be underinvestment in information acquisition in a market economy, there is likely to be overinvestment in information collection by private agents when opportunities for speculation exist. Some aspects of Hirshleifer's model are open to criticism, but his observation that the private value of information may exceed its social value is an important one.

The proposition was, in a sense, anticipated by Samuelson (1957). Samuelson poses the question, Do speculators always deserve the profits they obtain? He concludes they do not by giving the example of a speculator who obtains information only a short time before his competitors. The speculator, however, appropriates all the speculative profits through trading, leaving no speculative profits for his competitors. Yet the difference in social value from having, say, information on the impact of frosts on the Brazilian coffee crop one day earlier, would be very small.

It is true in this example that both the private and the social value of information acquired by speculators who are not first is zero. The potential for overinvestment and possible wasteful duplication of informaton networks arises from the "rush to be first." The source of market failure is the *common-property* nature of undiscovered information. It is thus a variant of the "over-fishing" model, or the "rent-seeking" model.[22] The divergence between private and social values arises because as more speculators (fishermen) enter the market (fishing ground), part of their "catch" of new information (fish) would have been "caught" in any event by the speculators (fishermen) already there. With free entry, expected average (private) returns for each firm must equal average cost, whereas optimality requires that marginal social return be equated with marginal cost. Under competitive conditions of free entry, the incentive stucture is then such that speculators (fishermen) will enter the market (fishing ground) up to the point where the rents are dissipated. Hence when speculative markets exist, there can be no presumption that the provision of information in a pure market economy will be socially insufficient. Indeed, there may be both wasteful duplication of information networks and an excessive supply of information.

Futures markets exist for most agricultural commodities, with rice being the major exception.[23] A serious deficiency of the traditional theoretical literature on price stabilization is that it focuses on spot prices and has generally ignored the crucial role played by futures markets. It is now widely recognized that futures markets serve two major functions: They generate information, and they facilitate the sharing and transfer of risk. The earliest theories of futures markets explained their existence solely in terms of their risk-transfer function. In particular, it was proposed that to induce speculators to accept the transfer of price risk, hedgers would need to pay speculators a risk (insurance) premium. As a consequence, futures markets would typically exhibit normal backwardation and futures prices would provide a biased estimator of future spot prices.[24] The issue of whether or not a risk premium (and associated market bias) exists has received fairly continuous attention in the empirical futures-market literature. It is sufficient to observe here that for most futures markets in major agricultural commodities, the hypothesis of zero risk premium and bias is a reasonable one. This, of course, does not mean that futures markets are an unimportant institution for facilitating risk transfer and sharing. Rather, it indicates that the risk transfer is accomplished without the necessity for one group of traders (hedgers) to pay another group (speculators) a risk premium.

The particular significance of information in price discovery and formation for agricultural commodities can, in large part, be attributed to the biological nature of the production process and the typically large number of individual producing (and consuming) units. For grain and other continuously stocked commodities, any new supply-demand information that affects expectations of future spot prices will jointly shift the whole constellation of futures-market prices in conjunction with the current spot price. For example, if a group of traders acquires information that causes them to revise downward the expected size of a future wheat crop, they will trade in the futures market until futures prices have moved upward to reflect the expectation of a smaller crop. The higher futures prices will in turn provide a signal to storage operators to store more (release less for current consumption), thus raising the current spot price. The linkage between spot and futures prices for continuously stocked commodities is supported by empirical research, which reveals that spot and futures prices are in general equally variable. The emergence of information and consequent revision of prices is a continuous process, and since the flow of new information tends to be random, so too does the resultant movement of spot and futures prices.[25]

The information conveyed by futures markets is valuable to all market participants (storage operators, farmers, processors, transporters, and so forth). The largest users of futures markets are storage operators; this suggests that the most important single service performed by futures markets is to facilitate the intertemporal distribution of consumption of a commodity. Results based on a theoretical model developed by Turnovsky (1978), however, suggest that the benefits of a futures market in facilitating better production decisions are likely to be at least as great as those resulting from better storage decisions.[26]

In the earlier discussion on the private and social value of information, I stated that in some circumstances there may be a wasteful tendency toward duplication of information networks. The USDA is a major producer of monthly crop-outlook information, making size-of-crop forecasts up to one year in advance. A number of writers on futures markets, including Working (1958), Caves (1977–1978), Morgan (1979), and De-

Canio (1980), give evidence of substantial private networks acquiring crop-outlook information. A major motivation for some of these private firms is apparently to acquire information before the release of the official USDA crop forecasts.[27] The earlier work of Holbrook Working (1958, p. 38) indicates that some agents specialize in this aspect of market information.

> Some traders concentrate on getting pertinent information quickly, ahead of others. Instead of waiting for the publication of official crop estimates, for example, they have their own networks.

Although Working did not criticize this apparent duplication of information networks as potentially inefficient, it appears to provide an example of a situation in which the speed and timing of acquiring (or releasing) information induces a significant divergence between its private and social value. There is too much private incentive for greater speed and frequency of forecasts and perhaps too little private incentive for improvements in the quality and accuracy of a particular forecast. Bradford and Kelejian (1978) obtain a similar result in their study on the U.S. wheat crop. They conclude that the social returns to increases in the frequency of data collection appear to be substantially less than the returns associated with comparable improvements in the accuracy of the collected data on which to base less frequent forecasts.[28]

Empirical Testing of the Informational Efficiency of Futures Markets

There was a lengthy debate following World War II on whether or not speculation was stabilizing. Economic theory suggested that profitable speculation had to be stabilizing. Questioning the empirical validity of the theoretical proposition led to the early statistical studies of speculative markets. Most of these studies focused on the stock market, but markets in commodities, bonds, and foreign exchange were also analyzed.[29] Working (1949) first wrote about economic expectations and commodity futures markets. He classed market errors into two groups: (1) "necessary inaccuracy" and (2) "objectionable inaccuracy." An efficient market is one that contains only necessary inaccuracies; that is to say, the forward-pricing errors are solely attributable to the emergence of new information that comes randomly. The resultant price changes are thus unpredictable and unavoidable. Objectionable inaccuracy is the remaining portion of the total forward-pricing error and likely results from the poor forecasting ability of speculators or perhaps some form of noncompetitive market behavior.

Muth (1961, p. 316) was the first to argue that a theory of market expectations ought to assume rational, maximizing behavior.

> . . . expectations, since they are informed predictions of future events, are essentially the same as the predictions of the relevant economic theory.

An economist would make, say, a commodity-price forecast by calculating the minimum-variance unbiased forecast based on a rational stochastic model of the market. Muth asserts that rational agents in speculative markets do the same. If market expectations were not moderately rational, there would be opportunities for economists and other market analysts to make profits from commodity speculation (for example, futures trading) or by selling commodity-outlook information.

Muth's paper on rational expectations spawned very substantial economics literature on the issue of whether or not speculative commodity (and other) markets collect, process, and disseminate information efficiently. In the late 1960s, Fama (1970) and others built on Muth's fundamental contribution and developed a theory of "efficient markets." This theory indicated new testable hypotheses and motivated new statistical studies. Fama classified empirical tests into weak, semistrong, and strong forms. This classification has been widely used in empirical research on foreign-exchange and bond markets but has received little attention by agricultural economists.

A *speculative market* is defined as being weakly efficient if the current price always completely discounts (reflects) the information contained in the history of past prices. A market exhibits semistrong efficiency if, in addition to the information contained in the history of past prices, the market accurately evaluates and reflects all widely held information such as government crop reports. Finally, a market exhibits strong efficiency if it accurately discounts and reflects all information, including that held by only small numbers of "informed" market participants.

Most of the empirical tests of market efficiency on agricultural commodities have been implicitly of the weak efficiency form. The hypothesis most commonly tested is the random-walk hypothesis, namely that successive price changes are independent, identically distributed random variables, so that the sequence of price changes is a random walk.[30] The general conclusion that emerges from most of the empirical studies (for example, Labys and Granger [1970] and Praetz [1975]) is that the random walk probably best describes the movement of futures prices for the major agricultural commodities, although there were sometimes small discrepancies. The most significant evidence of some nonrandomness in price movements that I am aware of is in the study by Cargill and Rausser (1975). These researchers found that around 10 percent of futures contracts exhibited nonrandom behavior in tests on the Chicago Board of Trade Exchange for corn, wheat, soybeans, and oats. Cargill and Rausser are careful to point out the limitations of the statistical tests used and the fact that the rejection of the random-walk model does not necessarily imply that a commodity market is inefficient, as many writers have inferred.

Samuelson (1965) clearly shows that the random-walk model conventionally used to test efficiency in commodity futures markets is a special case of an efficient capital market. In particular, there is a need to distinguish between the more general martingale models and the special random-walk model. While both imply that expected profits cannot be increased by application to historic prices of ". . . chart or any other esoteric devices of magic or mathematics" (Samuelson 1965, p. 44), it is nevertheless still possible for certain types of serial correlation to exist in an efficient market. Currently available statistical tests generally are not able to discriminate between more general martingale models and the special random-walk version and have, in effect, tested only the random-walk model. The empirical studies taken together support the hypothesis that futures markets for the major agricultural commodities generally meet Fama's "weak-efficiency" criterion.

A related but distinct approach to testing the weak form of the efficient market hypothesis is the use of mechanical filters or trading rules. While the random-walk model implies that no mechanical trading rule can be used to increase expected profits, there is no simple relationship between the degree of serial correlation and the expected profits derived from the application of mechanical trading rules. Cox (1976) attempted to find profitable trading rules for each of six agricultural commodities, both for periods when there was no futures trading in the commodity and for periods during which the commodity was traded in a formal futures market. In periods when futures markets were absent, Cox concludes that prices did not fully reflect the information contained in the history of past prices for any of the six commodities. In periods with futures trading, the prices of four commodities behaved as if market information were fully reflected in current prices. Analysis of price data for the remaining two commodities showed a substantial increase in the information content of prices with futures trading, but prices did not fully reflect available information.

DeCanio (1980) estimates the economic losses from forecasting error associated with the production of wheat and corn in Kansas over the period 1874 to 1933. Over the entire period, the statewide median losses from forecasting error and consequent suboptimal production decisions averaged approximately 2.5 percent of gross income. Throughout the period, there is a general trend toward an increasingly stable (smaller variance) wheat-corn price ratio and an associated declining trend in losses from forecasting error. This trend is attributed in part to the growth and refinement of futures markets. In particular, DeCanio observes a strong correlation between rapid growth in the volume of wheat and corn futures contracts throughout the late nineteenth century and a significant decline in the variance of the wheat-corn price ratio. The Cox and DeCanio studies provide empirical evidence that lends support to the hypothesis that the existence of futures markets increases the informational efficiency and stability of commodity markets.

There has been very little empirical research on testing the semistrong form of market efficiency for agricultural commodities. In a recent semi-strong efficiency test of the live-hog futures market, Leuthold and Hartman (1979) compare price forecasts they derive from an econometric model with futures-market prices. They find that although the futures market is the more efficient predictor overall, there are periods when the econometric model provides more accurate forecasts than does the futures market. They conclude that the live-hog futures market has not consistently utilized all the available market information and has consequently not always exhibited semistrong market efficiency. The inference Leuthold and Hartman place on their results is questionable. Given the stochastic nature of the equilibrium in agricultural-commodity markets, speculators with generally poor forecasting ability will, on occasion, make profits at the expense of speculators with generally good forecasting ability, but on average the converse will be true. The relevant test is surely whether an econometric model can be developed that will overall (on average) provide superior forecasts to those given by futures markets.

Rausser and Just (1979) compare the forecast accuracy of the commodity-price predictions given by the U.S. commercial econometric models with those of futures markets for corn, wheat, soybean oil, soybean meal, cotton, live cattle, and hogs. Their main conclusion is that futures markets generally provide more accurate price forecasts than do the commercial econometric models, although the evidence is not overwhelmingly in favor of either.[31] Some of the econometric forecasts, for instance, seemed to be superior to futures prices for livestock commodities. This result is consistent with Leuthold and Hartman's results and also with the research by Giles and Goss (1981), which revealed that the Australian (Sydney) futures prices were efficient estimators of future spot prices for wool but not for live cattle beyond a three-month time horizon. There are thus some indications that futures prices provide better spot price forecasts for continuous inventory commodities like wheat and wool than for noncontinuous (effectively nonstorable) commodities like live cattle and hogs.

It is now pertinent to consider Fama's strong efficiency condition, although no empirical work has explicitly attempted to apply this test to agricultural-commodity futures markets. When information is costly to acquire, will prices determined in speculative markets accurately reflect *all* available information held by market agents, including information acquired by small numbers of "informed speculators?" Grossman and Stiglitz (1980) argue that prices will not fully and instantaneously reveal all information, since if they did, it would not pay anyone to invest in the acquisition of information. They conclude that where the market for information acquisition is competitive, the market price must reveal just enough of the costly information that participants are indifferent to incurring the cost of becoming "informed" or remaining "uninformed" and simply using market prices to guide their decisions.

The Grossman-Stiglitz paper sets up a straw man in that their implied benchmark for an efficient market is one in which information is costless. In a world of costly information, the observation that market prices require a short interval to adjust (attain a new equilibrium) to reflect each new bit of information does not constitute a serious efficiency argument against speculative commodity markets. If futures prices were to instantaneously adjust to new information, the improvement in major areas of resource allocation, such as production and storage decisions, would appear to be minimal.

While a substantial body of empirical and theoretical research now exists that lends support to the hypothesis that futures markets increase the amount of market information as well as the informational efficiency of commodity markets, futures prices do not convey all information held by "informed" traders to other market participants. For example, the futures price represents a single-valued point estimate, yet market participants who are risk-averse (or risk-preferrers) would value information on the expected probability distribution of prices, together with a measure of the expected forecast error associated with a futures price. Furthermore, market participants commonly desire explicit information on the anticipated states of nature underlying each expected futures price. All agents involved in the spot market for a commodity (particularly farmers) would value information on whether a commodity's price at a particular time is high (low) because of "temporary" or "permanent" phenomena. Is the underlying state of nature causing a high price, for instance, poor weather conditions, or is it an expected permanent upward shift in the demand schedule because of the emergence of a new market? If futures contracts existed for periods of, say, five years or more, the temporary or permanent nature of a price change would be revealed by the time profile of futures prices. Futures contracts do not generally extend beyond a maximum period of eighteen months, however, and the great bulk of trading is in contracts of six months or less. Ideally, producers would like to have long-term price forecasts, including estimates of a commodity's average price over the next five or ten years.

Considerations for the Future

Many important issues pertaining to the costs and benefits of organized futures markets remain to be resolved. Certain pertinent questions deserve to be raised.

First, very little is known about how the nature of futures trading reacts to and interacts with different forms of givernment intervention. Telser and Higinbotham (1977) claim that U.S. government price-support programs in peanuts and tobacco have stifled interest in futures trading in these commodities and that trading in cotton was extremely low at times when government stocks were large and growing. On the other hand, reasonably active trading in wheat (wool) futures has continued to take place when the U.S. and Canadian governments (the Australian Wool Commission) have been holding substantial buffer stocks. It seems that if a commodity's price is highly stable due to governmental policies, an active futures market is unlikely to exist. But if, even with government intervention, a commodity's price is reasonably variable—as has been the case for wool and wheat—this appears to be compatible with an active futures market.

Second, if it were desirable for government to attempt to attain greater stability of spot prices, should this be done through use of a futures fund to intervene in futures markets rather than a buffer-stock fund? Houthakker (1967) and McKinnon (1967) have both proposed that direct intervention in futures markets by government is likely to be a less costly means to reduce the variability of farm-commodity prices than is the operation of buffer-stock schemes. McKinnon observed that futures contracts do not generally extend beyond a maximum period of eighteen months, and his proposal was for the government to make a market in "distant" futures prices. This would, in particular, facilitate production decisions and enable primary producers to hedge their future income.[32]

Response to Houthakker's and McKinnon's suggestions has been rather unfavorable. Powers and Tosini (1977) suggest it is not possible for a futures market to survive if there is substantial government participation in futures trading. Peck (1976) considers that government purchase of futures could only be a temporary substitute for the accumulation of physical stocks and not an alternative method of stabilizing price. These objections would presumably not extend to statutory marketing organizations like the Australian Wheat Board and Canadian Wheat Board trading on the U.S. wheat futures market.

At present, neither the futures markets nor the commercial econometric forecasts extend beyond a period of eighteen months. If a government believes it can make more distant price forecasts at reasonable cost (superior to simply using the eighteen-month futures price as a predictor of more distant spot prices) it should publicly announce such price forecasts, together with estimates of the expected probability distribution and forecast errors.

Third, should government encourage setting up futures markets in developing countries? Data given by Powers and Tosini does not support the contention held by some that foreigners have lacked access to U.S. commodity futures markets. At the same time, foreign futures traders on the U.S. markets (especially those from less developed countries) appear to rank only marginally above U.S. farmers in their direct participation in futures markets. It seems clearly desirable that foreign access to the U.S. futures exchanges be kept as open as possible. Also, a real possibility exists for the development of regional futures markets on the fringes of major developing country areas such as Hong Kong and Malaysia-Singapore. At present, crop forecasts made during the growing season in many developing countries are extremely inaccurate. A major potential benefit of the development of regional futures markets would be the stimulation of greater investment by developing countries in forecasting the size of their crops. Powers and Tosini (pp. 982–983) are cautious, however, about the general possibilities for setting up efficient futures markets in developing countries. They state

> It takes time and a great deal of educational effort to build credibility, confidence, and understanding of an exchange and its role.

Also, they express concern that some developing countries want futures exchanges for the wrong reasons and that they are not sufficiently developed to support them.

Finally, more research is required to analyze the distributional effects of improvements in commodity outlook information, and, to test Caves's (1977–1978) claim that futures trading is perfectly competitive.

Summary

A major conclusion of the large body of theoretical literature that has followed in the Waugh-Oi-Massell tradition is that price stabilization will always improve net economic welfare. This literature, however, ignores the role of private storage and of futures markets and makes no attempt to identify potential sources of market failure. In contrast with the result from traditional stabilization literature, practical experience with public buffer stocks provides no evidence of net economic welfare gains from public stockpiling at levels in excess of those that, in the absence of government intervention, would have been undertaken by the private-storage market. In the absence of any clearly identified area of market failure, it is not surprising that government-controlled buffer-stock schemes that seek to provide greater price stability than that attained by the private storage sector will have operating losses.

Two potential areas of market failure that could lead to excessive commodity-price instability were analyzed in this chapter. First, a number of advocates of government-controlled, or subsidized, buffer stocks have based their case on the supposed divergence between social and private risk aversion to the risks inherent in commodity stockpiling. The major conclusion to emerge from the analysis in this section is that in a mature stock-market economy like that of the United States, good opportunities exist for the pooling of financial risk within the private sector. In the United States, with its highly developed capital market and mature futures markets on which stockpiles can be hedged, the case is weak on pure efficiency grounds for subsidizing private stockpiling or for using a discount rate for public stockpiling lower than that used by the private sector. In developing countries where capital markets are not as highly developed and futures markets are rare, the use of a lower discount rate for publicly held stocks or the subsidization of private stockpiling may be justified.

The second potential area of market failure is related to whether or not speculative agricultural commodity markets collect, process, and disseminate information efficiently. A traditional view says that in the absence of government intervention, there will be underinvestment in the production of information because of its public-good characteristics. While it is true that commodity-outlook information has public-good characteristics and that there is an inevitable trade-off between production and consumption inefficiency, the degree of market failure attributed to this has typically been exaggerated. To the extent that government appears to have a comparative advantage in the provision of some forms of information (for example, expected crop-size forecasts and probability distributions), the first-best course of government action is to assume responsibility for ensuring an optimal information supply. The traditional theoretical literature that contrasts no stabilization with perfect price stabilization through costless public buffer stocks assumes away the crucial role of information.

The view that there will be underinvestment in the production of information in a private-market economy because of its public-good characteristics is apparently based on the premise that in order to profit from the provision of, say, commodity-outlook information, firms must sell the information. There is a more recent view that when opportunities for speculation are taken into account, some types of information may have high private value but low social value, and there can be no a priori presumption that the provision of information in a pure market economy will be socially insufficient.

Analysis of the information supply in agricultural-commodity markets inevitably leads to a consideration of futures markets. The view is widely held that U.S. futures markets are the dominant institution for price discovery and formation in the U.S. and world grain market. A substantial body of empirical and theoretical research on futures markets now exists. The general thrust of the results of this research supports the hypothesis that futures markets increase the supply of market information and the informational efficiency of agricultural-commodity markets, although there are a number of important issues pertaining to the costs and benefits of organized futures markets that remain to be resolved.

In formulating policy, it should be recognized that marginal social benefits are a decreasing function of increases in the accuracy of quantity and price forecasts. There are some indications that in developed countries, the benefits of reducing existing forecast errors are likely to be small.[33] The main conclusion that emerges from this chapter is that from a microeconomic perspective, there is no compelling evidence of excessive world-price instability that is the result of major agricultural-commodity markets in developed countries being informationally inefficient, or of there being significant risk aversion among private stockpilers. Developing countries are, however, increasingly important actors in the major staple-food markets. And there appear to be significant potential benefits to be gained in some of these countries from improvements in the quality of commodity outlook information, particularly domestic-crop forecasts. The selective establishment of regional futures markets on the fringes of major developing-country areas could contribute toward greater food security by stimulating investment in size-of-harvest forecasts and other commodity-market information.

Notes

1. In addition to the survey paper by Turnovsky (1978), see the studies by Just (1977), Smith (1978), and Harris et al. (1978).

2. For a comprehensive survey of the empirical studies on international grain reserves, see Houck and Ryan (1979). For recent studies, see Morrow (1980) and Kennedy (1979).

3. Taylor and Talpaz (1979) and Gardner (1979) also reach similar conclusions for stabilization of wheat prices, but Gardner cautions that it is not possible to be confident about distributional conclusions. The need for caution is borne out by the results of a recent study of U.S. wheat reserves by Burt et al. (1980). This study, using a differently specified model, concluded that U.S. producers gain from a wheat storage program, while

domestic and foreign consumers are relatively small and large losers, respectively.

4. Random disturbances in supply (production variability) are the dominant source of price instability for food grains.

5. Part of the explanation for the oversight may stem from the fact that in the United States the massive grain stockpiles held throughout most of the 1950s and 1960s led to the virtual extinction of private stockholding.

6. The storage problem formulated by Gustafson (1958) can best be solved by dynamic programming or optimal control-theory techniques. For a good recent study that has built on Gustafson, see Gardner (1979).

7. For simplicity, marginal costs of storage are assumed here to be constant, so that producer surplus does not accrue to private or public storage operators.

8. The confusion that this has generated is illustrated in the exchange between Samuelson (1972a and 1972b), who independently analyzed the economic consequences of the random disturbances, and Oi (1972).

9. For example, another means of reducing the impact of the disturbances is by biological research that increases the resistance of plant and animal species to rainfall and temperature fluctuations and to diseases and pest attacks.

10. The same point has also been made by Newbery and Stiglitz (1979).

11. The Hazell and Scandizzo (1975) study was an exception. These authors proposed that if price stability is increased, risk-averse farmers will increase supply and that if this aspect of risk is ignored, the economic benefits of price stabilization will be underestimated. More recently, Schmitz et al. (1981) have examined the case of a risk-averse single- and multiproduct firm, assuming that a firm maximizes its expected utility from profits rather than maximizing expected profits. The authors show how Oi's results can be reversed, although they do not consider long-term supply responses.

12. Newbery and Stiglitz (1979) indicate that their paper forms one chapter of a comprehensive book on the theory of commodity stabilization; its publication was forthcoming at the time of this writing.

13. GSA stands for the General Services Administration, the government agency that administers U.S. tin stockpile transactions.

14. Since initially making this observation, I have read the study by Morrow (1980). Morrow's analysis indicates that the world carry-over stocks, which were dominated by U.S. stockpiling, were substantially above Pareto-efficient levels throughout the 1960s.

15. These estimates of carry-over stocks are given in Morrow (1980, table 4). Morrow also claims that the Soviet decision to maintain its grain consumption in 1972–1973, through substantial imports, was based on a

desire to maintain the program of livestock production begun in the mid-1960s.

16. This estimate is based on Australian wool sales to eight OECD countries—Japan, the United States, Belgium, West Germany, France, Holland, Italy, and the United Kingdom—that take some 70 percent of Australia's raw-wool exports.

17. If a buffer-stock scheme is to attain highly stable prices, some insight into the very large capital reserves required is provided by a simulation study of an international buffer-stock scheme for rice. Chaipravat (1978) estimates that a U.S. $13 to $37 billion capital reserve would be required to assure a 70 percent chance of successfully stabilizing the world price of rice within a 5 percent margin around its "normal" value over a simulated twenty-year period. This figure may be compared with the value of the total annual international rice trade in 1976 of $2.5 billion. The total value of world trade in rice, however, accounts for only 4 to 5 percent of the total value of annual world rice production.

18. This article is a memorandum by John Maynard Keynes, dated April 1942, that was discovered by Dr. Lal Jayawardene in the archives of the U.K. Treasury after he had seen reference to such a memorandum in Sir Roy Harrod's biography of Keynes. It is clear that Keynes envisaged three world institutions for the postwar period—the International Monetary Fund (IMF), the International Bank for Reconstruction and Development (IBRD), and a Commod Control. Only the IMF and IBRD were subsequently established. The international body called the Commod Control was envisaged by Keynes as controlling a series of commodity buffer stocks that would not only ameliorate short-period price fluctuations but also would make a significant contribution to the cure of the Trade Cycle itself.

19. Contrary to the conclusion reached by Gardner (1979, chapter 4), that (among other reasons) the incentives for private storage are insufficient because taxation of net returns from storage places pretax returns above the social discount rate, I would argue that a public storage authority should also "imitate" private investment in this respect. If public investment were to be justified wherever "gross" rates of return could be attained that were higher than the net-of-tax rates of return earned by the private sector, most of the private sector would be "crowded out" by government investment.

20. The aim of this section is to provide a compact discussion of some of the main points relating to the issue of the informational efficiency of commodity markets. A more comprehensive treatment of the topic is given in Chisholm (1980 and 1981).

21. See Martin (1980) for a highly critical analysis of the provision of weather information in the United States.

22. See Hirshleifer and Riley (1979).

23. The absence of a futures market for rice could be attributable to it being the only major food commodity whose production has traditionally been concentrated in developing countries, with a very small production (around 5 percent) entering world trade. In recent years, the United States has become a major rice exporter, and it is interesting to note that at the time of this writing, an attempt was being made to set up a rice futures market in New Orleans.

24. This result is formally derived in the paper by Danthine (1978).

25. For some interesting studies on this aspect of futures markets see Tomek and Gray (1970) and Tomek and Robinson (1977). Despite the many good theoretical and empirical studies of futures markets, it seems fair to say that a vigorous comprehensive conceptual formulation is still lacking that fully explains their evolution and success for some commodities but not others, as well as the precise mechanism of information aggregation and price formation.

26. There has been surprisingly little empirical work that has sought to determine how well futures prices explain commodity supply. In the only study of which I am aware, Gardner (1976) found that futures-market prices performed at least as well as the Nerlovian adaptive-expectations model in explaining soybean and cotton supply in the United States. Results from a study undertaken by Pashigian (1970) suggest that adaptive expectations may commonly be, in practice, a reasonable approximation to rational expectations.

27. The *Leslie Report,* for example, is a privately produced monthly crop estimate that is released just before the public release of the monthly USDA crop estimates.

28. For a further study on the economic value of improved crop forecast information for storage decisions, see Bradford and Kelejian (1977).

29. For a useful historical outline of the debate on speculative markets, see Poole (1976).

30. This assumes, of course, that there is no seasonal component in the price series. Samuelson (1965) was the first to provide a rigorous proof that properly anticipated prices fluctuate randomly.

31. In the only other study of this kind I know of, Marquardt (1979) tests whether futures prices are more accurate predictors of subsequent spot prices than forecasts contained in "outlook letters" disseminated by private advisory agencies, government, and land-grant college sources. The tests are made on wheat, corn, soybeans, hogs, and cattle futures contracts. Marquardt found that futures markets were generally a more accurate source of forecasts, both in terms of having lower average forecast errors and in better predicting direction of price movements. Further-

more, the futures markets provide a more frequent and timely forecast about future conditions than the outlook letters. The studies by Rausser and Just and by Marquardt do not discuss the issues of the likelihood of information contained in econometric forecasts and of outlook letters being incorporated into futures prices. If futures markets were functioning efficiently, any useful information contained in econometric forecasts and outlook letters would become imbedded in futures prices. Rausser and Just do indicate, however, that the results of their study suggest that econometric and futures price forecasts contain some independent information that may be valuable when combined to form composite forecasts.

32. Massell (1970) makes some comparisons between the reduction in the variability of producers' incomes likely to be attained under McKinnon's futures-market proposal with that under a buffer-stock scheme. The proposal made by Houthakker is somewhat different from McKinnon's. Houthakker suggests that government should buy and sell futures contracts to reach target prices, based on three-year moving averages of past prices, for the six- to nine-month contract. He envisaged this as a means of lessening the capital required to operate a buffer-stock scheme.

33. Freebairn (1976), for example, estimates that a 50-percent reduction in the forecast error of expected prices, on which production decisions of some Australian agricultural commodities are based, would increase economic surplus by less than 1 percent of the gross value of the commodities produced. These estimates do not include any increase in welfare attributable to improved storage decisions.

Bibliography

Aiyagari, S.R., Eckstein, Z., and Eichenbaum, M. 1980. "Rational Expectations, Inventories and Price Fluctuations." Economic Growth Center Discussion Paper No. 363, Yale University.

Arrow, K.J. 1971. *Essays in the Theory of Risk-Bearing*. Chicago, Ill.: Markham Publishing Co.

Arrow, K.J., and Lind, R.C. 1970. "Uncertainity and the Evaluation of Public Investment Decisions." *American Economic Review* 60:364–378.

Bradford, D.F., and Kelejian, H.H. 1977. "The Value of Information for Crop Forecasting in a Market System: Some Theoretical Issues." *Review of Economic Studies* 44:519–532.

______. 1978. "The Value of Information for Crop Forecasting with Bayesian Speculators: Theory and Empirical Results." *Bell Journal of Economics* 9:123–144.

Brennan, M.J. 1958. "The Supply of Storage." *American Economic Review* 48:50–72.

Brito, D.L., and Oakland, W.H. 1980. "On the Monopolistic Provision of Excludable Public Goods." *American Economic Review* 70:691–704.

Burmeister, E. 1978. "Is Price Stabilization Theoretically Desirable?" In *Stabilizing World Commodity Markets* ed. F.G. Adams and S.A. Klein. Lexington, Mass.: Lexington Books, D.C. Heath and Company, pp. 189–191.

Burt, O.R., Koo, W.W., and Dudley, N.J. 1980. "Optimal Stochastic Control of U.S. Wheat Stocks and Exports." *American Journal of Agricultural Economics* 62:172–187.

Campbell, R., Gardiner, B., and Haszler, H. 1980. "Revenue Effects of Wool Price Stabilization in Australia: Initial Results." *The Australian Journal of Agricultural Economics* 24:1–15.

Cargill, T.F., and Rausser, G.C. 1975. "Temporal Price Behavior in Commodity Futures Markets." *Journal of Finance* 30:1043–1053.

Caves, R.E. 1977–1978. "Organization, Scale, and Performance of the Grain Trade." *Food Research Institute Studies* 16:107–123.

Chaipravat, O. 1978. "International Rice Buffer Stock Operations: A Simulation Study." In *Stabilizing World Commodity Markets* ed. F.G. Adams and S.A. Klein. Lexington, Mass.: Lexington Books, D.C. Heath and Company, pp. 63–81.

Chisholm, A.H. 1980. "The Economics of Information in Agricultural Commodity Markets, Working Paper WP-80-3, Resource Systems Institute, East-West Center, Honolulu, Hawaii.

———. 1981."Production and Utilization of Information in Speculative Commodity Markets: With Applications to Agriculture." Paper presented to 51st ANZAAS Congress, Brisbane, Australia.

Corden, W.M. 1979. "The NIEO Proposals: A Cool Look." Thames Essay No. 21, Trade Policy Research Centre, London.

Cox, C.C. 1976. "Futures Trading and Market Information." *Journal of Political Economy* 84:1215–1237.

Danthine, J.P. 1978. "Information, Futures Prices and Stabilizing Speculation." *Journal of Economic Theory* 17:79–98.

DeCanio, S.J. 1980. "Economic Losses from Forecasting Error in Agriculture." *Journal of Political Economy* 88:234–258.

Dusak, K. 1973. "Futures Trading and Investor Returns: An Investigation of Commodity Market Risk Premiums." *Journal of Political Economy* 91:1387–1406.

Fama, E. 1970. "Efficient Capital Markets: A Review of Theoretical and Empirical Work." *Journal of Finance* 25:43–63.

Feder, G., Just, R., and Schmitz, A. 1977. "Storage with Price Uncertainty in International Trade." *International Economic Review* 18:553–568.

Freebairn, J.W. 1976. "The Value and Distribution of the Benefits of Commodity Price Outlook Information." *Economic Record* 52:199–211.

Gardner, B.L. 1976. "Futures Prices in Supply Analysis." *American Journal of Agricultural Economics* 58:81–84.

_______. 1979. *Optimal Stockpiling of Grain*. Lexington, Mass.: Lexington Books, D.C. Heath and Company.

Giles, D.E.A., and Goss, B.A. 1981. "Futures Prices as Forecasts of Commodity Spot Prices: Live Cattle and Wool." *Australian Journal of Agricultural Economics* 25:1–13.

Gislason, C. 1960. "Grain Storage Rules." *Journal of Farm Economics* 42:576–595.

Grossman, S.J., and Stiglitz, J.E. 1980. "On the Impossibility of Informationally Efficient Markets." *American Economic Review* 70:393–408.

Gustafson, R.L. 1958. "Carryover Levels for Grains: A Method for Determining Amounts That Are Optimal under Specified Conditions." Technical Bulletin No. 1178, U.S Department of Agriculture, Washington, D.C., October.

Hanock, G. 1974. "Desirability of Price Stabilization or Destabilization." Harvard Institute of Economic Research, Discussion Paper 351.

Harris, S., Salmon, M., and Smith, B. 1978. "Analysis of Commodity Markets for Policy Purposes." Thames Essay No. 17, Trade Policy Research Centre, London.

Hazell, P.B. R., and Scandizzo, P.L. 1975. "Market Intervention Policies When Production is Risky." *American Journal of Agricultural Economics* 57:641–649.

Head, J.G. 1977. "Public Goods: The Polar Case Reconsidered." *Economic Record* 53:227–238.

Helmberger, P., and Weaver, R. 1977. "Welfare Implications of Commodity Storage under Uncertainty." *American Journal of Agricultural Economics* 59:639–651.

Hillman, J., Johnson, D.G., and Gray, R. 1975. "Food Reserve Policies for World Food Security: A Consultant Study on Alternative Approaches." Food and Agricultural Organization of the United Nations, ESC/72/2, January.

Hirshleifer, J. 1966. "Investment Decision under Uncertainty: Application of the State-Preference Approach." *Quarterly Journal of Economics* 80:252–277.

_______. 1971. "The Private and Social Value of Information and the Reward to Inventive Activity." *American Economic Review* 61:561–574.

Hirshleifer, J., and Riley, J.G. 1979. "The Analytics of Uncertainty and Information—An Expository Survey. *Journal of Economic Literature* 17:1375–1421.

Hirshleifer, J., and Shapiro, D.L. 1970. "The Treatment of Risk and Uncertainty." In *Public Expenditure and Policy Analysis* ed. R.H. Haveman and J. Margolis. Chicago, Ill.: Markham Publishing Co.

Houthakker, H. 1967. "Economic Policy for the Farm Sector." American Enterprise Institute, Washington, D.C., November.

Houck, J.P., and Ryan, M.E. 1979. "Economic Research on International Grain Reserves: The State of Knowledge." Station Bulletin No. 532, University of Minnesota.

Johnson, D.G. 1975. "World Agriculture, Commodity Policy, and Price Variability." *American Journal of Agricultural Economics* 57:823–828.

———. 1976. "Increased Stability of Grain Supplies in Developing Countries: Optimal Carryovers and Insurance." *World Development* 4:977–987.

Johnson, D.G. and Sumner, D. 1976. "An Optimization Approach to Grain Reserves for Developing Countries." In *Analysis of Grain Reserves: A Proceedings* ed. D.J. Eaton and W.S. Steele. Economic Research Service Report No. 634, U.S. Department of Agriculture, Washington, D.C., August.

Just, R.E. 1977. "Theoretical and Empirical Possibilities for Determining the Distribution of Welfare Gains from Stabilization." *American Journal of Agricultural Economics* 59:912–917.

Just, R.E., Lutz, E., Schmitz, A., and Turnovsky, S. 1977. "The Distribution of Welfare Gains from International Price Stabilization under Distortions." *American Journal of Agricultural Economics* 59:652–661.

Kenndy, J.O.S. 1979. "Optimal Buffer Stock Policies for Wheat at the World Level." *Australian Journal of Agricultural Economics* 23:163–175.

Keynes, J.M. 1938. "The Policy of Government Storage of Foodstuffs and Raw Materials." *The Economic Journal* 68:249–260.

———. 1974. "The International Control of Raw Materials." *Journal of International Economics* 4:299–315.

Konandreas, P.A., and Schmitz, A. 1978. "Welfare Implications of Grain Price Stabilization: Some Empirical Evidence for the United States." *American Journal of Agricultural Economics* 60:74–84.

Labys, W.C., and Granger, C.W.J. 1970. *Speculation, Hedging and Commodity Price Forecasts*. Lexington, Mass.: Lexington Books, D.C. Heath and Company.

Leuthold, R.M., and Hartman, P.A. 1979. "A Semi-Strong Form Evaluation of the Hog Futures Market." *American Journal of Agricultural Economics* 61:482–489.

McKinnon, R.I. 1967. "Futures Markets, Buffer Stocks and Income Stability for Primary Producers." *Journal of Political Economy* 75:844–861.

Marquardt, R. 1979. "An Evaluation of the Relative Price-Forecasting Accuracy of Selected Futures Markets." In *Commodity Markets and Futures Prices* ed. R.M. Leuthold. Chicago, Ill.: Chicago Mercantile Exchange.

Martin, D.M.G. 1980. "Weather Information Services: Public and Private

Suppliers.'' Paper presented at the Meeting of the American Economics Association, Denver, Colo., September.

Massell, B.F. 1969. ``Price Stabilization and Welfare.'' *Quarterly Journal of Economics* 83:284–298.

———. 1970. ``Some Welfare Implications of International Price Stabilization.'' *Journal of Political Economy* 78:404–417.

Morgan, D. 1979. *Merchants of Grain*. New York: Viking Press.

Morrow, D.T. 1980. *The Economics of the International Stockholding of Wheat*. Research Report No. 18, International Food Policy Research Institute (IFPRI), Washington, D.C.

Muth, J.F. 1961. ``Rational Expectations and the Theory of Price Movements.'' *Econometrica* 29:315–335.

Newbery, D.M.G., and Stiglitz, J.E. 1979. ``The Theory of Commodity Price Stabilization Rules: Welfare Impacts and Supply Responses.'' *The Economic Journal* 89:799–817.

———. 1981. *The Theory of Commodity Price Stabilization*. Oxford: Oxford University Press.

Oakland, W.H. 1974. ``Public Goods, Perfect Competition, and Underproduction.'' *Journal of Political Economy* 82:927–939.

Oi, W.Y. 1961. ``The Desirability of Price Instability Under Perfect Competition.'' *Econometrica* 29:58–64.

———. 1972. ``The Consumer Does Benefit from Feasible Price Stability: Comment.'' *Quarterly Journal of Economics* 86:494–498.

Pashigian, B.P. 1970. ``Rational Expectations and the Cobweb Theorem.'' *Journal of Political Economy* 78:338–352.

Peck, A.E. 1976. ``Futures Markets Supply Response and Price Stability.'' *Quarterly Journal of Economics* 98:407–423.

———. 1977–1978. ``Implications of Private Storage of Grains for Buffer Stock Schemes to Stabilize Prices.'' *Food Research Institute Studies* 16:125–140.

Peck, A.E., and Gray, R.W. 1980. ``Grain Reserves—Unresolved Issues.'' *Food Policy* 5:26–37.

Poole, W. 1976. ``Rational Expectations in the Macro Model.'' *Brookings Papers on Economic Activity* 2:463–514.

Powers, M.J., and Tosini, P. 1977. ``Commodity Futures Exchange and the North-South Dialogue.'' *American Journal of Agricultural Economics* 59:977–985.

Praetz, P.D. 1975. ``Testing the Efficient Markets Theory on the Sydney Wool Futures Exchange.'' *Australian Economic Papers* 14:240–249.

Pratt, J.W. 1964. ``Risk Aversion in the Small and in the Large.'' *Econometrica* 32:122–136.

Rausser, G.C., and Just, R.E. 1979. ``Agricultural Commodity Price Forecasting Accuracy: Futures Markets versus Commercial Econometric Models." Working Paper No. 66, Department of Agricultural Economics, University of California, Berkeley.

Reutlinger, S. 1976. "A Simulation Model for Evaluating Worldwide Buffer Stocks of Wheat." *American Journal of Agricultural Economics* 58:1–12.

Samuelson, P.A. 1957. "Intertemporal Price Equilibrium: A Prologue to the Theory of Speculation." *Weltwirtschaftliches Archiv* 79:181–221. Reprinted in *The Collected Scientific Papers of Paul A. Samuelson,* Vol. 2, Ed. J.E. Stiglitz. Cambridge, Mass.: MIT Press.

———. 1965. "Proof That Properly Anticipated Prices Fluctuate Randomly." *Industrial Management Review* 6:41–49.

———. 1972a. "The Consumer Does Benefit from Feasible Price Stability." *Quarterly Journal of Economics* 86:476–493.

———. 1972b. "Rejoinder." *Quarterly Journal of Economics* 86:500–503.

Sandmo, A. 1974. "Discount Rates for Public Investment under Uncertainty. In *Allocation Under Uncertainty: Equilibrium and Optimality* ed. J.H. Dreze. London: Macmillan.

Sarris, A.H., and Taylor, L. 1978. "Buffer Stock Analysis for Agricultural Products: Theoretical Murk or Empirical Resolution?" In *Stabilizing World Commodity Markets* ed. F.G. Adams and S.A. Klein. Lexington, Mass.: Lexington Books, D.C. Heath and Company, Pp. 149–159.

———. 1976. "Cereal Stocks, Food Aid and Food Security for the Poor." *World Development* 4:467–976. Reprinted in *The New International Economic Order: The North-South Debate* ed. J.B. Bhagwati, Cambridge, Mass.: MIT Press.

Schmitz, A., Shalit, H., and Turnovsky, S.J. 1981. "Producer Welfare and the Preference for Price Instability." *American Journal of Agricultural Economics* 63:157–160.

Smith, G.W. 1978. "Commodity Instability and Market Failure: A Survey of Issues." In *Stabilizing World Commodity Markets* ed. F.G. Adams and S.A. Klein. Lexington, Mass.: Lexington Books, D.C. Heath and Company, pp. 161–188.

Smith, G.W., and Schink, G.R. 1976. "The International Tin Agreement: A Reassessment." *The Economic Journal* 86:715–728.

Solow, R.M. 1977. " 'Comment' on Cereal Stocks, Food Aid, and Food Security for the Poor." In *The New International Economic Order: The North-South Debate* ed. J.B. Bhagwati. Cambridge, Mass.: MIT Press.

Stein, J.P., and Smith, R.T. 1977. "The Economics of the United States Stockpiling." Report for Council on International Economic Policy, R-1861-CIEP, The Rand Corporation.

Taylor, C.R., and Talpaz, H. 1979. "Approximately Optimal Carryover Levels for Wheat in the United States." *American Journal of Agricultural Economics* 61:32–40.

Telser, L.G., and Higinbotham, H.N. 1977. "Organized Futures Markets: Costs and Benefits." *Journal of Political Economy* 85:969–1000.

Tomek, W.G., and Gray, R.W. 1970. "Temporal Relationships among Prices on Commodity Futures Markets: Their Allocative and Stabilizing Roles." *American Journal of Agricultural Economics* 52:372–380.

Tomek, W.G., and Robinson, K.L. 1977. "Agricultural Price Analysis and Outlook." In *A Survey of Agricultural Economics,* Vol. 1 ed. L.R. Martin. University of Minnesota Press, pp. 329–409.

Townsend, R.M. 1977. "The Eventual Failure of Price Fixing Schemes." *Journal of Economic Theory* 14:190–199.

Turnovsky, S.J. 1978. "The Distribution of Welfare Gains from Price Stabilization: A Survey of Some Theoretical Issues." In *Stabilizing World Commodity Markets* ed. F.G. Adams and S.A. Klein. Lexington, Mass.: Lexington Books, D.C. Heath and Company, pp. 119–148.

_______. 1979. "Futures Markets, Private Storage, and Price Stabilization." *Journal of Public Economics* 12:301–327.

Turnovsky, S.J., Shalit, H., and Schmitz, A. 1980. "Consumer's Surplus, Price Instability and Consumer Welfare." *Econometrica* 48:135–152.

Waugh, F.V. 1944. "Does the Consumer Benefit from Price Instability?" *Quarterly Journal of Economics* 58:602–614.

Willig, R.D. 1976. "Consumer Surplus without Apology." *American Economic Review* 66:589–597.

Wilson, R. 1975. "Informational Economies of Scale." *Bell Journal of Economics* 6:184–195.

Working, H. 1949. "The Investigation of Economic Expectations." *American Economic Review* 39:150–166.

_______. 1958. "A Theory of Anticipatory Prices." *American Economic Review* 48:188–199.

Wright, B.D. 1979. "The Effects of Ideal Production Stabilization: A Welfare Analysis Under Rational Behavior." *Journal of Political Economy* 87:1011–1033.

5 Commodity-Price Theory and Public Stabilization Stocks

Alexander H. Sarris

Primary commodity markets dominated by private traders exhibit very large interyear and intrayear price variability. This fact, which has been observed for many decades, has repeatedly led to calls for government intervention in these markets with the purpose of buying and selling stocks so as to avert extreme price fluctuations. Keynes was one of the earliest proponents of such schemes, and it seems that his major concern was not with year-to-year price fluctuations but with within-year price variability arising from the limited ability of the many and small market participants to withstand speculative runs.

The subsequent voluminous and still expanding theoretical literature that began with the path-breaking papers of Waugh (1944), Oi (1961), and Massell (1969), and that has been surveyed by Turnovsky (1978b) has taken for granted that the public authorities can stabilize the price with adequate buffer stocks, either at some mean level or around a price band. In all of these studies, the public stocks are viewed as being additional to any private stocks held by farmers, merchants, speculators, processors, and other market participants. The usual conclusion is that stabilization is beneficial to society but that the distribution of benefits is dependent on a host of factors and not unambiguously determined a priori.

The recent interest in national and international grain reserves, rekindled by the 1973–1974 world food crisis, has renewed the calls for public interference in grain and other primary commodity markets with the objective to stabilize year-to-year extreme price fluctuations and to ensure grain availability in years of low world supplies. Although much has been written on the subject, one of the major issues that has been left unresolved is the reaction of the private trade to public interference in grain markets through stockpiling (Stein and Smith 1977; Peck and Gray 1978). If the private trade reduces carry-over stocks by as much as the public authorities' stockpile, then no extra price stability is induced by government intervention. If, on the other hand, the substitution is not perfect, there is room for public intervention only if the private trade stockpiles in a suboptimal way. These questions will be investigated subsequently.

That there is substitution between private and public stocks is well recognized in the private grain trade, as illustrated by the following quote from an experienced trader:

> We used to also carry enough to make sure that people would eat if the following year's production were to be a partial failure, but Uncle Sam does that for us now (Wiese 1978, p. 3).

The empirical results of Peck (1977–1978) show that the substitutability between private and public stocks is much less than one for one. A casual observation of the yearly (ending May 31) wheat stocks in the United States shows that, indeed, whenever government-owned stocks are very large, the private trade tends to stockpile less. A simple, ordinary least-squares (OLS) regression of privately owned year-end wheat stocks (SP) on government-owned, year-end stocks (SG) from 1951 until 1978 (both in million bushels) yields the following equation (figures in parentheses denote standard errors):

$$\underset{}{SP} = \underset{(58.5)}{611.03} - \underset{(.09)}{.39}\,SG \qquad \begin{aligned} R^2 &= .42 \\ DW &= .63 \end{aligned}$$

Peck, taking into account charges, finds a negative coefficient of −.12 in a similar regression. It is clear that the underlying sources of this trade-off must be analyzed so that better estimates can be incorporated in models designed to test market-stabilization schemes.

Some recent theoretical and empirical studies (Helmberger and Weaver 1977; Gardner 1977; and Turnovsky 1979) have attempted to incorporate private storage in investigations of price stabilization. All of these studies, however, assume a competitive private-storage trade. Under these conditions, it is shown later that there is one-to-one substitution between public and private trade. Hence, public intervention will not affect the overall level of storage or price stability. The real issues concern imperfections in the private-storage trade, as Smith (1978) has also emphasized.

This chapter examines the trade-off between public and private storage under different assumptions about the markets and the information available to participants. It will be shown that the degree of substitution of public for private carry-overs depends on the amount of uncertainty or "noise" in the market as well as on the risk aversion of market participants. It will also be shown that the assumption of perfect competition renders public intervention completely ineffective. The role of information in the formation of expectations will be examined, and the theory of the supply of storage will be seen to be compatible with the model and, furthermore, to yield some testable hypotheses.

Optimal Social Storage in a Simplified Two-Period Model

Before the private trade is considered, it will be useful to define socially optimal carry-overs for later comparisons. Gustafson (1958) has provided a detailed analysis of both the definition of the intertemporal social-welfare function and a numerical method for obtaining the rules for socially optimal carry-overs. His analysis will not be repeated here; however, the same definition of a social-welfare function will be used.

The market price in periods 1 and 2 will be given by the following linear equations, which are to be interpreted as inverse-demand functions:[1]

$$p_1(x) = a - bx = a - b\,(H_1 - I) \tag{5.1}$$

$$p_2(y) = a - by + w = a - bI + w. \tag{5.2}$$

In equations 5.1 and 5.2, H_1 is the period-1 harvest that is known with certainty; I is the carry-over from period 1 for consumption in period 2; and w is a random variable. It might be convenient to think of w as equal to $-bH_2$ where H_2 is the unknown value of period 2 harvest. However, w does not have to be restricted in this way.

The model, specified by equations 5.1 and 5.2, has also been used in different theoretical contexts by Grossman (1977) and by Bradford and Kelejian (1977). They seem to offer the simplest nontrivial model for the theoretical analysis of storage problems.

If the social discount rate is r and the marginal variable storage cost is constant and equal to c, the social-welfare function to be optimized is given by:

$$W(I) = \int_0^{H_1 - I} p_1(x)\,dx + \rho \int_0^{I} p_2(y)\,dy - cI \tag{5.3}$$

where $\rho = 1/(1 + r) < 1$.[2]

A risk-neutral government will maximize the expected value of $W(I)$ with respect to I. Substituting 5.1 and 5.2 in 5.3, taking expected values and differentiating with respect to I, the solution for the socially optimal carry-overs—subject to nonnegativity of I—is given by the following expression:

$$I^s = \max\left[0,\ \frac{-a\,(1 - \rho) + bH_1 - c + \rho E\,(w|\Omega)}{b\,(1 + \rho)}\right]. \tag{5.4}$$

In 5.4, Ω is the information available in period 1 about the realization of the random variable in period 2. This can take the form of forecasts of harvest size, export demand, utilization, and so forth. If the discount rate is zero, the variable storage cost is negligible, the Ω has no information except the a priori beliefs about w, and the assumption is made that $w = -bH_2$, the optimal social carry-over would be equal to

$$I^s = \max \left(0, \frac{H_1 - EH_2}{2}\right) . \tag{5.5}$$

This oversimplified expression accords well with intuition. The future uncertainty induces a carry-over of about one-half the excess of current production over expected average production next period, thus splitting the uncertainty about the future in half.

The first-period price implied by 5.4 is

$$p_1 = \max \left[a - bH_1, \frac{2\rho a - \rho b H_1 - c + \rho E\,(w/\Omega)}{1 + \rho} \right] . \tag{5.6}$$

The optimal rule shown in 5.4 is piecewise linear. The optimal multiperiod rules for a stationary problem, as analyzed by Gustafson (1958) and Gardner (1977), have a similar break below which the optimal carry-over is zero and a monotonically increasing but slightly nonlinear subsequent part. The nonlinearity is induced by the nonnegativity constraints of future periods. Figure 5–1 illustrates the shapes of the rules. No attempt is made to compare the shapes empirically, the point being that for theoretical analysis the two-period rule is likely to be a reasonable approximation to the multiperiod one.

It might be interesting to point out that, under the informational assumptions made, the following relation holds in equilibrium under optimal social storage:

$$\rho E\,(p_2|\Omega) - p_1 - c \leq 0 \qquad (= \text{when } I^s > 0). \tag{5.7}$$

This can be easily shown by substituting, in the left-hand side of equation 5.7, equations 5.1, 5.2, and 5.6. What equation 5.7 brings out is the fact that optimal social storage, when positive, equates the difference between the discounted expected price and the current price to the marginal variable storage cost.

The task now is to compare storage under different market structures to the socially optimal one given by equation 5.4.

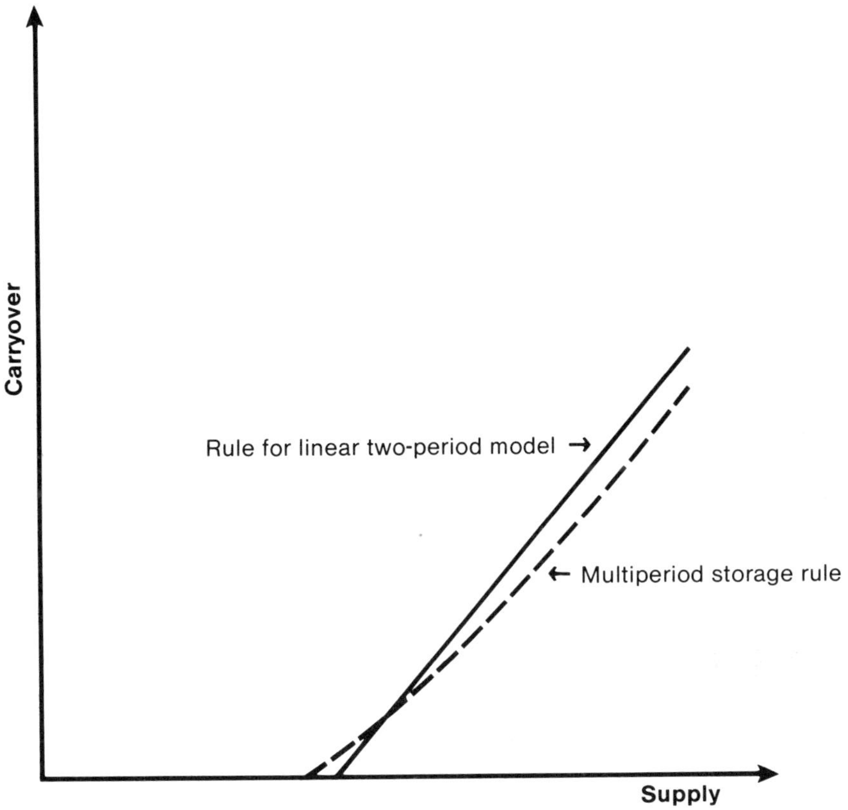

Figure 5–1. Approximate Shapes of Multiperiod and Two-Period Optimal Storage Rules

Private Monopolistic Storage

Consider one private monopolist carrying out the intertemporal storage function. The situation is unrealistic for the United States or for any other country in which storage is performed by many firms. Certain countries, however, may have a single firm or a few large firms controlling a large amount of the available binspace and hence have a large influence on market price. The model will approximate reality in those circumstances in which market power exists on the part of one or more storers who furthermore exploit that power. The model is also applicable to situations wherein markets are segmented and localized. The model will serve as a basis for later analysis.

The monopolist will be assumed to maximize a Von Neumann-Morgenstern utility function of profits with constant absolute risk aversion, ϕ,

$$U(\pi) = -e^{-\phi\pi} \tag{5.8}$$

where π denotes the profits from storage. When π is a normal random variable, maximizing the expected value of the above utility is equivalent to maximizing the function,

$$V(\pi) = E(\pi) - \frac{\phi}{2} \text{ var } (\pi). \tag{5.9}$$

It will be assumed here and in the concluding section that firms maximize 5.9.

The realized profit from speculative storing I from period 1 to 2 is given by

$$\pi = (\rho' p_2 - p_1) I - c'I \tag{5.10}$$

where $\rho' = 1/(1 + r')$ with r' equal to the private discount rate and c' the private marginal variable storage cost.

Substituting 5.10 in 5.9 and setting the derivative with respect to I equal to zero, the optimal monopolistic storage is

$$I^m = \max \left[0, \frac{\rho' E(p_2 | \Omega_m) - p_1 - c'}{\phi\rho'^2 \text{ var } (p_2 | \Omega_m)}\right]. \tag{5.11}$$

Here, Ω_m denotes the information set of the monopolist. From the original equations 5.1 and 5.2, eliminating I yields

$$\rho' E(p_2 | \Omega_m) - p_1 = -(1 + \rho') p_1 + 2\rho' a - \rho' bH_1 + \rho' E(w/\Omega_m) \tag{5.12a}$$

$$\rho'^2 \text{ var } (p_2 | \Omega_m) = \rho'^2 \text{ var } (w | \Omega_m). \tag{5.12b}$$

If 5.12a and 5.12b are substituted in 5.11 and then 5.11 is substituted in 5.1, the equilibrium value of p_1 can be found to be

$$p_1 = \max \left\{ a - bH_1, \frac{(a - bH_1) \phi\rho'^2 \text{ var } (w | \Omega_m) + b[2\rho' a - \rho' bH_1 - c' + \rho' E(w | \Omega_m)]}{\phi\rho'^2 \text{ var } (w | \Omega_m) + b(1 + \rho')} \right\} \tag{5.13}$$

while the profit-maximizing value of I^m is

$$I^{m} = \max \left[0, \frac{-a\,(1 - \rho') + bH_1 - c' + \rho' E\,(w \mid \Omega_m')}{b\,(1 + \rho') + \phi \rho'^2 \operatorname{var}\,(w \mid \Omega_m)} \right]. \tag{5.14}$$

Comparing 5.14 with 5.4, the conclusion that follows can be immediately reached.

Proposition 1

If the private marginal variable storage cost and discount rate are equal to their social values, and if the information of the monopolist is the same as public information, then a profit-maximizing, risk-averse speculative storage firm will stockpile less than that which is socially optimal.

Given the previous formulae, it is easy to show that the discounted expected future price contains a risk premium.

$$\rho' E\,(p_2 \mid \Omega_m) - p_1 - c' \leq \phi \rho'^2 \operatorname{var}\,(w \mid \Omega_m) \cdot I^m \; (= \text{when } I^m > 0). \tag{5.15}$$

If the monopolist is risk neutral—that is, $\phi = 0$—then there is no risk premium, but the optimal storage is indeterminate. In fact, a slight bullish change in the expectations will entail an infinite amount of desired storage. Under these conditions, a wealth constraint will be the limiting factor in stockholding.

A wealth constraint could also be built into the relation 5.14. Since the stockholding will either be risk constrained or wealth constrained, the parameter ϕ could be made large enough so as to make the wealth constraint not binding. Hence, wealth effects could be built into the model by enlarging the value of ϕ. In any case, the point is that ϕ must be greater than zero for realistic description of the market, and hence suboptimal storage will be implied under monopoly.

The expression for the optimal storage given in relation 5.14 brings out all the factors that can contribute to suboptimal private stockholding, namely, different discount rates, different marginal variable storage costs, risk aversion, and different information sets. Indeed, it can be easily seen that if $c' > c$ or $\rho' < \rho$, then $I^m < I^s$ where I^s was found in the previous section. These differences will be neglected from now on, and concentration will center on the implications of the parameter ϕ. The fact that in reality the private and social discount rates most probably diverge will only strengthen the conclusions.

Storage with Many Private Traders

Consider now the situation in which storage is performed by many private risk-averse firms, each one maximizing a function of profit like 5.9. It is assumed that the discount rate and the marginal variable storage cost are the same for all and equal to the social values.

Denote by I_i the storage of each firm; ϕ_i, its coefficient of absolute risk aversion (which, as already discussed, is assumed large enough to render the wealth constraint not binding); and Ω_i, its information set. Then the previous analysis shows that each firm's storage rule will be the following:

$$I_i = \max \left[0, \frac{\rho E(p_2 | \Omega_i) - p_1 - c}{\phi_i \rho^2 \operatorname{var}(p_2 | \Omega_i)}\right]. \qquad (5.16)$$

In the sequel, only the situations in which $I_i > 0$ are considered in order to simplify the notation.

If p_1 is the same for all traders, the equilibrium condition is[3]

$$p_1 = a - bH_1 + b\sum_i \left[\frac{-(1+\rho)p_1 + 2\rho a - \rho b H_1 - c + \rho E(w | \Omega_i)}{\phi_i \rho^2 \operatorname{var}(w | \Omega_i)}\right]. \qquad (5.17)$$

If the assumption is made that all market participants have the same information about w in equilibrium,[4] the resulting p_1 and aggregate storage can be easily found from 5.17 and 5.16 and are given by the following equations:

$$p_1 = \frac{(a - bH_1)\hat{\phi}\rho^2 \operatorname{var}(w | \Omega) + b[2\rho a - \rho b H_1 - c + \rho E(w | \Omega)]}{\hat{\phi}\rho^2 \operatorname{var}(w | \Omega) + b(1+\rho)} \qquad (5.18)$$

$$I^{\mathrm{P}} = \sum_i I_i = \frac{-a(1-\rho) + bH_1 - c + \rho E(w | \Omega)}{b(1+\rho) + \hat{\phi}\rho^2 \operatorname{var}(w | \Omega)} \qquad (5.19)$$

where Ω is the common information set and

$$\frac{1}{\phi} = \sum_i \frac{1}{\hat{\phi}_i}. \qquad (5.20)$$

These expressions are identical to the ones in 5.13 and 5.14—if $\Omega = \Omega_m$—except for the aggregate risk-aversion parameter $\hat{\phi}$. The previous section discussed the dual role of ϕ_i as a risk-aversion parameter and, at the same time, as a wealth parameter. If it is assumed that each individual storer has small wealth, then each ϕ_i must be assumed large. If there are many storers, each having small wealth, it is possible that $\hat{\phi}$ becomes smaller than the ϕ of the monopolist. Hence, the market with many participants has the potential to attain a socially more efficient level of storage than does a monopolist. In the limit, as the number of participants becomes infinite, the expression for I^p in 5.19 reduces to the expression for the socially optimal carryover. Thus the following proposition, well known since Gustafson (1958), is obtained.

Proposition 2.

If all private storage firms have an information set equivalent to the one available to society at large and if their number is large enough, then aggregate private carry-over is equal to the social optimum.

Notice that if the number of firms is large enough, risk aversion does not matter, since no matter how small $1/\phi_i$ is, the sum of many of these will yield a large number, hence forcing $\hat{\phi}$ close to zero. Moreover, it does not matter whether one or few traders are large relative to the others since information is assumed the same for all, and entry is free.

It is also easy to show that

$$\rho E-(p_2|\Omega) - p_1 - c \leq \hat{\phi}\rho^2 \text{ var } (w|\Omega)\cdot I^p \text{ (= when } I^p > 0), \quad (5.21)$$

an expression analogous to 5.15. Hence, there is a risk premium in this case, and it is a function of $\hat{\phi}$ and I^p.

Public Storage in the Presence of Private Speculative Stockholding

In the previous sections it was shown that the private sector will not hold optimal stocks when risk aversion, wealth constraints, or divergences between the social and private discount rates and storage costs are present. Suppose the government decides to interfere with the intention to improve on the private stockholding activities. In the two-period model of this chapter, the intervention is carried out as follows. The public authority charged with the stockholding function purchases an amount I^g in the first period and sells it in the next. The amount purchased, as well as the government's intention to sell it in the next period, is publicly announced.

Given this intervention, the new equilibrium conditions are found just as before.

$$p_1 = a - bH_1 + bI^g + b \sum_i I_i \tag{5.22}$$

$$p_2 = -p_1 + 2a - bH_1 + w. \tag{5.23}$$

Equation 5.23 is found from 5.2 by substituting $I^g + \Sigma I_i$ for I from equation 5.1. It is here that the assumption of *known* government stocking rules is important. The private trade knows that the amount I^g purchased by the government will be sold in the next period. This induces the relation 5.23 and renders w the only random variable.

The private traders now behave just as they did in the previous section; that is, they maximize their individual utility functions. The speculative stockholding rule is identical to 5.16. Substituting 5.16 in equation 5.22, the equilibrium values of p_1 and the private carry-over (again under the assumption of the same information set) are found to be

$$p_1 = \max \left\{ a - bH_1 + bI^g, \frac{(a - bH_1 + bI^g)\, \hat{\phi}\rho^2 \operatorname{var}(w \mid \Omega) + b\,[2a\rho - \rho bH_1 - c + \rho E(w \mid \Omega)]}{\hat{\phi}\rho^2 \operatorname{var}(w \mid \Omega) + b\,(1 + \rho)} \right\} \tag{5.24}$$

$$I^p = \sum_i I_i = \max\left[0, \frac{-a\,(1 - \rho) + bH_1 - c + \rho E\,(w \mid \Omega) - b(1 + \rho)\, I^g}{\hat{\phi}\rho^2 \operatorname{var}(w \mid \Omega) + b\,(1 + \rho)}\right] \tag{5.25}$$

The coefficient of I^g in the expression of I^p (when $I^p > 0$) can be seen to be

$$\frac{dI^p}{dI^g} = -\frac{b\,(1 + \rho)}{\hat{\phi}\rho^2 \operatorname{var}(w \mid \Omega) + b\,(1 + \rho)}. \tag{5.26}$$

Notice that if $\hat{\phi} \to 0$, the trade-off between public and private storage becomes equal to -1. In other words, when there are many traders, (5.26) implies that for every addition to public stocks there is an *equal reduction in private stocks*. In more detail, one finds:

Proposition 3.

In the presence of a risk-averse private-storage industry, there is a trade-off between public and private storage. This trade-off is, in general, less than one-to-one, and, under the ideal conditions of infinite traders, it becomes one-to-one.

The implications of this proposition are particularly important. It means that if the private-storage industry is composed of many traders, *public stockholding with a known rule will have no effect at all on total carry-over.*

It can also be easily shown from 5.25 and 5.4 that, if the public stocks are larger than the socially optimum, the numerator of the fraction in 5.25 becomes negative; hence, the private trade carries no stocks.

It was just shown that a market with a large number of private-storage operators renders public intervention unnecessary. Under conditions other than these, what does 5.26 imply about total stocks, both public and private? The following is obtained from 5.25:

$$I^p + I^g = \max\left[I^g, \frac{-a(1-\rho) + bH_1 - c + \rho E(w|\Omega) + \hat{\phi}\rho^2 \operatorname{var}(w|\Omega) I^g}{\hat{\phi}\rho^2 \operatorname{var}(w|\Omega) + b(1+\rho)}\right] \tag{5.27}$$

The second term in the above expression is now compared with the socially optimal value of stocks from 5.4 and, after some rearrangement, the following is obtained:

$$I^s - I^g - I^p = \frac{\hat{\phi}\rho^2 \operatorname{var}(w|\Omega)}{\hat{\phi}\rho^2 \operatorname{var}(w|\Omega) + b(1+\rho)}(I^s - I^g). \tag{5.28}$$

From this expression, the following proposition can be readily shown.

Proposition 4.

When the public storage is less than the social optimum, then the aggregate stocks remain less than the social optimum. When the public storage is equal to the social optimum, then the private stocks are zero and, hence, the aggregate is equal to the optimum.

In general, if $I^g < I^s$, the following is true:

$$I^p < I^p + I^g < I^s.$$

Proposition 4 means that public intervention contributes toward optimality when the number of traders is finite. Unless the public sector takes over the whole storage trade and stocks optimally, however, the mixed performance of the private and the public sectors together is less than optimal.

By taking the derivative of aggregate stocks in 5.27 with respect to I^g, we find that:

$$\frac{d\,(I^{p} + I^{g})}{dI^{g}} = \frac{\hat{\phi}\rho^{2}\,\mathrm{var}\,(w\,|\,\Omega)}{b\,(1+\rho) + \hat{\phi}\rho^{2}\,\mathrm{var}\,(w\,|\,\Omega)} < 1. \qquad (5.29)$$

This expression shows that government stockpiling *is not additional* to private carry-over. In fact, under the assumption of infinite traders, this derivative becomes equal to zero and, hence, the government contributes nothing extra toward stabilization. This implies that much of the theoretical literature on the welfare effects of price stabilization must be revised to take into account the contribution of private trade.

The most crucial assumption made here is that the private trade *knows* the public-stockholding *rule*. This assumption will be relaxed in a later section and its implications examined.

A Multiperiod Extension for the Perfectly Competitive Case

The result that with infinite private-storage operators the government stocks are a perfect substitute for private stocks is not restricted to the simple two-period model. In this discussion, Gustafson's multiperiod model is considered, and the fact that the result carries over to the general case is demonstrated.

In Gustafson's model, consumption in year t is given by

$$C_t = I_{t-1} + H_t - I_t, \qquad (5.30)$$

and the multiperiod welfare criterion whose expected value is to be maximized is given by

$$W = \sum_{t=t_0}^{T} \rho^t W_t, \qquad (5.31)$$

where

$$W_t = \int_0^{C_t} p_t(x)\,dx - cI_t \qquad (5.32)$$

and

$$p_t(x) = a - bx. \qquad (5.33)$$

The author's model, as can be seen, is a two-period version of the above. Gustafson shows that if H_t is a sample drawn from the same distribution every time, then for $T \rightarrow \infty$, the socially optimal stockholding policy is given by a function, $\Theta(\cdot)$, of the yearly available supply, $I_{t-1} + H_t$, which is independent of t. In terms of the notation used here

$$I_t^s = \Theta^s \left(I^s_{-1} + H_t \right) . \tag{5.34}$$

The form of $\Theta(\cdot)$ is as shown by the dotted line in figure 5–1. Gustafson showed that the optimal law (5.34) implies the following equation:

$$\rho E \left(p_{t+1} \middle| \Omega_t \right) - p_1 - c = 0, \tag{5.35}$$

where Ω_t denotes the information set in period t. It was on the basis of this equation that Gustafson concluded that a perfectly competitive storage trade would behave in an optimal fashion since it would tend through intertemporal arbitrage to satisfy 5.35. Samuelson (1972) also used 5.35 as a definition of intertemporal optimality. The only rule that satisfies 5.35 is the optimal one.

It should now be clear that, if the government intervenes in the storage trade with its own rule, $\Theta^g(\cdot)$, so that $\Theta^g(x) \leq \Theta^s(x)$ for all x, as shown in figure 5–2, a perfectly competitive storage trade (which assumes many traders)—*if it knows* the rule $\Theta^g(\cdot)$—will again stock so as to satisfy 5.35. Since $\Theta^s(\cdot)$ is the only rule that satisfies 5.35, the private trade will store

$$\Theta^p(x) = \Theta^s(x) - \Theta^g(x) \tag{5.36}$$

the difference for all x. In other words, if the private-storage trade knows the government policy, then its rule will be an exact complement of the government rule.

The result given in 5.35 implies that if one is interested in finding how a perfectly competitive private storage trade behaves in the presence of a publicly announced rule (for example, a price band one), all one has to do is translate the public rule in the format $\Theta^g (I_{t-1} + H_t)$—namely, a function with the available supply as the argument—and then subtract it from the optimal rule $\Theta^s(\cdot)$.[5]

Trade-Off between Public and Private Storage in the Presence of Policy Uncertainty

Attention is now focused on the two-period model of the earlier sections. It has been assumed that the public storage rule was announced and was

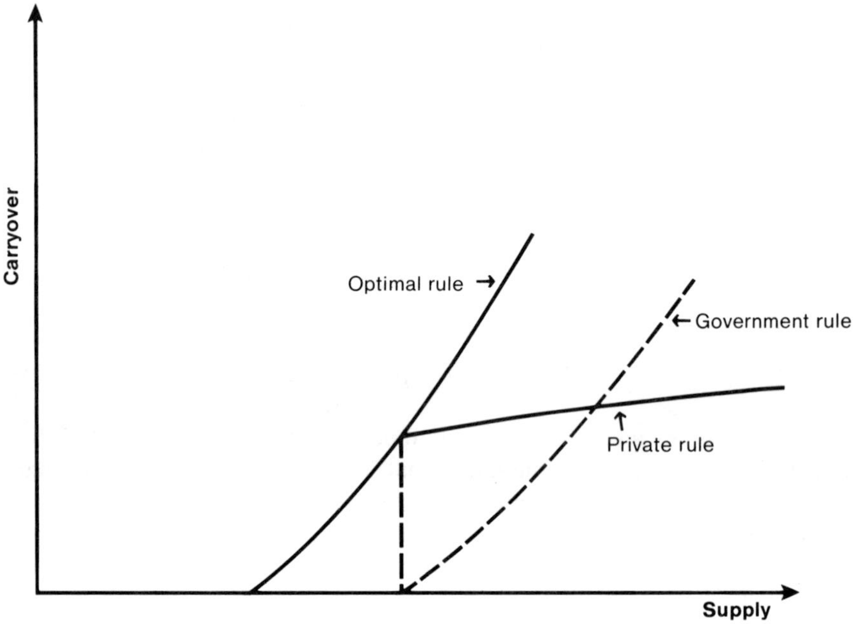

Figure 5–2. Optimal Carry-Over Rule for Multiperiod Problem and Two Possible Suboptimal Government and Private Rules

binding on the public authority. It is often the case, however, that while the government announces its intention to do something, it changes policies shortly afterward when conditions change. This induces additional uncertainty in the system. In the simple model of this chapter, the way this public-policy uncertainty will be modeled is as follows. The storage authority will purchase in period 1 I^g with the intention of selling it in period 2. There is a chance, however, that it will change its mind in period 2 and either purchase more or sell less of the public stock. In essence, what is being considered is uncertainty in the policy rule. The question is, how will the private trade react to this added uncertainty?

The first- and second-period price equations 5.22 and 5.23 will be modified as follows:

$$p_1 = a - bH_1 + bI^g + b \Sigma I_i \tag{5.37}$$

$$p_2 = -p_1 + 2a - bH_1 + w + w_g. \tag{5.38}$$

In 5.38 the added random variable w_g (which here will be assumed normal) denotes the uncertainty in the policy rule. It will be assumed that w and w_g

are independent. After following the earlier analysis, we arrive at the formula below for the total private stocks, which is analogous to 5.25.

$$I^p = \max\left\{0, \frac{-a(1-\rho) + bH_1 - c + \rho[E(w|\Omega) + E(w_g)] - b(1+\rho)I^g}{\hat{\phi}\rho^2[\text{var}(w|\Omega) + \text{var}(w_g)] + b(1+\rho)}\right\} \tag{5.39}$$

The coefficient of I^g in this expression is found to be

$$\frac{dI^p}{dI^g} = -\frac{b(1+\rho)}{\hat{\phi}\rho^2[\text{var}(w|\Omega) + \text{var}(w_g)] + b(1+\rho)}. \tag{5.40}$$

Comparing 5.40 with 5.26, the following conclusion is immediately reached.

Proposition 5

If there is uncertainty about the public storage rule, the trade-off between private and public stocks is smaller in the presence of risk-averse traders.

In other words, the private trade responds *less* to government interference. Does this mean that the public can induce combined stocks closer to the social optimum for the same amount of public carry-over? Before this question is analyzed, it is useful to compare 5.39 with 5.25. The comparison shows that, for the same amount of public stocks, if the policy uncertainty parameter w_0 has zero mean, *less total private* stocks will be carried if the government rule is uncertain. This is easy to rationalize since the risk-averse stockholders are faced with larger uncertainty in the present case.

Proposition 6

In the presence of an uncertain public policy rule of zero mean, a given public stock will induce a total (public plus private) carry-over that is farther away from the social optimum than if the public rule were known with certainty. Furthermore, to achieve the same level of total stocks, a larger public carry-over is needed.

For the proof of this proposition, see the chapter appendix. The main implication is that if the government policy is unpredictable, private trade will move to a position farther away from the optimum, and the public authority must then devote more resources to achieve the same degree of optimality. The obvious policy recommendation that can be made is that whatever rule the government decides to follow, it should announce it and stick to it; otherwise, by losing its credibility in the minds of the private trade, it makes its stabilization effort more difficult.

Storage with Different Information Sets

Until now, the focus of this chapter has been on the market imperfections induced by risk aversion, wealth effects, and to a lesser extent, differences between the private and social discount rates and storage costs. For each one of these imperfections, the case can be made for government intervention to improve on the stockholding practices of the private trade. It has been assumed throughout the discussion that all participants have the same information set.

Decisions about carry-overs, however, are not usually made until at least some information about the next year's production is available. This means that instead of using the prior probability distribution function for w, an informed posterior density should be used; these posterior densities might not be the same for the public and the private trade. A Bayesian stance will be taken. Let the prior probability density function for w be normal[6] with mean $\bar{w}$ and variance σ^2. The information Ω consists of a forecast y of the realization of w,

$$y = w + u, \tag{5.41}$$

where the random variable u denotes the precision of the forecast and is assumed normal with mean zero and variance σ_u^2.

The posterior density of w, given y, will be normal with mean and variance given by the expressions

$$E\,(w \mid y) = \frac{\bar{w}\sigma_u^2 + y\sigma^2}{\sigma^2 + \sigma_u^2} \tag{5.42}$$

and

$$\text{var}\,(w \mid y) = \frac{\sigma^2\,\sigma_u^2}{\sigma^2 + \sigma_u^2} \tag{5.43}$$

It can be clearly seen from 5.42 and 5.43 that only if $\sigma_u^2 \rightarrow \infty$ will $\bar{w}$ represent the best guess about the realization of w.

Suppose now that the socially best information available is y with precision (namely, variance of u) of σ_s^2, while the private trade—although it makes the same point forecast y—consistently underestimates its precision so that its perceived variance of u is $\sigma_p^2 > \sigma_s^2$. Obviously, this is only one particular way an informational inefficiency arises. Under these assumptions, the socially optimal carry-over is given by (see equation 5.4)

$$I^s = \frac{A + \rho\,(\bar{w} + yx_s)/(1 + x_s)}{B} \tag{5.44}$$

where

$$A = -a\,(1 - \rho) + bH_1 - c$$
$$B = b\,(1 + \rho)$$

and

$$x_s = \sigma^2/\sigma_s^2.$$

If it is assumed that the private trade is composed of many traders so that the aggregate $\hat{\phi}$ parameter can be neglected as very close to zero, then the informational assumptions above yield the following expression for the total private-trade carry-over (see equation 5.19):

$$I^p = \frac{A + \rho\,(w + yx_p)/(1 + x_p)}{B} \tag{5.45}$$

where $x_p = \sigma^2/\sigma_p^2$ and A and B are as in equation 5.44.

The difference $I^p - I^s$ is now formed and its sign investigated. After some algebraic manipulation, the following is obtained:

$$\text{sign}\,(I^p - I^s) = \text{sign}\,(x_p - x_s)\,(y - \bar{w}). \tag{5.46}$$

From the original assumptions, $x_p > x_s$. The forecast y can be on either side of its mean value $\bar{w}$; the probability that it is exactly $\bar{w}$ will be zero if a continuous distribution of y is assumed. Therefore, proposition 7 is arrived at.

Proposition 7
A private storage market that consistently underestimates the precision of the socially optimal forecast will never (that is, with probability zero) carry stocks equal to the optimal amount.

Note that the risk and wealth aspects have been neglected, and concentration has been on the informational aspects only.

Earlier, we saw that under a many-actor private storage trade, the trade-off between public and private stocks is exactly one-to-one. This result interpreted in the informational inefficiency context, however, means that the government cannot improve the storage situation by storing less than optimally (as was seen to be the case in proposition 4). If government wants to improve the system, it must take over the whole operation because only then will the private trade cease to operate, and optimality will be achieved.

Thus we see that information inefficiencies imply the need for a complete takeover of the private carry-over trade by the government.[7] Note that the discussion does not concern intrayear storage or working stocks but stocks to take care of unforeseen year-to-year production fluctuations.

If we assume that the private and social forecasts y are different, but the size of the forecast errors is the same, we obtain a similar conclusion to that given by proposition 7.

The issue of informational efficiency of different markets, particularly capital markets, has been the subject of considerable discussion and empirical testing. In the context of commodity markets, this topic was reviewed by Chisholm in chapter 4.[8] In this case, the usual tests are based on equations like 5.7 or 5.21. From these equations, we can see that the efficient-markets test jointly tests the informational efficiency as well as the perfect competitiveness of the market. This is so because informational efficiency would provide a unique definition of the expectations in 5.7 or 5.21, and the perfect competition assumption would set $\hat{\phi}$ equal to zero. It seems, therefore, that separate tests of each hypothesis are needed.

Considerations from the Theory of the Supply of Storage

Investigations of private carry-overs of wheat led Working (1948, 1949, 1953) to establish the theory of the supply of storage, which Brennan (1958) later elaborated on. According to the theory, the private supply of storage—namely, the quantity I^{p} in the present terminology—ought to be related to the difference between future expected and current price in the fashion shown by curve A in figure 5–3.

An examination now of equation 5.21 shows that it is compatible with a supply storage curve like B. Such a theoretical curve denotes that if the expected price appreciation is less than or equal to $ON = c$, no carry-overs in excess of working stocks will be carried into the next crop-marketing year. At expected price appreciations larger than c, an increasing amount of extra stocks will be carried over.

Notice, however, that risk aversion or wealth constraint (namely, a $\hat{\phi}$ parameter greater than zero) implies from 5.21 a *positive slope* for the supply of storage curve above I^{w}.[9] The data that Brennan (1958), Peck (1977–1978), and Peck and Gray (1978) present to estimate the supply of

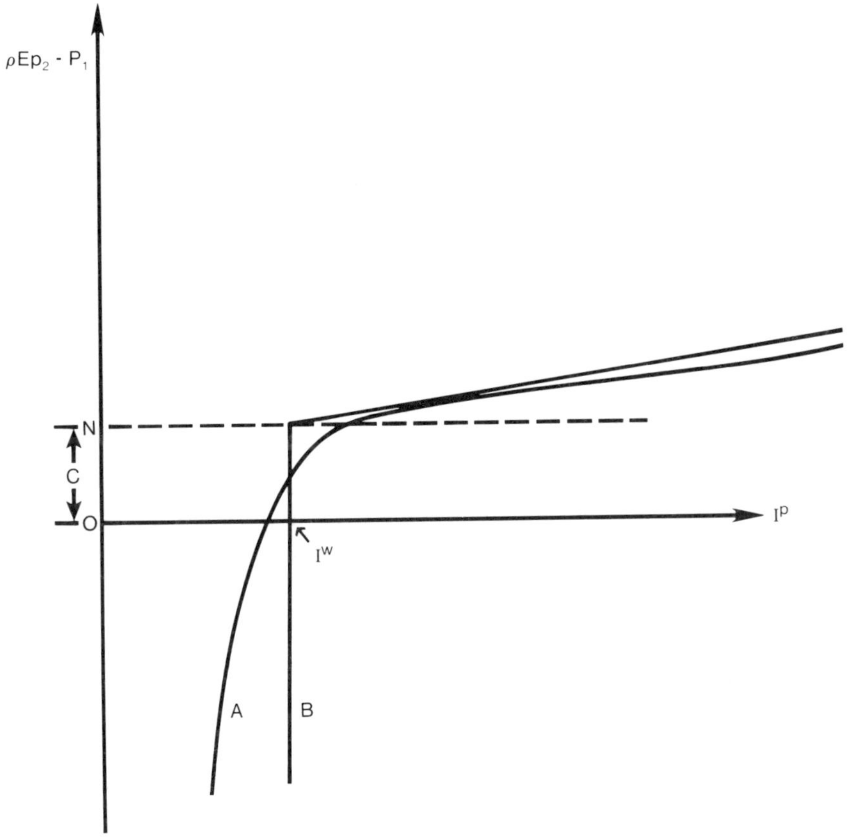

Figure 5–3. Supply-of-Storage Curves

storage curve show few points in the upper half of the diagram and a slight positive slope but no test of the hypothesis.

The discussion shows that a test of the nonzero value of the slope of the supply of the storage curve in the upper half of the diagram might provide firm conclusions about the existence of risk and wealth constraints in the storage industry.

The theoretical discussion here does not say anything about what might happen if there are inverse carrying charges. The empirical investigations of Working (1948, 1949) and Brennan (1958) have shown that the private stocks diminish even further in the presence of negative carrying charges. The theoretical results presented here, although neglecting this point, are certainly not incompatible with this empirical conclusion.

The tests leading to empirical estimates of the supply-of-storage curves have almost invariably been carried out using differences between futures prices as the indicators of carrying charges. Such a use implicitly assumes that the futures prices are informationally efficient. The validity of this hypothesis has recently been questioned (see, for example, Danthine, 1978), but empirical results are still nonexistent.

It seems that if good measures of aggregate market-expected prices could be found, a test of the nonzero slope hypothesis as outlined above could provide some insights into the structure of the private storage trade and a better rationale for government stockpiling.

Summary

This chapter has focused on the conditions under which the private trade stores in a socially suboptimal fashion and on the contribution public stockpiling can make toward improving the various market imperfections.

In defining the social optimum, society was assumed to be risk-neutral. This has been assumed in all previous work, and the validity of this assumption has not been questioned here nor has that of the weaker but equivalent assumption that society is less risk averse than are private individuals.

The analysis showed how divergences between private and social discount rates and storage costs could lead to generally lower private carry-overs than the social optimum. The argument was made that risk aversion in the context of a market with a finite number of participants will, under informational efficiency, lead to suboptimal private stockholding. It was also shown that the government will exacerbate the inefficiency if it varies its stockpiling policy in an unpredictable fashion.

Next, the chapter examined the possible inefficiency of the private trade in processing information and showed that under such an assumption the private-trade behavior diverges from the optimum. Does this imply that the government ought to publish, in addition to its regular crop-production forecasts, estimates of the reliability of each forecast? Is it true that the government can make better estimates of uncertain future events than the private trade? The empirical answers to these questions might make the case for public stocks or the provision of commodity-outlook information stronger.

The supply-of-storage theory was seen to be compatible with the author's simplified theoretical analysis, and with the multiperiod analysis developed by Gustafson that leads to rules depicted in figure 5–1. In addition, the theory offers the promise of empirical tests of the hypothesis that the private storage trade is nearly perfectly competitive.

An outstanding result of the analysis in this chapter that has important implications for public policy is the finding that a private storage industry with many traders will carry socially optimal stocks and that, more importantly, in the presence of such private storage trade, public stocking intervention will be completely ineffective. Hence, the arguments for interyear buffer stocks, strongly advocated in recent years, must be made only after a clear-cut case is established that the private storage trade is not behaving in a nearly perfectly competitive fashion. In the presence of a less than one-to-one trade-off of private for public stocks, a case for public intervention can be made.

All of this implies that the storage trade may behave in a way far from an idealized many-trader market. More empirical research needs to be done not only to make or break the case for public storage but also to understand how such intervention can be carried out in the best fashion.

Notes

1. The demand function defined by equation 5.1 is to be interpreted as a general equilibrium price-quantity relationship. All productive capacity in the economy except for the quantity of x available is kept constant, and the price level of all other goods is kept constant although relative prices of other goods can vary (see Gustafson 1958. p. 14).

2. It might seem surprising that the upper limit of the second integral is I instead of the total consumption. The results, however, remain unaffected if the upper limit is $H_2 + I$ where $w = -bH_2$, H_2 is the uncertain harvest of period 2, and a slight generality is maintained by 5.3.

3. This equilibrium condition is found by going through a procedure similar to the one used in deriving 5.13 and 5.14. The equilibrium condition is nothing but equation 5.1 in which the expressions for I, and the expectation and variance of p_2 have been substituted in.

4. In equilibrium, if the participants include p_1, as well as other observations in their information sets, they will indeed all have the same conditional expectations of w. The proof is quite complicated, however, and is omitted. For a proof in a slightly different context, see Grossman (1977).

5. If the government rule does not satisfy $\Theta^g(x) \leq \Theta^c(x)$ for all x, then whenever $\Theta^g(x) > \Theta^c(x)$, the rule of the private trade will be equal to zero.

6. Normality implies that there is a small but finite probability of realistically unlikely events such as, for example, negative production. In empirical investigation, the error implied can be easily corrected; in a theoretical investigation, it affects the analysis very little.

7. One might argue that the private trade has better information about

the uncertainties than does the government. In this case, the social optimum might be defined with respect to this "better" information set. The private many-actor trade would then carry optimal stocks, and the government would not, as proposition 7 (properly reinterpreted) shows. In the presence of a finite number of traders, depending on the definition of the social optimum, government intervention will then be beneficial at times and detrimental at others.

8. For a survey of the informational efficiency of capital markets, see Fama (1970).

9. A positively sloped supply-of-storage curve could also be due to increasing marginal costs of storage.

Bibliography

Bradford, D.F., and Kelejian, H.H. 1977. "The Value of Information for Crop Forecasting in a Market System: Some Theoretical Issues." *Review of Economic Studies* 44:519–531.

Brennan, M.J. 1958. "The Supply of Storage." *American Economic Review* 48:51–69.

Danthine, J.P. 1978. "Information, Futures Prices, and Stabilizing Speculation." *Journal of Economic Theory* 17:79–98.

Fama, E.F. 1970. "Efficient Capital Markets: A Review of Theory and Empirical Work." *Journal of Finance* 25:383–417.

Gardner, B.L. 1977. "Optimal Stockpiling Models and the Effects of Public on Private Storage." *Proceedings, American Statistics Association, Business Economics Statistics Section.* Pp. 77–83.

Grossman, S.J. 1977. "The Existence of Futures Markets, Noisy Rational Expectations, and Informational Externalities." *Review of Economic Studies* 44:431–439.

Gustafson, R.L. 1958. *Carryover Levels for Grains: A Method for Determining Amounts That Are Optimal under Specified Conditions.* USDA Technical Bulletin 1178, Washington, D.C., October.

Helmberger, P., and Weaver, R. 1977. "Welfare Implications of Commodity Storage under Uncertainty." *American Journal of Agricultural Economics* 59:639–651.

Keynes, J.M. 1938. "The Policy of Government Storage of Foodstuffs and Raw Materials." *Economics Journal* 48:449–460.

Massell, B.F. 1969. "Price Stabilization and Welfare." *Quarterly Journal of Economics* 83:284–298.

Oi, W.Y. 1961. "The Desirability of Price Instability under Perfect Competition." *Econometrica* 29:58–64.

Peck, A.E. 1977–1978. "Implications of Private Storage of Grains for Buffer Stock Schemes to Stabilize Prices." *Stanford Food Research Institute Studies* 16:125–140.

Peck, A.E., and Gray, R.W. 1978. "Grain Reserves: Some Unresolved Issues," mimeo. Stanford Food Research Institute Studies, Palo Alto, California.

Samuelson, P.A. 1972. "Stochastic Speculative Price." In *Collected Scientific Papers of Paul A. Samuelson,* Vol. 3, ed. R.C. Merton. Lexington, Mass.: Lexington Books, D.C. Heath and Company, Pp. 894–896.

Smith, G.W. 1978. "Commodity Instability and Market Failure: A Survey of Issues." In *Stabilizing World Commodity Markets* ed. F.G. Adams and S.A. Klein. Lexington, Mass.: Lexington Books, D.C. Heath and Company.

Stein, J.P., and Smith, R.T. 1977. "The Economics of United States Grain Stockpiling." Rand Corporation R-1861-CIEP, March.

Turnovsky, S.J. 1978. "The Distribution of Welfare Gains from Price Stabilization: A Survey of Some Theoretical Issues." In *Stabilizing World Commodity Markets: Analysis, Practice and Policy* ed. F.G. Adams and S. A. Klein. Lexington, Mass.: Lexington Books, D.C. Heath and Company, Pp. 119–148.

_______. 1979. "Futures Markets, Private Storage, and Price Stabilization." *Journal of Public Economics* 12:301–327.

Waugh, F.V. 1944. "Does the Consumer Benefit from Price Instability?" *Quarterly Journal of Economics* 58:602–614.

Wiese, V.A. 1978. "Introduction to Hedging." In *Readings in Futures Markets,* vol. 3, *Views from the Trade* ed. A.E. Peck. Chicago, Ill.: Board of Trade.

Working, H. 1933. "Price Relations between July and September Wheat Futures at Chicago Since 1885." *Wheat Studies* 9:187–238.

_______. 1948. "Theory of the Inverse Carrying Charge in Futures Markets." *Journal of Farm Economics* 30:1–28.

_______. 1949. "The Theory of the Price of Storage." *American Economic Review* 39:1254–1262.

Appendix 5A:

Proof. Consider the difference $I^s - I^g - I^p$. By using 5.39, after some rearrangement the following is obtained:

$$I^s - I^g - I^p = \frac{\hat{\phi}\rho^2 \, [var\,(w \mid \Omega) + var\,(w_g)]}{\hat{\phi}\rho^2 \, [var\,(w \mid \Omega) + var\,(w_g)] + b\,(1 + \rho)} (I^s - I^g). \quad \text{(A.1)}$$

Denote this difference by d_1. As can be readily seen, the difference d_1 is positive for $I^g < I^s$. Denote by d_2 the similar difference in 5.28 in the absence of policy rule uncertainty resulting in

$$d_1 - d_2 = \left(\frac{x_1}{x_1 + B} - \frac{x_2}{x_2 + B} \right) (I^s - I^g), \quad \text{(A.2)}$$

where x_1 is defined as the numerator in 5.41, $B = b\,(1 + \rho)$ and the definition of x_2 is analogous. Carrying out the calculation in the first parenthesis:

$$d_1 - d_2 = \frac{B\,(x_1 - x_2)}{(x_1 + B)\,(x_2 + B)} (I^s - I^g). \quad \text{(A.3)}$$

Since $x_1 > x_2$, it is clear that $d_1 > d_2$ whenever $I^g < I^s$.

The second part of the proposition can be easily shown by setting $I^p + I^g$ from 5.27 equal to $I^p + I^g$ in this case (computed from 5.39) and comparing the corresponding I^gs. Denote by subscript 1 the case with added uncertainty and by subscript 2 the earlier situation. By simplifying the notation, as above, and furthermore setting A equal to $-a\,(1 - \rho) + bH_1 - c + \rho E\,(w \mid \Omega)$, 5.39 and 5.27 imply

$$I_1^p + I_1^g = \frac{A + x_1 I_1^g}{B + x_1} = I_2^p + I_2^g = \frac{A + x_2 I_2^g}{B + x_2}, \quad \text{(A.4)}$$

where $x_1 > x_2$. By rearranging terms, A.5 is obtained.

$$\left(I_1^g - I_2^g \right) x_1\,(B + x_2) = B\,(x_1 - x_2) \left(\frac{A}{B} - I_2^g \right). \quad \text{(A.5)}$$

By the notation used here, however, $A/B = I$, the socially optimal carry-over. Since $I_2^g < I$, it is implied that $I_1^g > I_2^g$.

6 Rural Food Security

James Roumasset

What Is Food Security?

Food security is commonly regarded as the ability to meet target consumption levels in the face of fluctuating production, prices, and incomes.[1] A fourth risk is often added to this list of problems: namely, the possibility that food supplies will be unavailable at any price. In this chapter, food unavailability is not distinguished from the risk of high prices. During times of unexpectedly low production or high consumption, it is possible that spot markets in key grain commodities may become very thin or even disappear altogether. This means that the asking price on spot markets exceeds the buying price, not that grain cannot be purchased at any price.

The risk of *food insecurity (RFI)* may be defined as the probability that the value of the production deficiency *(VS)* is greater than the relevant exchange entitlement *(EE)*. That is,

$RFI = Pr\ (VS > EE)$ where

$VS = P(\bar{R} - R_p)$

P = gross import price of grain (including internal as well as external marketing costs)

$\bar{R}$ = consumption requirement

R_p = production

EE = the sum of liquid assets and other income (Y) that can be used in exchange for grain (R)

A subsequent question is, "food security for whom?" Much of the food-security literature focuses on food security from a national perspective. This chapter discusses food security from the perspective of the rural household. Sen (1981) has shown that famines are primarily a rural phenomenon. We can assume the same is likely to be true for food insecurity. In particular, rural households are more prone to suffer from a combination of high food prices and low entitlements. The risk of food insecurity is interpreted here with respect to a rural household, although the definition could also be applied at more aggregate levels.

I have benefited from extensive discussions with Jock Anderson, some of which were relevant for this paper. I also wish to thank Rodney Tyers for helpful comments on a previous draft.

The definition helps to classify sources of food insecurity according to whether they affect the price, the household's production, or the household's purchasing power. The relevant price to the household, for example, may be affected not only by international prices but also by local supply and demand conditions and transportation costs. It also facilitates consideration of various risk-management strategies available to the household such as diversification, storage, and saving.

From a policy perspective, however, it is difficult to see aspects of food security rooted in short-term fluctuations as well as separated from the secular problems of rural poverty. Therefore, both the short-run and long-run issues are discussed. First, the sources of food insecurity that relate to the definition given are dealt with. Next, some of the long-run issues in food security are taken up. Finally, policy options are covered, and some preliminary conclusions are drawn.

Short-Term Food Security

Figure 6–1 illustrates some of the major sources of food insecurity facing a rural household with a small endowment of land. The household is viewed as facing two exogenously determined prices for the staple commodity, say, rice. P_s is the net price that the household members receive for selling rice after deducting any marketing costs that they must incur. P_b is the gross buying price. The difference between P_b and P_s reflects transportation and marketing costs between the rural household and the market center as well as other transaction costs. Thus the wedge between prices is idiosyncratic; it depends on the location of the household and other factors. The model is thus analogous to a competitive equilibrium with individualized taxes.

S_1 represents the household's supply curve of rice for an average year. The representative household is shown as selling a small market surplus, the difference between S_1 and D, both evaluated at P_s. If supply is S_2, however, then the relevant shadow price of rice to the family is P_b. This illustrates how, unlike the conventional neoclassical model, a local domestic shortfall can result in a price increase.

Suppose, for example, that figure 6–1 portrays a representative household in a village hit by a flood or drought. If the village usually exports rice, then the institutions for importing may not be well established. This implies a large wedge between the buying and selling price so that a natural disaster may result in a large price increase even if supplies are plentiful at the market center. This fits Sen's description of the 1943 Bengal episode as a "boom famine," that is, famine in the midst of increased national production.

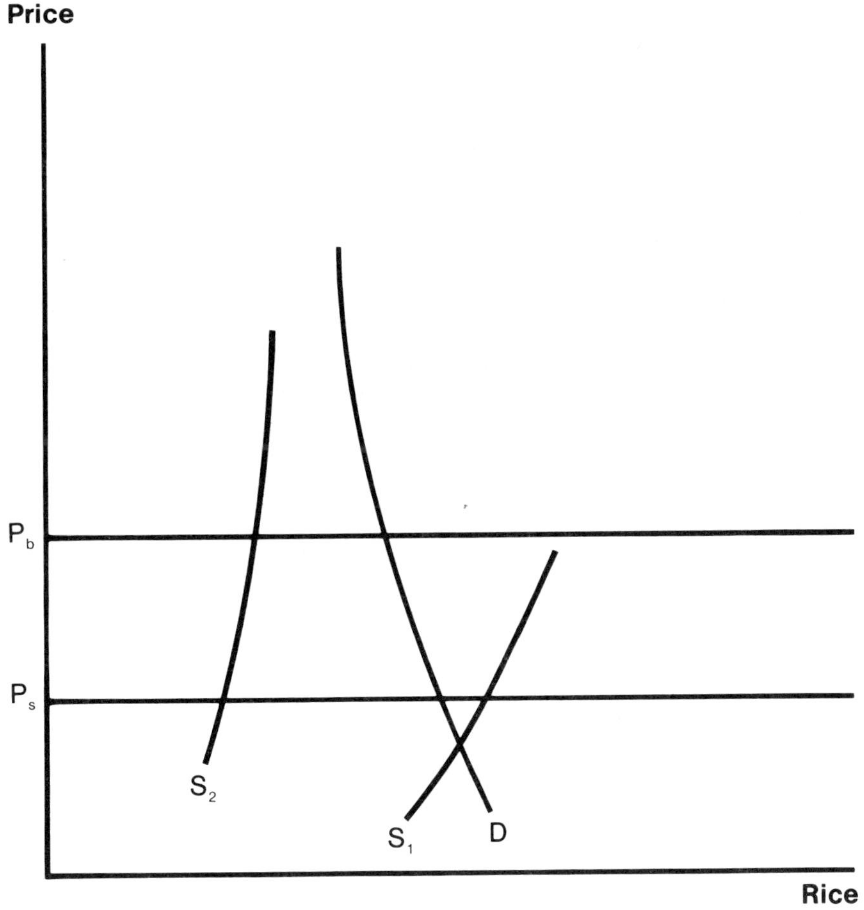

Figure 6–1. Effects of a Domestic Shortfall on Price

The household in figure 6–1 is hit by a double whammy. At the same time that the household's real income is low, the buying price of the major staple has risen sharply. This simple graph can also be used to represent other sources of food insecurity. For example, a price increase in the market center—perhaps induced by a higher world price—could cause a further increase in P_b. A fall in other sources of income, due, for example, to lower wages or to unemployment, could cause a backward shift in effective demand, perhaps to a level below some minimum nutritional requirement.

Figure 6–1 also describes the types of the 1943 Bengal famine and the 1974 Bangladesh famine as described by Sen (1981). In both cases, the famine victims were concentrated in rural areas and were hit by the combination of higher prices and lower incomes. It seems likely that household production and consumption practices have some built-in flexibility, for example, in the form of savings or durable goods. Perhaps households can survive either a fall in income or a rise in prices. It is the combination of major changes in both situations that may bring disaster, especially when repeated over more than one period.

What kind of indigenous mechanisms may insulate the household from the kinds of fluctuations just described? Any strategy the household can use to translate fluctuating prices and incomes into a smooth consumption stream has the potential for preserving food security in the face of substantial risks. Storage of food is perhaps the most direct of such mechanisms. If the costs of storage—including spoilage and the interest rate—are high, however, then it is quite possible that the accumulation of liquid assets is a more efficient strategy than that of food storage. Well-developed formal or informal credit markets can also mitigate against the destabilizing effects of fluctuating production.

Another important set of strategies for household management of food risk is diversification of production and consumption activities. Diversification into uncorrelated income-earning activities, for example, will reduce the variance of total income. Supply-side diversification includes diversifying in alternative cash crops, spreading labor between household and market activities, and diversifying production for home use.

The last example implies some flexibility in home consumption. This strategy is often neglected in academic discussions but is, in fact, quite important. At the national level, China used demand management to its advantage in 1974, actually increasing rice exports in the face of the rice shortage and trading for relatively cheaper wheat. The same strategy can be employed at the household level. For example, in Indonesia, the household may diversify production into rice, corn, and cassava and then adjust consumption according to price fluctuations. In a full neoclassical model, production and consumption decisions are independent. Thus, for example, consumption can be adjusted according to fluctuating prices without diversifying production. Once different buying and selling prices are admitted, however, the household shadow price of commodities depends on production as well as on market developments. Thus it is quite common for households in upland Java, for example, to diversify production in order to smooth the consumption stream of calories.[2]

This multiplicity of instruments implies that the household faces what is analytically equivalent to a portfolio management problem. To the extent that these options are not highly covariant, the optimal strategy may employ simultaneous use of several instruments.

If there were universal markets, including futures markets and markets for spreading risks, then resource allocation would be Pareto optimal despite the presence of fluctuations and the existence of poverty. Once incomplete markets and transaction costs are entered into the picture, resource allocation is no longer efficient in the first-best sense. That is, the use of storage, liquid assets, and other "smoothing" instruments are costly relative to the use of state-contingent futures markets.

Nonetheless, there is no a priori reason for believing government intervention would improve efficiency; government must face many of the same transaction costs as are faced by the private economy. A case for intervention rests on showing that the government has a comparative advantage in dealing with these transaction costs. Even if there is a collective demand for poverty reduction, the justification of intervention requires that government mechanisms for poverty reduction be shown to be more efficient than private ones. These themes will be discussed in the last section of this chapter.

Long-Run Food Security

Long-run food security is essentially a problem of decreasing poverty. As population growth brings increasing pressure on a limited or declining resource base, a greater number and even percentage of households may earn average real incomes below the poverty line. For a substantial fraction of the rural poor, this is a problem of the secular decline in real wages.

An apparent decline in real agricultural wages has been documented for the early 1970s in several Asian countries (Asian Development Bank, 1977). The moderating influence of relatively stable food prices appears to have eased the situation in the late 1970s. Nonetheless, substantial pockets of poverty exist where the supply of labor has grown faster than the demand and where out-migration has been insufficient to prevent real wages from declining.[3]

To some observers, the decline or stagnation of real wages has come as a surprise in the face of what appeared to be breakthroughs in agricultural technology. One way of reconciling the persistence of poverty with the new high-yielding rice varieties and other technological gains has been the hypothesis of "institutional constraints."

According to this view, agricultural production is organized under a set of inappropriate and exploitative institutions that combine the worst aspects of feudalism and capitalism. The institution of share tenancy, the notorious inverse relationship between productivity and farm size, and "the emergence of the rural proletariat" are all thought to provide a priori evidence of inefficiency and exploitation. It is now apparent that all these observations are consistent with models that rest only on individual rationality and which abstract from the various sources of divergence between individual and social efficiency. This new class of models, which extends neoclassical microeconomics to incorporate transaction costs, is sometimes called "the new institutional economics."[4]

The phenomenon of proletarization, that is, the rapid growth of a landless class of workers, has been confused with polarization, the bifurcation of society into classes of rich owners of large capitalistic farms and their landless workers.[5] Recent research in rural Asia has shown that the rapid growth of a landless class can be explained by the fact that optimal labor inputs per hectare have risen faster than farm size has declined, a tendency that is augmented by land-saving technological change. Land ownership and cultivation rights are more widely diffused throughout the economy, however, not increasingly concentrated in the hands of a few.[6]

Figure 6–2 illustrates how population pressure induces a transition from family to hired labor. D_L^1 and D_L^2 are the demand curves for labor by the family farm before and after technological change. For example, switching to high-yielding rice varieties increases the demand for labor

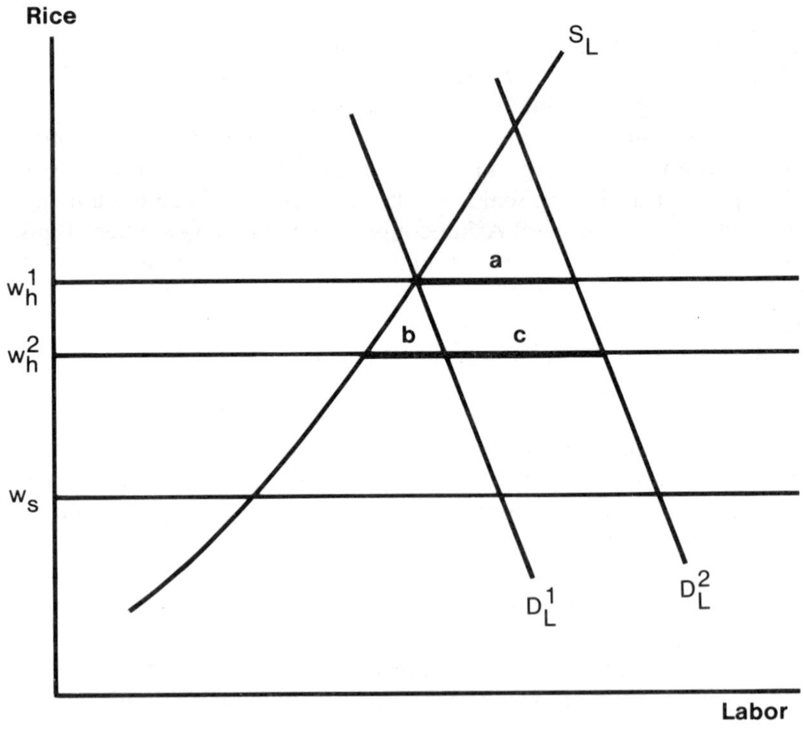

Figure 6–2. Supply and Demand for Labor for the Farm-Household Unit

because of the higher marginal product of weeding labor. The farm household takes the market wage and transaction costs as parameters. For example, w_h^1 is the gross hiring wage before the technological change. This is the per unit cost of labor to the employer, including the market wage and transaction costs of employment such as hiring and supervision costs.

Before the technological change, our hypothetical farm household is self-sufficient, but just on the verge of hiring labor. After the technological change, the demand for labor exceeds the supply by the quantity, a, that is, the amount of hired labor. If transaction costs also fall, then the increase in hired labor is augmented by the additional quantity, b, which is associated with the fall of the hiring wage from w_h^1 to w_h^2.

In the case of Laguna, Philippines, the increase in hired labor following the introduction of new varieties was quite dramatic. From 1965 to 1975, total preharvest labor for a sample of farmers studied by the International Rice Research Institute (IRRI) increased by 200 percent. As a fraction of total labor, hired labor increased from one-third to two-thirds during the same period.[7] The transition from family to hired labor was partly facilitated by a rapid increase of in-migration to the study villages. As the new migrants established bonds of trust and reputations for reliability (called "F- connections" by Ben-Porath, 1980), the transaction costs of employing landless workers were reduced. Economies of scale in supervision also contributed to the reduction in w_h. In many cases, teams of workers provided their own internal supervision and were paid by piece rates.[8]

What is the role of population growth in this scenario? In the perspective of induced innovation (Binswanger and Ruttan 1978), the development of high-yielding varieties is a land-saving innovation and can itself be viewed as a response to land scarcity created by rapid population growth. As is clearly the case with the high-yielding varieties, the technological change will only stimulate the demand for labor in certain parts of the country. For high-yielding varieties in the Philippines, the increased demand is concentrated in irrigated areas. Thus the increased demand for labor will tend to be met by the migration of workers from less favored regions. It is impossible to say, in general, whether the negative forces of population growth and in-migration on wages will be offset by the positive effect of appropriate technological change. In the Laguna case, real wages appeared to remain about constant from 1965 to 1975 and then rose somewhat from 1975 to 1978, reflecting perhaps the additional "pull" effect of the growth of the nonagricultural sector and of capital accumulation.[9]

It is possible, of course, that various sources of inefficiency, such as monopoly power, contributed to the rapid growth of the landless class in the Philippines. What has been shown is that the transition to hired labor is not proof of the existence of exploitation and inefficiency. Indeed, the transition may be viewed as an institutional response to changing factor prices and, as such, represents a positive rather than a negative force on wages. Thus the observation of a correlation between declining wages and the incidence of hired labor does not imply that capitalism produces poverty. The causation may be at least partially the other way around. That is, population pressure induces the spread of labor markets and other "capitalist" institutions.

It is now widely recognized that share tenancy is not necessarily a source of inefficiency as the so-called Marshallian authors have suggested, but rather that it tends to compensate for the transaction costs that inhibit the functioning of a full set of markets.[10] Share tenancy economizes on supervision costs, spreads risks, gives incentives for management, and helps select appropriate workers.[11]

The widely documented inverse relationship between farm size and yield per hectare has also been taken as evidence of efficiency. The argument is that different yields per hectare imply a different marginal productivity of labor and this, by definition, is characteristic of inefficient allocation of labor. This conclusion rests on two fallacies. First, yield per hectare may be substantially different on farms with the same marginal productivity of labor simply because the inherent productivity of the land is different. In fact, for family farms, a tendency often exists to adjust farm size to help equalize the marginal productivity of labor across farms of different quality.[12] Thus small family farms tend to be of higher average quality than large family farms (Roumasset 1976, chapter 4). The land quality/farm size relationship appears to diminish, however, as population pressure induces a transition to hired labor.

Even if the marginal productivity of labor on large commercial farms tends to be higher than on small family farms, as is alleged to be the case, this does not imply inefficient allocation of labor. Returning to figure 6–2, imagine a household with a large supply of household labor relative to its endowment of land. The equilibrium shadow price of labor to such a household would be w_s, that is, the monetary wage minus any transaction costs borne by the worker (for example, journey to work). Such a family would hire out the difference between the household supply and demand for labor, both evaluated at w_s. Thus this model predicts that the marginal product of labor for farms that hire workers is equal to the actual wage plus the transaction costs borne by the employer. The marginal product of labor for small subsistence farms, on the other hand, is equal to the actual wage minus the transaction cost borne by the worker. Thus, even in the same locality, marginal productivities across farms will differ according to the sum of these transaction costs. If data are analyzed across localities, then those additional transaction costs (especially the costs of migration) that prevent full market clearing in the usual neoclassical sense must be added.

These observations point to the need for further research on the existence, nature, and causes of inefficiency in rural labor markets. Observations such as the inverse relationship between farm size and yield per hectare appear to be consistent with both efficiency and inefficiency explanations. Additional hypotheses or predictions can be inferred from the model that can provide an empirical basis for discrimination.

The policy implications of efficiency and inefficiency models differ dramatically. If agricultural institutions act as constraints to development, then the door is open for a wide variety of institutional reform, intervention, and "development planning." If, on the other hand, the models described do capture the main determinants of agricultural organization, then policymakers should be cautious about attempts to replace indigenous institutions with planner's dreams.

The efficiency models do not, however, support a continuation of the status quo. The forces of supply and demand and induced technological and institutional change work to promote development and reduce poverty only to the extent that these forces are not stifled by excessive government regulations and distortions. A variety of government activities, including protective tariffs, usury laws, subsidized credit, and government marketing monopolies, have been designed and implemented by well-meaning policymakers but have retarded development (ILO 1974; and Bautista and Power 1979). The liberalization of these regulations and distortions may prod development into moving again.

Agricultural development may also be promoted by investing in agricultural research and extension work oriented toward generating technology that is appropriate to the wide diversity of physical and economic conditions that prevail. Irrigation and other infrastructure projects are also legitimate public goods and may well represent an efficient use of resources. Government may also actively promote justice, not by violating the rights of the rich, but by protecting the rights of the poor.

Toward a Framework for a Rational Food Policy

The first section of this chapter focused on the effects of fluctuations in production, income, and prices on the nutritional well-being of the low-income household. Next, a critical issue in long-term food security—the possibility of a secular decline in real wages—was examined. In particular, the role of institutions and institutional change in either causing or ameliorating the decline in wages was examined. A comprehensive food policy must presumably deal with both of these issues.

The policy instruments discussed for smoothing the consumption stream in the face of fluctuating incomes and prices all involve some deviation from the first-best optimum. Grain storage, liquidation of assets, borrowing money, and diversification of production all involve substantial costs. The rational household will tend to invest in these activities up to the point where the marginal benefits from stabilization equal the marginal cost. Accordingly, the optimum consumption path for low-income households will not necessarily be stable. Government policies and activities designed to increase stability beyond what the household is able to provide for itself may well have costs that outweigh the benefits. There is no a priori reason to believe that the government has a comparative advantage in stabilization activities beyond what can be achieved by the private market and nonmarket sectors.[13]

Since an ample body of literature focuses on the potential benefits of stabilization, the following discussion focuses on some of the costs. In particular, it seems appropriate to point out the potential conflict between government policies that offset short-term fluctuation and their programs to ameliorate the depressing effect of rapid population growth.

The most obvious conflict is that the scarce government revenue for poverty reduction that is used for stabilization may to some extent replace investments in long-term poverty reduction. The numerous simulation studies that compare buffer stocks with stabilization through trade have highlighted the large costs of maintaining stable consumer prices (typically at prices lower than average free-market prices). The simultaneous use of producer and consumer subsidies not only drives a wedge between marginal social costs and benefits but also requires large government revenues with the attendant tax friction or fiscal drag. The use of imports to support low and stable consumer prices may put a large burden on scarce foreign reserves. In the words of Vernon Ruttan (referring to Indonesia's use of oil exports to finance subsidized rice imports), this is "like burning down your house to keep warm."

Perhaps a less obvious cost of stabilization is the reduction in domestic production induced by moral hazard. Without costly producer subsidies, stabilization policies that put a ceiling on consumer prices will also lower prices received by producers. This is true not only for large producers but also true for small farm households such as the one depicted in figure 6–1. Stabilization programs will typically reduce P_b or both P_b and P_s. In either case, the distribution of possible prices will be lowered, resulting in a negative supply response. Somewhat paradoxically, this negative response will be larger to the extent that farm households are risk averse.

Despite the emphasis given to the costs of stabilization, such programs are not necessarily socially inefficient. It is possible that the government's welfare objective has the nature of a consumption externality and that an efficient way to subsidize food consumption to the poor involves some extent of stabilization or food aid. Trying to offset cyclical fluctuations is much like treating the symptoms of a malnourished patient, however. The patient who is malnourished and in poor health is susceptible to a wide variety of diseases and symptoms. Treating these symptoms as they appear will only provide a temporary cure. Other symptoms and diseases will inevitably appear. What is needed is a more long-term and holistic approach. The same is true of rural poverty. The symptoms of poverty will be most noticeable during crisis periods. But responding to only the crisis itself may detract from a more permanent cure.[14]

Some stabilization policies, however, may also contribute to the reduction of poverty in the long run. For example, at the national level, creative portfolio management and aggressive pursuit of commodity agreements seem to be fruitful candidates for both increasing stabilization and improving efficiency. A suitable combination of diversified foreign-exchange reserves, financial assets, loans, debts, and contractual assets and liabilities may go a long way toward facilitating a smoother national consumption stream in the face of fluctuating domestic production, income, and international prices. These activities involve a movement toward the pattern of production and consumption that would prevail if there were universal markets. The types of activities more conventionally discussed, such as diversification and storage, represent a movement away from such patterns. Suppose, for example, that some countries diversify agricultural production in order to avoid fluctuating export prices while others diversify to mitigate the effects of fluctuating import prices. A commodity agreement between countries could potentially reduce price fluctuations without causing a diversion from comparative advantage.

In summary, short-term food security, at least for developing countries, should not be bought at the expense of the long-term battle with hunger and poverty. Consumer-price-stabilization schemes that lower average producer prices and buffer programs that dull the cutting edge of comparative advantage come at a high cost. Policy tools that promote both types of food security should be encouraged. These include international risk management and domestic investment in the research/extension network, irrigation, and other aspects of the agricultural infrastructure.

Notes

1. See, for example, Siamwalla and Valdes (1980).
2. See McCauley (1982).
3. While several researchers have noted this impression, clear documentation is hard to find. One of the problems is that as hired labor has

increased, the composition of skill levels has changed. In particular, the skill of the average hired worker appears to have increased (also the percentage of adult males). This implies that wage data even after adjusting for inflation overstates the improvement in rural welfare.

4. See Roumasset (1978), Roumasset and Uy (1980), Roumasset and Smith (1981), and Ben-Porath (1980). For an earlier and less neoclassical version of the new institutional economics, see Williamson (1975).

5. See Hayami and Kikuchi (1981).

6. See Roumasset and Smith (1981) and Hayami and Kikuchi (1981).

7. See Roumasset and Smith (1981).

8. See Roumasset and Smith (1981) and Roumasset and Uy (1980).

9. See Roumasset and Smith (1981).

10. See Newbery and Stiglitz (1979).

11. See Roumasset (1976, chapter 4), Hallagan (1978), Reid (1979), and Newbery and Stiglitz (1979).

12. Some authors have attempted to control for land quality by including some proxy for land quality as an independent regressor. Most of these proxies (for example, market value, soil type, irrigation type) may be only weakly related to the inherent productivity and profitability of a particular farm.

13. Results to the contrary rest on inappropriate specifications of the private economy, such as the implicit assumption that private storage is zero. For a fuller discussion of these issues, see Anthony Chisholm's chapter 4 in this volume.

14. First, stabilization programs use scarce resources that could have been employed to increase productivity. Second, consumer-price stabilization often results in lower average producer prices and lower future production. In chapter 12, Bouis and Herdt treat the second point as a trade-off between short-run and long-run objectives.

Bibliography

Anderson, J.R. 1981. "Food Risk and the Poor." Mimeo., World Bank.

Asian Development Bank 1977. *Rural Asia: Challenge and Opportunity.* Hongkong: Federal Publications.

Bautista, R., and Power J. 1979. *Industrial Promotion Policies in the Philippines.* Manila: Philippine Institute for Development Studies.

Ben-Porath, Y. 1980. "The F-Connection: Families, Friends, and Firms and the Organization for Exchange." *Population and Development Review* 6, no. 1:1–30.

Binswanger, H., and Ruttan, V., Eds. 1978. *Induced Innovation: Technology, Institutions and Development.* Baltimore, Md.: Johns Hopkins University Press.

Hallagan, W. 1978. "Self-Selection by Contractual Choice and the Theory of Sharecropping." *The Bell Journal of Economics* 9, no. 2:344–354.

Hayami, Y., and Kikuchi, M. 1981. *Asian Village Economy at the Crossroads.* Los Baños, Philippines: International Rice Research Institute (IRRI).

International Labour Organization (ILO). 1974. *Sharing in Development: A Programme of Employment, Equity and Growth for the Philippines.* Geneva.

McCauley, D. 1982. *Explaining Investments in Conservation Practices: The Case of Subsistence Farmers in Upland Java.* Ph.D. dissertation, Department of Agricultural Economics, University of Hawaii.

Newbery, D., and Stiglitz J. 1979. "Sharecropping, Risk Sharing and the Importance of Imperfect Information." In *Risk Uncertainty and Agricultural Development* ed. J. Roumasset, J. Boussard, and I. Singh. Los Baños, Philippines: SEARCA and A/D/C.

Reid, J. 1979. "Sharecropping and Tenancy in American History." In *Risk, Uncertainty and Agricultural Development* ed. J. Roumasset, J. Boussard, and I. Singh. Los Baños, Philippines: SEARCA and A/D/C. Pp. 283–309.

Roumasset, J.A. 1976. *Rice and Risk: Decision Making among Low-Income Farmers.* Amsterdam: North-Holland Publishing Co.

_______. 1978. "The New Institutional Economics and Agricultural Organization." *Philippine Economic Journal* 17, no. 37:331–348.

Roumasset, J.A., and Uy, M. 1980. "Piece Rates, Time Rates and Teams: Explaining Patterns in the Employment Relation." *Journal of Economic Behavior and Organization* 1:343–360.

Roumasset, J.A., and Smith, J. 1981. "Population, Technological Change, and Landless Workers: The Extent of the Market is Limited by Specialization." *Population and Development Review* 7, no. 3:401–419.

Sen, A.K. 1981. "Ingredients of Famine Analysis: Availability and Entitlements." *The Quarterly Journal of Economics,* 46:433–463.

Siamwalla, A., and Valdes, A. 1980. "Food Insecurity in Developing Countries." *Food Policy* 5, no. 4:258–272.

Williamson, O.E. 1975. *Markets and Hierarchies.* New York: The Free Press.

Part II
Perspectives on Food Security in Asian Countries

7 Promoting National Food Security: The Indonesian Experience

Soegeng Amat

Rice is of paramount importance in the national economy of Indonesia, occupying more than one-third of the cropped area and providing the staple food for the bulk of the population. Production is still, however, insufficient to meet the domestic requirements, and thus substantial quantities of rice have to be imported every year. With annual imports varying between 1.2 and 2.0 million tons, Indonesia has been the single largest rice-importing country in the world. It is not surprising, therefore, that government food policy has emphasized this major cereal. The assurance of adequate availabilities of basic foodstuffs, particularly rice, to meet the increasing needs of the country's large and growing population (estimated at 143 million in mid-1979)[1] is an objective accorded the highest priority.

Substantial technical and financial support is provided each year by the government in order to promote the country's output of rice, especially under the National Rice Intensification Program (BIMAS), whereby guidance, production inputs (seeds of high-yielding varieties, fertilizers, and pesticides), and credit are provided to the farmers on concessional terms. Such support is further complemented and strengthened by the government rice-price policy, which guarantees the farmer a minimum price for his product, while also taking into consideration the limited purchasing power of the consumers at large. Another important government objective is to improve the nutritional standards of the population. Government policies with respect to rice and other staple foods are thus oriented toward consumption and nutrition and are implemented through production incentives and supply management in order to maintain stable prices.

A bumper rice crop in 1980 and the expectation that the crop for 1981 will also be excellent have introduced a dramatic change in Indonesia's food situation and prospects. While there have been no major increases in either the area cultivated or the yields of secondary crops during the past three years, average rice yields grew by more than 10 percent between 1979 and 1980 (table 7–1). This sudden improvement culminates a decade during which rice production grew at an annual average rate of 3.8 percent. However, the demand for rice in Indonesia has simultaneously grown rapidly, reflecting widespread income growth, the people's preference for rice over secondary staple foods, population growth, and the success of the government's programs to stabilize prices. Consequently, import require-

Table 7–1
Harvested Area, Yield, and Production of Rice and Secondary Food Crops, 1978, 1979, and 1980

	Harvested Area (1,000 ha)			*Yield (ton/ha)*			*Production (metric tons)*		
Crop	*1978*	*1979*	*1980*	*1978*	*1979*	*1980*	*1978*	*1979*	*1980*[b]
Rice[a]	8,929	8,803	9,018	1.96	2.02	2.24	17,525	17,970	20,250
Maize	3,025	2,594	2,771	1.33	1.39	1.45	4,029	3,606	4,012
Cassava	1,383	1,439	1,414	9.30	9.60	9.60	12,902	13,751	13,532
Sweet potatoes	301	287	287	6.90	7.60	7.70	2,083	2,194	2,193
Soya beans	733	784	726	0.84	0.87	0.89	617	680	642
Peanuts	506	473	507	0.88	0.90	0.94	446	424	476

Note: Statistics were drawn from the government of Indonesia, Central Bureau of Statistics and Department of Agriculture.

[a]Yield and production in terms of milled rice.

[b]Provisional.

ments have also risen, from 0.6 million metric tons in the late 1960s to 2 million tons in 1980 (table 7–2).[2]

In addition to this substantial deficit, Indonesia has also been faced with the problem of instability in supplies. During the period from 1960 to 1978, the domestic output of rice fell short of the trend in nine out of eighteen years, with the largest shortfall reaching almost 10 percent in 1967. This instability in output is caused by a variety of factors, in particular, the dependence on weather and timely rains, the effects of natural hazards like droughts and floods, and the vulnerability of the crop to pests and diseases. Uncertainty has existed in the supply of some of the key inputs (like fertilizers and pesticides). In addition, the weakness of the marketing system and difficulties of transport and communication in an archipelago (consisting of more than 13,000 islands spread over 5,000 kilometers from east to west) further add to the instability in local rice supplies.

The flow of the needed external supplies (imports) has also not always been dependable. This was demonstrated in 1972–1973 when an acute shortage developed on the international market as a result of a worldwide decline in production. The experience was particularly painful for Indonesia since the substantial reduction in domestic and world output of rice coincided with an ususually low level of stocks within the country.

The Rice Stabilization Program

As part of the government's food policy, a Rice Stabilization Program has been developed that emphasizes supply management through government

Table 7–2
Rice Production (Actual Compared with Trend Production) and Rice Imports, 1960–1962 to 1978

Year	Production (million tons)	Deviation from Trend Production (%)	Imports (million tons)
1960–1962	10.01	13.49	0.97
1962	10.28	10.90	1.01
1963	9.16	−5.80	1.07
1964	9.61	−5.50	1.02
1965	10.24	−3.60	0.14
1966	10.75	−2.60	0.24
1967	10.40	−9.70	0.35
1968	11.67	−2.50	0.63
1969	12.25	−1.40	0.60
1970	13.14	2.10	0.96
1971	13.72	3.00	0.49
1972	13.29	−3.50	0.73
1973	14.61	2.70	1.66
1974	15.28	4.20	1.09
1975	15.18	0.50	0.67
1976	15.84	1.80	1.28
1977	15.94	−0.50	1.96
1978	17.52	6.40	1.85
1979	17.87	5.30	1.95
1980[a]	20.25	14.20	2.03

Note: Statistics were drawn from the government of Indonesia, Central Bureau of Statistics, and the National Logistics Agency (BULOG).
[a]Provisional.

stocks and imports, with the objective of maintaining stable and acceptable domestic prices. A minimum or floor price (for paddy and rice) and a maximum or ceiling price (for rice) have been established, between which the market prices are permitted to fluctuate during the year. These price controls are implemented through the domestic procurement of rice at the floor price and subsequent injections of rice from the national stock into the market (so-called market operations) to prevent prices from exceeding the ceiling. Both the holding and maintenance of an adequate buffer stock are essential prerequisites for such an operation. Rice from domestic procurement is combined with imports in maintaining the national stock.

To help implement this policy, imports of rice are facilitated by exempting them from any import duties, levies, or tariffs. Rice exports are prohibited. The National Logistics Agency (BULOG) is entrusted by the government with the implementation of the Rice Stabilization Program and is also designated as the sole importer of rice in the country.[3] A detailed account of BULOG's operations under the Rice Stabilization Program is given in Appendix 7B.

Setting Floor and Ceiling Prices

Under the Rice Stabilization Program, the levels of the floor and ceiling prices are reviewed every year. The new floor price becomes operative as of February 1 each year, that is, when domestic procurements are initiated with the start of the first harvest of the main crop.[4] The level of the floor price is determined on the basis of the incremental benefit/cost ratio facing farmers who choose to enter BIMAS (the ratio between the increase in benefit and the increase in cost to the farmers from participating in the program).[5]

There is only *one* floor price set each year for *all* varieties of rice, irrespective of locality. This price is based on one quality standard, however, (distinguished by moisture content and degree of purity). It is usually announced late in the preceding year in order to give farmers the opportunity to make production decisions, based on a firm expected floor price at harvest time. It is *not* illegal for farmers or merchants to sell rice for less than this price. But BULOG must continue purchasing rice from the farmers as long as the market price is below it. This implies that the quantity of rice BULOG eventually purchases domestically in a given year is primarily determined by the level of the floor price set and not necessarily by the level of stocks that BULOG chooses to build up or maintain.

In determining the level of the ceiling price, consideration is given to factors such as the following: (1) the cost of storage; (2) the need to promote both interseasonal, as well as interregional (or interisland), trade; and (3) the purchasing power of the population in certain regions. Regional price differentials are normally introduced at the level of ceiling prices, reflecting the relative economic strength of the various regions as well as their relative food self-sufficiency. Price differentials have also been introduced for a limited number of major widely circulated varieties of rice. It is *not* illegal for farmers or merchants to sell rice for more than the ceiling price. Its significance is derived from the continual pressure on BULOG to release supplies onto the market as long as there is danger of the ceiling price being exceeded by market prices. Thus the size of BULOG's market operations in a given year is primarily determined by the level at which the ceiling price is set.

As can be seen from table 7–3 and figure 7–1, a constant and substantial increase has occurred in the level of both floor and ceiling prices over the years. The floor prices for paddy and milled rice have increased by fivefold during the last ten-year period. The increase in the ceiling price of rice has been slightly more modest, reflecting the desire of the government to reduce the inflationary effect of rising market prices of rice. In some years, however, when stocks have been found temporarily inadequate to meet the demand on the domestic market at the ceiling price, consumer

Table 7–3
Floor and Ceiling Prices of Rice

	1969–1970 to 1972–1973	*1973–1974*[a]	*1974–1975*	*1975–1976*	*1976–1977*	*1977–1978*	*1978–1979*[b]	*1979–1980*	*1980–1981*
Floor price of									
Paddy (Rupiah (Rp)/kg)	20.90	25.55	41.80	58.50	68.50	71.00	75.00	85.00–95.00	105.00
Increase (%)	—	22.20	63.60	39.90	17.10	3.60	5.60	13.30–26.70	10.5–23.5
Milled rice (Rp/kg)	36.00	45.00	68.50	97.00	108.00	100.00	119.50	140.00–158.00	175.00
Increase (%)	—	21.60	52.20	41.60	11.30	11.30	19.50	17.10–32.20	10.8–25.0
Ceiling price of									
Milled rice (Rp/kg)	50.00	—	110.00	125.00	135.00	140.00	145.00	175.00	225.00
Increase (%)	—	—	—	13.60	8.00	3.70	3.60	20.7	28.6

Source: National Logistics Agency (BULOG).

Note: The new floor prices become operative as of February 1, whereas the new ceiling prices are announced later in the year with the approach of the lean months. In 1979–1980, the floor prices were raised two times, the second price becoming effective as of May 2, 1979.

[a]During 1973–1974, so-called floating ceiling prices were maintained because of the temporary inadequacy of stocks to meet demands on the market.

[b]The 1978 floor prices for paddy and milled rice were, respectively, 359 and 323 percent of the 1969 prices. If this increase is deflated, according to the simultaneous rise in prices of 8 basic nonrice commodities, then the corresponding real price increases would be reduced to 165 and 146 percent for paddy and milled rice, respectively.

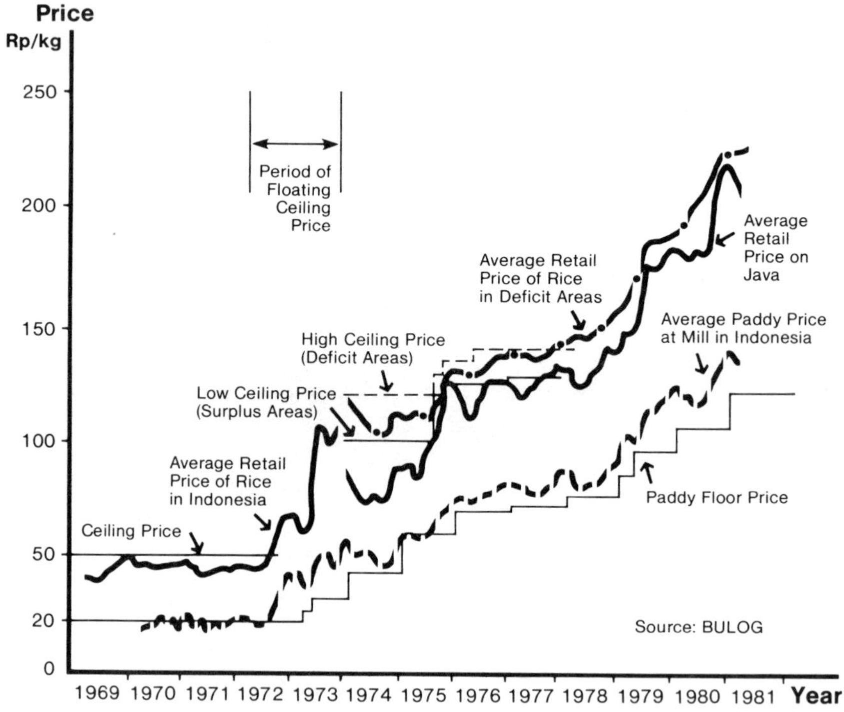

Figure 7–1. Comparison of Average Retail Rice Price and Paddy Price at Mill with "Ceiling" and Floor Prices, 1969–1981

Source: National Logistics Agency (BULOG).

prices have been permitted to "float" in order to equate demand with the available supply. This policy became necessary during the international food crisis of 1973–1974. In more recent years, when stocks have approached full capacity, prices have been permitted to "float" downward. During this period, the overriding concern of the government has been the control of inflation, a consequence of a currency devaluation in November 1978 and a decision in 1980 to allow domestic oil prices to increase by 50 percent. Therefore, between 1978 and 1980, a portion of the surplus of total supply over demand at the ceiling consumer price was marketed rather than stored.

Domestic Procurement

Domestic procurement of paddy and milled rice, as undertaken by the government through the village cooperatives and private rice traders (normally millers), usually amounts to between 350,000 and 540,000 metric tons (milled rice equivalent) per year, or between 2.5 and 3.5 percent of the national crop. With the bumper crop in 1978, however, total procurement during the fiscal year 1978–1979 April/March reached the record level of 881,000 tons, or 5 percent of the harvested crop. Then in 1980–1981, another bumper crop pushed procurement to the extraordinary level of 1.65 million tons—over 8 percent of the total rice crop (table 7–4).

One of the important factors affecting the amount of paddy and milled rice that BULOG is able to procure in the country is the level of floor prices. More important, however, is the size of the marketed surplus, which depends on the size of the crop (or more accurately, the total output per capita). With regard to how much of this marketed supply is eventually procured by the government, the most important factors are the financial and technical capability of the village cooperatives and rice traders and the need for cash among the farmers.

The volume of marketed produce has been estimated through field surveys at 25 to 30 percent of the total crop (Department of Agriculture 1970; and Hasan 1976). There are indications, however—based on more recent but incomplete surveys—that this share may have increased significantly to 40 percent or even more (Department of Agriculture 1979; and BULOG 1979). The increase has generally been interpreted as reflecting the increasing need for cash within the farm community (for instance, due to the growing number and variety of consumer goods being offered to the villagers). There is also the possibility that the increased interseasonal stability in rice prices has encouraged farmers to sell more of their produce on the market, with the expectation that they will be able to buy rice when needed later in the season at comparatively reasonable prices.

Releases from the National Stock

Releases from the national stock are made by BULOG to meet the following purposes or needs:

1. Regular supplies for the so-called budget group (rice rations to military and civil service personnel), as well as for a number of state enterprises.
2. Injections into the market (the so-called market operations), the volume of which fluctuates from year to year, depending primarily on the size of the crop in a particular year.
3. Supplies for emergency relief, usually of relatively small amounts each year.

Table 7–4
Rice: Per Capita Production, Level of Floor Price, and Domestic Procurement by National Logistics Agency (BULOG)

	1969–1970 to 1973–1974 Average	*1974–1975*	*1975–1976*	*1976–1977*	*1977–1978*	*1978–1979*	*1979–1980*	*1980–1981*[a]
Per capita production (kg milled rice)	112	120	116	118	116	125	124	137
Floor price of milled rice (Rupiah/kg)	40.92	68.50	97.00	108.00	110.00	119.50	140.00–158.00	175.00
Domestic procurement (1,000 tons milled rice)	349	536	539	410	404	881	431	1,650
Procurement as a percentage of production	2.6	3.5	3.6	2.6	2.5	5.0	2.4	8.1

Source: National Logistics Agency (BULOG).
Note: Table lists domestic procurement data on fiscal year basis (April/March).
[a]Provisional.

From the point of view of achieving price stability, injections of rice into the market are the most important and the most characteristic of BULOG's operations under the Rice Stabilization Program. As stated earlier, their main objective is to prevent prices from exceeding the ceiling. These operations averaged 364,000 tons a year during the First Five Year Development Plan period (1969/70 to 1973/74), but have tended to increase every year thereafter. A record 2,006,500 tons were injected in 1977–1978, mainly due to the stagnation of production over the preceding three years. With the "bumper" crop in 1978, injections declined to 1,032,000 metric tons, as indicated in table 7–5.

Another important factor affecting the volume of market operations, in addition to the size of the crop, is the level of ceiling prices set every year and hence the margin within which market prices are allowed to fluctuate in a given year. A more detailed study is needed in order to quantify the relationship between these two major factors and the size of the market operations.

Releases for purposes of emergency relief are generally small, normally not more than 50,000 metric tons a year. Emergency food shortages occur every year as a result of poor crops or complete crop failures caused by floods or drought. They also occur as a result of other calamities such as earthquakes and pest infestations. Except for the food crops of 1972–1973, however, they have tended to be localized, and most often special food assistance has been needed only for a short period of time. Even so, they can cause severe hardship for the people concerned. Therefore, strengthening the country's early warning system for possible food shortages—not only at the national level, but even more so at the subnational level—will contribute to alleviating such recurring hardship.

The Size of the National Stock

The implementation of stabilization measures has been facilitated by the growing level of rice stocks under the direct control of the government. In 1972, before the global food crisis, these stocks were at an all-time low level (168,000 metric tons). The advent of a very poor rice crop nationwide and the relative unavailability of adequate rice imports from the world market resulted in the need to allow the ceiling price to float to relatively high levels and left the government unable to respond fully to acute local food shortages. By the end of 1976–1977, the national stock had been strengthened to 579,000 tons. With the massive market operations needed in 1977, however, it declined to 460,000 tons. The bumper crop of 1978 brought relief from pressure on the national stock, which then increased to 1.3 million tons. Since that time the crop has fallen below 1 million metric

Table 7–5
Rice: Production per Capita, Margin between Floor and Ceiling Prices, and Size of Market Operations

	1969–1970 to 1973–1974 Average	*1974–1975*	*1975–1976*	*1976–1977*	*1977–1978*	*1978–1979*	*1979–1980*	*1980–1981*
Per capita production (kg milled rice)	112	120	116	118	116	125	124	137
Margin between floor and ceiling price (Rupiah/kg)	13.00	41.50	28.00	27.00	40.00	25.00	22.00–40.00	45.00
As percent of floor price	39	61	29	25	40	21	11–25	29
Domestic procurement (1,000 tons milled rice)	349	536	539	410	404	881	431	1,650
Market operations (1,000 tons milled rice)	364	342	559	979	2,006	1,032	2,036	1,630

Source: National Logistics Agency (BULOG).

tons only in 1979 (when the level declined to 800,000 tons). The most recent bumper rice crops have strained the country's storage capacity since the quantity stored has climbed toward 3 million tons.

The recent growth in the national rice stock has necessitated the accelerated expansion of the nation's storage capacity. While private storage capacity has remained relatively static, BULOG has recently expanded the storage facilities under its control by constructing 323 modern warehouses in strategic locations throughout the archipelago, with a total capacity of 1.1 million tons. Several smaller warehouses are currently under construction, each providing an additional 1,000 tons of capacity.[6] The expanding role of village cooperatives as stockholders of rice is expected to continue to increase. All these contributions to the expansion of the country's storage capacity are particularly important steps toward reducing the risk of disruptive supply shortfalls caused by either crop failure or inaccessibility of imports. The role of stocks is especially important when it is considered that less than 40 percent of the annual product is usually marketed by farmers. When total production fluctuates from year to year, the marketed surplus undergoes proportional changes more than twice as large. Consequently, the availability of stocks widely distributed throughout the country is critical to the needs of the ever-increasing share of the population dependent on the marketplace for their food supply.

Control of Post-Harvest Grain Losses

The prevention or reduction of post-harvest grain losses has been increasingly recognized as being of major importance in the achievement of national food security. Surveys undertaken by BULOG in 1971 suggest that up to 25 percent of the rice crop can be lost in the various stages of the post-harvest system. Even if a 10 percent loss is assumed, the annual loss would still exceed 1.7 million metric tons of rice, about the amount Indonesia has needed to import to be able to meet domestic requirements.

Increased efforts are therefore being made to reduce post-harvest grain losses. The Rice Stabilization Program itself deals only with the handling and storage aspect of the whole post-harvest system, through which it has contributed substantially to the prevention of losses. BULOG's investment in the construction of the modern storage facilities referred to earlier is one good example. With the aim of further promoting and strengthening national efforts to limit postharvest grain losses, BULOG has recently entered into an agreement with The Food and Agricultural Organization (FAO) that provides for a loss-assessment survey to be undertaken on a national scale. In addition, BULOG's Rice Laboratory is to be developed into a national training institution capable of providing training in the field of rice processing and in storage at the national level.

National Food Security and Economic Stability

The Rice Stabilization Program has, during the past decade, demonstrated a positive contribution to the achievement of two important development objectives: (1) the assurance of adequate supplies of rice at all times and hence national food security and (2) the promotion of wider economic and political stability. The improvement in price stability achieved during the mid- and late 1970s is evident from the trend in the range between the lowest and highest rice price in each year. Between 1969/70 and 1973/74, this range averaged 45.6 percent. Since 1976, however, it has never exceeded 15.8 percent (table 7–6). Given that rice has been accorded a weight of about 31 percent in Indonesia's cost-of-living index, this improved stability in rice prices has clearly contributed to the country's more general economic stability.[7] The decline in Indonesia's inflation rate since the late 1960s has been significant, following the trend in rice price stability. It declined from 85.5 percent in 1968 to 25.9 percent in 1972 and further to 11.8 and 6.7 percent in 1977 and 1978, respectively. At the time of this writing, the consumer price index is 11.9 percent above its value of one year ago.[8] This increased stability of prices is all the more remarkable when one considers that Indonesia's currency was devalued against the U.S. $ by approximately one-third in November 1978.

Problems Requiring Further Study

Although the Rice Stabilization Program has been successful in Indonesia, room for improvement remains in the implementation of this program and others that are important for the maintenance of both national food security and the food security of the Southeast Asian region. Important areas for additional research are the efficiency of BULOG's market operations across the country as well as the accuracy of forecast information on crops and on the international market that is essential to food-policy implementation.

The Optimal Level of BULOG's Market Operations

The Rice Stabilization Program has been costly to the Indonesian government, both in terms of foreign-exchange requirements for rice imports and of the domestic currency cost of its implementation. The most important priority facing the program is to improve the efficiency with which it is able to provide adequate supplies of rice at stable prices. Market operations are a particularly large cost component. The quantity of rice that has been

Table 7–6
Market Prices of Milled Rice, 1969–1970 to 1980–1981

	1969–1970 to 1973–1974 Average	*1974–1975*	*1975–1976*	*1976–1977*	*1977–1978*	*1978–1979*	*1979–1980*	*1980–1981*
Monthly average prices during (Rupiah/kg)								
Harvest months	42.54	85.06	95.71	120.07	126.12	130.92	167.81	182.02
Lean months	61.96	95.16	123.24	127.72	133.49	146.13	183.76	210.80
Range (Rupiah/kg)	19.42	10.10	27.53	7.65	7.37	15.21	15.95	28.78
Range in percent of lowest prices	45.60	11.90	28.80	6.40	5.80	11.60[a]	9.50	15.80

Source: government of Indonesia, Central Bureau of Statistics, *Indicator Ekonomi*, January issues, 1978, 1979, 1980, and 1981.

[a]The widening of the range between the monthly average, lowest and highest, in 1978–1979 was caused by the devaluation of the rupiah as of November 15, 1978.

released from the national stock has increased from an average of 1.2 million metric tons for the period 1969–1974 to 2.8 million tons in 1977–1978. Further research is needed to determine the minimum share of the domestic rice market that must be controlled by BULOG in order to achieve the government's policy objectives. This level, once determined, could then be combined with a quantitative assessment of the risk that rice supplies abroad might be inadequate to meet Indonesia's import needs in order to calculate the optimal level of both carry-over and working stocks.

Crop Forecasting and Market Information

The most important factor determining the total amount of rice the government should control each year is the size of the crop. As a large importer, Indonesia is faced with the problem of planning for future imports in advance of its own harvests. The need to contract in advance for large rice purchases from abroad led to total imports exceeding 2 million metric tons in 1980, despite the bumper crop of that year (see table 7–2). Since procurement reached record levels that year, the national stock has risen in 1981 to above 2 million tons. Given the extraordinary level of the national stock, only about one-half million tons of imports have been contracted during 1981.

As the domestic crop forecasting system improves in Indonesia, import decisions will be based on better information about future domestic requirements. Since the archipelago is quite heterogeneous with respect to local supply deficits and risk of weather-related calamities, a well-organized early-warning system to alert BULOG that emergency stocks must be acquired internationally or be moved to local areas suffering from food shortages must be an integral part of Indonesia's agricultural information system.

The Management and Geographical Distribution of the National Stock

The decision to release rice from the national stock is not made annually but continuously. Releases from and additions to the stock are related to the seasonal nature of domestic production. Releases are normally very small during the harvest months but relatively large during the lean season. Additions to the national stock have depended not only on the size of domestic procurement but also on the availability of supplies from abroad. Timely purchases of rice from abroad, especially in years when Indonesia is to import a large share of the rice available for export elsewhere in the world, can result in minimal disturbance to the international rice market and therefore minimize foreign-exchange requirements.

The minimum level of stocks at any given time is presently maintained at about three months of expected releases. During the past ten years, depending on the size of the crop, the appropriate level of minimum stock has been found to be between 300,000 and 500,000 metric tons during harvest seasons and 700,000 to 1.2 million tons during lean seasons. The most appropriate level for these stocks and their distribution around the country depends on: (1) the level of uncertainty with which expected releases in future months are determined, (2) the average reorder interval in each location, and (3) the uncertainty with which BULOG estimates the reorder interval. With improved knowledge of the probability distributions of monthly releases and reorder intervals at specific storage locations, minimum stock levels can be calculated that will result in an acceptably low probability of a "stockout" in each location.

Minimizing Post-Harvest Losses

A variety of measures have already been taken by the government agencies concerned to reduce food losses in the post-harvest system. There appears to be, however, an urgent need to consolidate these somewhat fragmented efforts and to promote instead the development and implementation of a more integrated program. As a first step, an inventory must be made of all ongoing as well as planned programs and activities by national agencies as well as their collaborative international organizations. The national-scale loss-assessment survey presently being undertaken with FAO assistance can be expected to provide a good basis for future integrated operational and research programs.

Consumption Diversification

While rice is clearly the staple food for the bulk of the population in Indonesia, substantial quantities of other important basic food commodities are also produced and consumed in the country. As can be seen from table 7–1, the production of these foods amounts to about 4 million tons of maize, 13 million tons of cassava, 2 million tons of sweet potatoes, 0.6 million tons of soybeans, and 0.4 million tons of peanuts. The yields of these crops are presently low by international standards, and prospects for a substantial increase in production are favorable. As incomes have risen, however, the per capita consumption of these so-called secondary foodstuffs has tended to decline (with the exception of sweet potatoes), whereas the consumption of rice has continued to increase.[9] Nevertheless, the government has sought to promote national food security by encouraging a more diversified pattern of consumption toward more secondary foodstuffs and away from rice.

The achievement of this objective, which is being given a great deal of emphasis in the country's present Five Year Development Plan, will require a careful examination of the traditional preferences of the population at large for rice and the adoption of an appropriate pricing policy for secondary staple foods. Improvements in the processing of maize, cassava, and sweet potatoes into more attractive as well as more nutritious foodstuffs (including the development and promotion of possible composite flour products) should help to increase the demand for these secondary foodstuffs and thereby improve Indonesia's food self-sufficiency. An expanded discussion of this issue is provided by John Dixon in chapter 11.

Food Security at the Regional Level

The five members of the Association of Southeast Asian Nations (ASEAN)—Indonesia, Malaysia, the Philippines, Singapore, and Thailand—have agreed to establish an emergency food-supply facility called the ASEAN Food Security Reserve. Given that the international community has failed to establish such a facility at the global level such as was recommended at the United Nations World Food Conference in Rome in 1974) the establishment of such a facility by ASEAN represents a particularly innovative step toward international food security.

The reserve comprises regionally coordinated stocks of rice, which are maintained by each member country within its borders. At present, the agreement covers 50,000 tons of rice, of which the responsibility for storage is distributed among the members in accordance with their levels of production, consumption, and storage capacities.[10] The operation of the reserve is examined empirically by Somporn Hanpongpandh in chapter 13, and the original text of the ASEAN Food Security Reserve Agreement is reprinted as Appendix 13A.

Although the size of the internationally coordinated reserve is small by comparison with annual rice consumption in the ASEAN region, the contribution of each member country is part of a significantly larger national stock. The purpose of the reserve is to establish a capacity to move rice throughout the region to cover short-run emergencies that would otherwise overtax the national stock. The reserve is therefore of special significance to Indonesia, the region's largest importer of rice, since it provides a capacity to meet requirements in the short run when the national stock is low and when imports cannot be quickly delivered from elsewhere in the world.

Conclusion

The Indonesian experience with national food-security policies has centered on its Rice Stabilization Program. To achieve the objective of providing adequate supplies of rice throughout the country and throughout the year at stable prices, the government, through its National Logistics Agency (BULOG), has become the largest single participant in the domestic rice market, controlling about 10 percent of all rice consumed and about 30 percent of all rice marketed. Prices are not legislated, however, and the market behavior of private traders is not otherwise restricted.

This program has been very successful in maintaining a relatively stable domestic rice market. The effect it has had on general economic stability is considerable, since a large share of the nation's disposable income is spent on rice. This economic stability, combined with the improved reliability of urban markets as a source of staple foods throughout the year, has contributed significantly to Indonesia's economic growth and political stability during the past decade.

At present, an important priority of the government is the improvement of the program's efficiency of operation. Through the analysis of the minimum necessary share of the market to be controlled by BULOG, improvements in agricultural and market forecasting systems, more appropriate geographical distribution of storage facilities, technical improvements in post-harvest processing and the design of efficient incentives to encourage the continued diversification of the Indonesian diet, the effectiveness of this program can be maintained while decreasing the share of the government's budget it absorbs. The resulting cost burden can be further controlled through participation in international agreements that potentially have the effect of stabilizing the supply of food from abroad. The ASEAN Food Security Reserve Agreement constitutes a positive step in this direction.

In the long run, however, there can be no substitute for improved performance in the domestic production of staple foods. The bumper rice crop of 1980, followed by another excellent crop in 1981 (as currently forecast), has brought about a dramatic change in the overall food situation and the prospects of the country. It has enabled the government to reduce its rice imports from the record 2 million tons in 1980 to about 0.5 million tons in 1981, while providing for the expansion of domestic rice procurement by BULOG to a new record of 1.6 million tons in 1980–1981—almost twice as large as the earlier record of 0.88 million metric tons in 1978–1979. These exceptional increases in rice output in 1980 (13 percent) and in 1981 (8 percent) have been the result of a combination of factors including the following:

1. Expansion of the area under BIMAS—particularly under a new type of

Intensification Scheme (INSUS)—whereby between twenty-five and fifty farmers participate in the program as a group.

2. Further expansion of high-yielding varieties of rice resistant to the brown planthopper, which has been a major inhibitor to production growth with earlier varieties.
3. An extraordinary increase in the consumption of fertilizer and pesticides.
4. Improved availability of controlled water supply through a rehabilitated and expanded irrigation network.
5. Some strengthening of the network of agricultural extension and plant-protection brigades.
6. Favorable weather and adequate rains.

Although it is certainly too optimistic to expect the country to soon achieve rice self-sufficiency, there appears to be a distinct possibility that during the present decade Indonesia may have occasional rice surpluses. Deficits must still be expected in some years, however, since unfavorable weather and the possible limited recurrence of pests like the brown planthopper affect the size of the rice crop. Consequently, the government must continue to pursue not only its policy aimed at achieving overall self-sufficiency in staple foods but also its effort to maintain stable domestic markets through the operation of the national food reserve.

Notes

1. The November 1980 census indicates a population of 147.4 million at the time of the census and implies an annual growth rate of 2.34 percent during 1971–1980.

2. The effect of bumper crops in 1980 and 1981 has been to greatly increase government stocks and thus reduce import requirements in 1981 to about one-half million tons.

3. BULOG's specific responsibilities and activities are detailed in Appendix 7A, together with a review of Indonesia's institutional structure as it affects agriculture, food trade, marketing, and distribution.

4. There are generally two crops per year—the main crop being harvested in the months from February to June and the second from August to October.

5. The concept of the incremental benefit/cost ratio is detailed in Appendix 7C.

6. The new storage capacity is also designed to carry other products, including maize and soybeans.

7. The weighting given to rice in the cost of living index declined during 1979 with the introduction of a new index covering seventeen cities and an increased number of goods and services.

8. See *Far Eastern Economic Review* (1981), p. 121.

9. Per capita consumption of maize and cassava over the last ten years has declined from 26 to 20 kg and from 88 to 85 kg, respectively. Per capita consumption of rice, on the other hand, has increased from 98 to about 125 kg.

10. Of the ASEAN member countries, the Philippines and Thailand have been net exporters of rice, while Indonesia, Malaysia, and Singapore are net importers.

Bibliography

Department of Agriculture, Goverment of Indonesia. 1970. "Analysis of Sawah Rice Farms and Rice Marketing in West Java During the 1968/69 Season." Internal report, Jakarta.

________. 1979. "Implementation of Intensification of Rice and Secondary Food Crops, 1971–1978." Unpublished report, Jakarta.

Far Eastern Economic Review. 1981. Week of December 4–10.

Hasan, I. 1976. "Rice Marketing in Aceh: a Regional Analysis." Ph.D. dissertation, University of Indonesia.

National Logistics Agency (BULOG), Government of Indonesia. 1979. "Report of the Study on Marketed Surplus of Rice in West Java, Wet Season 1978." Unpublished report, Jakarta.

Appendix 7A: Institutional Structure Affecting Agriculture, Food Trade, Marketing, and Distribution

The basic responsibility for promoting agricultural *production* and thereby improving the income and well-being of farmers and fishermen lies with the Department of Agriculture, whose field of competence covers: (1) food crops, (2) commercial crops (small holder and plantation), (3) livestock and animal production, (4) fisheries (agriculture and marine fisheries), and (5) forestry. Promotion of *trade* in general falls within the responsibility of the Department of Trade and Cooperatives, while the Department of Health holds responsibility over matters relating to *nutrition*.

One of the basic elements in the government *food policy* is the assurance of adequate food supply at stable prices for the country's large and growing population. The achievement of this policy objective is pursued through the National Food Price Stabilization Program, the implementation of which is entrusted to BULOG. Established in 1969, BULOG is a nondepartmental agency reporting directly to the President of Indonesia. Its principal task is the maintenance of national stocks of basic food commodities and the management of buffer-stock operations. Today, BULOG's field of responsibilities covers the commodities and activities shown in table 7A–1.

The relationship between BULOG and other Agencies/Departments is as follows:

1. *Financing of BULOG's operations.* BULOG's operations are *not* financed out of the State Budget, but by credits from the Central Bank (Bank of Indonesia) on the basis of a budget annually submitted by BULOG and approved by the Minister of Finance.
2. *Determination of the floor price.* This is done by the government annually, based on proposals by an Inter-Agency Team representing the Departments of Agriculture, Finance, Trade, and Cooperatives, National Planning (BAPPENAS), and BULOG.
3. Domestic procurement. This is undertaken by BULOG as far as possible through the Village Cooperatives, the latter receiving loans from the People's Bank.
4. *Import planning.* BULOG is primarily responsible for staple-food import planning, based on crop forecasts. Account is taken of recom-

mendations from the Department of Agriculture and the Central Bureau of Statistics, as well as from the Department of Trade and Cooperatives.

As of March 1978, the Chairman of BULOG has been appointed by the President as State (Junior) Minister of Cooperatives.

Table 7A–1
BULOG's Responsibilities and Activities

Responsibilities and Activities	*Rice*	*Sugar*	*Wheat and Flour*	*Maize*	*Soybean*	*Peanut and Mungbean*	*Meat*
Monitoring of prices	X	X	X	X	X	X	X
Maintenance of stock	X	—	—	X	X	X	—
Domestic procurement at floor price	X	—	—	X	X	X	—
Import							
Control	X	X	X	X	X	X	—
As sole importer	X	X	X	—	—	—	—
As one of several importers	—	—	—	X	X	—	—
Stock releases							
Market operations	X	—	—	X	X	X	—
Distribution	—	X	X	—	—	—	—
Coordination of supply for some cities in some months of the year	—	—	—	—	—	—	X

Source: National Logistics Agency (BULOG).

Appendix 7B: Rice Stabilization Program

Table 7B–1
BULOG's Operations under the Government Rice Stabilization Program: Pelita I, Pelita II, and the First Three Years of Pelita III
(metric ton)

	Pelita I	*Pelita II*				*Pelita III*		
	Annual Average	*1974–1975*	*1975–1976*	*1976–1977*	*1977–1978*	*1978–1979*	*1979–1980*	*1980–1981*[a]
Supply								
Beginning stock	317.1	417.9	782.7	536.0	579.0	459.5	707.8	885.7
Procurement								
Domestic	348.7	536.1	539.0	410.4	404.3	881.2	430.8	1,635.3
Import	912.9	1,147.5	667.4	1,505.9	2,308.3	1,277.0	2,579.9	1,213.2
PL-480	252.3	—	—	401.2	239.8	305.0	352.5	
Food aid	208.4	168.7	—	10.0	192.7	12.1	312.0	299.0
Grant	5.0	—	6.0	12.0	5.6	2.5	13.8	
Commercial	447.2	978.8	861.4	1,082.7	1,870.2	957.4	1,901.6	914.2
Total	1,578.9	2,101.5	1,969.1	2,452.3	3,291.7	2,617.8	3,718.6	3,734.2
Releases								
Budget group	681.4	662.7	659.5	668.6	611.2	613.2	634.0	606.5
State enterprises	109.4	95.2	89.7	86.8	81.8	105.8	90.2	88.7
Market injections/operation	364.1	342.5	569.5	979.3	2,006.5	1,031.5	2,036.3	1,628.3
Emergency relief	54.9	168.6	101.0	84.2	92.7	112.2	64.7	215.3
Total	1,209.8	1,269.0	1,409.7	1,818.9	2,792.3	1,862.7	2,825.2	2,538.8
Loss/waste	41.5	49.8	43.5	54.3	39.9	47.3	7.7	11.5
Closing stock	327.4	782.7	536.0	579.0	459.5	707.8	885.7	1,183.9

Source: National Logistics Agency (BULOG).
Note: Pelita is an acronym for the Five Year Development Plan.
[a]Provisional as of the time of writing.

Appendix 7C: The Concept of the Incremental Benefit/Cost Ratio

The government (BULOG) domestic rice procurement year is from February (the start of the main harvest) to January. For stalk paddy, paddy, and milled rice, purchases are made at floor or minimum prices that are announced at the beginning of the foregoing (main) planting season (October/November). These prices, which are reviewed every year, have since 1973–1974 been based on the concept of an incremental benefit/cost ratio. Prior to 1973, the concept of cost of production was used. This was found unsatisfactory, however, mostly because of the large variation in cost from location to location and between different types and intensities of farming. This does not mean that the benefit/cost ratio concept is fully satisfactory. It also has undergone some modifications since its implementation.

The incremental benefit is defined as the increase in return the farmer receives as a result of his participation in BIMAS. The incremental cost is the increase in cost the farmer has to bear on account of his participation in the program. This incremental cost is evaluated based on the value of the so-called BIMAS package (consisting of HYV-seed, fertilizer, chemicals, and a certain amount of cash) made available to the participating farmer on a credit basis.

A simplified version of the formula used in the determination of the floor price is as follows:

$$\frac{B}{C} = \frac{\text{Benefit per hectare (BIMAS)}}{\text{Cost per hectare (BIMAS)}}$$

$$= \frac{\text{(Increase in yield of stalk paddy per hectare)} \cdot \text{Price}}{\text{Cost of BIMAS package per hectare}}$$

where

1. The increase in yield is calculated net of land tax (5%) and the cost of harvesting, mostly in kind (16%).
2. The cost of the BIMAS package includes credit interest.
3. The benefit/cost ratio should at least be 1.5, in order that the floor price should be attractive enough to farmers. (In fact, the benefit/cost ratio adopted since 1974–1975 has consistently exceeded 2.0.)

The floor price of stalk paddy for the 1976–1977 procurement year was calculated as follows:

1. The increase in yield associated with program participation was estimated at 2,006 kg of stalk paddy per hectare.
2. The cost of the BIMAS package, including interest, was calculated to be Rp 36,851 per hectare.
3. The benefit/cost ratio was then calculated as follows:

$$\frac{B}{C} = \frac{0.79 \times 2{,}006 \times \text{Price}}{36{,}851}$$

4. Price of stalk paddy per kg is $\frac{36{,}851}{1{,}585} \cdot \frac{B}{C} = 23.2\frac{B}{C}$

5. The Inter-Agency Team, after having taken into account such important factors as the country's rate of inflation, proposed a benefit/cost ratio of 2.24, giving a floor price of Rp 52 per kg of stalk paddy.
6. On the basis of the prevailing conversion factors, the following prices were arrived at:

Rough rice (gabah) — Rp 68.50/kg
Milled rice — Rp 108.00/kg

8 Food Security in Sri Lanka: The Historical Record

Neville Edirisinghe

In the past, the government of Sri Lanka has attempted to feed the country's population through a strategy of importing sufficient food supplies and of subsidizing consumption. Attempts to maintain consumer welfare were part of an overall development plan aimed at ensuring adequate basic nutritional levels. Providing inexpensive food to consumers, however, became increasingly expensive for the treasury. With limited investment funds, the costs of these food subsidies eventually contributed to economic stagnation. As the population continued to grow, Sri Lanka found its traditional approach increasingly difficult to pay for and began a series of changes in its food-security system. This chapter examines the historical record—how the food-ration system developed and how it has changed over time.

History of Dietary Adequacy

Food data in Sri Lanka for the last two decades show a level of food availability generally considered to be adequate for nutritional needs. Per capita daily consumption of calories and protein, based on food balance sheets, is shown in table 8–1. The aggregate food balance-sheet data, as well as findings from a comprehensive cross-sectional survey, point to an average daily per capita supply of about 2,200 calories and 48 grams of protein. These amounts are considered adequate to meet the 1973 Food and Agriculture Organization (FAO)/World Health Organization (WHO)-recommended nutritional levels adjusted for the age distribution and body weight of the Sri Lankan population.[1] The average figures present a picture of adequate nutrition, and a close examination of food intake by different income groups reveals little malnourishment or undernourishment (table 8–2). It is striking that even in the lowest household income class, both calorie and protein consumption are 84 percent or more of the recommended daily allowance for Sri Lanka. Calorie consumption increases only slowly as incomes rise; protein consumption, on the other hand, increases more rapidly as wealthier consumers purchase higher-quality, and more costly, protein-rich foods. The equitable distribution and

Table 8–1
Sri Lanka: Apparent per Capita Daily Calorie and Protein Consumption, 1955–1960, 1965–1973, and 1979–1980

	Food Balance Sheets, 1955–1960[a]				*Food Balance Sheets, 1965–1973*[b]				*Socio-Economic Survey, 1969–1970*[b]			
	Calories	*Percent*	*Protein (gm)*	*Percent*	*Calories*	*Percent*	*Protein (gm)*	*Percent*	*Calories*	*Percent*	*Protein (gm)*	*Percent*
Cereals	1,200	56.4	22.6	47.7	1,289	57.9	28.3	59.2	1,220	53.8	27.5	51.8
Rice	950	44.7	16.3	34.4	976	43.8	19.0	39.7	917	40.5	17.8	33.5
Other cereals	250	11.7	6.3	13.3	313	14.1	9.3	19.4	303	13.3	9.7	18.3
All other foods	925	43.5	24.7	52.3	936	42.0	19.5	40.7	1,044	46.1	25.5	48.1
Total	2,125	100.0	47.3	100.0	2,225	100.0	47.8	100.0	2,264	100.0	53.0	100.0

[a]Statistics drawn from T. Jogaratnam and T.T. Poleman, "Food in the Economy of Ceylon," *Cornell International Agriculture Development Bulletin* 11, October 1969. Reprinted with permission.

[b]Statistics drawn from Neville Edirisinghe and T.T. Poleman, "Implications of Government Intervention in the Rice Economy of Sri Lanka," *Cornell International Agriculture Mimeograph* 48, January 1976. Reprinted with permission.

Table 8–2
Percentage of per Capita Adequacy of Some Nutrients, by Household Income Classes (All Island), Socio-Economic Survey 1969–1970

Nutrients	*Per Capita Daily Recommended Allowances for Sri Lanka*	*Household Income Classes (All Island) (Rupees)*									
		Below 100	*100–140*	*150–199*	*Below 200*	*200–399*	*400–599*	*600–799*	*800–999*	*Over 1,000*	*All Class*
Energy (cal)	2,200	88	95	98	94	103	110	114	115	120	103
Protein (gm)	48	84	94	98	99	113	122	127	130	136	112
Calcium (mg)	519	—[a]	—	—	—	—	—	—	—	—	72
Iron (gm)	23	—	—	—	83	86	93	94	97	97	86
Vitamin A (mcg)	642	—	—	—	109	109	112	121	121	131	111
Riboflavin (mcg)	1,220	—	—	—	51	56	62	69	75	82	57
Percent of total population		8.1	16.8	17.7	(42.6)	37.7	12.0	4.1	1.6	2.0	(100)

Source: Department of Census and Statistics, "Socio-Economic Survey of Sri Lanka, 1969/70—A Special Report on Food and Nutritional Levels in Sri Lanka," mimeo, Columbo, October 1972.

Note: The adequacy of the diet in respect to any nutrient is determined by expressing consumption of the nutrient as a percentage of the recommended allowances on a daily per capita basis. The recommended allowances for Sri Lanka are shown in the first column, and the adequacy for each nutrient is given under each income class.

[a]Detailed breakdowns not available for computing adequacy.

high level of calorie consumption in Sri Lanka is in large part due to the government's staple food-ration and subsidy program.

Cereals play the dominant role in meeting energy and protein needs. On the average, rice and wheat contributed nearly 57 percent of total calories, with rice alone accounting for 44 percent (see table 8–1). Other locally grown cereals, roots, and tubers have contributed less than 3 percent to the total calorie supply. Cereals are also an important source of protein, accounting for about one-half of the total supply.

The role of rice cannot be overemphasized; historically, it has been the preferred staple food. More recently, the introduction of wheat flour into the national diet has been a major change, especially since no wheat is grown in Sri Lanka. The growth in importance of wheat has been the direct result of attempts by successive governments to maintain adequate food supplies by relying on imports. Figure 8–1 depicts the relative importance of food imports (rice and wheat) in maintaining adequate food supplies from 1950 to 1970. The size of rice imports has been influenced by the

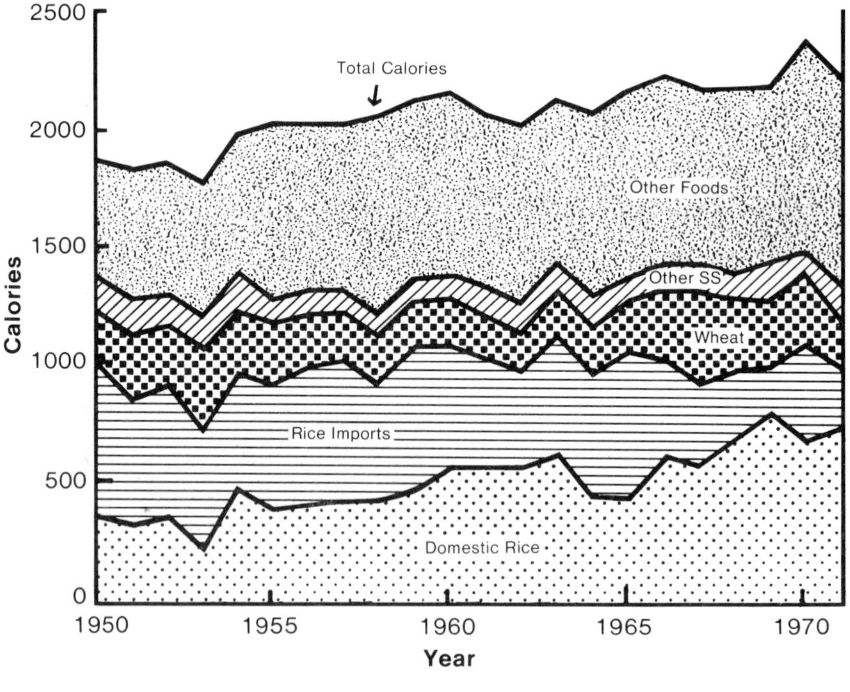

Figure 8–1. Sri Lanka: Per Capita Daily Supply of Calories, 1950–1971

Source: Central Bank of Ceylon, *Annual Reports*. Department of Census and Statistics, *Statistical Abstracts*. FAO, *Food Balance Sheets* (1955).

requirements for rice distribution under the rationing scheme. The carbohydrate deficit has been met by wheat imports. For most of this period, wheat prices have had a relative price advantage over rice in the international market (figure 8–2). Since rice and wheat contain similar amounts of calories and protein, it made economic sense to import lower-cost wheat calories when additional imported staple-food calories were required. Along with an increasing population and a larger demand for food, wheat imports increased substantially.

During the past three years, the volume of rice imports decreased significantly due to reductions in rice rations and increased domestic rice production. Price changes in the international market, however, have largely prevented the financial benefits expected from reduced imports. The maintenance of adequate consumption through rice and wheat imports has caused a heavy drain on scarce foreign exchange. Figure 8–3 depicts the key relationships that determine the level of welfare for most of the country's population—including the exports of tea and other commodities in order to finance the importation of foodstuffs. Sri Lanka's government has been importing nearly one-half of the country's food requirements, and a large share of foreign-exchange earnings is used to pay for these imports.

Consumption Subsidies

Sri Lanka has an outstanding record of successfully operating a nutrition-intervention program through direct participation of the state. Originally, public distribution of food arose as a wartime measure in response to

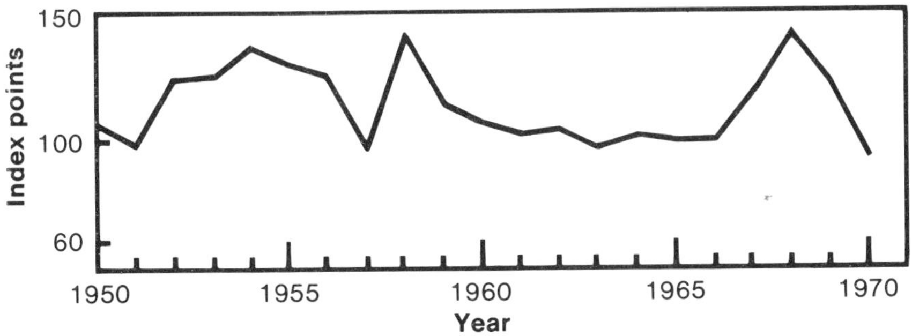

Figure 8–2. Sri Lanka: Index of Rice/Wheat Flour Cost Ratio, 1950–1970 (1946–1949=100)

Source: Central Bank of Ceylon, *Annual Reports*. Department of Census and Statistics, *Statistical Abstracts*. FAO, *Food Balance Sheets* (1955).

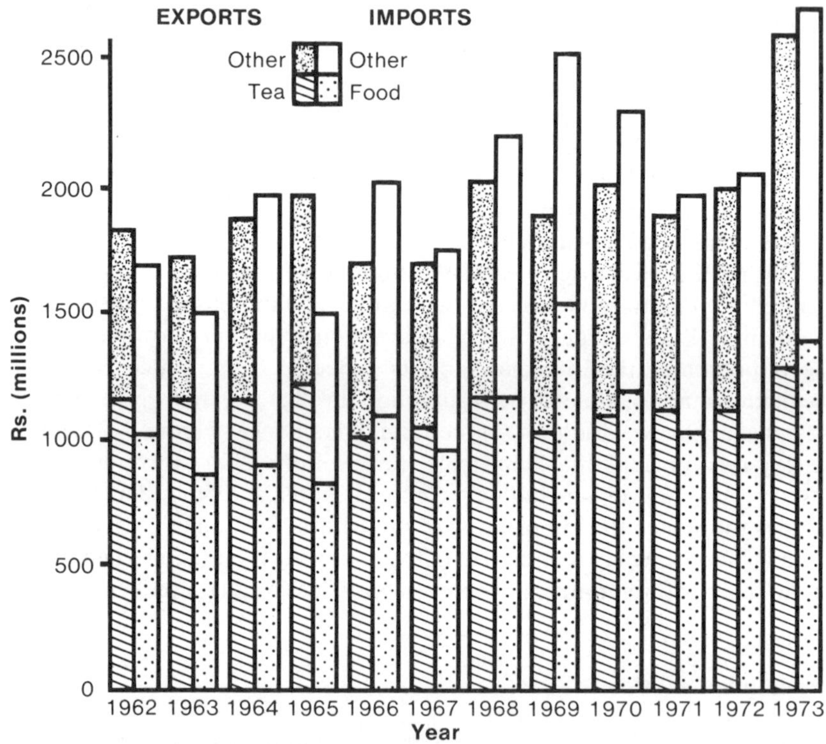

Figure 8–3. Sri Lanka: Value of Exports and Imports, 1962–1973

Source: Central Bank of Sri Lanka, *Annual Reports.*

reduced food imports. Measures to ensure equitable distribution of available supplies had to be implemented, and these resulted in the rice-rationing scheme and a food subsidy. With the end of World War II, the removal of controls combined with pent-up demand and an excess money supply caused postwar inflation. The cost of living increased rapidly. In order to prevent these forces from affecting low-income groups too adversely, the food subsidy was continued. Continuation of the rice-rationing scheme was the logical consequence. The subsidy on rice forced the government to continue rationing so that the rich would not unduly benefit by a subsidy meant for the poor.[2] Yet the rich did enjoy the subsidy, both directly and indirectly. For nearly two decades, almost everyone—rich and poor alike—was entitled to the rice ration; only a small minority of the population dispensed with the entitlement. The availability of large quantities of rice at low prices left little demand for nonration rice. Even prices of quality rice tended to remain relatively low.

In order to procure domestic supplies for the rationing scheme, the government made direct purchases of paddy from producers. These two forms of direct government involvement—rice procurement and rice distribution—have continued as the cornerstones of government policy. Changes in these programs have occurred from time to time, largely as a direct result of movements of wheat and rice prices in the international market. More specifically, whenever the world price of rice increased sharply, it was followed both by a change in the rice ration (either in the quantity issued and/or the price charged) and by a further intensification of the domestic food production effort.

Ration rice was distributed weekly to consumers who held ration books or token cards. In the late 1950s, four pounds of rice per person per week were issued under the ration at a heavily subsidized price. In late 1966, the government reduced the basic ration by 50 percent, but in order to relieve the pressure on low-income groups, the ration entitlement of two pounds of rice was issued free of charge. Additional amounts could be purchased at reduced prices. During the food crisis in 1973–1974, the basic ration was further reduced, and the free ration was only provided to non-income taxpayers. These changes in the income requirements meant that only about 50 percent of the population was eligible to receive the free ration. (For a fuller explanation of the ration system, see Gavan and Sri Chandrasekera, 1979.)

The rice subsidy is basically the loss to the government in the purchase and distribution or sale of ration rice. The concept of a net food subsidy arises because the government engages in the purchase and sale of a number of food items such as sugar, wheat flour, lentils, and dried fish, some of which are sold at a profit. The losses due to the sale of rice constitute the bulk of the gross food subsidy. Since the profits from the sale of other foodstuffs have always been minimal, the net food subsidy has continuously increased. Three basic factors contribute to higher food subsidies: (1) rising import prices, (2) larger producer subsidies associated with increased guaranteed prices for domestic rice, and (3) expansion in the number of food items receiving a subsidy.

The Economic Dilemma

Food-consumption subsidies form only part of a long-standing, broad-based program of social welfare. The other main components are free education and free health services. The wartime introduction of food subsidies has already been discussed. Free education was introduced in 1944 and broad-based health care even earlier. With Sir Lanka's independence in 1948, these forms of social welfare gathered greater momentum, resulting in the large-scale allocation of resources to these programs. Coverage was extensive, and almost everyone had access to these welfare programs.

Development economists have long debated the results of the large expenditures on social welfare. Among the positive effects are the changes in social indicators, including improved life expectancy, lowered mortality, and improved literacy rates. The average life span of a Sri Lankan increased from little over 40 years in 1946 to around 66 years by the beginning of the 1970s. During the same period, the crude death rate decreased from about thirty-eight per thousand to eight per thousand. Improvements in the adult literacy rate, to 78 percent of the population, were equally impressive.[3] Compared to the rapid population growth rate of the early 1950s (approximately 3 percent per year), the annual rate of growth has now declined to around 2 percent.

Together with a host of other factors, adequate nutrition contributes directly toward raising the quality of life, to which the state-sponsored programs of food distribution make a substantial contribution. The rice-rationing scheme has assured a regular supply of certain amounts of the staple food at a subsidized price to almost the entire population. After 1967, a portion of the ration was provided free of charge. Table 8–3 records the share of ration rice in total calorie intake between 1955 and 1970. Prior to 1967, rationed rice contributed one-third or more of total calorie consumption. The contribution since 1967, although lower in terms of percentage, is significant because of the role of free rice in that period. The free or subsidized rice ration is, in effect, an income transfer. Low-income consumers could increase their total food consumption as a result. Table 8–4 shows the contribution of rationed rice to various income groups in 1969–1970. Those in the lower-income groups received the largest calorie benefits, both in terms of ration-rice calories and ration calories as a share of total consumption. Other social-welfare policies—free eduction, free health services, subsidized public transport, and regulations affecting wage rates—also contributed indirectly toward maintaining relatively stable and satisfactory nutritional standards by increasing the amount of disposable income available for food purchases.

Those who argue that the past performance in Sri Lanka has been a development failure consider that the past development policy is a classic example of economic mismanagement, resulting in a reversal of the order of priorities usually considered essential for economic growth. They argue that resources have been misallocated by financing massive social-welfare programs and thereby undermining the incentives needed to accelerate development.[4]

Table 8–3
Sri Lanka: Consumption of Ration Rice, 1955 to 1970

Year	*Per Capita Ration Rice Consumption (lb./year)*	*Ration-Rice Calories Calories Per Day from Ration Rice*	*Proportion of Ration As a Percentage of Total Calories (%)*	*Proportion of Ration Rice in Total Rice Consumption (%)*
1955	149	664	31	72
1956	161	718	33	72
1957	163	727	34	73
1958	167	744	36	80
1959	174	776	37	72
1960	179	798	37	74
1961	180	802	38	77
1962	179	798	40	81
1963	188	838	40	74
1964	185	825	40	85
1965	192	856	40	81
1966	181	807	36	78
1967	98	437	20	48
1968	96	437	20	48
1969	97	432	20	44
1970	112	499	21	47

Source: Department of Census and Statistics, *Statistical Abstracts,* Colombo.

Table 8–4
Sri Lanka: Apparent per Capita Daily Calorie Intake from Rice, by Income Class, 1969–1970
(cal)

	Income Class (Rupees)						
	0–200	*200–399*	*400–599*	*600–799*	*800–999*	*1,000 and over*	*All Groups*
Rationed rice	430	424	403	393	368	323	417
Nonrationed rice	416	515	591	593	617	597	500
Total calorie intake	2,064	2,272	2,436	2,512	2,540	2,641	2,264
Calories from rationed rice as a percent of total calories	20.8	18.7	16.6	15.6	14.5	12.2	18.4
Percentage of total population	42.6	37.7	12.0	4.1	1.6	2.0	(100)

Source: Department of Census and Statistics, *Preliminary Report on Socio-Economic Survey of Ceylon 1969/70,* Colombo, 1971.

The opportunity cost of the food subsidy has been a matter of grave concern. The arguments against recurrent heavy expenditure on subsidy payments are based on the belief that the resources available for expenditure on development were largely determined by the subsidy on rice.[5] The Central Bank of Ceylon at one stage pointed out that by 1952, the rate of actual spending on rice and flour subsidies had exceeded that of the total of the government's development projects under the Colombo Plan.[6]

The concern over the food subsidy arises from the fact that the social programs in general and the food-subsidy program in particular accounted for a substantial percentage of total current expenditures incurred by government. Between 1963 and 1977, some 15 to 20 percent of total current expenditures went to meet the net food subsidy; 40 to 45 percent went to meet total current social services and net food subsidies.[7] An examination of the food subsidy in relation to other government financial operations leads to one reasonable conclusion: A diversion of resources from any form of welfare expenditure—be it the food subsidy or the health or education bill—to capital expenditure might have led to greater economic growth. Some economists have doubted whether resources diverted to capital expenditure would actually find their way to developmental activities. They argue that the resources would be drained away through other forms of consumption that would have benefited a smaller number of people than in the case of the food subsidy.[8]

The conflict between equity and growth is complex and not easy to resolve. Sri Lanka attempted and at least partially succeeded in adopting a poverty-oriented growth strategy aimed at meeting certain basic needs and at decreasing income disparities. This occurred before development economists began to recommend such growth strategies for developing countries. Sri Lanka's experience shows that population will continue to increase, although not at the high rates observed in the past. Some projections indicate at least 20 million people will inhabit the island by the turn of the century.[9] Feeding a larger population is one problem; gainfully employing the increasing numbers is another. Both problems have already reached serious proportions. Annual addition to the labor force has been at a rate over 1.6 percent. Nearly 1 million (out of a labor force of over 7 million) are already seeking their first jobs.[10]

The Problem: Food Security or Self-Reliance

An important question is the extent to which subsidized food has affected domestic food production. Large quantities of food at heavily subsidized prices may have had a dampening effect on open-market prices, and low market prices would adversely affect output. There has, however, been substantial growth of output in the paddy sector. This growth is due in part to an incentive price scheme and the provision of certain input subsidies, such as the subsidy on fertilizer.

Production incentives and direct assistance take many forms. These include the large-scale opening up of land and settlement schemes, expansion of irrigation facilities, subsidies on inputs, credit facilities through government institutions, extension services, guaranteed floor prices for farm produce, and crop-insurance schemes. The guaranteed floor-price scheme is particularly interesting. It ensures that if paddy prices fall below the floor level, farmers can sell their surplus to government-sponsored agencies. In general, the domestic paddy floor price has been higher than the equivalent price of imported rice.

Rice has been the focus of production incentives because of the latitude for import substitution in the rice sector. The greater the domestic rice supply, the lesser the need for imports that use scarce foreign exchange. The rice sector also has the largest potential for employment generation. The population census of 1971 showed that of a total agricultural sector employment of 1.8 million (agriculture, forestry, and fishing), the paddy sector employed 0.8 million people, while the export sector (including tea, rubber, and coconut) employed 0.74 million people.

The overall impact of government investment and farmers response can be seen in the growth rates of output, area, and yields. Table 8–5 shows the rates of growth during the period 1961–1975 for paddy and major subsidiary food crops. During this period, the area prepared and made available for paddy cultivation increased by 30 percent, with paddy output registering a 44-percent increase. The rate of growth of total output was 2.6 percent per annum, a result of the growth rates of 1.06 and 1.53 percent for net harvested area and yield per acre, respectively. The growth in production of the subsidiary nonrice crops has been impressive. While their total share in calorie consumption is still small, the importance of nonrice crops to certain subsets of the rural population is probably considerable. In particular, cassava (manioc) has become a major rain-fed crop. Production in 1975 was 770,000 tons, or about 235,000 metric tons rice-equivalent.

Since most emphasis has been on rice, self-sufficiency is usually viewed as rice self-sufficiency. A narrow but commonly used definition of the self-sufficiency ratio is the proportion of locally produced rice in total supply (imports plus domestic supply). A more practical concept for planning imports and production would be to consider the total cereal requirements against the domestic potential to meet them. In the 1950s, the cereal self-sufficiency ratio was around 40 percent; this ratio increased substantially and was around 60 percent in the early 1970s.

Growth rates required to meet the increasing demand for food grains are given in table 8–6. Given a minimum constant rate of cereal consump-

Table 8–5
Sri Lanka: Growth Rates of Paddy and Subsidiary Food Crops, 1961 to 1975

	Acreage			*Production*		
	1961	*1975*	*Growth Rate*	*1961*	*1975*	*Growth Rate*
	(1,000 acres)		*(percent)*	*(1,000 tons)*		*(percent)*
Paddy						
Total	1,179.0	1,535.8	1.9	910.0	1,306.0	2.6
Net harvested	1,216.0	1,425.8	1.06	—	—	—
Subsidiary crops						
Manioc	97.9	310.4	8.5	269.7	770.2	7.7
Potatoes	1.4	6.8	11.8	2.1	40.5	23.0
Maize	27.7	91.2	8.8	8.1	18.0	5.8
Green grain	9.3	16.1	3.9	1.7	5.0	7.7
Sorghum	3.5	9.1	7.0	1.0	2.9	7.5
Cowpea	6.8	16.3	6.3	1.0	3.7	9.6

Sources: Department of Census and Statistics, *Statistical Abstracts,* Colombo. Department of Agriculture, *Agricultural Statistical Information,* 1976. Central Bank of Ceylon, *Economic and Social Statistics of Sri Lanka,* 1978.

Note: 1961 is the average for the period 1960–1962; 1975 is the average for the period 1974–1976.

Table 8–6
Sri Lanka: Growth Rates Required to Achieve Given Rates of Cereal Consumption in 1990

Per Capita Cereal Consumption (kg)	*Required Cereal Output (paddy equivalent) (metric tons)*	*Required Growth Rate*[a] *(%)*
132[b]	3.6	6.8
154[c]	4.2	8.2
100[d]	2.7	5.0
115[e]	3.1	5.9

[a]Base year as 1975 (average 1974–1976) with 1.3 million tons paddy output.
[b]Per capita total cereal consumption observed in the past.
[c]Per capita cereal consumption to meet 110 percent of energy requirements.
[d]Per capita rice consumption observed in the past.
[e]Per capita rice consumption of 50 percent of wheat consumption is to be reduced.

tion of 132 kg per capita per year and population growth at 2 percent, the paddy equivalent of cereals in 1990 would be 3.6 million metric tons. If the paddy output growth rates seen during the fifteen years prior to 1975 are expected to continue during the fifteen years after 1975, the output in 1990 would be only 2 million metric tons, leaving a deficit of approximately 1.6

million metric tons of paddy or 1 million tons of rice. To replace all imported wheat with locally produced rice as well as to eliminate rice imports, paddy output would have to grow at a rate of 6.8 percent annually—a leap of over 4 percent from past achievements. If incomes increase, leading to higher per capita levels of food-grain consumption, even faster growth in output would be required. To be self-sufficient in rice alone, the rate of growth of paddy output would have to increase from the historical rate of 2.6 percent (see table 8–5) to 5 percent per annum (see table 8–6).

In the past, sizable improvements have occurred in paddy area, yields, and output. Given the expansion of irrigated areas and other forms of incentives and assistance, however, the rice sector has performed poorly. Sri Lanka's poor performance in the use of available land and relatively low levels of productivity (compared with some other Asian countries) are generally pointed to as indications of the rice sector failing to keep pace with expectations. The total area under paddy has increased from 900,000 acres in 1952 to 1.5 million acres in 1976; the cropping intensity (the ratio of annually sown area to total paddy area) has increased only from 120 percent in 1952 to 136 percent in 1974. Average paddy yields, although increasing, have not yet reached a level of one ton per acre. If Sri Lanka is to be self-reliant in rice, it is imperative that productivity increase. Given the emphasis placed on the rice sector for food output and employment, a review of the performance of the rice sector at all levels is required in order to identify the constraints on maximizing land use and yields.

If rice is to have any serious impact on the consumption of imported wheat, a massive leap in domestic rice production is required. One major project in this direction is the Mahaweli Ganga Development Scheme. According to the scheme's master plan, development of 890,000 acres (360,000 hectares) under irrigation, including about 640,000 acres (260,000 hectares) of newly opened land, are planned. Even under the present program to accelerate the completion of the scheme, it may take a decade or more before its full effects are felt.

Conclusion

This chapter has discussed the evolution of government food-security policies in Sri Lanka. Beginning with wartime rationing requirements, the postindependence governments have continued to supply rice rations as a part of a comprehensive social-welfare program. The results have been impressive: education, health, and nutritional levels are all higher than in most other countries with similar low levels of per capita income.

These results are not without cost, however. The burden of large and increasingly costly rice imports has been coupled with the need to establish domestic rice-producer incentives and subsidies. As the size of the net food subsidy grew, changes were made in the ration system by changing the eligibility requirements, the amounts available, and the proportion to be issued for free distribution and by using wheat as well as rice.

Domestic rice production has not been as large as hoped for. After a spurt in production in the 1960s, production peaked in 1970 and remained stagnant for the next seven years, only increasing again after 1977. In the search for sufficient food grains to meet the needs of the ration-shop system, both rice and wheat were imported. Large investments in the agricultural sector, such as the Mahaweli Ganga Development Scheme, are just beginning to produce results.

Although the impact on overall economic development of diverting scarce resources to the ration system and other social-welfare programs is still being debated, the effect on food security of these policies has been fairly clear. As seen in tables 8–1 and 8–2, the average level of calorie and protein consumption has generally been low but adequate. The distribution of that consumption, however, has been very equitable, and the ration system has played an important role in that distribution. Between 1955 and 1970, for example, rationed rice ranged from 50 to 80 percent of the total rice consumed and provided from 20 to 40 percent of all calories in the diet. While all consumers benefited from the system (see table 8–4), the poorer consumers received the largest benefits. Recent developments in Sri Lanka's food-security system are discussed by John Dixon in the Postscript to this chapter.

The historical record of Sri Lanka's government-implemented food-security ration system has shown that such a system can have major impacts on food consumption. The costs of such a program, however, are large, and resources devoted to food subsidies are not available for capital investment. Recent changes in government policy have, in part, been in response to the rising costs of these subsidies. The trade-offs are complex: massive social-welfare expenditures versus capital investment, subsidized staple foods versus producer incentives, import dependence versus self-sufficiency for basic cereals. The effects of alternative development strategies on food-consumption levels, welfare, and economic growth are only now being tested. Sri Lanka's historical record, however, has provided a unique example of a comprehensive public commitment to food security by a low-income country.

Notes

1. See de Mel and Jogaratnam (1977).
2. See Rasaputram (1964).
3. See Isenman (1980).
4. See Marga Institute (1976).
5. See Karunatileka (1971).
6. See Central Bank of Ceylon, *Annual Reports,* 1952, 1971, 1974.
7. See Isenman (1980), p. 245.
8. See Karunatileka (1971), p. 36.
9. See del Mel and Jogaratnam (1977).
10. See Central Bank of Ceylon, *Annual Reports,* 1952, 1971, 1974.

Bibliography

Central Bank of Ceylon. *Annual Reports,* 1952, 1971, 1974, Colombo.

_______. 1978. *Economic and Social Statistics of Sri Lanka,* Colombo.

de Mel, B.V., and Jogaratnam, T. 1977. "Population Growth, Nutrition and Food Supplies." *MARGA* 4.

Department of Agriculture, Government of Sri Lanka. 1976. *Agricultural Statistical Information,* Colombo.

Department of Census and Statistics, Government of Sri Lanka. Various years. *Statistical Abstracts,* Colombo.

_______. 1971. *Preliminary Report on Socio-Economic Survey of Ceylon, 1969/70,* Colombo.

_______. 1972. "Socio-Economic Survey of Sri Lanka, 1969/70—A Special Report on Food and Nutritional Levels in Sri Lanka." Colombo, October.

Edirisinghe, N., and Poleman, T.T. 1976. "Implications of Government Intervention in the Rice Economy of Sri Lanka." Cornell International Agriculture Mimeograph 48. Ithaca, N.Y., January.

Gavan, J.D., and Sri Chandrasekera, I. 1979. *The Impact of Public Foodgrain Distribution on Food Consumption and Welfare in Sri Lanka.* Research Report 13, International Food Policy Research Institute (IFPRI), Washington, D.C.

Isenman, P. 1980. "Basic Needs: The Case of Sri Lanka." *World Development,* Vol. 8. London: Pergamon Press.

Jogaratnam, T., and Poleman, T.T. 1969. *Food in the Economy of Ceylon.* Cornell International Agricultural Development Bulletin No. 11. Ithaca, N.Y., October.

Karunatileka, H.N.S. 1971. *Economic Development of Ceylon.* New York: Praeger.

Marga Institute. 1976. *Participatory Development and Dependence,* mimeo. Colombo.

Rasaputram, W. 1964. ''Influence of Foreign Trade on the Level and Growth of National Income in Ceylon, 1926–1957.'' Central Bank of Ceylon Research Studies, Colombo.

Postscript

John A. Dixon

According to most social-welfure indicators, Sri Lanka should be a much richer country than it in fact is. Sri Lanka ranks in the middle of the World Bank's list of low-income countries, with a 1979 per capita GNP of U.S. \$230 (slightly ahead of India at \$190 and behind China at \$260). On a social-welfare basis, however, it has literacy and health levels more common to countries with per capita GNPs five to ten times as large (world Bank 1981). The Physical Quality of Life Index (PQLI) calculated by the Overseas Development Council is 81 for Sri Lanka, compared to 43 in India and 71 in China. Among the developing countries of the Asia-Pacific region, only Taiwan and South Korea have higher PQLI indices.[1]

A major reason for this high level of well-being in a low-income country is the government's historic commitment of resources to food, health, and education programs. Aspects of the food-security system have been discussed by Neville Edirisinghe. As he indicates, the rising costs of the social-welfare program, especially the food-security program, have put increasing pressure on Sri Lanka's foreign-exchange reserves and the national budget.

Although Sri Lanka's population is small (about 15 million people as of 1980), the country's imports of rice and wheat flour have been large. Between 1970 and 1978, Sri Lanka imported, on the average, about 380,000 metric tons of milled rice and 480,000 tons of wheat flour each year.[2] When these quantities are added to domestic rice production (which averaged 995,000 tons per year during this period), we can see that imported rice provided about one-fifth and imported wheat about one-quarter of the total cereal calories consumed. Domestic rice supplied just slightly more than one-half of these basic staple-food calories.

Although some of these cereal imports were provided on concessional terms or in barter agreements, the bulk of imports were on a commercial basis and placed a heavy burden on the earnings of traditional exports such as tea, rubber, coconut products, and gems. As prices fluctuated in the international markets, the expected values of exports and costs of imports varied widely. While Sri Lanka's percentage share of food in total merchandise imports decreased from 39 percent in 1960 to 30 percent in 1978, it remains the highest percentage when compared among the 124 countries listed in the 1981 *World Development Report*.[3]

During the 1970s the combination of large and increasing cereal imports, fluctuations in export commodity prices, drought-induced domestic production variations, and increasing prices for many imported goods (including petroleum, sugar, and grains) contributed to a reevaluation of government policies in the food-security area. This reevaluation began in the early and mid-1970s when the free rice ration was reduced from two pounds per person per week to one pound, and the paid ration was reduced from two pounds to one. After 1973, income taxpayers were no longer eligible for the free ration. Wheat was distributed through the ration system between 1973 and 1975 at a lower price than ration rice. In 1977, just before the parliamentary elections, the paid rice ration was increased to three pounds, and total rice imports were over 540,000 tons, while wheat-flour imports were about 530,000 tons (Gavan and Chandrasekera 1979; and USDA various years).

In July 1977, the government changed; the more socialist Sri Lanka Freedom Party was routed and replaced by Jayewardene's United National Party (UNP). The UNP had campaigned on a platform of economic relief, restoration of basic rights, and a clean administration [Far Eastern Economic Review (FEER) 1978]. The new government encouraged a return to a free market economy, dismantled many exchange and import controls, and reduced government food subsidies.

While education and health programs were not affected, the food-ration system was phased out. In September 1979, a food- and kerosene-stamp scheme was introduced. The old rice subsidy was eliminated, and the poorest 40 percent of the population received food stamps that could be exchanged for a basket of goods including rice, wheat flour, dried and condensed milk, and kerosene (FEER 1980). The value of the food stamps was determined by the size and age composition of each family. Younger children received a greater value of stamps than did older children and adults; this was in recognition of both the greater nutritional needs of young children and their limited income-earning capacity.[4] Although a means test is used to determine which families should receive food stamps, indications are that considerable underreporting of household incomes occurs. More families receive the stamps, therefore, than would be the case if incomes were accurately reported. Those in the population who do not receive food stamps have been faced with sharply higher staple-food prices.

Although it is too early to determine the nutritional results of this change, some worsening of the food-consumption levels of the poorest consumers will probably occur. Since the food stamps were not indexed—that is, their value did not change with inflation—their real purchasing power decreased rapidly over time.[5] The real cost to the government of the food-stamp program also declined as inflation increased. The government's move to price imported rice, wheat, and sugar at cost meant that their prices increased sharply and thereby contributed to inflation. In early 1980 wheat flour prices went to world levels, and in late 1980 the price of rice increased as both paddy-procurement prices for domestic producers were raised, and retail prices went up.

These price changes—especially the rise in wheat prices relative to rice—resulted in sharply lower per capita wheat consumption and reduced wheat imports in 1980. Rice imports also decreased to about 225,000 metric tons in 1980 and are projected at 190,000 tons in 1981, in part due to increased domestic production (USDA 1981a). In fact, domestic rice production has increased rapidly in the past few years and has averaged over 1.3 million metric tons per year in 1979 and 1980, which constitutes a 30 percent increase over the 1970–1978 average level of production. Increased production has been in part attributed to attractive open-market rice prices that led to increased use of inputs and expanded cultivated area. In 1980, favorable weather, combined with increased use of fertilizer and improved varieties, led to a record rice production of almost 1.5 million metric tons (Central Bank of Ceylon 1981).

Since July 1977, Sri Lanka has undergone major changes: A free-market-oriented government has taken office, rice production has increased sharply, food rations and subsidies have been eliminated, inflation and balance of payments deficits have become major problems, and a food-stamp scheme has been introduced. The net effect on Sri Lanka's historical record of support of basic consumption levels by all segments of the population is not yet known.[6] If resources released by decreased food-subsidy payments are channeled into growth and not just into increasingly expensive petroleum and other consumer-goods imports, a rising standard of living may continue to ensure adequate consumption levels. The distribution of increased income and its translation into effective demand are therefore crucial challenges faced by Sri Lanka in the 1980s.

Notes

1. The Physical Quality of Life Index (PQLI) is based on three main factors: infant mortality, life expectancy at age one, and degree of literacy (IADS 1981). Taiwan's PQLI (87) and South Korea's (83) are only slightly higher than Sri Lanka's (81).

2. Year-to-year imports fluctuated quite widely as a result of variations in domestic rice production. Rice imports ranged from a high of 543,000 metric tons of milled rice in 1970 and 1977 to as low as 187,000 tons in 1978 (USDA 1980). The high level of imports in 1977 is in part due to the general election held in July of that year and the government's attempts to increase food availability before the election. Wheat imports have usually been larger than rice imports and have followed a rising trend from 1970 to 1978 (USDA 1981, and USDA various years).

3. The only other larger countries with similar food-import shares in 1978 were Haiti (28 percent) and Egypt (26 percent) (World Bank 1981, table 10).

4. In an eligible household, each adult received stamps worth Rs 15 per month, children under eight received stamps worth Rs 25, and children between eight and twelve received stamps worth Rs 20.

5. Inflation has increased sharply in the past few years. In 1979, inflation was about 14 percent, and in 1980 it reached 20 percent or more (FEER 1980). The Colombo Consumers' Price Index, which is designed to measure retail prices, increased by 26 percent in 1980, compared to 11 percent in 1979, 12 percent in 1978, and only 1 percent in 1976 and 1977 (Central Bank of Ceylon 1981).

6. For some background on the economic parameters affecting food consumption in Sri Lanka, see Alderman and Timmer (1980).

Bibliography

Alderman, H., and Timmer, C.P., 1980. "Consumption Parameters for Sri Lankan Food Policy Analysis." *Sri Lanka Journal of Agrarian Studies* 1 (2), Colombo.

Central Bank of Ceylon. 1981. *1980 Review of the Economy,* Colombo.

Far Eastern Economic Review (FEER). 1978. *Asia 1978 Yearbook,* Hong Kong. Pp. 308–312.

———. 1980. *Asia 1980 Yearbook,* Hong Kong. Pp. 279–284.

Gavan, J.D., and Sri Chandrasekera, I. 1979. *The Impact of Public Foodgrain Distribution on Food Consumption and Welfare in Sri Lanka.* Research Report No. 13, International Food Policy Research Institute (IFPRI), Washington, D.C.

International Agricultural Development Service (IADS). 1981. *Agricultural Development Indicators,* New York.

United States Department of Agriculture (USDA), Economic Research Service. 1981a. *Rice—Outlook and Situation,* RS-38, Washington, D.C., September.

United States Department of Agriculture (USDA), Economics, Statistics and Cooperatives Service. Various years. *Agricultural Situation—Asia, 1973, 1974, 1976, 1977, 1978, 1979,* Washington, D.C.

United States Department of Agriculture (USDA), Foreign Agricultural Service. 1980. *Reference Tables on Rice Supply—Utilization for Individual Countries,* FG-38-80, Washington, D.C., December 19.

———. 1981b. *Reference Tables on Wheat, Corn, and Total Coarse Grains Supply—Distribution for Individual Countries,* FG-4-81, Washington, D.C., January 28.

World Bank. 1981. *World Development Report 1981,* Washington, D.C.

9 India's Food Security: Supply, Demand, and Signs of Success

John A. Dixon and *Rodney Tyers*

India has a population of 660 million and a land area of 3.3 million square kilometers of which about half are cultivated. Among Asian countries, India is second in size and population; only China is bigger or more populous. Despite its size and immense resources, India is also one of the poorest countries in Asia, its per capita income was recently estimated at about U.S. $190 per year.[1] The agricultural sector is very large, contributing 38 percent of the gross domestic product and employing 71 percent of the national labor force. After three decades of planning, with heavy emphasis on industrial growth, the agricultural sector is still 40 percent larger than the industrial sector but employs almost seven times as much labor. However, the industrial sector has grown, on average, over twice as fast as the agricultural sector during the past twenty years.[2]

India's most important staple foods are rice and wheat, although a variety of coarse grains, such as corn, millet, and sorghum, are important in many rural and urban areas. Although total production of grains has kept pace with population growth during the past decade, both weather-induced fluctuations in agricultural output and the immense cost of financing sudden large increases in grain imports have led to serious shortfalls in domestic food availability, most notably in 1966, 1967, 1973, and 1975. Such shortfalls have resulted not only in widespread physical hardship but also have interrupted progress in overall economic development through their effect on agricultural income and the resulting curtailment of savings and investment.

The agricultural sector, while having a fairly low growth rate (1.9 percent per annum from 1960 to 1970 and 2.1 percent per annum from 1970 to 1979), is still of overwhelming importance to India's economy because of the large proportion of total population involved. As a result, an agricultural production shortfall causes a significant decline in purchasing power and hence in the effective demand for food and other goods, especially in rural areas. Consequently, even if the government is able to finance sufficient imports to stabilize domestic supply, food consumption inevitably falls, especially among the very poor.

Relatively sound agricultural-development policies combined with favorable weather have resulted in a series of record grain crops in recent years, and large grain imports have not been required. In fact, since 1979, India has become a substantial rice and wheat exporter, and domestic food-grain stocks are at record levels. Although these developments have resulted in reduced exposure to the risks of disruptive foreign-exchange requirements for importing staple foods, there remain important difficulties in assuring adequate food intake. When India was a major food-grain importer, and government stocks were low, policies to address this food-insecurity problem were easier to motivate. Now that there are record food-grain harvests, large government grain stocks, and sizable rice and wheat exports, the question of continuing nutritional needs within India has become more pronounced.

This chapter examines the broad patterns of food-grain production and consumption in India, the major changes in those patterns in the past two decades, and the government's involvement in food-security programs. A major goal of these programs has been the improvement of the nutritional status of the Indian population. The problem of adequate nutrition can be examined from two basic perspectives: the supply side and the demand side. On the supply side, India has demonstrated remarkable progress in increasing total food-grain production in the past five years. The demand side—that is, the ability of all consumers to meet their basic nutritional needs at a reasonable price—has been more problematic. The low purchasing power of large numbers of consumers has meant that many people have not been able to increase their food intake and that inadequate nutrition continues to coexist with production "surpluses."

Patterns of Food-Grain Production and Consumption in India

Given that India's land area spans several thousand kilometers from north to south and from east to west (figure 9–1), it is not surprising that its diversity of agroclimatic zones and of cultures has led to nonhomogeneous food production and consumption patterns. Throughout the country, however, production of the staple grains—rice, wheat, and certain coarse grains—dominates the organization of agriculture. While the different relative emphasis given to each has depended primarily on agroclimatic comparative advantage and local consumption tastes, changes in cropping patterns during the past decade and a half have been extensively influenced by the revolution in grain productivity resulting from the adoption of high-yielding varieties (HYVs) of wheat and rice.

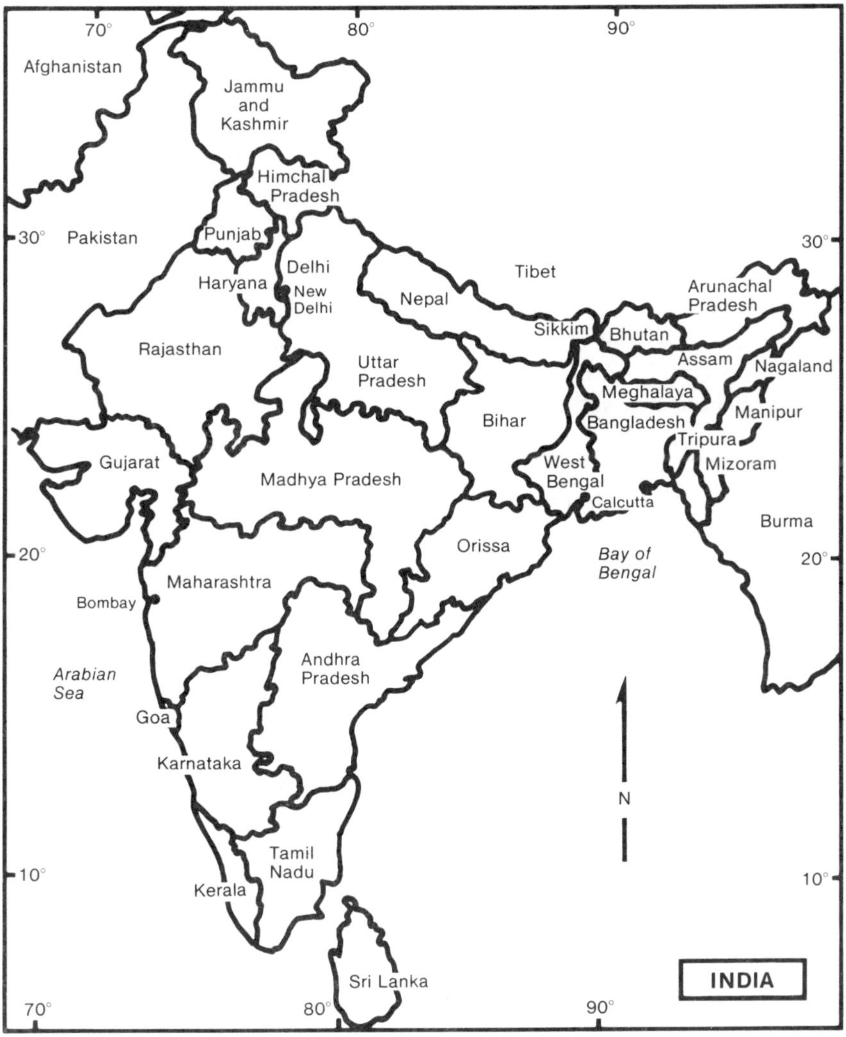

Figure 9–1. Map of India Showing States and Three Major Cities

Changes in Total Production

Improved wheat productivity led the green revolution in India during the 1960s and early 1970s with an improvement in average wheat yield of 43 percent between 1964/1965 and 1970/1971. Because of this improvement, during the late 1960s and early 1970s, the area cultivated in wheat, especially under irrigated conditions, expanded at rates far in excess of that for rice.[3] Moreover, rice yields themselves increased much more slowly than those for wheat. In the 1970s, total area planted to both rice and wheat increased slowly, and expansion of wheat was slightly faster (table 9–1). Yields, especially for rice, varied considerably from year to year because of weather fluctuations but were on a general upward trend. The main reason for the change was the rapid increase in use of high-yielding varieties for rice and wheat.

Between 1970/71 and 1979/80, the share of total rice area planted with HYVs increased from 15 to 40 percent and, because of higher yields from HYVs, the HYV share of total rice production increased from 28 to 70 percent. Wheat production from HYVs began the 1970s at a higher level, in 1970–1971 over 35 percent of wheat area and 65 percent of total wheat production had already come from HYVs. By 1979–1980, these shares had increased to 70 percent of area and constituted 80 percent of total wheat production (see table 9–1).

Rice, wheat, and the coarse grains such as corn, barley, millet, and sorghum provide the major source of calories and protein in the Indian diet. Coarse grains constitute 25 to 30 percent of all cereals produced in India. They are usually grown under rain-fed conditions or with limited irrigation and their production fluctuates considerably from year to year (see table 9–1). Together with pulses (lentils), they are the foods most important for the food security of India's poor. The pulses usually provide less than 10 percent of total food-grain consumption by weight, but they are a major source of protein. There has been a long-run secular decline in pulse production as the area cultivated in more profitable crops, including rice and wheat, has expanded. Because of the role of pulses in providing low-cost protein, this decline is a continuing problem for the Indian agricultural sector.

From this examination of trends in grain-cropped area and production from 1970 to 1980, the following five points emerge:

1. The total area cultivated in cereals has not varied much and has fluctuated around 100 million hectares.
2. Wheat's share of the total area cultivated in cereals has grown slightly, while the share of coarse grains has declined.
3. The share of HYVs in total production has increased rapidly, reaching 70 percent for rice, 80 percent for wheat, and 33 percent for coarse grains.
4. Average yields increased by about 15 percent for wheat and have remained unchanged for coarse grains. Rice yields have fluctuated widely[4], causing much of the year-to-year variation in total cereal production[5].

Table 9–1
India: Area and Production of Cereals, High-Yielding Varieties (HYVs) and Traditional Varieties (TVs), 1970–1971 to 1979–1980 (July/June)

	Area		*Production*		*Average Yield (kg/ha)*		
Crop	*Total (1,000 ha)*	*Share HYVs (%)*	*Total (metric tons)*	*Share HYVs (%)*	*HYVs*	*TVs*	*Total*
Rice							
1970–1971	37,593	14.9	42,225	28.4	2,147	944	1,123
1971–1972	37,758	19.6	43,061	30.9	1,995	981	1,141
1972–1973	36,688	22.3	39,245	36.7	1,765	871	1,070
1973–1974	38,285	25.4	44,051	37.9	1,718	957	1,151
1974–1975	37,887	28.5	39,578	44.2	1,623	815	1,018
1975–1976	39,475	32.4	48,740	51.7	1,970	882	1,235
1976–1977	38,511	35.1	42,055	55.9	1,741	742	1,092
1977–1978	40,283	35.8	52,737	77.2	2,066	888	1,309
1978–1979	40,196	38.1	53,829	70.9	2,052	899	1,339
1979–1980	38,000	40.3	43,500	70.6	1,667	793	1,145
Wheat							
1970–1971	18,241	35.5	23,832	65.5	2,407	700	1,307
1971–1972	19,139	41.1	26,410	63.5	2,135	854	1,380
1972–1973	19,464	52.3	24,735	71.2	1,729	768	1,127
1973–1974	18,583	58.7	21,778	72.6	1,448	779	1,172
1974–1975	18,010	62.3	24,104	70.9	1,525	1,048	1,338
1975–1976	20,454	66.8	28,846	72.8	1,537	1,156	1,410
1976–1977	20,922	68.8	29,010	73.8	1,486	1,167	1,387
1977–1978	21,203	68.9	31,749	76.9	1,671	1,113	1,497
1978–1979	22,220	66.6	34,982	77.2	1,824	1,076	1,574
1979–1980	21,500	69.8	32,500	80.0	1,733	1,000	1,512
Coarse grains							
1970–1971	45,950	7.2	30,547	18.0	1,658	588	665
1971–1972	43,153	6.7	24,138	17.8	1,483	493	559
1972–1973	40,868	8.9	22,157	24.1	1,463	452	542
1973–1974	46,221	11.3	28,828	23.6	1,308	537	624
1974–1975	38,326	11.9	26,129	26.8	1,529	567	682
1975–1976	43,798	13.5	30,409	30.3	1,561	560	694
1976–1977	41,940	14.1	28,879	32.2	1,574	543	689
1977–1978	42,226	14.5	30,014	32.7	1,607	560	711
1978–1979	42,157	14.7	30,389	36.2	1,774	539	721
1979–1980	41,500	14.9	26,800	36.6	1,581	482	646
Total cereals							
1970–1971	101,783	15.1	96,604	34.3	2,151	735	949
1971–1972	100,050	18.2	93,607	36.7	1,892	723	936
1972–1973	97,020	22.7	86,137	43.4	1,698	650	887
1973–1974	103,094	25.1	94,657	41.5	1,552	716	918
1974–1975	94,223	28.2	89,811	46.3	1,565	713	953
1975–1976	103,727	31.2	107,995	51.3	1,712	734	1,041
1976–1977	101,373	33.4	99,944	54.2	1,603	677	986
1977–1978	103,712	33.8	114,500	55.9	1,822	737	1,104
1978–1979	104,573	34.8	119,200	58.3	1,912	729	1,140
1979–1980	101,000	36.1	102,800	59.6	1,679	643	1,018

Source: U.S. Department of Agriculture, Economics, Statistics and Cooperatives Service, 1980, *Agricultural Situation: Asia, Review of 1979 and Outlook for 1980,* Supplement 2 to WAS-21, Washington, D.C., p. 12. Based on Government of India, 1978/79 Economic Survey, letters and reports from Agricultural Counselor, American Embassy, New Delhi, and ESCS estimates for production of HYVs and TVs and yields calculated by Asia Branch, IED, ESCS.

Whereas in the early 1970s total food-grain production had ranged from 100 to 108 million metric tons (Gavan and Dixon 1975), the 1975-to-1977 average had improved to 116.6 million metric tons, and was followed by a bumper crop of 128 million tons in 1978. Weather fluctuations caused drops in rice and wheat production in 1979 and 1980, respectively, but total production is expected to be higher in 1981 (table 9–2). It appears that Indian agriculture is moving to a new, higher productivity level compared to five to ten years previously and that weather-induced production variations are now more moderate than in the past.

Changes in Location of Production

As wheat cultivation has expanded, it has spread from the traditional wheat lands of the western states into the more traditional rice-producing areas in the east. The expansion of wheat into Bihar and Uttar Pradesh is notable: between 1967/1970 and 1975/1978, wheat production in these two states increased 58 percent, or by over 4 million metric tons. In comparison, in Haryana and the Punjab (the home of the wheat green revolution), production increased by 50 percent, or 3 million metric tons, during the same period (table 9–3 and figure 9–1).

Table 9–2
India: Area and Production of Selected Food Grains
(1,000 metric tons)

	Area (1,000 hectares)				*Production (1,000 metric tons)*			
Commodities	*1975–1977 Average*	*1978*	*1979*	*1980*[a]	*1975–1977 Average*	*1978*	*1979*	*1980*[a]
Rice (milled)	39,423	40,482	38,974	40,500	47,797	53,773	42,185	54,000
Wheat	19,795	21,456	22,641	21,964	27,320	31,749	35,508	31,564
Coarse grains	42,967	42,401	41,301	41,350	30,042	30,611	27,256	28,620
Cereals	102,185	104,339	102,916	103,614	105,159	116,133	104,949	114,184
Pulses	23,154	23,497	23,657	21,750	11,471	11,972	12,183	8,371
Food grains	125,339	127,836	126,573	125,364	116,630	128,105	117,132	122,555

Source: U.S. Department of Agriculture (USDA), Economics and Statistics Service, *Agricultural Situation: Asia, Review of 1980 and Outlook for 1981,* Supplement 2 to WAS-24, Washington, D.C., 1981a, p. 8.

Note: The difference between tables 9–1 and 9–2 arise from use of the calendar year in table 9–2 and the agricultural year (July–June) in table 9–1. The main rice harvest falls in September to October/November, while the main wheat harvest is from February to April. In the agricultural year, the main rice and wheat crops are combined (say, for July 1979 to June 1980), while the bulk of the rice was produced in 1979, and most wheat was harvested in 1980. Coarse grains cover both periods.

[a]Estimated.

Table 9–3
Regional Share in Rice and Wheat Production in India, 1967–1970 and 1975–1978

	Rice				*Wheat*			
	Average Area (1,000 hectares)		*Average Production (1,000 metric tons)*		*Average Area (1,000 hectares)*		*Average Production (1,000 metric tons)*	
States	*1967–1970*	*1975–1978*	*1967–1970*	*1975–1978*	*1967–1970*	*1975–1978*	*1967–1970*	*1975–1978*
Jammu, Kashmir, and Himachal Pradesh	332.5	350.1	523.8	521.9	516.8	495.8	495.7	446.2
Punjab and Haryana	572.3	1,025.2	790.3	2,795.3	2,936.5	3,858.9	5,926.6	8,911.0
Rajasthan	113.1	165.7	83.7	224.3	1,226.8	1,797.4	1,257.5	2,399.8
Uttar Pradesh and Bihar	9,876.4	10,087.4	7,885.0	9,617.2	6,293.9	8,441.4	7,204.8	11,424.3
Assam, Meghalaya, Manipur, Tripura, and West Bengal	7,512.6	8,298.6	8,558.4	9,845.9	165.0	602.0	262.4	1,181.1
Madhya Pradesh	4,293.5	4,636.5	3,133.0	3,678.8	2,964.1	3,244.2	2,035.0	2,665.0
Gujarat and Maharashtra	1,878.0	1,936.1	1,792.8	2,803.8	1,372.4	1,894.4	1,030.5	2,202.6
Andhra Pradesh and Orissa	7,631.6	8,160.6	8,828.3	9,583.0	28.7	88.7	20.4	126.3
Tamil Nadu, Kerala, and Karnataka	4,659.2	4,449.1	7,471.5	8,408.9	314.9	379.8	143.6	252.9
Rest of India	158.8	220.0	200.9	298.6	41.5	56.9	72.8	118.8
All of India	37,028.0	39,329.3	39,267.7	47,777.7	15,860.6	20,859.5	18,428.3	29,728.0

Source: Government of India, Ministry of Agriculture and Irrigation, Directorate of Economics and Statistics, "Estimates of Area and Production of Foodgrains," 1979, reported in Majumdar, 1979b.

Although high-yielding varieties of both rice and wheat depend on the use of artificial fertilizers, pesticides, and improved water control, large productivity increases in rice depend most heavily on the control of irrigation water. The rice land and irrigation systems of the southern and eastern states have tended to be rain-fed or dependent on diversion schemes that are frequently inadequate for realizing the maximum benefits from modern rice varieties. The large Eastern Gangetic plain has significant potential for improved water use and control, however, principally through the conjunctive use of both surface and ground water. A further problem inhibiting growth in rice yields is the greater agroclimatic and organizational diversity of India's rice production, which spans the country from north to south and throughout the eastern states. The concentration of wheat in the northwest simplified the early development of research and infrastructural support systems appropriate to high-yielding wheats. Because of their spatial and agroclimatic diversity, delivering the needed support to rice producers has been a more difficult task, although significant potential for improved rice productivity remains.

The increased cultivation of wheat in traditional rice-producing states is a consequence of the greater productivity of wheat with respect to India's most scarce factors of production—land and water. The effects of government intervention in grain distribution at the state level, a relatively poor national transportation system, and the emphasis on subsistence farming all result in a highly segmented national market for grain. These factors have not prevented the overall growth of wheat's role in the food economy, however.

Food-Grain Availability and Consumption Patterns

The expansion of wheat in both production and consumption has not significantly increased food-grain availability per capita. Some substitution has occurred among grains, however, especially as wheat began to replace production of coarse grains. As shown in table 9–4, the three-year average of total food-grain availability per capita actually decreased slightly between 1960/1962 and 1976/1978.[6] Most of the decrease was caused by reduced availability of gram (split peas) and pulses during this period. Wheat's share rose rapidly between 1960/62 and 1970/72, from less than 30 kg per capita per year to over 40 kg. During this same ten-year period, the shares of both rice and coarse cereals declined. Rice is still dominant, but wheat has replaced the combined coarse cereals as the second most important staple food.

Staple-food consumption patterns in India, especially with respect to the preferred grains rice and wheat, show major regional variations

Table 9–4
Average per Capita Net Availability of Food Grains in India, 1960–1962, 1966–1968, 1970–1972, 1976–1978
(kg per year)

	Foodgrains					
Period[a]	*Rice*	*Wheat*	*Coarse Cereals*	*All Cereals*[b]	*Pulses and Gram*	*All Food Grains*[c]
1960–1962	72.1	29.4	42.5	144.0	34.3	168.0
1966–1968[d]	60.8	34.3	41.9	137.1	24.6	154.6
1970–1972	70.7	40.4	39.9	151.0	25.7	169.3
1976–1978	67.8	42.4	38.0	148.3	23.9	165.2

Source: Ministry of Agriculture and Irrigation, Directorate of Economics and Statistics, Government of India, *Bulletin on Food Statistics,* New Delhi, 1979, p. 168.

[a]The periods are three-year averages.

[b]All cereals equals the sum of rice, wheat, and coarse cereals.

[c]All food grains equals all cereals plus pulses (lentils) and gram (split pea).

[d]The 1966–1968 period included two very bad agricultural years—the drought years of 1966 and 1967.

reflecting regional production patterns. As shown in figure 9–2, the drier western states rely heavily on wheat and other coarse grains, and rice provides less than 20 percent of the total food grains. The states along the east coast of India on the Bay of Bengal are major rice-producing and consuming areas; over one-half of all food-grain calories come from rice. The middle states on the Deccan Plateau and to the north have a mixed staple-food diet consisting of rice, wheat, and coarse grains. These trends are also shown by the regional production figures of table 9–3.

Details of regional rice and wheat consumption are presented in table 9–5. These data refer to 1973–1974 or to the period after the large increases in wheat consumption of the 1960s (see table 9–4). Several things are striking: The wheat-dominated states reported higher levels of per capita income (consumption) than other areas, and food grains constituted a smaller percentage of total consumption. In contrast, in the densely populated, rice-dominated states, the share of food grains in total consumption was significantly larger, reflecting the lower levels of per capita income. Where agroclimatic conditions are suitable, the promotion of the more resource-efficient wheat technology in these less-developed states might provide the improvements in overall agricultural productivity necessary to achieve growth in income and employment opportunities.

It is important to recognize, however, that rice remains the predominant Indian cereal and that improvements in rice technology will still lead to proportionally larger increments to national grain production than would equal improvements in the productivity of wheat or coarse-grain technol-

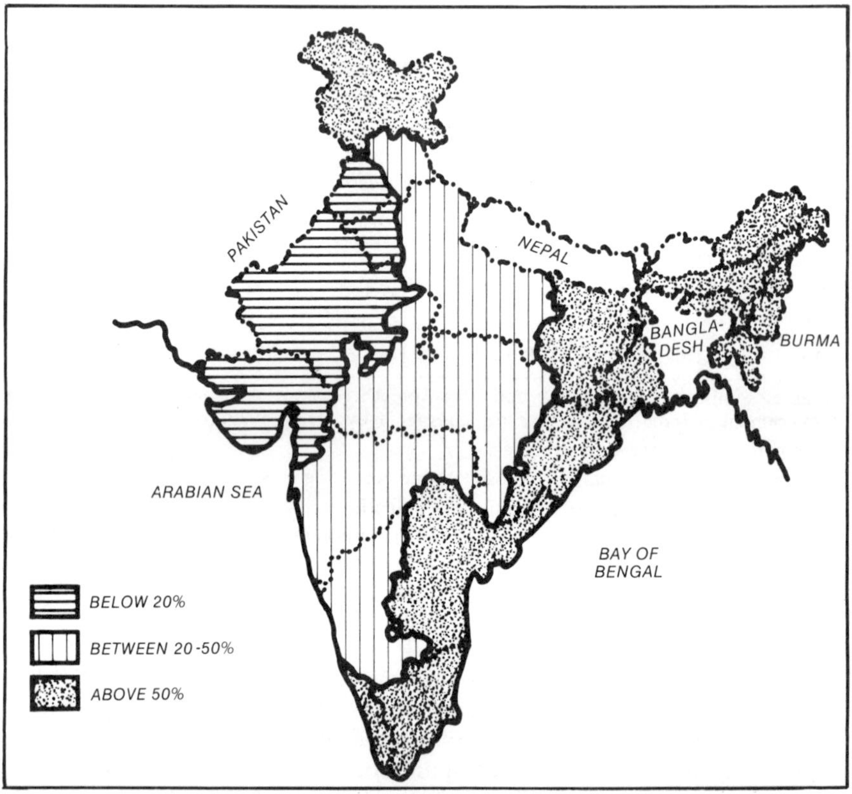

Figure 9–2. India, Showing Regional Consumption of Rice (As Percentage of Total Food Grains)

ogy. More important from the viewpoint of food security is the resilience of the technology in the face of changes in weather conditions. From table 9–1 it is clear that the critical food-grain supply shortfalls of the 1970s were induced by sudden declines in rice production. The potential returns (in the form of improvements in national grain productivity and resilience) from the expansion and upgrading of rice irrigation systems were recognized by the Indian government during the 1970s. Investments of this type, combined with appropriate price incentives and good weather, have contributed to record grain crops in 1977/1978 and 1978/1979. The improvement in productivity has been so great that even with the drought-induced curtailment in cereal production of 1979–1980, the cereal crop was considerably larger than that achieved during the equally serious droughts of the early 1970s.

If these changes in food-grain production and consumption are placed in perspective, the major change in the past decade has been the increase in

Table 9–5
Rice and Wheat Consumption Pattern in India, 1973–1974

			Rice		Wheat			
States[a]—Rice as percent of Foodgrains	*Total Monthly Per Capita Consumption (Rs)[b]*	*Food Grains as Percent of Total Consumption*	*As Percent of Total Consumption*	*As Percent of Food Grain Consumption*	*As Percent of Total Consumption*	*As Percent of Food Grain Consumption*	*Population (million) (1971 census)*	*Population Density (no/Km²)*
Rice constituting less than 20 percent of food grains								
Gujarat	57.9	39.5	6.6	16.8	11.6	29.3	26.7	136
Haryana	73.1	27.3	1.6	6.0	17.3	63.1	10.0	227
Punjab	78.2	21.7	1.8	8.3	14.1	64.8	13.6	269
Rajasthan	64.9	37.5	1.1	2.8	11.7	31.3	25.8	75
Delhi	85.6	17.7	2.1	12.1	12.8	72.5	4.1	2,738
							80.2	
Rice constituting 20–50 percent of food grains								
Himachal Pradesh	73.6	35.9	9.0	25.1	10.2	28.4	3.5	62
Karnataka	55.8	46.6	19.9	42.8	1.4	3.1	29.3	153
Madhya Pradesh	53.2	48.7	17.9	36.7	15.6	31.9	41.7	94
Maharashtra	62.0	34.9	7.6	21.9	5.3	15.3	50.4	164
Uttar Pradesh	53.1	46.8	13.1	28.1	20.6	43.9	88.3	300
							213.2	
Rice constituting more than 50 percent of food grains								
Andhra Pradesh	53.5	43.7	31.6	72.2	0.7	1.5	43.5	157
Assam	53.9	51.5	47.3	91.9	1.2	2.4	15.0	150
Bihar	57.3	59.3	33.9	57.2	11.1	18.7	56.4	324
Jammu and Kashmir	54.4	33.5	22.6	67.3	4.2	12.7	4.6	NA
Kerala	57.9	38.5	30.6	79.6	0.8	1.9	21.3	549

Table 9–5 continued

States[a]—Rice as percent of Foodgrains	Total Monthly Per Capita Consumption (Rs)[b]	Food Grains as Percent of Total Consumption	Rice: As Percent of Total Consumption	Rice: As Percent of Food Grain Consumption	Wheat: As Percent of Total Consumption	Wheat: As Percent of Food Grain Consumption	Population (million) (1971 census)	Population Density (no/Km²)
Manipur	54.9	55.1	52.9	96.2	0.1	0.1	1.1	48
Meghalaya	65.9	42.2	38.5	91.4	1.8	4.2	1.0	45
Orissa	45.1	51.9	46.1	88.8	1.5	2.9	21.9	141
Tamil Nadu	51.8	41.7	31.6	75.7	0.4	0.9	41.2	317
Tripura	53.6	44.5	41.5	93.2	0.9	2.1	1.6	149
West Bengal	55.9	47.1	36.0	76.4	7.5	16.0	44.3	504
Pondicherry	57.7	39.8	35.0	87.9	0.4	1.1	0.5	983
							251.9	
All of India	56.6	43.9	21.3	48.5	9.1	20.8	548.0	178

Note: Table is based on government of India, National Sample Survey (28th Round) data for the period October 1973 – June 1974 on household consumption. Population statistics are from government of India, Registrar General and Census Commissioner, Pocket Book of Population Statistics, 1972, reported in Majumdar, 1979b.

[a]All the states in the country have not been included.

[b]Rs 8.3 = U.S. $1.00.

the importance of wheat. Of special significance is wheat's ability to sustain production with less year-to-year variability in total output than is the case for rice. In terms of food security, this has allowed more orderly operation of government food programs (discussed later in the chapter), as well as a reduction in food-grain imports. Although weather-induced production fluctuations still exist, wheat has helped ease the impact of these fluctuations in total food-grain availability.

All of the data presented so far have been aggregated at the national or state level. Consumption is a micro phenomenon, and considerable segments of the Indian population have food consumption below the recommended levels. Since India has been successful in increasing overall food-grain supply and availability, adequate consumption levels depend on the regional availability of foods and the ability of consumers to purchase the foods they need.

Problems in Food-Grain Distribution

Most rural people obtain their staple foods directly from their own on-farm production or through local markets. Some agricultural laborers are paid in kind. Urban residents are dependent on marketed supplies, and, therefore, the procurement, distribution, and marketing of food grains are particularly important in urban areas.

The distribution of food grains in a large and poor country such as India poses special problems, most arising from the thin margin between the quantity of grain available and the amount required to meet the minimum average nutritional needs of the population. Whatever public distribution system is adopted, some degree of inequity does result, and some relatively underprivileged groups do suffer physical hardship. Gavan and Dixon (1975) estimated that the poorest 30 percent of the population consumed between 1,460 and 1,670 kcal per capita per day, significantly less than their estimate of the average minimum nutritional requirement (1,955 kcal per capita per day). Current practice by the Indian Planning Commission is to set a poverty-line income level according to minimum nutritional requirements and other basic needs. In 1978, this level was set at Rs. 61.8 (U.S. $7.45) per capita per month in rural areas and Rs. 71.3 (U.S. $8.59) per capita per month in urban areas.[7] About 46 percent of the total population of India was estimated to have earnings below this poverty line in 1977–1978.

In India, as in many developing countries, there is a widespread distrust of private entrepreneurship activity, a distrust that is most acute where food distribution is concerned.[8] Consistent with India's overall economic development strategy over the last three decades, which has emphasized centralized control of capital markets and industrialization through state-run enterprises, the distribution system adopted for grains has also been state-run and highly centralized. The principal administrative branch of the bureaucracy at the central level has been the Food Corporation of India (FCI). The FCI is responsible for international food-grain trade, storage, and interstate movements.

A complete government monopoly in grain distribution and marketing would require immense resources and is thus impractical in a country such as India. Instead, from 3 to 20 percent of all grain consumed has been either procured domestically or imported and then marketed at controlled prices by the government (table 9–6). Total public distribution has always been substantial. As early as 1952, over 6 million metric tons of food grains were handled by the public distribution system, and peaks occurred in 1966 and 1967, years of major drought and food scarcity (see table 9–6). Before 1970–1971, imports were very important in meeting distribution requirements; in the 1970s, domestic procurement increased in importance, and the central and state governments were able to build up sizable stocks. In the late 1970s, these stocks totaled almost 20 million metric tons, or enough food grains for almost two years of public distribution at current distribution rates.

The distribution system is composed of many parts: internal procurement, imports and exports, changes in stock levels, internal grain movements, and final distribution. In the 1970s, the central and state distribution system handled about 10 to 12 percent of all food grains consumed. Wheat was the major grain used in the system, both in terms of total domestic procurement and total distribution. Since the international trading price of wheat has tended to be significantly lower than that of rice, the sale of some high-value rice abroad and the emphasis on wheat in imports and distribution have acted to reduce the foreign-exchange burden associated with the government's food policy. In addition, in the past, large quantities of U.S. wheat were imported at concessional terms under the Public Law 480 Program. By adjusting the relative quantities of rice and wheat procured and imported, the government can take advantage of shifts in their relative international trading prices. Although India has not exploited this potential to the extent that China did in the early 1970s, as the numbers of people whose staple food diet constitutes a mix of rice and wheat increase, India's ability to adjust grain imports and exports as international prices change should be enhanced.

As Gavan and Dixon (1975) indicate, much of the problem of food distribution has not been due to difficulties in importing grain but rather in the management of its movement from surplus to deficit areas across the country.[9] Production and consumption are frequently spatially separated. Between 1976 and 1978, for example, the state of Punjab alone provided 6

Table 9–6
Internal Procurement, Public Distribution, and Closing Stocks in India, 1952–1978
(1,000 tons)

	Internal Procurement					
Year	Total	Percent Wheat	Total Public Distribution (Central and State)	As Percent of Net Food Grain Availability	Total Closing Stocks	Per Capita Net Availability of Food Grains (kg/year)
1952	3,477	—	6,800	13.1	1,948	140.7
1954	1,430	—	2,154	3.4	1,667	167.1
1956	37	—	2,082	3.3	319	157.6
1958	526	—	3,980	6.4	906	149.2
1960	1,275	—	4,937	6.9	2,801	164.6
1962	479	—	4,365	5.7	2,281	168.2
1964	1,430	—	8,665	11.1	1,016	165.4
1966	4,009	—	14,085	19.2	2,216	149.0
1967	4,462	—	13,166	17.8	1,956	146.5
1968	6,805	—	10,221	11.8	3,991	168.4
1970	6,714	47.4	8,841	9.9	5,569	166.1
1971	8,857	57.4	7,816	8.3	8,137	171.1
1972	7,665	65.5	10,487 + 909[a]	10.9	3,443	170.7
1973	8,424	53.8	11,414	12.9	3,134	154.2
1974	5,645	33.4	10,790	11.1	2,730	164.6
1975	9,563	42.9	11,253	12.6	8,289	148.4
1976	12,853	51.5	9,174	9.0	19,032	165.7
1977	9,974	51.8	11,729	11.8	17,406	158.7
1978	11,098	49.3	10,183	9.3	17,136	171.1

Source: Ministry of Agriculture and Irrigation, Directorate of Economics and Statistics, Government of India, *Bulletin on Food Statistics,* New Delhi, 1979, tables 4, 11.
[a]Sent to Bangladesh.

million metric tons of rice and 9.4 million tons of wheat to the internal procurement system and received back less than 20,000 tons of rice and 730,000 tons of wheat from the food distribution system (Government of India 1979a, p. 29). In fact, since 1970, about 50 percent or more of total domestic food-grain procurement has come from Haryana and the Punjab.

The physical problems with transporting food grains over long distances and the political problems in crossing state boundaries can be major. For example, in 1973, the prevailing rapid inflation and pessimism regarding economic prospects provided incentives to hoard grain. These incentives were then exacerbated by the government's attempts to procure at less-than-market prices. Political constraints to the movement of grain from some surplus states to deficit states led to severe shortages in Gujarat, Madhya Pradesh, Orissa, Rajasthan, and West Bengal. Similar problems also developed in Gujarat during the drought of 1975, resulting in food riots and the dissolution of the state government.

Central to the public food-distribution system is the sale of grains through fair-price shops located throughout the country. Their number has increased from 122,000 in 1970 to over 235,000 today, or, in theory, one shop for every 2,500 people (Government of India 1979a, p. 55). Fair-price shops are most common in urban areas (especially Bombay and Calcutta), which is not surprising given the total dependence of the urban population on marketed grains. Some states have also undertaken extensive rural food-security schemes.[10] Despite this attention to the needs of urban consumers, there is evidence that some truly needy urban dwellers still do not have access to government food supplies. One reason for this failure has been the regulation requiring that ration-card holders have a fixed residence, thereby rendering the cards inaccessible to street and slum dwellers.[11]

A further means of distributing food to the needy is the Food for Work Program. This activity has been largely funded by the United Nations, although it has received support from the Indian government. It functions as a public-works program in all respects except that wages are paid in the form of imported grain. Since 1977, the government of India has augmented this international scheme with a program to further improve rural infrastructure. Labor is compensated with imported and procured wheat and *milo* (sorghum). The cost of imports and procurement are borne by the federal government, although the food is distributed by the states. In 1979, a planning commission evaluation of this program surveyed its performance over 80 villages in 10 states, finding that despite irregular arrivals of the grain for distribution, significant improvements in the level of living of the most underprivileged had been achieved.[12] Although activities of this type augment local grain supplies and contribute to the abatement of poverty, their scale is too small to have a significant effect on the wider problem of inadequate food consumption. Mellor (1976) compares planned public-works expenditures with the size of the transfer that would be required to raise India's poor to the level of the poverty line predetermined by the planning commission. He concludes that less than 3 percent of the required transfer might be achieved in this way.

The food distribution system in India is thus a blend of the following: on-farm consumption and private marketing (85 percent of total consumption), a public procurement and rationing system (10 to 12 percent), and public-works programs. Despite the problems encountered in each, there is little argument that a net improvement in food security for the poor has in fact resulted from government activities. What is in greater dispute is the efficiency of the system. The cost of the procurement and ration-shop program is very high, especially in those years when national food supplies fall short of the long-run trend. The gap between procurement and ration-shop prices widens in these years and, at the same time, the government has to carry the cost of increased imports.[13]

Regardless of the food-security system adopted, the twin problems of adequate food-grain supply and effective demand remain. India has made dramatic progress in increasing the overall level of food-grain production and decreasing the weather-induced variations, largely through improved water control. Government-held stocks have been at record high levels, and sizable rice and wheat exports have taken place.[14] The problem of creating effective demand has been harder to solve. Poverty and malnutrition still exist, and large numbers of people lack the purchasing power to meet their basic nutritional needs. The creation of more productive jobs in agriculture, industry, and the service sector is crucial for ensuring that effective demand will be adequate. In the longer run, continued improvements in agricultural productivity are essential both to raise food consumption levels and to achieve sustained economic development.

The Long-Term Remedy: Employment-Oriented Economic Growth

Despite almost three decades of planning, India's real income per capita has shown sluggish improvement, averaging 1.4 percent per year between 1960 and 1979. A major problem has been population growth; India's population increased by 220 million people during the past twenty years. Although the rate of population growth fell from 2.3 percent per year during the 1960s to 2.1 percent per year during the 1970s, the annual net increase continues to be of the order of 13.8 million, or about the size of the entire population of Australia, Malaysia, or Sri Lanka (World Bank 1981). Even with the continuance of the gradual decline in fertility observed in the1970s, India's population has been projected to grow to about 1 billion by the end of the century and to ultimately stabilize at about 1.6 billion.[15] In order to reduce poverty and increase nutritional well-being, the strategy chosen for economic development must provide access to income through employment to at least one-half of this immense population.

In the past, India's economic development strategy emphasized capital intensive industrial growth. Domestic resources were combined with foreign aid and invested primarily in large- and medium-sized enterprises engaged in the production of fuels, electricity, metals, and chemical products for industrial use. The share of investment, value-added, and employment in smaller scale, and more labor-intensive industries producing primarily consumer goods for domestic consumption or export, all declined from 1950 through the mid-1960s. Two especially labor-intensive industries—textiles and food processing—suffered significant declines in their shares of investment and value-added during these years, despite their employment of more than 40 percent of the labor force in manufacturing.[16]

The average annual growth rate of Indian industry was 5.5 percent in the 1960s and 4.4 percent in the 1970s or over twice that in agriculture. The share of employment by sector did not change, however. In 1960, only 11 percent of the total population was employed in industry and 74 percent in agriculture; twenty years later the figures were almost identical: 11 percent in industry and 71 percent in agriculture (World Bank 1981). While many more people have been employed in both sectors as the total population has grown, the modern industrial sector has not increased its employment in proportion to its increased role in the economy. In terms of food security, therefore, rapid industrial growth has had a limited impact on employment generation and the consequent creation of effective demand for food. The more sluggish agricultural sector has had to provide jobs for the bulk of the increase in the labor force, and these have tended to be low-paying and low-productivity jobs.

Two other characteristics of India's early development strategy were (1) the emphasis on self-sufficiency in industrial and consumer goods production and (2) the only limited attempts to realize benefits from India's comparative advantage in labor-intensive products in the international market. This led to very tight foreign-exchange controls, these foreign-exchange shortages in turn constrained food imports in deficit years. In more recent years, greater emphasis on employment generation has characterized Indian planning; policies emphasizing the promotion of labor-intensive exports are now being considered (Raipuria 1980). Such policies are necessary elements of any long-run strategy for the alleviation of poverty.

In the medium term, however, the income of India's poor majority will continue to depend on agriculture. A further element necessary to the strategy for poverty reduction is therefore a set of policies designed to improve the productivity of the most scarce resources: land and water. As Mellor (1976) argues, advances in agricultural technology not only improve the overall supply of food but also increase income to cultivator classes, thereby boosting the demand for nonagricultural consumer goods. This results in expanded employment of wage labor and, subsequently, favorable growth in the demand for food and other agricultural products. Larger wage incomes should then lead to increased demand for highly income-elastic labor-intensive agricultural products such as vegetables, fruits, nuts, and dairy products, thereby resulting in the further absorption of rural labor. Increased diversification of agricultural activity, combined with improved access to jobs in decentralized manufacturing industries, will help moderate the effects of overemployment in rural areas during certain seasonal periods and underemployment at nonpeak times.

Thus an employment-generating strategy is required that emphasizes support to both agriculture and industry. Agriculture can be supported through reliable supplies of fertilizers and other inputs, improved water control, expanded research and training, and favorable price policies. Labor-intensive manufacturing can be supported by the improvements in infrastructure required for the maintenance of a competitive system of small-scale enterprises. In addition, exports serve to provide an expanded market for manufactured products and, at the same time, to mitigate any shortage in foreign exchange that might limit access to necessary imports such as petroleum and, in the event of weather-induced supply disturbances, international food-grain supplies.

India's mass poverty problem cannot be solved quickly, however. In the Draft Five Year Plan for 1978–1983, the target improvement in food consumption by those below the poverty line would eliminate 75 percent of their prior deficiency relative to minimum nutritional requirements.[17] By 1987–1988, however—even with full employment—planning commission studies indicate that the eradication of povery is an impossible task.[18] Some further improvement in the incomes of the rural landless might be achieved through the more vigorous pursuit of land reform. Majumdar (1979a) shows that a successful land reform program, wherein 10.5 million landless families would receive 1 acre (0.47 hectare) each of surplus land, would reduce the Gini coefficient of food consumption inequality by about 0.06. This result, however, would not raise to the poverty line the average income of those currently below it.

A long-term perspective plan has been developed by the government of India to examine the pattern of land use that will be necessary to provide sufficient food production beyond this century, when the population is expected to stabilize. The plan is based on the results of a linear programming model designed to address a range of long-run planning problems, including the transition from dependence on nonrenewable energy and on other resources to renewable alternatives.[19] By using estimates of India's ultimate capacity for land and water use based on the Report of the National Commission on Agriculture (1976), it is possible to derive from the model corresponding estimates of the potential for future food-grain production. The projections are mixed and some show India producing large exportable surpluses, while other scenarios point to serious food-grain production problems. The end result in 20 or 50 years will depend on many variables. The use of Fertilizer and HYVs, the progress in improving irrigation systems, the production mix between rice and wheat, intensity of multiple cropping, and the weather. If production gains continue to be realized, they will be crucial in raising the average level of rural and urban income and thereby in increasing food-grain consumption significantly above the presently defined poverty line by the end of the century.

Summary

The dependence of three-quarters of India's population on agricultural income, the relatively low labor productivity in Indian agriculture, and the random effects of weather on agricultural production and income all contribute to widespread rural poverty and undernourishment in average years and to serious nutritional problems in years of unfavorable weather.[20] Furthermore, India's large physical size, its dispersed rural population, and its poor infrastructure contribute to the occurrence of local shortfalls in food supply even in years when the country as a whole has a normal or above-average grain supply. Obviously, food security is still a major concern in India.

Food security can be approached from two directions: (1) assuring that adequate supplies of food grains are available within the country and (2) assuring that incomes are sufficient to ensure effective demand. India has made remarkable progress on the supply side. Whereas food-grain production fluctuated around a level of just under 100 million metric tons between 1968 and 1975, the past five years have seen major improvements and rapid growth in total output. The rapid gains in wheat and, to a lesser extent, rice production have more than offset the fluctuations in coarse cereals and stagnating pulse production.

Several factors have contributed to this rising level of productivity, including infrastructure investments, government price policies, and the use of new varieties and the required agricultural inputs. The role of the high-yielding varieties, especially for wheat, has been very important. When weather is good and when water and fertilizer are adequate, rice and wheat HYVs yield up to twice as much as traditional varieties. In fact, during the past decade the area sown to cereals has not increased significantly, and total production advances are largely due to the increasing share of that area planted to HYVs (see table 9–1).

Sizable food-grain imports, a feature of Indian food-security planning for almost thirty years, have been largely eliminated, and exports of rice and wheat have taken place. Food-grain imports are still occasionally required when droughts affect production and domestic procurement. Government grain stocks now average between 15 and 20 million metric tons, compared to the levels ranging between 2 and 3 million tons, which have been common in the past (see table 9–6).

The creation of an effective demand for food grains and other foods has been a greater problem than that of increasing their total availability. Government food programs in India use fair-price shops and other means to distribute about 10 percent of the total food grain consumed. These programs are heavily concentrated in urban areas. In order to meet basic nutritional needs, however, adequate supplies have to be available in all parts of the country, and poor people must have adequate incomes (or entitlements) to translate need into effective demand.

Since government food-grain distribution can only meet a small part of the total food-grain demand, most people have to rely on either their own food production or their ability to purchase foods in local markets. Employment generation and income growth, especially for the poorest groups, will therefore be major factors in assuring food security in India. Government studies have found that significant shares of both the urban and rural populations fall below the officially defined poverty line. Moreover, the food security of this group is especially vulnerable to local production shortfalls and price increases. Both the public and private sectors must cooperate in the procurement and movement of foods from surplus to deficit areas.

Agricultural growth should lead to higher rural incomes. A major effort to expand labor-intensive, nonagricultural employment is essential, however, to improve overall food security. More employment opportunities in higher-productivity jobs are needed, the attainment of which will necessitate that manufacturing and processing output be geared to both the domestic and international markets. An ultimate goal is widely distributed self-sustaining economic development, whereby agricultural production and domestic demand both grow rapidly and reinforce one another. India's rapid population growth makes this goal more difficult to achieve. A continuation of the important increases in food-grain production of the past few years, however, combined with further efforts to improve effective demand should make its achievement attainable while at the same time making possible increased food security for India's poor.

Notes

1. See the *World Development Report, 1981* published by the World Bank (1981) for a general discussion of global trends, as well as for the useful World Development Indicators found in the annex. The indicators compare one hundred twenty four countries in a series of tables.

2. See tables 2, 3, and 19 of the *World Development Report, 1981*, Annex (World Bank 1981).

3. During the 1960s, the total area cultivated in wheat grew at 2.3 percent per year, compared with 1.0 percent per year for rice. Irrigated wheat grew at 6.4 percent per year, compared to 1.0 percent per year for rice. See Mellor (1976), P. 52.

4. Rice is more dependent on irrigation and precise water control than is wheat; many wheat-growing areas, especially in Haryana and the Punjab, have benefited from the rapid adoption of tubewells to supply irriga-

tion water to a greater extent than in rice areas. Tubewells, while costly to install and operate, have provided a greater degree of control over water timing and supply than the large irrigation systems common in rice-growing areas. Consequently, average rice yields have fluctuated with year-to-year variation in the quantity and distribution of rainfall.

5. During the 1970/71 to 1979/80 period, each of the major cereal shortfalls was associated with a major drop in rice production: 1972/73, 1974/75, 1976/77, and 1979/80 (table 9–1). Coarse grains, which usually depend on rainfall, also displayed a similar pattern. The per capita net availability of food grain data display the same trend (see table 9–6). For more information on Indian food grain production and on consumption data, see Sarma, Roy, and George (1979).

6. Population grew dramatically during this period. In 1961, the all-India population was 439 million; in 1978 it was estimated at 638 million—a 45 percent increase (Government of India 1979a). Yearly per capita food grain availability is shown in table 9–6.

7. See Government of India, Planning Commission (1978). A number of studies have addressed the question of poverty in India, including the classic study by Dandekar and Rath (1971). Two recent presidential addresses by incoming Presidents of the Indian Society of Agricultural Economics have considered food-security issues: B.S. Minhas (1976) and C.H. Shah (1980). The Shah paper presents some interesting concepts and contains an extensive bibliography.

8. See Griffin and James (1978).

9. See also Rao (1977).

10. A successful case is the program adopted in the relatively poor but progressive state of Kerala in the Southwest. This program is said to reach 97 percent of the combined urban and rural population. See George (1979) and Kumar (1979).

11. See Srinivasan (1974).

12. See Government of India, Planning Commission, Program Evaluation Organization (1979).

13. Donaldson and Lewis (1981) quote estimates of the cost of government distribution programs of between U.S. $75 and U.S. $100 per metric ton of grain distributed. Urban fair-price shops are frequently used by both rich and poor consumers (Wall 1978). Three factors tend to ensure that low-income consumers receive most of the benefits: the location of fair-price shops in poor neighborhoods, long lines, and the lower quality of grain provided when compared to that of open markets.

14. Shlomo Reutlinger argues in chapter 2 that the relatively high cost of maintaining large emergency reserves renders more attractive the option of importing the quantity of grain needed to stabilize domestic supplies. In the past few years, India's grain exports have been considerable: 400,000 to

700,000 metric tons of wheat and similar quantities of rice. Some of the rice exports have been part of a rice-for-petroleum barter arrangement with the USSR (USDA 1981a). Weather-induced production fluctuations still necessitate imports. In July 1981, India announced its first major wheat imports since 1977 with the purchase of 1.5 million tons from the United States (USDA 1981b, p. 31). This wheat will be used to rebuild government stocks, depleted by the effects of the 1979 drought and poor 1981 procurement.

15. See World Bank (1981), annex, table 17. The stable population projected by the Government of India, Planning Commission (1979b) is 1.3 billion, significantly below the estimate published by the World Bank.

16. Mellor (1976) estimates that a more balanced investment strategy could have achieved 2.3 times as much employment in manufacturing industries as was actually achieved by the mid-1960s.

17. See Government of India, Planning Commission (1978 and 1979a).

18. See Alagh and Majumdar (1978).

19. The model used to develop the Perspective Plan is described in detail in Majumdar (1979b).

20. There is a saying that India's budget is "a monsoon gamble." In many ways, this is true: a poor monsoon usually most seriously affects the *kharif* (summer) rice crop and consequently grain production falls. In order to meet public distribution requirements, government stocks are depleted, and imports are thus usually required, thereby placing large, and unbudgeted, demands on scarce foreign exchange. A good monsoon (and resulting good grain crops) reverses these effects: domestic procurement is easier, government stocks can be increased, and grain exports are sometimes possible.

Bibliography

Alagh, Y.K., and Majumdar, K.C. 1978. "The Input-Output Model Used for the 1978–83 Draft Plan—A Brief Outline." Paper presented to the Sixth Input-Output Conference, Bombay, June.

Dandekar, V.M., and Rath, N. 1971. *Poverty in India,* Bombay: Indian School of Political Economy.

Donaldson, G., and Lewis, C. 1981. "Food Security in Developing Countries—The Story of the 1970s." Mimeo World Bank, June.

Gavan, J.D., and Dixon, J.A. 1975. "India: A Perspective on the Food Situation." In *Food: Politics, Economics, Nutrition and Research* Ed. P.H. Abelson. Washington, D.C.: American Association for the Advancement of Science and *Science* 188 (May): 541–549.

George, P.S. 1979. "Public Distribution of Foodgrains in Kerala—Income Distribution Implications and Effectiveness." Research Report No. 7, Washington, D.C.: International Food Policy Research Institute.

Government of India. 1976. *Report of the National Commission on Agriculture,* New Delhi.

Government of India, Ministry of Agriculture and Irrigation, Directorate of Economics and Statistics. 1979a. *Bulletin on Food Statistics,* New Delhi.

———. 1979b. *Estimates of Area and Production of Foodgrains,* New Delhi.

Government of India, Ministry of Food and Agriculture. 1967. *Report of the Agricultural Prices Commission on Price Policy for Kharif Cereals in the 1965–66 Season,* New Delhi.

Government of India, Planning Commission. 1978. *Draft Sixth Five Year Plan, 1978–83 (revised),* New Delhi.

———. 1979a. *Interim Report of the Task Force on Projections of Minimum Needs and Effective Consumption Demands,* New Delhi.

———. 1979b. *Interim Report of the Working Group on Population Policy,* New Delhi, March.

Government of India, Program Evaluation Organisation. 1979. "Quick Evaluation Study of the Food for Work Programme." New Delhi.

Griffin, K., and James, J. 1978. "Supply Management Problems in the Context of a Basic Needs Strategy." Report prepared for the World Bank, February.

International Food Policy Research Institute (IFPRI). 1977. "Food Needs of Developing Countries: Projections of Production and Consumption to 1990." Research Report No. 3, Washington, D.C.

Kumar, S.K. 1979. "Impact of Subsidized Rice on Food Consumption and Nutrition in Kerala." Research Report No. 5, International Food Policy Research Institute, (IFPRI), Washington, D.C.

Lele, U. 1971. *Foodgrain Marketing in India: Private Performance and Public Policy.* Ithaca, N. Y.: Cornell University Press.

Lipton, M. 1977. *Why the Poor People Stay Poor.* Temple Smith.

Majumdar, K.C. 1979a. "Reduction of Disparity in Private Consumption, in Draft Five-Year Plan for 1978–83." Paper presented to the 18th Indian Econometric Conference, Kashmir, May.

Majumdar, K.C. 1979b. "Some Aspects of Food Security in India." Paper presented at the Working Group Meeting on Food Security in Asia and the Pacific, East-West Resource Systems Institute, East-West Center, Honolulu, June.

Mellor, J.W. 1976. *The New Economics of Growth—A Strategy for India and the Developing World.* Ithaca N.Y.: Cornell University Press.

Minhas, B.S. 1976. "Towards National Food Security." *Indian Journal of Agricultural Economics* 31, no. 4:8–19.

Myrdal, G. 1976. "Environment and Economic Growth." Institute of International Economic Studies Seminar Paper No. 57, Stockholm.

Narain, D., and Roy, S. 1980. "Impact of Irrigation and Labor Availability on Multiple Cropping: A Case Study of India." Research Report No. 20, International Food Policy Research Institute (IFPRI), Washington, D.C.

Raipuria, K.M. 1980. "Export-Led Growth: India's Strategy and Policy Options for the Eighties." Indian Institute of Foreign Trade, New Delhi, *Foreign Trade Review,* April-June. P. 42–84.

Rao, C.H.H. 1977. "Agricultural Growth and Rural Poverty," *Economic and Political Weekly,* Vol 12.

Sarma, J.S., Roy, S., and George, P.S. 1979. "Two Analyses of Indian Foodgrain Production and Consumption Data." Research Report No. 12, International Food Policy Research Institute (IFPRI), Washington, D.C.

Sen, A.K. 1977. "Starvation and Exchange Entitlements: A General Approach and its Application to the Bengal Famine." *Cambridge Journal of Economics* 1, no. 1, March.

Shah, C.H. 1980. "Food Preferences and Nutrition: A Perspective on Poverty in Less Developed Countries." *Indian Journal of Agricultural Economics* 35, no. 1:1–39.

Srinivasan, T.N. 1974. "Income Distribution: A Survey of Policy Aspects." In *Poverty and Income Distribution in India,* Ed. P.K. Bardhan and T.N. Srinivasan. Calcutta.

United States Department of Agriculture (USDA), Economics and Statistics Service. 1981a. *Agricultural Situation: Asia, Review of 1980 and Outlook for 1981.* Supplement 2 to WAS-24, Washington, D.C.

United States Department of Agriculture (USDA), Economic Research Service. 1981b. *World Agriculture: Outlook and Situation.* WAS-26, Washington, D.C.

United States Department of Agriculture (USDA), Economics, Statistics, and Cooperatives Service. 1980. *Agricultural Situation: Asia, Review of 1979 and Outlook for 1980.* Supplement 2 to WAS-21, Washington, D.C.

Wagstaff, H. 1979. "Food Policies and Prospects—Insights from Global Modeling." *Food Policy,* August. Pp. 155–168.

Wall, J. 1978. "Foodgrain Management: Pricing, Procurement, Distribution, Import and Storage Policy." In *India: Occasional Papers,* World Bank Staff Working Paper No. 279, Washington, D.C. November.

World Bank. 1981. *World Development Report,* Washington, D.C.

10 The Problem of Food Security in Japan

Saburo Yamada

Continuous and stable supplies of many goods and services are essential to the health of society. Of these goods and services, staple foods are among the most indispensable. They are of agricultural origin, leaving industrial societies like Japan without the option of manufacturing synthetic substitutes. Thus, in the event of scarcity, a significant reallocation of resources is required to ensure that sufficient supplies are available. Yet as total income grows, the demand for staple foods increases at a slower and declining rate. Consequently, the importance of staple-food supplies as a national-security issue becomes evident only in times when shortages threaten.

This chapter examines the problem facing Japanese policymakers in providing insurance against the possibility of a disruptive shortfall in national staple-food supplies and the adverse consequences of such a shortfall for Japanese consumers. A variety of possible supply disturbances are considered and alternative policy responses reviewed that would ensure access to sufficient quantities of staple foods throughout Japan. The first part of the discussion outlines trends in Japan's food production and imports. Next, Japan's vulnerability to disturbances in international food markets or in international trade regarding essential factors of Japan's food production, such as petroleum, is detailed. Then, policy measures for food-crisis avoidance or mitigation are reviewed in the context of Japan's overall national security. Specific measures Japan should take to avoid a food crisis are then covered. The chapter closes with a review of policies needed during a food crisis, should it occur.

Trends in Japan's Food Supply, Demand, and Import Dependence

Rapid economic growth since the 1960s has been associated with the conversion of Japan's food system from its earlier emphasis on staples

This paper is translated, edited, and revised with the consent of the publisher from an earlier manuscript, Wagakunino Shokuryo-mondai to Anzenhosho (Food Problems and Food Security in Japan), *Wagakuni Anzenhosho Nikansuru Kenkyukai Hokoku* (Report on Security Problems in Japan), Nihon Keizai Chosa Kyogikai (Japan Economic Research Institute), Tokyo, March 1980. Thanks are due to Hideki Uehara for his assistance in translation and to Rod Tyers for his help in revising an earlier draft.

(principally rice) to its present form, which focuses on high-value livestock products. Since Japan is poorly endowed with the resources required to provide feed for a growing livestock industry, the govenment has permitted producers and formula-feed manufacturers relatively unrestricted access to the international markets for cereals. The result has been a correspondingly rapid growth in imports of feed grains, soybeans, and other feed components (table 10–1). Domestic livestock production has still not kept pace with demand, and consequently, imports of livestock products have also grown rapidly. Their share of total agricultural imports rose by 1978 to 23 percent—equal to that for grains.

Except for a few commodities such as rice, final consumption is heavily dependent on imports. For the reasons already discussed, this is most pronounced in the cases of wheat, barley, corn, and soybeans (table 10–2). The apparently high rates of self-sufficiency implied by the consumption and trade statistics for refined sugar and livestock products disguise considerable dependence on imports of the principal raw materials: raw sugar and feeds. This high level of dependence on imports leaves Japan vulnerable to disturbances in international markets that might limit access to imports and that could be beyond Japan's powers of influence. Furthermore, this vulnerability to international-market conditions may be further exacerbated by the concentration of 60 percent of Japan's agricultural imports among only three suppliers: Australia, Canada, and most important, the United States.

Table 10–1
Trends in Japan's Agricultural Imports

	Import Value (million U.S. $)			*Share (%)*		
	1960	*1970*	*1978*	*1960*	*1970*	*1978*
Total agricultural imports	865	3,156	13,372	100	100	100
Total grain	291	1,046	3,038	34	33	23
Livestock products	132	448	3,015	15	14	23
Oils and fats[a]	186	542	1,769	22	17	13
Sugar	122	339	691	14	11	5
Other	134	781	4,859	15	25	36

Note: Import value statistics are drawn from Ministry of Finance, Customs Clearance Statistics for the years shown.

[a]Includes soybean imports.

Table 10–2
Japan's Food Balance Sheet for 1977
(thousand metric tons)

Commodity	Domestic Production	Foreign Trade: Imports	Foreign Trade: Exports	Stock Changes	Consumption
Total grains	13,585	22,709	104	2,391	33,799
Rice	13,095	71	100	1,583	11,483
Wheat	236	5,662	4	133	5,761
Barley	167	2,238	—	94	2,311
Rye	39	—	—	−2	41
Corn	8	9,313	—	597	8,724
Soybeans	111	3,602	—	−21	3,734
Vegetables	16,464	309	4	—	16,769
Fruits	6,588	1,473	87	173	7,801
Meat	2,552	769	3	−11	3,329
Eggs	1,901	59	—	—	1,960
Dairy products	5,847	1,016	—	178	6,685
Fish	10,065	1,848	852	742	10,319
Refined sugar	3,077	—	2	52	3,023
Vegetable oils	1,119	223	11	−9	1,340
Animal fats	362	192	116	−5	443

Source: Government of Japan Ministry of Agriculture, Forestry, and Fisheries (MAFF), 1977–1978.

Sources and Extent of Vulnerability to International-Market Disturbances

Although Japan faces a variety of potential sources of vulnerability to food-supply disruption, this discussion focuses on two themes underlying most of the public concern with food security. The first is the declining level of overall food self-sufficiency, coupled with increasing reliance on a single supplier. The second is a concern with the dependence of Japan's domestic food production on petroleum, another important raw material derived almost entirely from imports.

The Decline in Food Self-Sufficiency

It is doubtful that there could ever be a food shortage as acute as that experienced during and immediately after World War II. Yet even at that time, serious declines in the consumption of the basic nutritional components were avoided. Since then, however, the expansion of Japan's agricultural resource base has not kept pace with population growth and changing demands for food together with increases in income. The resulting decline in overall food self-sufficiency is an index of the increasing difficulty the country would face were food supplies ever again to be restricted to similar levels.

The aggregate food self-sufficiency ratio may be measured in a number of ways, three of which are illustrated in table 10–3.[1] The ratios for aggregate edible agricultural products and aggregate food include both livestock and fishery products. They are biased upward since they do not

Table 10–3
Trends in Food Self-Sufficiency in Japan
(unit percent)

	1960	*1970*	*1977*
Aggregated edible agricultural products self-sufficiency ratio[a]	90	76	71
Original calorie self-sufficiency ratio[b]	78	56	46
Aggregated food self-sufficiency ratio[c]	93	81	72
Self-sufficiency ratios for major foods[d]			
Total grain	83	48	40
Principal edible grains	90	79	77
Rice	102	106	114
Wheat	39	9	2
Soybeans	28	4	4
Fruits	100	84	84
Eggs	101	97	97
Dairy products	89	89	87
Meat[e]	91	89	77
Sugar[f]	18	23	20
Concentrated livestock feed[f]	67	33	25

Note: Self-sufficiency ratios for specific foods in 1960 and 1970 are based on MAFF statistics. Estimates of original calorie contents for these years are drawn from Norintokei Kyokai (1973), however. All estimates for 1977 are based on the author's calculations. Statistics for 1977 are drawn from MAFF (1977).

[a](Domestic production ÷ domestic consumption) × 100.

[b][$\sum$ (nonlivestock product calories × product self-sufficiency ratio) + $\sum$ (livestock product calories × product self-sufficiency ratio × feed calorie efficiency × feed self-sufficiency ratio)] × 100 / [total nonlivestock calories + livestock product calories × feed calorie efficiency]. Feed calorie efficiency is the ratio of the calorie content of the livestock product and the calorie content of all feeds used to produce it. A value of 7 percent is used in this calculation.

[c]This ratio includes fisheries products.

[d](Domestic production ÷ domestic consumption) × 100.

[e]Whale meat is excluded.

[f]1977 values are based on 1976 data.

account for the dependence of the livestock and fisheries industries on imported feeds. On the other hand, the original calorie self-sufficiency ratio is biased downward since both numerator and denominator include the calorific value of livestock feed, resulting in a heavy weighting on livestock-product self-sufficiency.

A more accurate method would not convert all livestock products consumed into original calories but would account for imported livestock products in terms of final calories only. When this method is used, the result for 1977 is 64 percent (including fishery products). The average of the three aggregate measures listed in table 10–3 is 59 percent. Thus it is clear that food self-sufficiency has declined markedly since 1960, to a point where Japan depends for about 40 percent of its staple-food supply on foreign countries whose export policies are largely beyond Japan's influence. The low self-sufficiency ratio for grains is of particular concern. The level of 40 percent in 1977 is below that for the United Kingdom prior to its entry into the European Economic Community (EEC), when 52 percent of its grain consumption was produced domestically.[2]

The Energy Intensity of Agriculture

The agricultural sector, which once depended primarily on land, human labor, and animal power, now depends heavily on advanced technology. Stable supplies of petroleum have become indispensable for the manufacture of fertilizers, for running agricultural machinery, and for heating greenhouses for winter vegetable cultivation. Petroleum is also used in food transportation and processing, as well as indirectly in the manufacture of agricultural machinery and transportation equipment. Greenhouse covers are made from vinyl sheets, which are also manufactured from imported petroleum. Thus to assess the vulnerability of Japan's food system to disturbances in the international petroleum market, it is necessary to undertake the difficult task of assembling a comprehensive energy account.

Such an account has been estimated by Udagawa (1978) for Japan's rice production (table 10–4). From these results it is clear that rice-production technology has become more energy intensive; the energy devoted to rice in 1950 would produce less than one-third of the food energy produced than if the technology of 1974 were used. More important, four times as much petroleum was required in 1974 to produce each calorie of food energy than was required in 1950. Petroleum use in rice production per cultivated hectare has correspondingly increased sixfold.

The production of other food commodities is also highly energy intensive. Estimates of petroleum energy per unit of food-energy output have

Table 10–4
Input and Output Energy in Rice Production

	1950	*1960*	*1970*	*1974*
Total energy input (10,000 kcal/ha)	914	1,942	3,696	4,701
Petroleum energy input[a]	756	1,825	3,621	4,641
Energy content of rice product	1,160	1,590	1,730	1,770
Output energy/input energy ratio	1.27	0.82	0.46	0.38
Petroleum input energy used per kcal of rice production	0.65	1.15	2.09	2.62

[a]Petroleum energy input includes fuel and petroleum-based electricity for operating machinery and for the manufacture of fertilizers and agricultural chemicals. Petroleum energy used in the manufacture of machinery and farm implements is also included.

been derived using methods different from that of Udagawa. The resulting values range from 2.0 for milk, 2.5 for pork, 3.0 for eggs and fruits, to 5.0 for beef, and 6.0 for pelagic fish.[3] This heavy dependence of Japan's domestic-food production on imported petroleum indicates the illusory nature of the self-sufficiency ratios derived in the previous discussion. Without a major reallocation of domestic energy resources, an international disturbance restricting Japan's access to petroleum supplies would drastically lower domestic-food-production potential.

Potential Impact of Reduced Food Imports on Domestic Consumption

The impact of a possible shortfall in Japan's access to imported food has been an important factor in the evolution of agricultural policy since the 1940s. It has made political action by farm groups in favor of increased protection from foreign competition less costly, resulting in support prices for many farm products well above border prices. In this context, the short-lived soybean embargo by the United States in 1973 was a particularly symbolic event, despite the minimal effects on domestic soybean consumption that actually resulted. For an objective assessment of Japan's vulnerability to a potential import shortfall, it is useful to estimate the impact on food-energy intake due to reductions of various sizes in the supply of food from abroad.

Assuming initially that there would be no domestic-supply response to the import shortfall, I have estimated the changes in overall food-energy consumption and dietary composition that would have accompanied reductions in all food imports by 10, 20, 50, and 100 percent had they occurred in 1977 (table 10–5). A complete cutoff in supplies from abroad results in a change in the average food consumption mix that depends only

Table 10–5
Impact of Reduced Imports on Food-Energy Consumption

Commodity	*Domestic Consumption (1,000 tons)*	*Imports (1,000 tons)*	*Share of Imports in Consumption (%)*	*Food-Energy Consumption per capita (cal/day) after reduction of imports by* 0%	10%	20%	50%	100%
Rice	11,483	0	0	802	802	802	802	802
Wheat	5,761	5,658	98	309	279	249	158	7
Barley	2,352	2,238	95	9	8	7	5	0
Corn	8,724	9,313	100	12	11	10	6	0
Soybean	3,734	3,602	96	58	52	47	30	2
Meat	3,329	766	23	127	124	121	113	98
Dairy products	2,989	1,016	34	41	40	38	20	27
Fish	7,504	328	4	101	101	100	99	97
Fishmeal and fertilizer made from fishmeal	2,815	667	24	—	—	—	—	—
Fats and oils	1,783	288	16	289	284	280	266	243
Eggs	1,960	59	3	62	62	62	61	60
Drinking milk	3,575	0	0	50	50	50	50	50
Sugar	3,023	(3,023)[a]	100	272	250	228	163	54
Other[b]	—			358	358	358	358	358
Nominal Total (A)				2,490 (100%)	2,421 (97%)	2,352 (94%)	2,131 (86%)	1,798 (72%)
Agricultural total (B)				2,389 (100%)	2,320 (97%)	2,252 (94%)	2,032 (85%)	1,701 (71%)
Deduction[c] (C)				0	18	36	90	179
Final total (A – C)				2,490 (100%)	2,403 (96%)	2,316 (93%)	2,041 (81%)	1,619 (64%)

Source: The table is based on data from Government of Japan, Ministry of Agriculture, Forestry, and Fisheries (MAFF), 1977.

[a]Eighty percent of raw sugar is assumed imported.

[b]Imports of other minor food products are ignored.

[c]A reduction of 75 percent is assumed in the calorie content of domestically produced meat, dairy products, raw milk, animal fats (excluding vegetable oils from the figures for fats and oils in the table), and eggs, resulting in a decline in food-energy supply from these commodities as feed imports are curtailed.

on prior commodity-specific self-sufficiency ratios. Average food energy consumption per capita falls to 1,619 calories per capita per day—65 percent of the actual average intake in 1977. Based on the analysis by the Food and Agriculture Organisation (FAO) (1952) and Poleman (1979), the minimum per capita food-energy requirement for Japan is probably in the range of 2,000 to 2,300 kcal per day.[4] Thus the present mix of foods produced domestically would not be sufficient to sustain Japan's present population, even if domestic food supplies were to be equitably distributed.

Although a complete cutoff of food supplies from abroad is highly unlikely, it is conceivable that any one of a variety of international disturbances or policy changes could result in a partial curtailment of food imports. The impacts of partial curtailments, ranging from 10 to 50 percent, are considerably more moderate than that of a complete cutoff (see table 10–5).[5] The reduction of imports by 20 percent drives average food-energy intake per capita down by 7 percent to 2,316 calories per day. Even with the curtailment of food imports by 50 percent, an equitable food-distribution program might still provide for minimum subsistence food-energy needs. Furthermore, the pattern of domestic production could not be expected to remain fixed. Such a curtailment would surely raise the prices of the staples capable of most efficiently delivering basic nutritional needs, reducing the commitment of domestic resources to luxury foods, and increasing the domestic availability of food energy.

Potential Impact of Reduced Petroleum Imports on Food Consumption

Even though Japan might manage to meet its basic nutritional needs in the event of a partial curtailment of food imports alone, the likelihood that such a major change in the international pattern of trade would not be accompanied by some curtailment of petroleum supplies is fairly remote. As with a shortage of food, however, reduced petroleum supplies would lead to a reallocation of domestic energy resources so as to mitigate the effects on the supply of the most basic necessities.

It is beyond the scope of this chapter to trace quantitatively the general economic effects of a petroleum-supply curtailment, since to do so would require the use of a general equilibrium model of Japan's economy. A significant petroleum-supply curtailment would result in general economic stagnation and, eventually, a significant labor surplus. The ultimate effect on food-production capacity would then depend on the degree to which this labor could be diverted to farm production.

Although data showing the share of staple-food agriculture in Japan's overall energy consumption are not available at the time of this writing, the significance of food in the overall energy account can be derived from a comparison of the energy consumption mix of rural villages with that for the nation as a whole (table 10–6). Aside from the quantity of liquefied petroleum gas, which is primarily used for cooking and other household purposes, a tentative estimate of agriculture's share in total petroleum use

Table 10–6
Consumption of Petroleum Products in 1977

	Total Consumption (1,000 cal)	*Farm Village Consumption (1,000 cal)*	*Farm Village Share (%)*
Volatile fractions (including benzene and gasoline)	31,516	4,530	14
Kerosene	24,011	3,250	14
Light oils	18,142	1,670	9
Heavy oils	28,848	1,440	5
Total fuels	229,340	10,890	5
Total lubricating oils	2,014	120	6
Total liquid petroleum	231,354	11,010	5
Liquified petroleum gas (thousand tons)	5,176	972	19

Source: Zenkoku Nogyo Kyodokumiai Chuokai, 1979.

is 5 percent. When the petroleum used for the manufacture of fertilizers and farm machinery is included, the share rises to, at most, 10 percent. Given the priority that would be placed on food production under conditions of reduced food and energy imports, a relatively minor reallocation of the remaining petroleum supplies would probably be sufficient to prevent a decline in domestic food output.

Even in the event that a reallocation of energy resources in favor of agriculture were not feasible, a reversal of the trend in agricultural output and energy use since 1960 would result in a proportional decline in food production much smaller than the proportional decline in energy inputs. Table 10–4 shows that the elasticity of rice production to energy input, measured over the period 1960–1974, was about 7 percent. If such technological retrogression were feasible, 93 percent of the food energy could be produced with the use of only one-half the petroleum. Although the reversibility of this technological progression would be limited in the short run by the conversion of land to nonagricultural uses and by lags in the reallocation of labor and other important factors of production, it is clear that the proportional impact on food production would be considerably smaller than the shortfall in overall petroleum supplies.

Nevertheless, the impact on Japan's economy and on the quality of the Japanese diet of reduced supplies from imports of staple foods and energy would be serious indeed. Whether domestic resources might be reallocated in time to stabilize the supply of staple foods would depend on the events responsible for the disruption of trade and also on the preparedness of the Japanese government. This preparedness depends on food-security policies that could be implemented in the present, although a major change in Japan's agricultural policy would require a stronger national consensus as to the problem of national vulnerability than exists today.

Some Potential Causes of a Food Crisis in Japan

A wide variety of possible events could result in reduced food availability in Japan. The likelihood that one or more of them will occur during a planning period of the next twenty years varies considerably. Only those that should be accounted for in Japan's agricultural and trade policy are considered in the following discussion.

Food-Supply Disturbances Caused by Weather

Periodic crop failures due to random weather effects are an inevitable characteristic of agricultural production throughout the world. Since these disturbances are not usually correlated between distant countries, their effects on international trade are generally offsetting, except in rare cases when several crop failures coincide with key political changes such as the opening of the U. S. grain trade to the Soviet Union after 1971 and the crop failures of 1972–1974. The result is some uncertainty as to the import prices of food commodities. Unlike many developing countries, however, Japan's relatively abundant foreign-exchange resources render year-to-year fluctuations in international market prices little more than a minor irritant.

A more important threat to Japan's food security would be long-run increasing trends in food import prices that result from lasting changes in the world's climate. Although average atmospheric temperatures have tended to decline in recent years, scientists are uncertain whether the heating effect of carbon-dioxide buildup will outweigh the cooling effect of additional particulates in the atmosphere over the next two decades. This considerable uncertainty about the direction of long-run climatic change leaves insufficient information on which to adjust present food policies.

Structural Changes in World Food Markets

A lasting decline in the export potential of one of the major food-exporting countries or a lasting increase in the excess demand of major importers would lead to a rising trend in real international food prices. In 1977–1978, the world's four largest cereal exporters—the United States, Canada,

Australia, and Argentina—shared 23 percent of world wheat production and 36 percent of coarse-grain production. Their shares of world exports were markedly higher, however, at 82 and 83 percent for wheat and coarse grains, respectively. Any decline in the capacity of these surplus countries to export would have a major effect on world prices. On the import side, centrally planned countries—including China and the Soviet Union—share one-third of all the world's imports of wheat, compared with Japan's 8 percent. As for feed grains, imports are not as concentrated, although Japan and the Soviet Union have tended to be the largest single importers. The principal uncertainty on the import side of world cereal markets is the future trend in the excess demands of the major centrally planned economies.

While there appears to be a consensus among analysts that real cereal prices are most likely to increase (O'Brien 1981), the amount of the increase depends on the supply responsiveness of the major exporters. Considering that the three largest exporters are industrialized countries in which agricultural-productivity growth has continued through the 1970s despite increased energy costs, significantly lower supply-responsiveness in these countries is unlikely in the foreseeable future. Fluctuations in import demand, which characterize Soviet grain imports, do discourage sustained supply response, although this problem is most likely to be solved through the use of contracts specifying limits on the quantities traded and through the management of carry-over stocks by both importers and exporters.

Political Disturbances Affecting International Trade in Food and Petroleum

The most serious form of political disturbance from Japan's viewpoint would be an international conflict sufficiently widespread that its commerce with the suppliers of food, energy, and raw materials are affected. Should Japan become involved, its dependence on the United States—its largest trading partner and principal political ally—would increase. Under such circumstances, Japan's wider national security would be at stake, an issue beyond the scope of this paper.

Should Japan's economic and political links with the major food exporters ever diminish, the food exporters' considerable combined market power could be used as a strategic tool, in the manner adopted by the United States against the Soviet Union during 1980–1981. This market power could also be used against all food importers in order to capture "economic rent" (Schmitz and McCalla 1981).

Food-Market Disturbances Originating in Japan

Two remote possibilities are evident whereby a domestic-food-supply shortfall could result from events within Japan. First, ill-designed agricultural policies could lead to a decline in staple-food self-sufficiency to the point where bad weather in Japan and in the major exporters could combine to render food supplies inadequate in the short run. Second, sluggish structural adjustment to further increases in petroleum prices could lead to a sequence of large current-account deficits, greatly increasing the social cost of food imports. It is highly unlikely, however, that food imports would ever be curtailed in order to correct a short-run imbalance in the current account. Should such a deficit persist in the longer run, the emphasis of national economic policies would need to fall more heavily on import substitution in the agricultural sector and export promotion in the manufacturing sector.

Policies for Avoiding Food Crises

During 1972–1974, unprecedented increases in international petroleum prices and a doubling of the prices of the staple foods imported by Japan occurred (table 10–7). These events constituted a true food crisis for many developing countries. Although these changes were costly for Japan, no shortage in staple-food supplies resulted. Thus, so long as international commerce continues uninterrupted, the overall strength of Japan's

Table 10–7
Prices of Grain Imported to Japan
(1,000 yen/metric ton)

Year	*Corn*	*Grain Sorghum*
1965	24.2	21.2
1970	25.5	22.8
1971	22.8	22.0
1972	19.9	19.4
1973	30.7	29.2
1974	46.2	41.7
1975	42.6	40.7
1976	37.7	35.1
1977	28.8	26.8
1978	23.7	21.8

Source: Zenkoku Nogyo Kyodokumiai Chuokai, 1979.

economy should in most cases protect it from serious food scarcity resulting from such a combination of events. To help avoid a damaging curtailment of international commerce or to reduce Japan's vulnerability to such an event, a variety of alternative policies are available.

A Flexible Plan for Food Supply and Distribution

A set of food and agricultural policies is required that would facilitate the ready adjustment of Japan's staple-food supply in the event of an impending curtailment of international commerce. These policies could be implemented within the framework of a general food-security master plan. Typical elements of such a plan would be policies to maintain the capacity of Japanese farms to switch their product mix toward staple foods at relatively short notice and policies to control the irreversible conversion of crop land to nonagricultural uses.

Research on the Most Appropriate Agricultural Technologies

Since improvements in technical efficiency are a major source of agricultural growth, continued research on the most appropriate alternatives for improving domestic output capacity is indispensable. The concern with national food security must be incorporated into the process that determines the best directions for this research so that the technologies used in Japanese agriculture can become more resilient. To achieve this, these technologies will need to become less intensive in imported factors of production, especially petroleum.

Incentives to Producers

Irrespective of the degree to which more resilient agricultural technologies and farming practices are advocated by the government, the degree to which private owners of rural land will respond will depend primarily on profitability. To be fully successful, the policies adopted need to be supported by a national consensus that includes farm groups and consumers. A delicate balance must be maintained between those policies that stimulate the adoption of appropriate farming practices, thus imposing a cost on producers, and those policies that favor greater domestic production and improved self-sufficiency, which reward producers and burden consumers. There are limits, however, to the improvement in Japan's food security that can be realized by these policies. In the case of improvements to self-sufficiency, the domestic output of wheat, feed grains, and soybeans, for example, is limited by the available land. Complete self-sufficiency in these commodities would require 9 million hectares of crop land, over and above the 5.5 million hectares on which all of Japan's crop agriculture is based (table 10–8).

Cooperation with Foreign Countries

Given that complete self-sufficiency must be unattainable without major changes in the mix and quantity of foods consumed and in the allocation of domestic resources, some dependence on trading partners is inevitable under all but the most extreme crisis conditions.[6] Furthermore, a very large share of the total output of Japan's economy depends on the continuance of

Table 10–8
Cultivated Land Required for Self-Sufficiency in 1977

Commodity	*Imports (1,000 metric tons)*	*Production per Hectare (metric tons)*	*Cultivated Land Needed (1,000 hectares)*	*Present Cultivated Area (1,000 hectares)*
Wheat	5,658	2.75	2,060	86
Barley and rye	2,238	2.64	850	78
Corn	9,313	2.63	3,540	0.3
Soybeans	3,602	1.40	2,570	7.9
Total	—	—	9,020	24.6

Source: Government of Japan Ministry of Agriculture, Forestry, and Fisheries (MAFF), 1979.

Table 10–9
Structure of Japan's Balance of Trade
(million U.S. $)

Year	*Total*	*Food*	*Raw Materials and Fuel*	*Industrial Products*
1971	4,295	−2,229	−10,643	17,166
1972	5,120	−2,941	−12,328	20,390
1973	−1,362	−5,136	−19,699	23,472
1974	−6,437	−7,270	−37,798	38,630
1975	−2,111	−8,051	−36,213	42,154
1976	2,698	−8,462	−40,438	51,599
1977	9,910	−9,198	−44,307	63,415

Source: Zenkoku Nogyo Kyodokumiai Chuokai, 1979.
Note: Trade balance is expressed in terms of the net value of exports.

free and profitable international commerce (table 10–9). To ensure that this lifeline is maintained, both political and economic relations with trading partners must be strong.

The achievement and maintenance of such good relations with all trading partners is not a simple task for Japan, as illustrated by the conflict in 1980 between Iran—then a major supplier of petroleum to Japan—and the United States, Japan's largest trading partner. The security interests of Japan dictated that, for a time at least, it could not comply with the U.S. request for economic sanctions against the new government of Iran. Such instances, however, only heighten the need for Japanese foreign policy to pay attention to the maintenance of political good will and to the prevention of serious international conflicts generally.

Participation to Increase Food Production in Developing Countries

Although participation in the international effort to improve food production in developing countries could be seen as part of a general commitment to international cooperation, the plight of food-deficit developing countries has special relevance for food-security policy. First, periods of internationl food scarcity and high grain prices bring greater hardship to countries with domestic food consumption near subsistence levels and limited foreign-exchange resources. At such times, large purchases by developed countries—although they may provide some insurance against worsening international supply conditions by increasing world stocks—only act to exacerbate the short-run situation for the developing importers. In order to prevent the resulting competition for grain between a demand driven primarily by livestock consumption in developed countries and by the subsistence needs of the poor in developing countries, Japan should assist in efforts to improve domestic supplies in poor countries.

Second, production levels in many poor countries are presently below potential because policies are adopted to keep food prices low to protect consumers. Tyers and Chisholm show in chapter 14 that a change to producer prices which equal border prices in these countries would result in a significant supply response. This not only reduces the cost of food imports to these countries but also lowers world trading prices, thus serving the interests of Japan and other large importers. Where resources can be committed to increased production incentives in poor countries, without exposing their consumers to unnecessary risk, it is appropriate for Japan to contribute in its own food-security interest.

Food-Security Reserves

The periods of international food scarcity that occurred in 1965–1966 and 1972–1973 were both associated with very low levels of world grain stocks (table 10–10). Had stocks been greater in periods immediately preceding the bad harvests of these years, the severity of the resulting shortages would have been mitigated. Grain stocks are a particularly expensive method of supply stabilization, however, and their level has depended heavily on storage subsidies associated with producer price-support policies in the major exporting countries. Since the 1960s, Japan has held relatively large stocks of rice that would constitute an emergency reserve in the event of a curtailment of grain imports. The high level of these stocks has, however, resulted mostly from the need to support domestic-producer rice prices through government purchases and the limited international demand for the Japonica varieties grown in Japan.

Policies for Coping with Food Crises

Preventive policies can only reduce the likelihood of a significant food supply shortage in Japan. The successful management of such events requires policies that can have a short-run impact on food supply and distribution patterns. Such policies should form part of the master plan referred to earlier.

Consumption Patterns and Food Distribution

A return to a diet intensive in staple foods would be essential in the event of a supply shortfall. Under extreme circumstances, tubers such as potatoes could be substituted for the preferred staple, rice.[7] At the very least, the consumption of livestock products must be reduced, releasing feed grains for direct consumption. Depending on the magnitude of the scarcity, these changes would probably take place as a consequence of domestic-market forces. Only if income is very unequally distributed and the high-income groups do not adjust their consumption patterns would government intervention be required. This intervention could take the form of government participation in food markets as a buyer and a seller to keep the consumer prices of staple foods from increasing excessively and to discourage hoarding. Should the staple-food-supply situation become more serious, the share of staple foods distributed by the government would have to increase to ensure that survival is the principal priority governing food distribution.

Table 10–10
Trends in World Grain Stocks
(million metric tons)

	Wheat			Coarse Grains		
Year	*Consumption*	*Closing Stock*	*Stock as Percent of Consumption*	*Consumption*	*Closing Stock*	*Stock as Percent of Consumption*
1960–1961	237	78	33	447	102	23
1961–1962	239	67	28	451	87	19
1962–1963	251	72	29	462	85	18
1963–1964	247	63	26	465	88	19
1964–1965	266	73	28	480	81	17
1965–1966	283	54	19	505	67	13
1966–1967	282	81	29	517	68	13
1967–1968	290	88	31	533	77	14
1968–1969	305	112	37	542	81	15
1969–1970	327	95	29	570	82	14
1970–1971	339	72	21	586	65	11
1971–1972	341	79	23	609	78	13
1972–1973	361	61	17	621	61	10
1973–1974	364	69	19	665	56	8
1974–1975	363	63	17	621	52	8
1975–1976	350	63	18	635	52	8
1976–1977	372	104	28	674	68	10

Source: U.S. Department of Agriculture, *Foreign Agriculture Circular*, 1977.

Supply Intervention and Management

If policies to sustain the ability of Japan's agricultural sector to adjust its product mix and output level in the event of a curtailment of imports are successful, then the reallocation of domestic resources in favor of staple-food production, once such a crisis occurs, might proceed smoothly with a minimum of government intervention. Land would need to be diverted from nonagricultural uses such as golf courses and playing fields and brought under cultivation. Labor and energy would need to be transferred from industrial production for export to agriculture. The result would be rapid structural change rendering the resources for industrial production considerably more scarce. Although such change would be resisted by political forces within the industrial sector, industries related to the agricultural sector would benefit considerably. According to the input-output table for Japan, value added in agriculture and imported food commodities is one-third of final consumer expenditure on food (table 10–11). If the fertilizer and agricultural-machinery industries were to be included, the value share of industry would be still larger. Thus rapid reallocation in favor of agricultural production would help to stabilize, if not expand. large elements within the industrial sector in the event of a food crisis.

The role of government in reorganizing the industrial and agricultural sectors would depend on the severity of the food-supply shortfall. Higher staple-food prices would inevitably result from a curtailment of imports. This, in turn, would stimulate a reallocation of land and labor in the short run as well as increase the domestic production of staples such as rice within a single season. If the supply shortfall is particularly serious, the government might need to invoke the Compulsory Land Purchase Act[8] to ensure that the nonagricultural lands most suitable for agriculture are converted in time to meet emergency food-production targets.

Conclusion

In choosing a strategy for the attainment of national food security, the government of Japan faces two dilemmas. First, steps to reduce vulnerability to a curtailment of food imports by improving food self-sufficiency will lead to increased agricultural energy use and increased petroleum imports. The result would be increased vulnerability to a possible cessation of petroleum imports, an event considered more probable in the present international political climate than in the past. Under such conditions,

Table 10–11
Trends in the Structure of the Food and Agricultural Sectors
(unit percent)

	1965	*1975*
Consumer expenditure on food (billion yen)	(6,989) 100.0	(25,253) 100.0
Value shares of agricultural commodities	41.4	33.4
Domestic production	37.2	29.2
Imports	4.2	4.2
Share of value added in food processing	30.9	26.8
Share of value added in distribution	20.9	25.2
Wholesaling and retailing	18.5	22.9
Transportation	2.4	2.3
Share of value added in restaurant service	6.6	14.6

Sources: Gyosei Kanricho hoka 10 Shocho, 1976, and Zenkoku Nogyo Kyodokumiai Chuokai, 1979.

reduced energy supplies would be particularly destructive, especially considering that a sudden return to very large food imports might not be feasible in the short run.

Second, by adopting the internationalist strategy of strengthening both political and economic ties with important trading partners, Japan's dependence on these countries as sources of food increases as does its vulnerability to changes in their trade policies. This vulnerability is particularly acute in the case of trade links with the United States, and the likelihood of potentially damaging changes in U.S. trade policy is not insignificant, as illustrated by the soybean embargo of 1973. However, the mutuality of Japan's overall economic interests with those of the large Pacific Rim exporters—the United States, Canada, and Australia—extends beyond agriculture and food to industrial raw materials and manufacturing. This mutuality of interests is such that events resulting in a significant curtailment of staple-food supplies in Japan are unlikely to be initiated within the Pacific Rim.

Nonetheless, policies both to prevent a major national food-supply shortfall and to mitigate the effects of such an event if it should occur must continue to be adopted as part of the overall management of Japan's food and agricultural sectors. The resilience of Japan's food system should be considered in the assessment of policies affecting the conversion of land to nonagricultural use and the adoption of energy-intensive agricultural technologies. The continued maintenance of emergency stocks of rice, soybeans, and petroleum is also important as a means of mitigating the damaging effects to possible food- or energy-supply curtailments. Such reserves also help to stabilize international markets and thus contribute to more internationalist strategies for attaining national food security.

Designing Japan's food and agricultural policies with too great a concern for unlikely events is analogous to the decision not to travel to work for fear of a traffic accident. The benefits derived through interdependence with trading partners are the principal source of Japan's present prosperity. Thus the concern with national food security must not be exploited for purposes of narrow isolationist goals. Food security can best be maintained through the internationalist strategy, emphasizing the reinforcement of political and economic ties with trading partners and the commitment of resources to improved incentives for agricultural production in the developing countries.

Notes

1. Alternative formulae for the self-sufficiency ratio include the total weight- or volume-based ratio and the agricultural land-based ratio. In the

case of the land-based ratio, the area of agricultural land used domestically is divided by the area that would be needed to produce all the food consumed if the prevailing domestic technology were used.

2. See Organization for Economic Cooperation and Development (OECD) (1975).

3. See Shokuryo Mondai Kenkyu-dai (Food Problem Research Group), 1975.

4. Poleman (1979) surveys the various much-disputed estimates of minimum daily requirements and concludes that the minimum requirements range from less than 2,000 kcal per capita per day in Asian developing countries to 2,700 kcal per capita per day in North America. The minimum average requirement for Japan is probably between 2,000 and 2,300 kcal per capita per day.

5. Estimates of the share of present food-energy consumption that would be sustained in the event of food-import curtailments of 10, 20, and 50 percent have also been derived by the Shokuryo-Nógyo Mondai Kenkyu-kai (Food Agriculture Problem Research Group), 1977. Their estimates are only slightly lower than those shown in table 10–5 at 95, 91, and 77 percent, respectively.

6. Even those who strongly advocate increased self-sufficiency set modest targets for achievement in this decade. Kondo (1976) sets a target self-sufficiency ratio of 60 percent for achievement by 1990.

7. Tubers were extensively substituted for rice during World War II.

8. In Japanese: Tochi Shuyo Ho.

Bibliography

Food and Agriculture Organization (FAO). 1952. *Second World Food Survey*. Rome, November.

Gyosei Kanricho ta 10 Shocho (Administrative Management Agency and ten other Agencies. 1976. *Sangyo Reukanhyo (Input-Output Table of Industries)*. Tokyo.

Kondo, Y. (Ed.). 1976. *Shokuryo Jikyuryoku no Gijutsuteki Tembo (A Technological Perspective on the Capacity for Food Self-Sufficiency*. Norintokei Kyokai (Agricultural Statistics Association). Tokyo.

MAFF (Ministry of Agriculture, Forestry and Fisheries). 1977. *Showa Gojyu Ninen Do Shokuryo Jyukyu Hyo (1977 Food Balance Sheet)*. Tokyo.

MAFF (Ministry of Agriculture, Forestry and Fisheries). 1979. *Norinsuisansho Tokeikyo, 1977–78 (Statistical Data Book for 1977–78)*. Tokyo.

Norintokei Kyokai (Agricultural Statistics Association). 1973. *Shokuryo Jikyu (Food Self-Sufficiency)*, Tokyo.

O'Brien, P.M. 1981. "Global Prospects for Agriculture." In U.S. Department of Agriculture, *Agricultural-Food Policy Review: Perspectives for the 1980s,* Economics and Statistics Service AFPR-4, April.

Organization for Economic Cooperation and Development (OECD). 1975. *Food Consumption Statistics, 1955–73.* Paris.

Poleman, T.T. 1979. "Quantifying the Nutrition Situation in Developing Countries." Cornell Agricultural Economics Staff Paper No. 79-33, September.

Schmitz, A., and McCalla, A.F. 1981. "Analysis of Imperfections in International Trade: The Case of Grain Export Cartels." In *Imperfect Markets in Agricultural Trade* ed. A.F. McCalla and T.E. Josling. Montclair, N. J.: Allanheld, Osmun & Co.

Shokuryo Mondai Kenkyu-kai (Food Problem Research Group). 1975. *Shokuryo Mondai Kenkyu-Kai Hokokusho (Report of the Food Problem Research Group).* Tokyo: August.

Shokuryo-Nogyo Mondai Kenkyu-kai (Food Agriculture Problem Research Group). 1977. *Shokuryo-Nogyo Mondai Kenkyu-Kai Hokokusho (Report of the Food Problem Research Group).* Tokyo: September.

Udagawa, T. 1978. "Nogyoseisan to Energy o Kangaeru (On Agricultural Production and Energy)." In *Norin Tokei Chosa (Inquiry into Agricultural Statistics).* November.

U.S. Department of Agriculture. 1977. *Foreign Agriculture Circular,* May.

Zenkoku Nogyo Kyodokumiai Chuokai (National Central Agricultural Cooperative). 1979. *1980 Nendai Nihon Nogyo no Kadai to Nogyo no Taisaku—Chiiki Kara no Nogyo Saihen o Mezashite (Problems in Japan's Agriculture and Agricultural Cooperatives—Countermeasures for the 1980s Based on Regional Development),* October.

Part III
Results from Empirical Analysis

11 Use of Expenditure-Survey Data in Staple-Food-Consumption Analysis: Examples from Indonesia

John A. Dixon

As many countries in the Asia-Pacific region continue to struggle with the problem of providing sufficient food—either from domestic production or from imports—to meet basic nutritional needs, increasing attention is being paid to the details of staple-food consumption and the economic parameters that influence that consumption. The realization that income or price policies might have very different impacts on different segments of the population has led to greater disaggregation of data for use in consumption analysis.

The cereal and root or tuber starchy staples provide a very large share of both calories and protein in many countries in the region. The ways in which these staples are consumed and the variations by residence (urban or rural), geographical location, season, and income groups all become important factors in local food security and must be accounted for in designing government policies that influence food availability and consumption. In order to analyze these patterns and trends in staple-food consumption, a number of data sets can be used. At the national aggregate level, Food Balance Sheets provide gross estimates of consumption (or availability) of many foods. These data are prepared yearly by the Central Bureau of Statistics and provide a broad overview of national consumption patterns. Many countries, however, also conduct national expenditure surveys, such as the National Sample Surveys in India and the National Socio-Economic Surveys *(Susenas)* in Indonesia. These surveys permit the detailed examination of consumption patterns by groups within the population and can be used to estimate various parameters useful for consumption and food-policy analysis.

This chapter examines the food situation in Indonesia and the use of Susenas data for consumption analysis. A quick overview of staple-food consumption patterns is given, and then the Susenas surveys are consid-

Much of the work for this paper was done while the author worked in Indonesia as a Project Specialist for the Ford Foundation (1978–1980).

ered in some detail. Techniques of analysis are discussed, as well as various biases and shortcomings in the data. The focus is on the major staple foods and special attention is given to the nonrice staples, principally corn and cassava.

The final part of the chapter presents empirical results based on the Susenas data set and interprets these results, especially with regard to the reservations raised in the preceding section. While Indonesia is the example used, the problems addressed and the approaches taken can be generalized to other countries in the region.

Staple-Food-Consumption Patterns in Indonesia

At the national level, the availability of calories and protein in Indonesia appears adequate to meet basic nutritional needs.[1] Based on Food Balance Sheet data, the per capita daily availability of calories has averaged between 2,150 and 2,400 calories in recent years; protein has ranged between 44 and 48 grams. The most striking fact, however, is the extremely large share of total calories, protein, and fats coming from vegetable sources (table 11–1).

Clearly, the nonanimal foods are of paramount importance in meeting basic food needs for calories and protein. The cereals and roots and tubers provide most of the calories and protein. As seen in table 11–2, these staples account for 78 percent of all calories and 72 percent of all protein. Within the staples, rice, corn, and cassava rank as the most important, although the other nonstaple food groups are necessary to provide required vitamins, minerals, and variety in the diet.

Further disaggregation of the Food Balance Sheet data is not possible; national figures are of limited use and conceal as much as they reveal.[2] The Susenas expenditure surveys are therefore used to examine variations in

Table 11–1
Per Capita Daily Food Availability for All of Indonesia, 1974 to 1978

	1974	*1975*	*1976*	*1977*	*1978*
Calories (kcals) total	2248	2150	2231	2314	2417
Percentage vegetable source	97.8%	98.0%	98.0%	98.0%	97.9%
Protein (gm) total	45.8	45.3	43.7	44.5	47.5
Percentage vegetable source	89.3%	88.2%	89.7%	90.0%	90.2%
Fats (gm) total	35.0	33.2	39.6	42.6	46.8
Percentage vegetable source	92.9%	93.6%	93.2%	93.3%	93.7%

Source: Government of Indonesia, Central Bureau of Statistics, *Food Balance Sheets, 1968–74, 1975, 1976, 1977, 1978,* Jakarta, 1977a, 1977b, 1978, 1979, and 1980.

Table 11–2
Percentage Distribution of Calories and Protein, by Food Groups, for All of Indonesia, 1974–1978

	Calories	*Protein*
Per Capita Daily Availability, 1974–1978	*2,272*	*45.4 gm*
Food group	*Percent of total*	*Percent of total*
Cereals[a]	66.5	67.4
Rice, corn	(53.5)	(49.4)
	(10.7)	(14.4)
Roots and tubers[b]	11.5	4.5
Cassava	(9.0)	(3.6)
Sugar	5.0	0.1
Pulses, nuts, and oilseeds[c]	7.3	14.8
Fruits	1.9	1.1
Vegetables	0.4	1.3
Meat	0.8	2.7
Eggs	0.1	0.4
Milk	0.2	0.5
Fish	0.8	7.0
Oils and fats[d]	5.5	0.0

Source: Government of Indonesia, Central Bureau of Statistics, *Food Balance Sheets, 1968–1974, 1975, 1976, 1977, 1978,* Jakarta, 1977a, 1977b, 1978, 1979, and 1980.

[a]Cereals include rice, corn, and wheat.

[b]Roots and tubers include sweet potatoes, cassava, and sago.

[c]Pulses, nuts, and oilseeds include groundnuts, soyabeans, and coconuts/copra.

[d]Oils and fats include groundnut oil, copra oil, palm oil, and animal fats.

consumption by residence, region, season, or income group. The susenas expenditure surveys have been conducted every few years since 1963–1964.[3] The fourth survey was carried out between October 1969 and April 1970; the fifth and sixth surveys covered the calendar years 1976 and 1978, respectively. The analysis presented in this chapter is primarily based on the 1976 survey, Susenas V.

When the data are disaggregated, interesting trends emerge. The differences in staple-food consumption between Java and the other islands (referred to as Off-Java) are shown in table 11–3. Per capita rice consumption in Off-Java is 25 percent higher than on Java, while the reverse is true for corn consumption. Cassava consumption is about the same in both areas. When the rural-urban differences are examined, however, the much greater role of corn and cassava in the rural areas is evident.[4] If the data are further broken down by per capita income and if the poorest half of the population (based on per capita expenditures for all goods) is considered separately, the differences between urban and rural areas are accentuated. In rural areas rice consumption decreases by a quarter, and corn and cassava consumption increases in importance; in urban areas, there is some decrease in rice consumption but little change in corn or cassava demand (see table 11–3).

Given that the poorest half of the population included almost 75 million people in 1980, these differences are very important when food-security issues, as well as government policy, are concerned. Since expenditure-survey data permit such disaggregated analysis, it is essential that the nature of these data, their possible biases and limitations, and the ways in which they can be used, are all understood.

Table 11–3
Average Weekly per Capita Consumption, 1976
(kg)

Region and Residence	*Rice*	*Corn*	*Cassava*	*Wheat Flour*
Java	2.02	0.26	0.94	0.01
Rural	2.01	0.31	1.12	0.01
Urban	2.07	0.01	0.14	0.02
Off-Java	2.49	0.16	0.90	0.04
Rural	2.50	0.18	1.03	0.04
Urban	2.47	0.03	0.30	0.06

Weekly Per Capita Consumption by the Poorest 50 Percent of the Population, 1976
(kg)

Region and Residence	*Rice*	*Corn*	*Cassava*	*Wheat Flour*
Java				
Rural	1.52	0.35	1.18	—
Urban	1.89	0.02	0.16	0.01
Off-Java				
Rural	1.93	0.21	0.95	0.01
Urban	2.11	0.04	0.26	0.02

Source: Government of Indonesia, Central Bureau of Statistics, *Susenas V, Pengeluaran Untuk Konsumsi Penduduk* (Population Consumption Expenditures), VU579-29, Jakarta, 1979.

Note: Rice includes rice, glutinous rice, and rice products. Corn includes corn kernels and corn flour. Fresh corn and dried corn with cover are not included. Cassava includes fresh cassava, dried cassava (*gaplek*), and cassava flour/starch. The last two forms are expressed in fresh root equivalents. Wheat is only wheat flour and does *not* include products such as breads, noodles, and cookies made from wheat.

The Fifth National Social Economic Survey: Susenas V, 1976.

Susenas V was carried out in three rounds in 1976, and each round covered a four-month period as follows: January to April, May to August, and September to December. Almost all of the provinces of Indonesia were covered, with the exception of Irian Jaya and Timor Timur. Each round had a sample size of about 18,000 households; the total sample, therefore, contained nearly 54,000 households composed of over 260,000 people. Since the Susenas surveys are expenditure surveys, information was obtained on the purchase of both food and nonfood items, services, and other expenditures.[5]

Most food groups were reported on in detail in both quantity and value terms. Cereal and cereal products, for example, were broken down into eight categories, while roots and tubers had six groupings.[6] Unfortunately, vegetables, beans and pulses, fruits, and prepared foods were reported in value terms only; no quantity figures were collected. When an item was nonpurchased home production, it was valued using local-market prices. The data were then presented in table form as consumption (or expenditure) per capita per week by monthly per capita expenditure groups. There were twelve expenditure groups, ranging from less than Rp 1,000 per capita per month (U.S. $2.40 at the prevailing exchange rate between the rupiah and the dollar) to Rp 30,000 and over (U.S. $72.30 per month).

While information was collected on total household expenditure and consumption, the data were reported per capita based on the total number of members in each household surveyed. Consumption was not converted to adult equivalents, and hence the average values presented implicitly reflect the age distribution in each grouping. (Unfortunately, information on the age distribution in different expenditure classes is not available.) The total population surveyed is the total number of persons reported in the households in each sample, including children as well as adults.

For most foods included in the survey (and all of the staples), both the per capita quantity consumed and the expenditure on that food are reported. Implicit prices are easily calculated and, as opposed to the aggregated Food Balance Sheets, the data are available by region, by urban or rural residence, by season (subround), and by income group. A problem, therefore, is how to handle such a rich, disaggregated data set in order to obtain information and results efficiently. Decisions have to be made on which foods or goods should be included in an analysis as well as the appropriate level of disaggregation.

The first level of disaggregation gives the percentage of total expenditure on food versus nonfood items and the distribution of food expenditures among various food groups. Because of the importance of the basic staple foods (rice, corn, and cassava) in Indonesia, this chapter will concentrate on these staples.

Graphical data display can highlight major patterns. If the log of consumption of a food is plotted against the log of total expenditures or income, expenditure elasticities can be directly read off the graph. As shown in figure 11–1, rice displays the classic quadratic shape of the Engel curve for a normal good: the slope (the expenditure elasticity) starts large and positive and decreases as incomes increase. If seasonal data are available, separate curves can be plotted and seasonal variations noted (see figure 11–1). In rural Java, for example, rice consumption is uniformly larger in the May to August postharvest period and lowest in the September to December period. The latter period occurs just before the main March-to-April rice harvest and coincides with seasonally high rice prices.

Such graphical analysis of grouped data can help in determining proper estimating equations for the relationships between food consumption and total expenditure noted and the appropriate equations chosen. In addition, whether or not a food is generally an inferior, normal, or superior food can

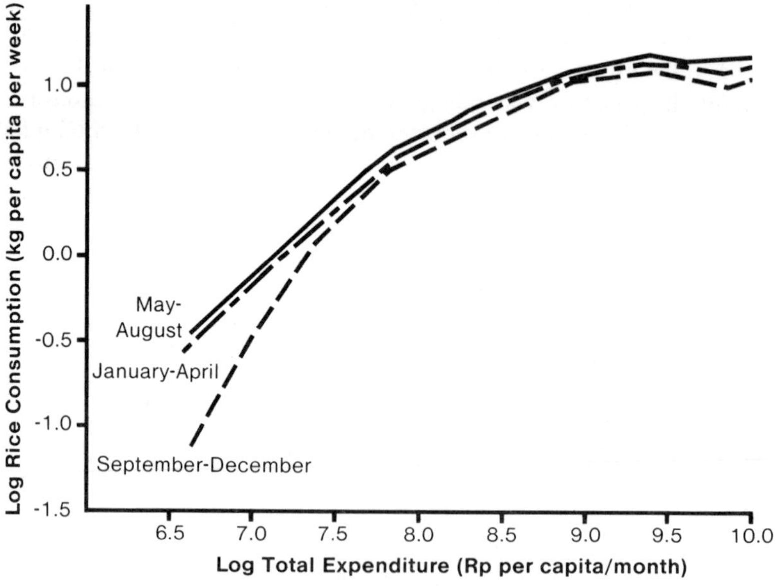

Figure 11–1. Natural Log of Rice Consumption and Natural Log of Total Expenditure: Java-Madura, 1976 (Rural)

Source: National Socio-Economic Survey (Susenas V), 1976.

also be determined.[7] If several similar foods are plotted on the same graph, substitution between and among them (such as the starchy staples of corn, cassava, and rice) is illustrated.

More than one type of information can be placed on a graph; for example, if two separate scales are used on the vertical axis, both the consumption of a food and the distribution of population can be graphed against the range of expenditure groups. A variation of this is to convert a set of staple foods into calories and plot both calories and population against expenditures. This double histogram presents a great deal of data and, by converting all staples to calories, avoids the "apples and oranges" (or more properly, rice and cassava) problem. Figure 11–2 is an example of such a histogram based on calories from six staple foods (rice, corn, wheat flour, fresh cassava, *gaplek,* and sweet potatoes) for an All-Indonesia sample. It clearly shows the large concentration of total population in the first four expenditure groups and the rather low levels of staple-food consumption (less than 1,400 kcals per day) by those groups.

Although graphical display can be very useful for getting a feel for data and an intuition about which questions are important, data can also be analyzed to estimate elasticities. For purposes of policymaking, three elasticities are particularly relevant: (1) the expenditure elasticity, (2) the own-price elasticity, and (3) cross-price elasticities.[8] These elasticities measure the effect of marginal changes in total expenditures, the food's own price, and the prices of other foods or goods on the consumption of that food.

Expenditure elasticities relate changes in demand to changes in expenditure levels. In Indonesia, the income-led change in total demand for a food depends on several variables: the size of the expenditure elasticities for various income groups, the average consumption of the food by each group, and the change in total expenditure for each group.[9] Expenditure elasticities can be either positive (normal goods) or negative (inferior goods). For normal foods such as rice, demand increases as incomes increase; for inferior foods such as dried cassava, demand decreases as incomes rise. Similarly, own-price and cross-price elasticities measure the effects on demand of changes in the price, either of the food itself or of other foods or goods.[10]

Elasticities are measured at the margin and predict reactions given marginal changes. For example, the demand effects of a 10 percent change in income or prices might be fairly accurately reflected using an elasticity while a 50 or 100 percent change might not. In addition, the Susenas surveys are cross-sectional surveys, and expenditure elasticities are fairly easy to estimate. Because of the subrounds within each survey, changes in price can be noted and own-price elasticities estimated; estimates of this type have generally been weaker than the expenditure elasticity estimates.

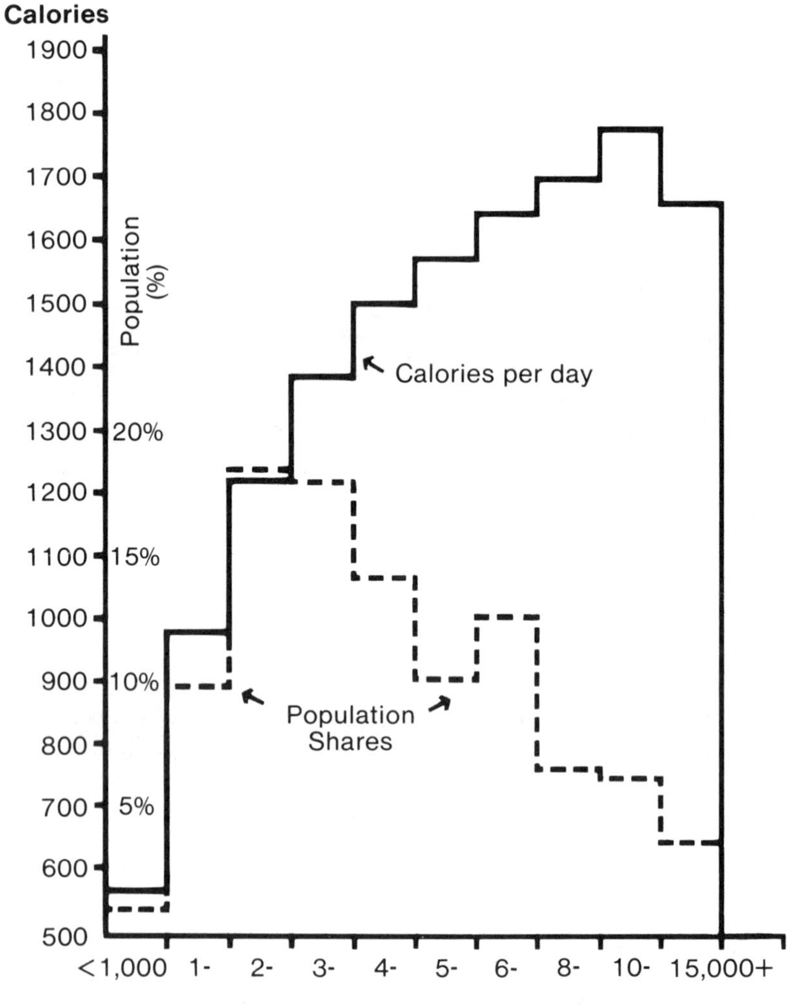

Figure 11–2. Double Histogram of Population Shares and Calories per Day (from Six Basic Starchy Staples), by Expenditure Groups

Source: National Socio-Economic Survey (Susenas), All-Indonesia, Urban plus Rural, Average of Rounds 1, 2, 3, 1976. The six starchy staples included are rice, corn, wheat flour, fresh cassava, *gaplek* (dried cassava), and sweet potatoes.

Estimates of cross-price elasticities have been poor; results have been confusing and are frequently not statistically significant.

Special Problems in Analyzing Expenditure-Survey Data

Expenditure-survey data have certain inherent biases and problems that should be recognized in order to properly interpret results. One set of biases relates to the fact that the surveys are just that: surveys of selected individuals. These surveys report expenditures on individual foods, goods, and services. The researcher must then work backwards to aggregate up and derive total expenditures (or income in the absence of savings). For poor people, expenditures are about equal to income since their low earnings are generally associated with a very high discount rate, leading to little or no savings. At high levels of income, expenditures tend to underestimate total resources available, since income either goes into savings or into durable, nonfood items that tend to be underreported (for example, land, jewelry, or cars). For example, the 1976 expenditure survey captured only 54 percent of the Central Bureau of Statistics estimate of per capita national product. This reflects the underreporting of expenditures and savings by individuals and the omission of retained business earnings.

A second set of biases and concerns relates to the quantities actually reported and used in tabulating the survey results. These problems may be grouped into three areas: *quality, hidden goods,* and the *own-production as income* question. *Quality* concerns are straightforward; for normal or superior foods, the quantity demanded increases with growth in total expenditure (or income). This increased demand often has two components: increased amounts of the food in question (rice, for example) combined with improved food quality and a higher purchase price per unit. In Indonesia, this is easily seen in the case of rice where the price of rice per kg increases steadily with increases in the level of income. Similar trends are observed for other normal foods such as meats, eggs, milk products, prepared foods, or drinks. If estimates of expenditure elasticities are based on expenditures on a food, not the actual quantities consumed, the elasticities estimated might be larger than they in fact are. In this analysis, the physical quantities demanded have been used; the derived expenditure elasticities are therefore slightly smaller than if expenditures on foods had been used as the dependent variable.

The first type of *hidden-goods* problem arises from the noninclusion of useful data or the indirect demand for foods when purchased in processed forms. For a number of foods reported in the Susenas surveys, only expenditures are reported (vegetables, pulses, and fruits); it is very hard to estimate calories and proteins derived from these foods other than by estimating a local-market price and calculating implicit quantities. For Indonesia, this is unfortunate because two major protein sources in the diet—*tahu* and *tempe*, both soybean products—were reported only in terms of expenditures prior to 1978. Calorie and protein estimates are possible but are quite imprecise. Prepared foods—the myriad of snacks and quick meals that can be a significant food source for many people—also fall in this category.

The second major hidden-goods problem, food consumption in processed form, is illustrated by wheat. No wheat is grown in Indonesia, so it is fairly easy to get a reliable estimate of total consumption based on wheat-import figures. Susenas reports consumption and expenditures of wheat flour, but this accounts for only a fraction of total demand; the balance is consumed as breads, noodles, biscuits, or cakes. These foods are grouped in the surveys in fairly broad categories that are reported only in value terms. Since these categories also include goods made of rice and cassava flour, it is difficult to separate out the role of wheat-based products by urban and rural areas and by expenditure groups. A possible solution is to include more detailed questions on wheat products in future Susenas surveys. There is a similar problem in the analysis of cassava consumption. A major use for fresh cassava on Java is the manufacture of starch. Most of this is then used in prepared foods. Therefore, even though indirect consumption of cassava in these forms is believed to be substantial, it is difficult to make precise estimates of this demand for which implicit expenditure and own-price elasticities of demand might be measured.

The last major problem is a serious one that can be called the *own-production as income* question. A large share of Indonesia's population is rural and consists of small farmers who rely directly on their own production for the bulk of their staple-food requirements. These farmers enter the market at various times during the year but depend heavily on home production to meet basic calorie needs. Since their "income" or total expenditure level in the Susenas survey is determined by the sum of reported consumption and since basic foods constitute a very large share of this consumption, especially for the poorest segments of the rural population, their apparent total expenditure level (or "income") increases as they consume more of their own production. In rural Java, for example, "food" accounted for over 70 percent of all expenditures in 1978, and the staple foods were about one-half of this amount. In the lowest income groups, the percent of total expenditures on both "food" and staple foods increases. For rice—the preferred grain—this is not a major problem since available data indicate very strong and positive expenditure elasticities for rice. If farmers had cash instead of rice they would probably demand more rice anyway. For nonrice crops, it is a problem; the data indicate that most Indonesians consider corn and dried cassava as inferior foods with negative expenditure elasticities.

In theory, a farmer can either consume what he produces, or he can sell his crops in the market and then purchase what he wants. In practice, farmers may not have the option of selling their staple-food output and purchasing other foods. The reason for this is economic: Farmers would have to go into the market at the low end (farm-gate prices) and then buy other foods at higher retail prices. The spread between farm-gate and retail prices is further increased because of the staples involved. Corn and cassava have relatively low value compared to rice; if a farmer sold corn or cassava in order to purchase rice, he would be paying a premium of 50 to 100 percent for the rice calories purchased.[11] Thus for corn and cassava—especially dried cassava (*gaplek*)—there is strong economic pressure to consume as much of one's own production as possible, especially if total income is low. By the same logic, as production of corn or cassava increases, consumption of those foods will also increase, and therefore positive expenditure elasticities for those foods would be estimated even though no real expenditures were involved.

Although one may argue that farmers are merely minimizing marketing costs, it is important to understand why certain consumption patterns are observed. Perhaps farmers consume corn and dried cassava because they like these staples, or purchase them because they are inexpensive. On the other hand, perhaps corn and dried cassava are consumed in rural areas because they are grown by upland farmers, and the calorie loss of selling these foods and buying rice is too large for poor farmers to bear.

In urban areas, the own-production-as-income problem does not arise, since all consumers purchase their food in the market (with the exceptions of those receiving government-issued rice or supplies from relatives in their home villages). Almost no own-production of food exists in cities, and hence consumer decisions reflect their preferences, given the availability and relative prices of foods in the market. In urban areas, consumption of corn and *gaplek* is very small (see table 11–3), and both commodities show strong negative expenditure elasticities. If purchases are made for cash, then true economic decision making is taking place, and the expenditure elasticities estimated are meaningful. The implications of this are that estimates of rural expenditure elasticities for own-produced staples might be high and should be evaluated with caution. This is important in Indonesia when government policymakers are trying to gauge the real role of corn and cassava in the food system, as well as the possibilities for switching consumption from rice to other foods. Estimates of expenditure elasticities in rural areas would be biased by the fact that reported income or expenditures increase as the consumption of own-produced corn or cassava increases. Own-rice elasticities would also be biased upward, at harvest time for corn and cassava their prices would fall, and rice would be relatively more expensive. The incentive would thus be to increase corn or cassava consumption, since the rice-calorie premium would be even larger than when the corn or cassava prices are higher. This would result in a positive own-price elasticity larger than if all foods were purchased in the market. Thus, one would expect a priori that both expenditure elasticities and own-price elasticities would be larger in rural areas than in urban areas, even if the population and taste patterns in both areas were similar.

This brief discussion of the data and possible problems encountered in their use is not meant to negate thevalue of such expenditure surveys but to point out some of the cautions necessary to obtain meaningful results from such surveys. These reservations are especially important when the non-preferred staples are involved (in Indonesia, corn and cassava), since they are largely produced and consumed on the farm, and, especially in the case of corn, only limited amounts are extensively marketed.[12] If markets are not well integrated, it is harder to determine a fair market price for valuing the consumption of own-produced food. Because of the own-production-as-income question, the value of this own-produced food may be very important in determining the family's income level. Much of the analysis is based on measured income/expenditure levels, and hence the implicit prices used are important.

Results from Indonesia

A number of researchers have examined the published results from the 1976 Susenas survey. Many researchers used regression analysis to estimate various elasticities and to examine questions relating to food-security or food-policy issues.[13]

In this analysis, the estimating equations used were of the following basic form:[14]

$$lnQ_i = B_0 + B_1 lnTX + B_2(lnTX)^2 + B_3 lnPr_i + B_4 lnPR_j + \sum_{k=1}^{5} B_{4+k} D_k + E$$

where

lnQ_i is the natural log of the quantity of good i consumed, in kg per capita per week.

$lnTX$ is the natural log of total expenditure (food and nonfood), in Rupiah per capita per month.

$lnPr_i$ is the natural log of the price of good i, in Rupiah per kg.

$lnPr_j$ is the natural log of the price of good j $(j \neq i)$, in Rupiah per kg.

D_k, $k=1, \ldots, 5$, are the dummy variables for Round 1, Round 2, West Java, Central Java, and East Java, respectively. These variables take only the values zero or one.

E is the error term.

The data were grouped, and separate runs were made for Java for both rural and urban areas. A further division was then made by dividing each data set (rural Java) into three income groups—low, medium, and high—based on calories consumed from six basic staples.[15] The shape of the estimating form used—linear or quadratic—was determined by an examination of graphs of the data (consumption on expenditures) and by experimentation. In general, all income subsets—the low, medium, and high groups—were estimated linearly, while the whole set (rural Java) was estimated with a quadratic formulation. This was true for normal or superior foods; when graphed, these foods displayed a strongly quadratic shape, as was seen for rice in figure 11–1. For corn, an inferior food, a linear function was fitted.

The results for Java are presented in table 11–4. The coefficients for the regional dummy variables are not given here.[16] The expenditure elasticities were all estimated log-log quadratic (except for corn) and are significant; rural own-price elasticities are also significant and negative except for corn. None of the other rural or urban cross-price terms are statistically significant, with the exception of corn and sweet potatoes. The corn expenditure elasticity is −0.55 and linear, while all the other foods have quadratic shapes, starting positive and then turning negative.

The anomalies in the own-price elasticity estimates—corn in rural areas and fresh cassava in urban areas—might have reasonable explanations. Corn is a very seasonal crop, and most consumption is from own-production. The peak period for corn consumption is from late December to early April; the period after the corn harvest and before the rice harvest. If farmers maintain or increase corn consumption just before the upland rice crop is harvested (in March or April), a positive own-price elasticity could be estimated. This happens because corn supplies available in the market that are used to value own-production increase in price as stocks are depleted and as cassava and rice prices rise. The strong positive cross-price elasticity with rice, indicating that corn and rice are substitutes, supports this view. The corn own-price elasticity illustrates the impact of own-product consumption and the use of market prices to value that consumption.

The positive own-price elasticity for fresh cassava in urban areas has another cause. In cities, many people consume fresh cassava as a vegetable or snack, and it has a positive expenditure elasticity for part of the sample. Because of the perishable nature of the roots, fresher better-quality roots command a higher price, and wealthier consumers might easily pay higher prices in their local markets. This could lead to a positive own-price elasticity: wealthier consumers demand more cassava and pay a higher average price.[17]

Earlier it was postulated that the various biases in the survey data would lead to larger estimates of expenditure and own-price elasticities in

Table 11–4
Staple-Food Regression Results, Java, 1976

	Regression Coefficients									
				Cross-Price Effects with:						
Food (kg)	*Own Price (Rp/kg)*	*TX (Rp)*	TX^2 *(Rp)*	*Rice*	*Corn*	*Cassava*	Gaplek	*Sweet Potato*	R^2	*Degree of Freedom*
Rural										
Rice	−0.84	4.10	−0.22	—	−0.05	0.01	0.02	−0.05	.94	68
	(4.0)	(11.5)	(9.9)	—	(0.8)	(0.3)	(0.3)	(0.5)		
Gaplek	−1.86	18.3	−1.2	−1.83	0.29	−0.15	—	—	.78	66
	(2.6)	(5.3)	(5.5)	(0.5)	(0.5)	(0.5)	—	—		
Fresh cassava	−0.82	7.76	−0.46	2.00	0.25	—	−0.07	−0.80	.55	66
	(4.8)	(4.1)	(4.0)	(1.1)	(0.7)	—	(0.2)	(1.6)		
Corn	1.03	−0.55	—	4.86	—	0.22	0.31	−2.30	.78	67
	(1.7)	(2.6)	—	(1.5)	—	(0.7)	(0.4)	(2.7)		
Urban										
Rice	−0.48	2.31	−0.12	—	0.04	0.06	—	0.06	.72	68
	(1.6)	(8.1)	(7.6)	—	(1.2)	(1.2)	—	(0.5)		
Fresh cassava	0.44	3.38	−0.20	1.05	0.18	—	—	−0.41	.43	66
	(1.5)	(1.7)	(1.8)	(0.5)	(0.8)	—	—	(0.5)		

Note: All variables in natural logs. TX is total reported expenditures, food and nonfood, in rupiahs per capita per month. T test is in parentheses. The round and regional dummy variables were included in the above regression but are not reported here.

rural areas when compared to urban areas. For own-price elasticities, this is definitely true for rice, the price elasticity of demand for which is −0.8 in rural areas versus −0.5 in urban areas (see table 11–4). Fresh cassava elasticities are not comparable because of the anomaly already mentioned. The rural expenditure elasticities for rice and fresh cassava are also considerably larger than urban elasticities. If the respective functions are evaluated at the average per capita expenditure level in rural (Rp 3,500, U.S. $8.45[1976]) and urban areas (Rp 6,200, U.S. $14.95[1976]), the sample expenditure elasticities for rice are 0.51 in rural areas and only 0.21 in urban areas. For fresh cassava, the sample expenditure elasticities are 0.25 in rural areas and −0.11 in urban areas. Even if the rural and urban elasticities are estimated at the same expenditure level—for example, Rp 3,500 or U.S. $8.45—the rural estimates are still considerably larger than the urban ones.

While the sizes of the elasticities conform with the earlier hypothesis, this does not prove that the survey biases are the sole cause or even one of the causes of this difference. Given the background of consumption in rural areas, however, the postulated direction of bias is reasonable. It appears probable, therefore, that estimates of expenditure and own-price elasticities in rural areas, especially for nonrice staples like corn and cassava, are overstated because of the biases mentioned earlier. Rice elasticities, as previously pointed out, are also affected. Although rice is the preferred staple food, the average level of consumption by higher-income groups is considerably larger in rural than in urban areas. Rural consumers demand more rice as their incomes rise, and if the rice is own-produced, their increased consumption is equated to increasing expenditures. This own-production-as-income phenomenon does not occur in urban areas, and the maximum level of rice consumption (as well as the estimated expenditure elasticity for rice) is lower than in rural areas.

To examine expenditure changes by different income classes, two approaches were used: (1) an estimation of separate linear expenditure elasticities for low, medium, and high expenditure subsets of the whole sample; and (2) an evaluation of the whole sample equations (see table 11–4) at the average expenditure levels in each subset. As seen in table 11–5, the two approaches gave reasonable results for rice but less satisfactory results for fresh cassava and *gaplek.* All three whole sample estimates were based on quadratic formulations. For rice, which displayed this form naturally, this was not a problem, and the two approaches produced similar results. For fresh cassava and *gaplek,* however, the separate linear estimates gave considerably different elasticities than did the whole sample approach. For fresh cassava, the differences were minor at low expenditure levels and more important later on. *Gaplek* results were quite biased; the whole sample figures underestimated expenditure elasticities at low

Table 11–5
Expenditure Elasticity Estimates for Separate Expenditure Subgroups, Rural Java, 1976

	Expenditure Subgroups					
	Low		*Medium*		*High*	
Average expenditure level (Rp per capita per month per U.S. $)	Rp 1,873 ($4.51)		Rp 4,160 ($10.02)		Rp 9,365 ($22.56)	
Population share (percent)	54.6		37.1		8.4	
Food	A[a]	B[b]	A[a]	B[b]	A[a]	B[b]
Rice	0.97	0.78	0.36	0.43	0.12[c]	0.08
Fresh cassava	0.77	0.83	0.48	0.09	−1.20[c]	−0.65
Gaplek	−0.46	0.22	−0.66	−1.70	−3.22[c]	−3.65

[a]Linear expenditure elasticity estimates made for separate expenditure subgroups.
[b]Expenditure elasticities estimated by evaluating the whole sample quadratic function (table 11–4) at the average expenditure level of each subgroup.
[c]Not statistically significant.

expenditure levels and overestimated the negative elasticities at higher levels.

The main lesson to be learned is that caution in the selection of a functional form and the data set used are important in estimating these elasticities. If a quadratic or linear shape is forced on data that are not suited to these forms, the results can be misleading. Estimating elasticities—whether expenditure, own-price, or cross-price—can be a useful way to examine reactions to changes in income levels or prices if sufficient care is taken, and the sensitivity of the results to alternative assumptions is recognized.

Food Security and Consumption Analysis

The Indonesian government is interested in the use of consumption analysis to help formulate its food security program. Growth in the demand for rice (in part due to government policy to make rice available at reasonable prices and minimize seasonal price fluctuations) has outstripped production for most of the past fifteen years. Rising rice imports from an uncertain world rice market have placed a financial burden on the government. Indonesian rice imports are large both in dollar terms (about U.S. $600 million or almost 8 percent of Indonesia's total import bill in 1979) and in the country's share of total world trade in rice. This has led to the increased interest in the role of nonrice staples and their place in the food system. As seen in tables 11–2 and 11–3, corn and cassava are important staple foods for many rural people.

A number of staple foods are presently part of the government's food-security system. Rice, Indonesia's primary source of calories and protein, is ably handled by the National Logistics Agency (BULOG); BULOG's activities are discussed in more detail by Soegeng Amat in chapter 7 of this volume. BULOG also handles all wheat and sugar imports and is marginally involved in the corn trade.

The government's food policy has had a national focus. This chapter has illustrated how production-based data (such as the Food Balance Sheets) and expenditure survey data (such as the Susenas surveys) can be used to understand the broad trends of staple-food consumption, as well as the interesting regional and income-group consumption patterns observed in disaggregated data. Some of the problems inherent in survey data have been mentioned: in particular, the bias toward higher estimates of expenditure and price elasticities because of the consumption of own-produced corn, cassava, and rice.

The importance of this type of analysis to Indonesian food security has several aspects. First, an understanding of variations in staple-food consumption is essential to rational food-policy planning. At present, corn and *gaplek* are rural foods with almost no demand in urban areas. Fresh cassava is consumed in both urban and rural areas, but urban demand appears to be less as a staple and more as a vegetable or snack. Urban demand is also small (see table 11–3). Rice is the one universal staple and has received the main share of government attention.

The econometric results give indications of the probable effects of changes in government policy. A policy to rapidly increase per capita incomes, especially for the poorest groups, will lead to large increases in rice consumption in both urban and rural areas. Even if rural expenditure elasticities are overestimated and are, in fact, no higher than the urban average (0.21), a 10 percent increase in income would lead to an extra 380,000 tons of rice being demanded.[18] If the income growth were to accrue primarily to the lower-income groups and if the rural elasticities were as estimated in table 11–5, the increased demand would be much larger.

Increased incomes would also lead to some increased fresh-cassava demand in rural areas but a fall in demand in urban areas. In rural areas, the demand for both corn and *gaplek* would decrease (tables 11–4 and 11–5). Since corn and *gaplek* are the two domestic nonrice staples most frequently mentioned as objects of food policies to diversify consumption away from rice, other methods would be needed to increase their consumption in rural areas. Price policies could be used: *gaplek* has a sizable negative own-price elasticity, and we can assume that the same would be true for corn if it were widely marketed.

The reservations raised earlier are important. If expenditure and own-price elasticities for corn and cassava are overstated, the impact of a price policy to switch consumption away from rice by raising its relative price would be less effective than implied by the sizable own-price elasticities for fresh and dried cassava.

The fact is that most poor urban residents, many of whom have recently come from rural areas, consume only very small amounts of corn and dried cassava, even though these staples could be purchased at prices considerably lower than those for rice. This strong rice bias is concealed somewhat in the expenditure survey data for rural areas because of the own-production-as-income phenomenon. Programs in rural areas to rapidly switch consumption from rice to corn and dried cassava need to be carefully evaluated and field-tested in order to ascertain the real degree of consumer response to changed market prices.

These reservations do not necessarily mean that price policies cannot be used to influence consumption in rural areas. The present mixed staple-food diets in these areas and their seasonal and regional variations all indicate consumer responsiveness to production, availability, and relative prices. Substantial amounts of rice, corn, and cassava are purchased in rural areas, and market prices are therefore important.[19] To overestimate the extent of the responsiveness to changes in the relative prices of the less-preferred staple foods, however, could lead to inappropriate recommendations for food-policy changes.

Although the variations in consumption patterns observed in disaggregated data imply that food security (and policies designed to assure it) will mean quite different things to different groups in the Indonesian population, the use of only aggregate, national-level data does not supply sufficient information to make realistic recommendations. At the very least, the consumption differences between urban and rural areas have to be considered, and disaggregation by rural income subsets is desirable. The foregoing discussion has illustrated ways in which expenditure survey data can be used to achieve this disaggregation. While this chapter has drawn attention to the need for caution in the analysis of disaggregated data, more widespread use of such information in developing countries will result in better government planning to meet food-security goals.

Notes

1. The question of minimal calorie requirements has been discussed by Sayogyo, Professor of Rural Sociology of the Bogor Agricultural University. Based on the 1973 FAO/WHO recommendations and on the distribution by age, sex, and body weight of the Indonesian population (infants, children, and adults), a minimal requirement of 1,910 calories and 39.2 grams of protein per day was calculated. This calculation is based on a

protein score of 62 and a slight increase in the body weights of adult men and women in the future. When these figures were further adjusted by a 10 percent loss factor, the result was a minimal daily requirement of 2,100 calories and 45.9 grams of protein. See Sayogyo (1978).

2. Food Balance Sheets for Indonesia are prepared each year by the Central Bureau of Statistics. They are based on production estimates and are adjusted for imports, exports, nonfood uses, seed, feed, and wastage. Figures are only available at the national level.

3. Of the first six Susenas surveys, consumption data are available from the Central Bureau of Statistics, Jakarta, for Susenas I (December 1963 to January 1964), Susenas II (November 1964 to February 1965), Susenas IV (October 1969 to April 1970), Susenas V (1976), and Susenas VI (1978). The published data from the last two surveys are the most complete. No published information on Susenas III (1967) is available.

4. Much of the corn and cassava in Java is grown in upland rain-fed areas. Some of these areas are among the poorest rural areas in Java, and local consumption patterns shift between and among the staple foods, depending on their availability and relative prices. For more information on diversity in the diet, see Dixon (1979b).

5. Food intake is recorded, based on consumption during the preceding week. For certain other consumer goods such as clothing, the preceding month was the reporting period; for consumer durables and major items (house repairs), the past three months were used. All purchases and consumption were then converted to per-week figures.

6. The eight cereals included were the following: milled rice, sticky rice, rice products, young corn, dried corn on the cob, corn grain, corn flour, and wheat flour. Roots and tubers had six groupings as follows: fresh cassava, *gaplek* (dried cassava), cassava starch, sweet potatoes, taro, and sago.

7. An economically inferior food has a negative expenditure elasticity: As income increases, purchases of the food decrease. In Indonesia, an example of an inferior staple for most income groups is *gaplek*. A normal food has an expenditure elasticity between zero and unity: As incomes increase, demand increases but at a lower rate. Rice is a classic normal food. A superior or luxury food has an expenditure elasticity greater than unity (1.0); meat and poultry products are luxury foods for many Indonesians.

8. Elasticities measure the change in demand for a good, given a change in income or expenditure, the price of the good, or the price of other goods. Elasticities are unitless numbers; an elasticity of 1.0 means that a 10 percent increase in income (or price of X or Y) will create a 10 percent increase in consumption of X (or demand for X).

9. If the expenditure elasticity for rice is 1.0 for a low-income group

that at present has total expenditures of rp 2,000 per capita per month and consumes 1.2 kg of rice per person per week, a 10 percent increase in expenditure (to rp 2,200) by this group would mean a 0.12 kg increase in rice consumption (to 1.32 kg per week). At higher expenditure levels (rp 10,000 per capita per month) with larger rice consumption (3 kg per person per week), the same 10 percent increase in expenditures (to rp 11,000) may result in a lower expenditure elasticity (0.5) but a larger absolute increase in rice consumption of 0.15 kg of rice per person per week when compared to the low-income groups.

10. Own-price elasticities should be negative (if the price of food *X* goes up, *with everything else unchanged,* a consumer would buy less of it), but cross-price elasticities can be either positive or negative, depending on whether or not the two goods (the one consumed and the one whose price has changed) are substitutes or complements. If they are substitutes and the price of one food increases, consumption may shift to the other food, and thus the elasticity is positive; an example could be brown sugar or refined sugar. For complements, the reverse is true, and the elasticity is negative. Complements are usually consumed together or at the same time (for example, tea and sugar); if the price of one food goes up, the demand for the complement decreases, and the cross-price elasticity is negative.

11. In general, corn, rice, and *gaplek* have similar calorie contents per unit weight (340 to 360 kcal per 100 gm). Fresh cassava, containing substantial amounts of water, has about one-third the calories of the other dry staples (110 kcal per 100 gms). Whereas corn and rice are similar in terms of protein content, cassava is devoid of protein. In rural Indonesia, corn and dried cassava have traditionally sold at much lower prices than rice, and so consumers have received a calorie bonus by purchasing corn and *gaplek*.

12. The market for cassava products, especially dried roots, is more integrated than the corn market because of the strong demand and the high prices for dried roots to be pelletized and exported to Europe for animal feed. The domestic starch industry is also based on fresh cassava and creates strong localized demand. For more information on cassava, see Dixon (1979a).

13. Much of this work is based on research done by C. Peter Timmer. Results from Timmer's analysis, based on a slightly different data set (*gaplek* not included), are presented in Timmer and Alderman (1979). For more analysis of the Indonesian food-policy question, see Alderman and Timmer (1980) and Timmer (1980).

14. The data used consist of the quantity and expenditure information from the Susenas surveys grouped by expenditure class, by urban or rural area, and by province. For the all-Indonesia sample, there are 1,800 possible observations or cells: twelve separate expenditure classes subdivided into three subrounds for twenty-five provinces by urban or rural areas.

Some of the cells are empty, and any observation with fewer than ten people in it (about two or three households reporting) was excluded. The remaining observations were weighted by the population reported in each cell.

15. The expenditure subgroups were based on levels of staple-food consumption. This was done because of the very wide variation in income distribution between urban and rural areas. The percent of urban or rural population in each expenditure subgroup is comparable, and each subgroup shares a common level of calorie consumption. The lower-expenditure group—in both urban and rural areas—has about 50 to 55 percent of total population in that area, the medium group has about 40 percent, and the high group, the remainder, about 8 percent.

16. Regional dummies have been very important. They reflect the different consumption patterns that prices alone do not account for; for example, West Java is a rice-dominated area, whereas the diets in Central and East Java have more corn and cassava. Within provinces, important dietary variations also exist that can be captured by disaggregating the data below the provincial level.

17. This market-induced result is partly due to the cross-sectional data used. If fresh cassava prices were to increase in any given market location, consumption would decrease, and a normal negative own-price elasticity would be estimated.

18. Based on a total Indonesian population of 150 million people and average per capita rice consumption (in all forms) of 120 kg per year.

19. Analysis of the 1976 Susenas survey indicated that substantial amounts of the staple foods consumed in rural areas were purchased: 63 percent of all rice, 60 percent of corn, 34 percent of fresh cassava, and 50 percent of *gaplek*. These numbers underestimate the true extent of own-production and self-sufficiency. Many farmers sell food at harvest time in order to repay debts or obtain cash and then repurchase the same or other staples later on. In urban areas, over 90 percent of staple foods were purchased; the remainder were from government distribution of rice rations, gifts, or own-production.

Bibliography

Alderman, H. and Timmer, C.P. 1980. "Food Policy and Food Demand in Indonesia." *Bulletin of Indonesian Economic Studies* 16, no. 3:83–93.

Central Bureau of Statistics, Government of Indonesia. 1977a, 1977b, 1978, 1979, 1980. *Food Balance Sheets, 1968–1974, 1975, 1976, 1977, 1978,* Jakarta.

———. 1966. *Susenas I, Pengeluaran Untuk Konsumsi Penduduk* (Population Consumption Expenditures), Report No. 2, Jakarta.

———. 1968. *Susenas II, Pengeluaran Untuk Konsumsi Penduduk* (Population Consumption Expenditures), Report No. 4, Jakarta.

———. 1973. *Susenas IV, Pengeluaran Untuk Konsumsi Penduduk* (Population Consumption Expenditures), Report No. 3, Jakarta.

———. 1978. 1979. *Susenas V, Pengeluaran Untuk Konsumsi Penduduk* (Population Consumption Expenditures), VUS 78–24, 78–25, 78–26 and VUS 79–29, Jakarta.

———. 1981. *Susenas VI, Pengeluaran Untuk Konsumsi Penduduk* (Population Consumption Expenditures), VUS 81–33, 81–34, Jakarta.

Dixon, J.A. (1979a). "Production and Consumption of Cassava in Indonesia." *Bulletin of Indonesian Economic Studies* 15, no. 3:83–102.

———. 1979b. "Diversity in the Diet and Staple Food Consumption Patterns in Indonesia (1969/70 to 1976)." *Kajian Ekonomi Malaysia* (Malaysian Economic Studies) 16, nos. 1, 2:137–152.

Sayogyo. 1978. "Tingkat Pendapatan Rumah Tangga dan Kecukupan Gizi." ("Household Income Levels and Nutritional Sufficiency"). Paper presented at the National Workshop on Food and Nutrition, Bogor, Indonesia, July 10–14.

Timmer, C.P. and Alderman, H. 1979. "Estimating Consumption Patterns for Food Policy Analysis." *American Journal of Agricultural Economics* 61, no. 5:982–987.

Timmer, C.P. 1980. "Food Prices and Food Policy Analysis in LDCs." *Food Policy,* August: 188–199.

12 Evaluating Trade-Offs and Complementarities among Public Investments in the Rice Sectors of Asian Countries

Howarth Bouis and
Robert W. Herdt

Prior to World War II, Asia as a whole was a net exporter of cereals. During the past thirty years, however, the region has become a net importer, depending increasingly on supplies from the major Pacific Rim exporters: Australia, Canada, and the United States.[1] A study by the International Food Policy Research Institute (IFPRI) projects that a fourfold increase in net cereal imports to Asian developing countries will occur between 1975 and 1990 (table 12–1). An increase in imports of this magnitude could hardly be sustained without a large increase in international cereal prices, in view of expected strong demand for feed-grain imports in middle- and high-income countries, which presently consume the bulk of world grain imports.

Several Asian importing countries have experienced high rates of population growth and rapid rural-to-urban migration; yet they confront a continued concentration of employment in agriculture. For many, the energy price increases of the 1970s have made imports more costly to finance, with the result that pressures for food self-sufficiency have increased.[2] Given the primary role of rice as the staple food throughout most of Asia, increased domestic rice production has been a major objective of agricultural policies in this region.

While an increase in the rate of growth of rice production is the overriding long-term rice policy objective in many low-income Asian countries, the short-run governmental objective is often primarily concerned with keeping the retail price of rice low.[3] That such a short-term policy runs counter to the long-run goal constitutes a classic trade-off in the distribution of income between consumers and producers. Only through a strategy of steadily increasing the efficiency of production is it possible to appease both groups concurrently. In land-scarce Asia, this means increasing yields.[4]

Governments committed to increasing the rate of growth of production are faced with an array of policy alternatives. The development of modern

Table 12–1
Projected Net Imports of Cereals by 1990 for Developing Market Economies
(thousand metric tons)

Region	*Actual 1975*	*Projected 1990*
Asia	7,780	32,000
South Asia	3,460	18,050
Bangladesh	800	5,300
India	1,180	14,650
Nepal	−70	410
Pakistan	550	−3,550
Sri Lanka	1,000	1,240
Southeast Asia	−710	2,280
Burma	−360	1,580
Indonesia	1,770	4,990
Malaysia	710	320
Philippines	230	1,200
Thailand	−3,060	−5,810
North Africa/Middle East	8,760	27,210
Sub-Sahara Africa	1,210	13,060
Latin America	0	−6,640
Total	17,750	65,630

Source: International Food Policy Research Institute (IFPRI), Food Needs of Developing Countries: Projections of Production and Consumption, Research Report No. 3, December 1977, Washington, D.C.

varieties of rice has created the opportunity for increasing the aggregate growth rate of yields in Asia. Investments in agricultural research may be made to better adapt existing modern varieties to environments where these varieties have already been introduced or to develop newer varieties with tolerances to environments not presently planted to modern varieties. Strong complementarities exist between availability of controlled supplies of water, fertilizer use, and the introduction of modern varieties. Investments in irrigation expand the type of environment to which modern varieties are best adapted. Studies conducted by International Rice Research Institute (IRRI) on the gap between experimental and farm yields indicate that applications of fertilizer are well below the profit-maximizing point, especially in the dry season. Depending on the region studied, this result could indicate potentially high returns to expenditures for extension, increased access to credit, and fertilizer subsidies.

What is the level of government investments in agriculture required to make up the projected regional shortfall in the supply of cereals indicated in table 12–1? What is the optimal mix of investments for research, land infrastructure, and institutional change? What would be the consequence of ignoring investments in any one of these three areas in order to concentrate on meeting short-run food needs at subsidized consumer prices?

These are long-range policy questions to which governments often give second priority in pursuing short-run objectives. What constraints do consumer-oriented price policies place on long-term growth, both as a disincentive to private investment and as a drain on scarce government resources? What are the government costs and short- and long-run production effects of producer-oriented price policies such as fertilizer subsidies or a guaranteed floor price? What are the costs of maintaining retail rice prices within a predetermined range? To what extent can governments rely on the international market for their import needs to achieve these target prices? Although the answers to these questions will vary among countries, the methodology best suited to their analysis will be similar in each. In this chapter some simple models are proposed for evaluating the trade-offs between short-run food security and long-run food and agricultural policy objectives that are the basis of a methodology for food policy analysis in Asian countries.

Modeling National Food Markets in the Short and Long Run

To quantify the separate impact of short- and long-run food and agricultural policies, it is necessary to link output both to short-run price (and hence profit) expectations and to the more gradual effects of investments in production technology. On the demand side, the effects of long-run changes in consumption taste that might occur within income groups are ignored, and final consumption is assumed to be a function of income and price only. Total consumption also depends on the demand for food by stockholders, which is in turn dependent on expectations regarding short-run price movements. To explain this behavior, an anticipatory price model is developed in which the total quantity of rice produced annually is distributed between periods in such a way as to equate marginal storage costs with expected gains to stockholders.

The short-run model would calculate consumption levels by month, by region, and possibly by income group. It could be used to measure the consequences of a government policy emphasizing free trade in rice, in which case prices would be exogenous, and imports or exports would be calculated. In the case of restricted private trade but predetermined levels of government imports or exports in which the government does not otherwise intervene, the model would calculate domestic prices. Were the government policy to emphasize control of the output price through a producer subsidy or buffer-stock scheme or the maintenance of input subsidies, the government expenditures required to pursue these policies would then be calculated.

A Long-Run Supply Model

At any point in time, the production of rice depends on the area sown to paddy and the yield. In this model of production, the area sown is linked to expected yields and farm prices. Expected yields are assumed to depend on the degree of water control, the type of technology, and the level of fertilizer applied.

In figure 12–1, four solid-line functions show yield response to applications of fertilizer to traditional and modern varieties under irrigated and nonirrigated conditions using presently available technologies. The two dashed-line functions suggest a future upward shift in the response curve as a result of agricultural research. By identifying where on each response curve (present and future) farmers operate and then multiplying the implied yields by the area planted to each of the four types of rice technology, total supply (present and future) is determined.

Within this framework, production is increased by (1) raising the yield potential of modern varieties and (2) increasing the percentage of the total rice area planted to modern varieties. These goals may be realized by identifying particular environmental factors that either limit yields or preclude the planting of modern varieties altogether and then either (1) adapting the environment to the genetic characteristics of existing modern varieties or (2) breeding newer varieties whose genetic characteristics are tolerant of these environmental constraints.

Environmental constraints may take the form of particular soil characteristics, topographical features, type of water supply, climatic conditions, biotic properties of indigenous plants and insects, and socioeconomic conditions.[5] Government irrigation projects or extension and credit programs may be characterized as expenditures to transform the environment. Expenditures for agricultural research obviously are characterized by the second strategy given but may also identify particular constraints that can best be overcome by using the first strategy.

To project short- and long-run production performance it is necessary to:

1. Determine total land planted to rice.
2. Determine the percentage of land planted to each of the four rice technologies.
3. Obtain estimates of the four fertilizer response functions shown in figure 12–1 for existing technologies.

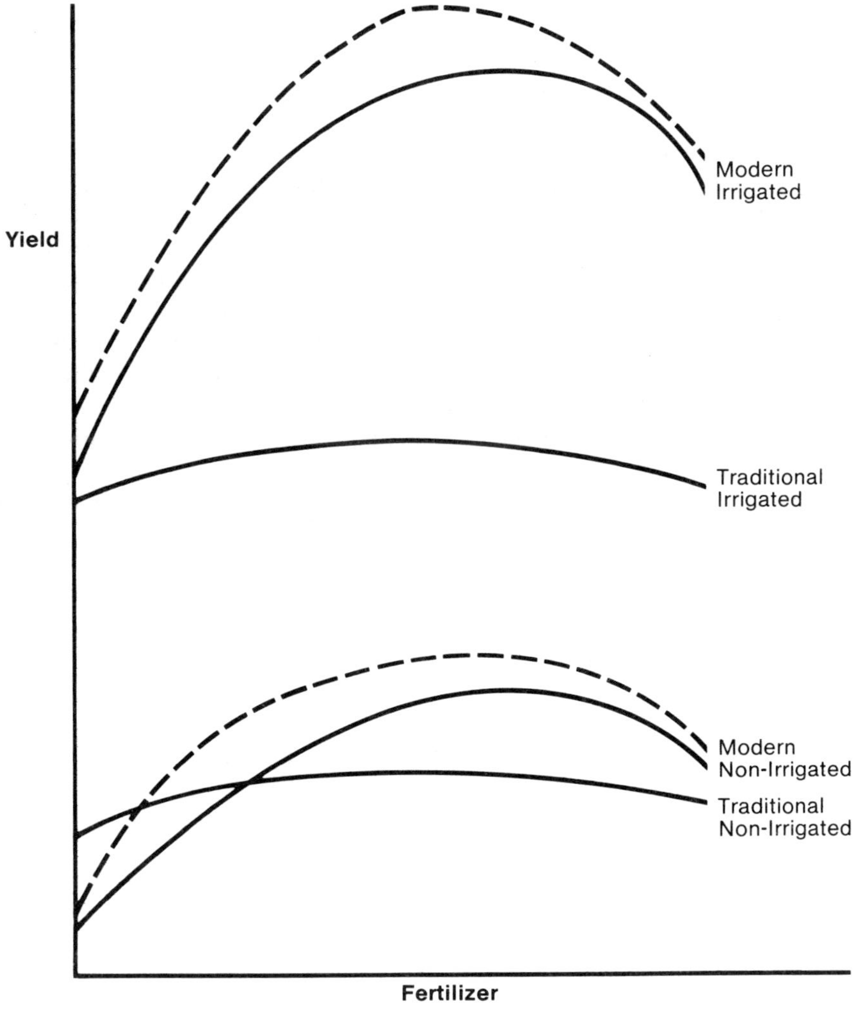

Figure 12–1. Yield Response to Applications of Fertilizer on Traditional and Modern Varieties under Irrigated and Nonirrigated Conditions Using Presently Available Technologies

4. Obtain projections of the two anticipated fertilizer response curves for future rice varieties and technologies.
5. Determine where farmers will operate on each of the six fertilizer response functions.[6]

Total area planted to rice may be determined as a function of lagged farm prices and lagged yields of rice and competing crops. Projections of the percentage of this land that is irrigated are then primarily a function of government expenditures on new irrigation and can be derived from the allocation of public investment resources among feasible irrigation projects and their projected costs. Expenditures for irrigation may also raise yields by upgrading existing irrigation systems.

Expenditures for agricultural research ultimately expand the area planted to modern varieties. They also shift the fertilizer response curves upward in areas where modern varieties are presently planted. In Asia, the development of high-yielding varieties that are early-maturing, drought-resistant, and tolerant of adverse soils, deep water, and low temperatures will significantly improve the appropriateness of modern varieties to more widespread use. Projections of the distribution of land between traditional and modern varieties must be based on an evaluation of the particular environmental constraints that at present preclude the planting of modern varieties. An assessment is also required of the prospects for developing newer varieties that overcome these constraints at various levels of research and development expenditure.

The development of varieties that are disease-, insect-, and drought-resistant will shift the fertilizer response curve upward. Projections of future upward shifts in these response functions are necessarily conjectural but may be based on past expenditures for research and past trends in yield growth.

Present fertilizer response functions may be estimated from farm-survey data or from experiments conducted on farmers' fields. In determining where on these fertilizer response curves farmers operate, it can be assumed that they operate at the profit-maximizing point, which may be calculated using the ratio of the fertilizer price and the paddy price. Farmers have been observed to operate below this point, however. One hypothesis explaining this is that farmers apply fertilizer below the profit-maximizing point because they are risk-averse. If this is the case, the probability distribution of the yield needs to be determined for each level of fertilizer application, along with farmers' risk preferences. A given fertilizer-to-paddy-price ratio will then determine a unique level of fertilizer application and yield as before but with farmers maximizing a utility function that includes risk as well as profit. Thus it may be alternatively assumed that farmers will approach the profit-maximizing point at a rate determined by the following: (1) the degree of yield uncertainty associated with the crop varieties in use and the production technology adopted, (2) their access to credit, and (3) the accuracy of their expectations regarding paddy and other product prices.

Implicit equations describing the proposed production model for a given time period, t, are listed as follows:

Area planted in rice:

$$A = A\ (P_{-rc}, P_{-a}, Y_{-rc}, Y_{-a}) \qquad (12.1)$$

Percentage of rice area under each technology:

Modern varieties: $PC_m = PC_m\ (G_{-r}, G_{-c}, G_{-e})$ (12.2)

Irrigation: $PC_i = PC_i\ (G_{-ir})$ (12.3)

Irrigated modern varieties: $PC_{m,i} = PC_m + PC_i - PC_m \cap PC_i$ (12.4)

Rain-fed modern varieties: $PC_{m,ni} = PC_m - PC_{m,i}$ (12.5)

Irrigated traditional varieties: $PC_{t,i} = PC_i - PC_{m,i}$ (12.6)

Rain-fed traditional varieties:
$PC_{t,ni} = 1.0 - PC_{m,i} - PC_{m,ni} - PC_{t,i}$ (12.7)

Yield under each technology:

Irrigated modern varieties:
$Y_{m,i} = Y_{m,i}\left(P_{-rc}, P_f, G_{-ir}, G_{-r}, G_{-c}, G_{-e}\right)$ (12.8)

Rain-fed modern varieties:
$Y_{m,ni} = Y_{m,ni}\left(P_{-rc}, P_f, G_{-r}, G_{-c}, G_{-e}\right)$ (12.9)

Irrigated traditional varieties: $Y_{t,i} = Y_{t,i}\left(G_{-ir}, G_{-e}\right)$ (12.10)

Rain-fed traditional varieties: $Y_{t,ni} = Y_{t,ni}\left(G_{-e}\right)$ (12.11)

Total supply:
$S = A\left(PC_{m,i}\, Y_{m,i} + PC_{m,ni}\, Y_{m,ni} + PC_{t,i}\, Y_{t,i} + PC_{t,ni}\, Y_{t,ni}\right)$ (12.12)

Key:
Exogenous variables: P = farm price; G = government expenditure

Subscripts: $-$ = distributed lag
rc = rice
a = crop substituting with rice in production
f = fertilizer
r = research
e = extension

c = credit
ir = irrigation
m = modern varieties
t = traditional varieties
i = irrigated land
ni = nonirrigated land

The Anticipatory-Price Model

In order to calculate the pattern of consumption and storage over time that would occur under given trade and domestic-price policies, an anticipatory-price model, based in part on earlier studies by Working (1958) and Goldman (1974), is proposed. For expository purposes, a simplified version of the proposed model is presented for the case of one commodity, a single region, and two time periods (semesters) and for which the level of imports or exports is determined exogenously according to government policy.

A supply, S_1, of the commodity is harvested in the first period. S_1 may be all that is produced during the entire year or a second crop, S_2, may be harvested in the second period. Periods 1 and 2 are selected such that S_1 is greater than S_2. Depending on (1) the position of the demand curve in the two periods, (2) the relative sizes of S_1 and S_2, and (3) the cost of storage, it may be profitable to store a part of S_1 for consumption in period 2. If it is assumed that the demand schedules in the two periods, D_1 and D_2, are known with certainty and that S_1 and S_2 are also known with certainty and will be entirely consumed within the year, it can be shown that the difference in price in the two periods will be equal to storage costs (figure 12–2).

In general, however, S_2 and D_2 are known with far less certainty than S_1 and D_1 in period 1, when inventory decisions are made. Some expectations of the magnitudes of S_2 and D_2 (call these expectations S_2^* and D_2^*) are formed on the basis of past experience. For any given demand schedule in period 2 (say, D_2^*), expected consumption in period 2, C_2^*, which is equal to inventories from period 1 plus S_2^*, implies an expected price in period 2, P_2^*. Competitive market forces set P_1 such that the difference between P_2^* and P_1 is equal to storage costs and such that $C_1 + C_2^*$ just exhausts $S_1 + S_2^*$.

Deviations of D_2 from D_2^* and S_2 from S_2^* will result in deviations of P_2 around P_2^*. P_2 may range above P_2^*, as shown in figure 12–2, resulting in unusually high profits to storage, or it may fall below P_2^*, resulting in losses to storage. Thus, while over a number of years the average of $P_2 - P_1$ should approximate storage costs, $P_2 - P_1$ for individual years may be substantially above or below storage costs.

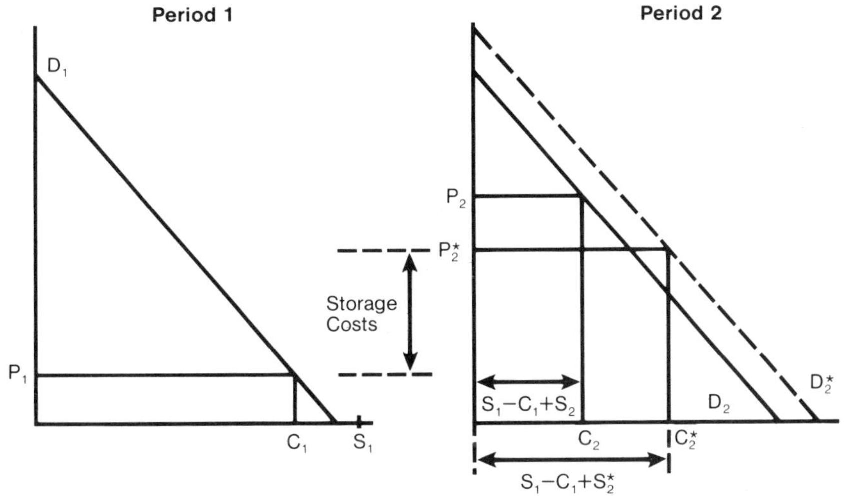

Figure 12–2. Difference in Price in the Two Periods

In applying this model to a national rice market, the following assumptions can be made:

1. The demand curves in periods 1 and 2 are known.
2. Price in period 1 is formed when S_1 is known.
3. No stocks are carried over across years.
4. Storage costs are determined as a markup, k, over the price in period 1.

$$P_2^* = P_1\,(1 + k) \tag{12.13}$$

The expected quantity available from production and imports in the second period, S_2^*, can then be calculated by adding the fitted value from an estimated supply function for the second period to the predetermined level of imports. If the demand curve for rice has intercept a and slope b:

$$P_1 = a - b\,C_1, \tag{12.14}$$

and

$$P_2^* = a - b\,C_2^*. \tag{12.15}$$

Substituting for P_2^* from (12.13):

$$P_1\,(1 + k) = a - b\,C_2^*. \tag{12.16}$$

Adding (12.14) and 12.16):

$$P_1 (2 + k) = 2a - b (C_1 + C_2^*). \tag{12.17}$$

Recalling that $C_2^* = S_1 - C_1 + S_2^*$:

$$P_1 = \frac{2a - b (S_1 + S_2^*)}{2 + k}. \tag{12.18}$$

Then consumption in the first period can be calculated:

$$C_2 = \frac{a - P_1}{b} \tag{12.19}$$

The amount stored between periods is then simply $S_1 - C_1$. Once the production in the second period is known with certainty, the levels of consumption and price in this period can be calculated as follows:

$$P_2 = a - b \left(S_1 - C_1 + S_2\right) \tag{12.20}$$

$$C_2 = \frac{a - P_2}{b} \tag{12.21}$$

Equations 12.18 through 12.21 provide the solutions for prices and consumption levels under the assumption that the government regulates the quantity of rice imported or exported but permits the domestic market to operate freely otherwise. If the government were to choose to stabilize domestic prices between predefined limits by manipulating public stocks and the level of imports, an additional iteration would be needed in the outlined calculation above where either P_1 or P_2 falls outside these limits. This additional iteration requires the formulation of a cost-minimizing decision rule for public stocks and government imports of the type discussed by Shlomo Reutlinger in chapter 2.

A More Disaggregated Model

Asian countries tend to be quite heterogenous with respect to consumption preferences, agroclimatic character, and income level. For models of the type discussed earlier to be useful in formulating agricultural policy in the short and long runs, disaggregation is required. Improvements to the anticipatory price model we are presently undertaking for the case of the Philippines include the following:

1. Disaggregation by region, income class, and source of income (farm or nonfarm).
2. The incorporation of commodities other than rice.
3. The separation of farm and consumer prices.
4. The further subdivision of the crop year into quarters or months.
5. The more detailed specification of alternative food and agricultural policies.

A more detailed account of these improvements is given by Bouis (1982). The data and parameters needed for the combined model include the following:

1. Estimates of own-price, cross-price, and income elasticities by commodity, income group, region, and farming and nonfarming occupations.
2. Estimates of transportation costs between regions and storage and milling costs by regions.
3. Estimates of total production of all competing cereals by region.
4. Estimates of the distribution of the grain harvested each month between carbohydrate substitutes in each region.

Links between the Supply and Anticipatory-Price Models

Both the long-run production model and the short-run anticipatory-price model can be simulated independently. Where only the long-run aggregate effects of various government investment policies are of interest, a national annual demand curve may be substituted for the anticipatory price framework. The combination of this demand curve with the supply model generates an annual price for any given year, which in turn becomes an argument in the supply equation for later periods. Where only the short-run costs and effects of a particular price or trade policy is of interest, exogenous supply projections can be used in the anticipatory price model.

When the long-run and short-run models are combined, they are linked by more than the recursive relationship between supply and price mentioned earlier. Different short-run price and trade policies cost different amounts to operate, leaving more or fewer resources to be spent on long-run investments.

In a combination of these models, the function suggested for allocating total government expenditures among short-run and long-run policies is a simplistic one. The government gives first priority to satisfying short-run needs and then invests what funds are left for increasing supply in the long run. In practice, budgets that support both short-run and long-run policies are usually fixed at the start of each fiscal year. The high cost of maintaining a buffer stock in a surplus year, for example, will not necessarily decrease expenditures for irrigation, extension, or credit. More complex relationships allocating funds among short- and long-run expenditures might be specified in later experiments with the combined model, since it is believed that the trade-off between these budgetary alternatives is perhaps the most important dilemma facing Asian agricultural policymakers.

Strengths and Limitations of the Models

The supply and anticipatory-price models described previously are designed to deal with a specific set of policy options. It is worth noting here the advantages of using these models individually and together in evaluating these alternatives as well as a few of their limitations.

The supply model emphasizes the complementarities among introduction of modern varieties, access to controlled supplies of water, and increased fertilizer applications in raising aggregate yields. Many countries in Asia no longer have the option of increasing rice production by bringing presently unused land under cultivation. This has led to the development and introduction of modern varieties to increase yields. Many farmers have not adopted modern varieties, and where they have been adopted, farm-level yields have been well below experiment-station yields. Studies have identified the principal causes for this as the following:

1. Modern varieties do not grow well under nonirrigated conditions.
2. Modern varieties do not grow well in various other microenvironments that are different from that of the experiment station.
3. Farmers do not have the necessary know-how to use the more complicated technology.
4. Farmers do not have sufficient access to credit to be able to afford the increase inputs that the new technology requires.

Functions incorporated in the supply model attempt to quantify the effect on yields of the relaxation of each constraint through government investments.

This approach, then, can identify a package of subgoals that various research, irrigation, credit, and extension programs must meet individually in order to attain some final objective in common. As to the important question of whether such a package of programs would be feasible given a particular matrix of political and social relationships among landless laborers, tenants, landowners, local government officials, and the national government, however, the model is of limited use. For example, the model may correctly indicate that increased training for farmers and access to credit will greatly increase fertilizer applications and yields. This does not guarantee the following: (1) that an extension agent will contact or be able to train all farmers who have been assigned to him, (2) that a credit program will be effectively administered, or (3) that fertilizer supplies will be available in the amounts required or at the program price.

The advantage of the anticipatory-price model lies in its ability to generate, as a direct result of its disaggregation, practical information for the administration of a government policy whose objective it is to control the price of rice. Examples of such information might include the following: (1) monthly peak handling and storage-capacity requirements for a buffer stock, (2) expected monthly cash-flow needs for regional purchasing and disbursement centers, (3) optimal location of storage facilities, or (4) scheduling of import disbursements. This model may also show the differential effects of various price policies in the consumption of cereals by different groups depending on their location, occupation, and income levels.

Supply-demand models aggregated at the national level on an annual basis are not appropriate for analyzing projected costs of a buffer stock where relatively large regional and seasonal price variations occur. Projected levels of injections or procurements necessary to maintain the annual national average price within the bounds of a price band may understate the levels of injections or procurements necessary to bring all regional and seasonal prices (which may fall considerably above or below the average price) within the band. In cases in which the width of the band is actually narrower than the range of normal intrayear regional and seasonal price variation, the government is forced to take over a part of the transportation and/or storage function of the private market and to buy and sell in the same year.[8] The best that an annual national model can do in such a situation is to project whether the government will be a net buyer or seller.

In combining the supply and anticipatory price models, this methodology provides a way to quantify the trade-off between short-run price stability and long-run growth in production. A primary difficulty with implementing this methodology is to link shifts in and movements along the fertilizer response curve to particular levels of expenditures for research, extension, and credit. The rate of productivity of agricultural research or the effectiveness of future extension and credit programs are particularly difficult to evaluate and project. Sensitivity analysis can at least indicate how accurate empirical forecasts must be in order that particular policy recommendations suggested by the model should remain valid.

An Analysis of Long-Run Supply Prospects in the Philippines

No function weighing policy objectives is proposed. Instead, simulation outcomes based on different assumptions regarding government policies and expenditures must be compared with respect to such objectives as the resulting level and stability of prices, production, and per capita rice consumption by income group.

A preliminary version of the supply model has been developed to study long-run production policies, independently of the short-run price effects, for the case of the Philippines. The results show types and sizes of long-run investments needed in the next decade in order to maintain the real price of rice at its present level. The analysis thus far stops short of asking how much such investments would cost, so that no trade-off is specified between expenditures for long-run investments and short-run price stability. For these limited purposes, the inclusion of the anticipatory price model is unnecessary.

Two alternative methods were used to project the exogenous variables: area sown in rice, shares of land planted to the four types of rice technology, the level of fertilizer use, and the size of the population consuming rice and domestically produced substitutes. The resulting projections are based on the following: (1) the Five-Year Philippine Development Plan 1978–1982 (the plan projections) and (2) the observed historical rates of change of exogenous variables (the trend projections).

Table 12–2 summarizes the price, output, and average yields projected by the model.[9] Projection 1, based on the development plan, indicates a slight increase in the real price by 1990. This increase, to Pesos 1.18/kg (U.S. $0.17), indicates that if the productivity of fertilizer, irrigation, and modern varieties remain at their present levels, demand will grow slightly more rapidly than supply, even with the rapid growth in input use assumed in the plan projections. In fact, under this set of assumptions, the shadow price ratio of fertilizer to rice declines from 9.0 in 1975 to 7.0 in 1980 to 3.3 in 1985 and becomes zero by 1990. This trend in the shadow price ratio implies that even if fertilizer were given away, production would not increase beyond the level shown.

Projection 2, based on the trend growth rates for exogenous variables, results in sluggish output growth, and the real rice price in 1990 is higher by a third than that resulting from the plan projection. To maintain the present real rice price through the decade, an expanded rate of implementation of

Table 12–2
Projections of Rice Price, Output, and Yield Using Alternative Models and Alternative Projections of Exogenous Variables for the Philippines

		1980			*1985*			*1990*		
Projection	*Exogenous Variable Projection*	*Price (Pesos/kg)*	*Output (1,000 metric tons)*	*Yield (metric tons/ hectares)*	*Price (Pesos/kg)*	*Output (1,000 metric tons)*	*Yield (metric tons/ hectares)*	*Price (Pesos/kg)*	*Output (1,000 metric tons)*	*Yield (metric tons/ hectares)*
1	Plan	1.10	7,127	1.96	1.06	8,258	2.22	1.18	9,022	2.28
2	Trend	1.23	6,812	1.92	1.28	7,687	2.10	1.58	8,097	2.13
3[a]	Plan	1.01	7,366	2.02	0.84	9,088	2.44	0.72	11,026	2.90
4	Trend	1.13	7,047	1.99	1.00	8.505	2.32	0.93	10,069	2.65

Source: Herdt, Te, and Barker, 1981.

Note: 1975 price was Pesos 1.21/kg at constant 1972 prices, output was 5,804 thousand metric tons, and yield was 1.65 tons per hectare.

[a]Differs from model in lines 1 and 2 by assuming a 10 percent increase in the linear fertilizer response coefficient every five years.

the advanced technology, at least to the rate projected by the development plan, would appear to be needed.

Projections 3 and 4 introduce the element of technological change into the analysis. For both projections there is an assumption that fertilizer response improves by 10 percent in each five-year period. Given this assumption, both projections result in slightly declining real prices, although the slower output growth in the case of the trend projections does lead to a slower rate of decline than in the case of the plan projection.

These results indicate that the present price of rice can be maintained or even lowered if their is an improvement in the productivity of input use. This objective will not be achieved, however, if only the rates of input use are increased.

Notes

1. The trend among Asian countries toward increased cereal imports and dependence on the large Pacific Rim exporters has been discussed in chapter 1.
2. See Falcon (1978).
3. See Timmer (1975).
4. Increased agricultural efficiency through land-saving technical innovation has been seen as a driving force in general economic development. See Johnston and Kilby (1975) and Mellor (1976).
5. See Herdt and Barker (1976).
6. This is the approach taken for all of Asia by Herdt, Te, and Barker (1978).
7. Roumasset (1976) has tested this hypothesis with a survey of farmers in Laguna and Albay provinces of the Philippines. His findings indicate that risk preferences are not major determinants of fertilizer-application rates. Farmers are probably behaving efficiently given the information at their disposal and the high cost of private credit or of gaining access to limited supplies of subsidized credit.
8. In the Philippines, the government has instituted a zero-width price band for rice. The stated floor price at the farm level of Pesos 65/cavan was equivalent in 1979 to a retail price of milled rice of Pesos 2.45/kg, just equal to the stated ceiling price.
9. The results in this section are drawn from Herdt, Te, and Barker, forthcoming.

Bibliography

Bouis, H. 1982. "Rice Policy in the Philippines." Unpublished doctoral dissertation, Food Research Institute. Stanford, Calif.: Stanford University, January.

Falcon, W.P. 1978. "Food Self-Sufficiency: Lessons from Asia." In *International Food Policy Issues, A Proceedings,* U.S. Department of Agriculture, Foreign Agricultural Service Report No. 143, January.

Goldman, R. 1974. "Seasonal Rice Prices in Indonesia, 1953–69: An Anticipatory Price Analysis." *Food Research Institute Studies,* 12:2. Stanford, Calif.: Stanford University.

Herdt, R., and Barker, R. 1976. "Networks, Environments and New Rice Technology for Farmers." Paper No. 76-10, International Rice Research Institute (IRRI), Department of Agricultural Economics.

Herdt, R., Te, A., and Barker, R. 1978. "The Prospect for Asian Rice Production." *Food Research Institute Studies,* 14:4. Stanford, Calif.: Stanford University.

———. 1981. "Prospects for Rice Production and Consumption in the Philippines—A Projection." *Journal of Agricultural Economics and Development* (the Philippines).

Johnston, B., and Kilby, P. 1975. *Agriculture and Structural Transformation.* New York: Oxford University Press.

Mellor, J.W. 1976. *The New Economics of Growth—A Strategy for India and the Developing World.* Ithaca, N.Y.: Cornell University Press.

Roumasset, J. 1976. *Rice and Risk: Decision Making Among Low-Income Farmers.* Amsterdam: North-Holland Publishing Co.

Timmer, C.P. 1975. "The Political Economy of Rice in Asia, Lessons and Implications." *Food Research Institute Studies,* 14:4. Stanford, Calif.: Stanford University.

Working, H. 1958. "A Theory of Anticipatory Prices." American Economics Association Papers and Proceedings, 70th Meeting. Supplement to Vol. 48, pp. 188–199.

13 Modeling the Impact of the ASEAN Food-Security Reserve

Somporn Hanpongpandh

The occurrence of the 1974 world food crisis has encouraged countries around the world to concentrate more on how to protect themselves in the event of possible global food shortages. The World Food Council, established by United Nations General Assembly Resolution in 1974, has made a number of proposals, one of which is global action on food reserves. The proposed system of international grain reserves would have set aside an equivalent of 50 days of world consumption in the principal exporting countries, either in the form of grain stocks or in idle cropland.

Startled by the same worldwide outbreak of food shortages and aroused by the global action on international food reserves, all five countries of the Association of South East Asian Nations (ASEAN), which includes Indonesia, Malaysia, the Philippines, Singapore, and Thailand, expressed their interest in the establishment of a food-security reserve system within the Southeast Asian region. Subsequently, it was recommended at the Second Meeting of the Committee on Food, Agriculture and Forestry (COFAF) of the ASEAN Economic Ministers in July 1977 that an ASEAN Food Security Reserve Working Group be established to evaluate all factors pertaining to the formulation of a suitable stockholding arrangement for ASEAN basic commodities.

Rice is the main staple food in the ASEAN region. It was therefore chosen as the first food item for inclusion in the regional food-security program. Having been the region's leading producer and exporter of rice, Thailand was selected to take the lead in a study to examine alternative ways to implement the program. With the close cooperation of the Iowa State University Agricultural Sector Analysis Team in Thailand, a simulation model was developed of rice production and trade within ASEAN and between ASEAN countries and the rest of the world.[1] This chapter describes this model and discusses the implications of its results for ASEAN food distribution and storage policies. The ASEAN Food Security Reserve Agreement incorporates the agreement to establish the ASEAN Emergency Rice Reserve and was signed at a meeting of ASEAN foreign

Thanks are due to Rodney Tyers and Thammanun Pongsrikul for their special assistance in revising an earlier draft.

ministers in New York in 1979. The text of the agreement signed at that meeting is reprinted as Appendix 13A.

Pattern of Rice Consumption and Trade in ASEAN Countries

Although rice is the dominant food grain throughout the ASEAN region, the degree to which each country is either in surplus or deficit in average years as well as the extent to which secondary staple foods can substitute for rice when relative prices change varies among countries. Other important staple foods include corn and cassava, although these are consumed as staples in only Indonesia and the Philippines.

Indonesia

Rice represents about 54 percent of the total food energy consumed in Indonesia, while corn and cassava provide about 11 and 12 percent, respectively. The relative importance of rice has increased as incomes have grown, while that of corn and cassava has declined. (See the detailed discussion of these trends by John Dixon in chapter 11.) Indonesia has been the world's largest importer of rice, with about 10 percent of final consumption purchased abroad. Although the rice crop has been extraordinarily good in recent years, the cost of rice imports has had an increasing trend through the 1970s, as has the cost of maintaining public food-security stocks. (See the review of Indonesia's rice stabilization program by Soegeng Amat in chapter 7.) Thus Indonesia has a significant interest in agreements, such as that with the other ASEAN countries, that might potentially stabilize access to rice on the international market. The trend in Indonesia's imports from Thailand is compared in table 13–1 with total imports and rice consumption for the period through 1975, on which the parameters of the model are based.

Malaysia

Malaysian consumers depend on rice for about 75 percent of their total food-grain requirements. Other important carbohydrate staples are wheat, the products of which make up about 20 percent of grain consumption, and corn, which is mostly fed to livestock. Through the mid-1970s, rice imports to Malaysia declined steadily (table 13–2). More recently, however, rice imports have leveled off at about 10 percent of annual consumption requirements.

Table 13–1
Population, Production, Imports and Distribution, and per Capita Domestic Disappearance of Rice in Indonesia[a]

			Distribution of Imports			*Domestic Disappearance*	
Year	*Population (1,000s)*	*Production (1,000 tons)*	*From Thailand (tons)*	*From Other Countries (tons)*	*Exports (tons)*	*Total (tons)*	*Per Capita (kg)*
1961	95,655	8,548	376,102	687,658	—	9,611,760	100.48
1962	97,765	7,855	266,166	829,881	—	8,951,047	91.56
1963	100,570	8,453	337,718	737,592	—	9,528,310	94.74
1964	102,426	7,537	452,453	571,998	—	8,561,451	83.59
1965	105,070	7,999	108,656	84,344	—	8,192,000	77.97
1966	107,789	8,434	166,974	139,026	—	8,740,000	81.08
1967	110,584	8,872	176,551	169,499	—	9,218,000	83.36
1968	113,459	8,594	44,517	662,583	—	9,301,100	81.98
1969	116,418	9,658	81,342	523,258	—	10,262,600	88.15
1970	119,467	10,109	143,991	812,139	—	11,065,130	92.62
1971	122,603	12,483	104,841	403,659	—	12,991,500	105.96
1972	125,826	12,131	164,360	569,940	—	12,865,300	102.25
1973	129,139	11,720	266,925	1,595,766	—	13,582,691	105.18
1974	132,544	14,236	129,092	1,002,981	—	15,368,073	115.95
1975	136,044	14,820	11,525	681,111	—	15,512,636	114.03

Sources: Population and production statistics are drawn from the FAO *Production Yearbook* (1970 through 1976). Total trade statistics are from the FAO *Trade Yearbook* (1970 through 1976) and the statistics on trade with Thailand are from the Bank of Thailand *Monthly Bulletin* 18, no. 1 (January 1978), and 20, no. 1 (January 1980).

[a]Domestic disappearance is here defined as the sum of production and net imports.

Table 13–2
Population, Production, Imports and Distribution, Exports Total, and per Capita Domestic Disappearance of Rice in Malaysia[a]

			Distribution of Imports			*Domestic Disappearance*	
Year	*Population (1,000s)*	*Production (1,000 tons)*	*From Thailand (tons)*	*From Other Countries (tons)*	*Exports (tons)*	*Total (tons)*	*Per Capita (kg)*
1961	8,083	698	248,107	175,771	20,552	1,101,326	136.25
1962	8,319	664	198,879	193,513	22,775	1,033,617	124.25
1963	8,561	738	250,599	226,667	9,784	1,205,482	140.81
1964	8,829	772	293,512	213,487	7,117	1,271,882	144.06
1965	9,040	717	217,037	117,229	36,524	1,068,742	118.22
1966	9,339	791	154,094	182,272	32,327	1,095,039	117.25
1967	9,607	790	204,431	189,187	10,157	1,173,461	112.15
1968	9,890	776	190,992	125,009	2,273	1,089,728	110.18
1969	10,170	931	151,427	164,829	6,605	1,240,651	121.99
1970	10,466	1,038	127,924	238,312	4,201	1,400,035	133.77
1971	10,770	1,091	117,546	133,059	4,300	1,337,405	124.18
1972	11,085	1,176	113,021	116,821	27,289	1,378,533	124.36
1973	11,409	1,187	28,262	270,883	26,282	1,469,863	128.83
1974	11,745	1,280	74,293	279,594	14,615	1,619,272	137.87
1975	12,093	1,334	18,438	190,944	14,600	1,528,782	126.42

Sources: Population and production statistics are drawn from the FAO *Production Yearbook* (1970 through 1976). Total trade statistics are from the FAO *Trade Yearbook* (1970 through 1976) and the statistics on trade with Thailand are from the Bank of Thailand *Monthly Bulletin* 18, no. 1 (January 1978), and 20, no. 1 (January 1980).

[a]Domestic disappearance is here defined as the sum of production and net imports.

The Philippines

Rice provides about 70 percent of total food-grain requirements in the Philippines. Corn is the second most important staple, meeting about 20 percent, while the remaining 10 percent is composed of wheat. During the fifteen-year period through 1975, the Philippines was a net importer of rice (table 13–3). Since 1977, however, self-sufficiency has been achieved, and net exports have been small but positive in the ensuing years.

Singapore

During the past two decades, Singapore has undergone greater proportional changes in its food consumption mix than any other ASEAN country. Approximately 60 percent of total food-grain requirements are currently met through the consumption of rice, while wheat makes up most of the remaining 40 percent. Rice consumption in Singapore has declined over the past decade as higher consumer incomes have led to increased consumption of meats and other luxury foods. Since Singapore produces no grain, its dependence on the international market for its supply of rice is complete (table 13–4).

Thailand

In contrast to the other ASEAN countries, Thailand is a major exporter of rice, corn, and cassava. Rice exports average between 1 and 2 million metric tons in most years, a large share of which have tended to go to other ASEAN countries (table 13–5). Rice is the principal staple food, and exports are taxed, partly to keep domestic food prices low in the interests of urban consumers.

Defining Food Security for the ASEAN Region

A variety of criteria by which food security might be measured have been discussed elsewhere in this book. According to most criteria, a critical yardstick is the degree to which consumers are insured against food risk. In many developing countries, such insurance is provided by the action of governments to regulate the domestic food supply (and hence domestic food prices) through control over trade and the maintenance of public stocks. The critical role played by rice in the ASEAN countries has led to considerable government intervention in the region's rice trade, as illus-

Table 13–3
Population, Production, Imports and Distribution, Exports Total, and per Capita Domestic Disappearance of Rice in the Philippines[a]

			Distribution of Imports			Domestic Disappearance	
Year	*Population (1,000s)*	*Production (1,000 tons)*	*From Thailand (tons)*	*From Other Countries (tons)*	*Exports (tons)*	*Total (tons)*	*Per Capita (kg)*
1961	28,727	2,079	140,838	46,962	53	2,266,747	78.91
1962	29,257	2,542	356	357,644	37	2,899,963	86.88
1963	30,293	2,579	71,428	184,572	90	2,834,910	93.58
1964	31,056	2,498	109,234	189,625	91	2,796,768	80.06
1965	32,030	2,595	129,899	429,661	26	3,154,534	98.49
1966	33,049	2,647	48,952	59,232	20	2,755,164	83.37
1967	34,113	2,661	99,872	190,580	1,054	2,950,398	86.49
1968	35,224	2,965	9	8	36,658	2,928,351	83.14
1969	36,387	2,889	5	5	550	2,888,460	79.38
1970	37,604	3,401	106	0	1,239	3,399,867	90.41
1971	38,875	3,473	213,088	157,320	5	3,843,403	98.87
1972	40,199	3,315	310,004	145,887	4,680	3,766,211	93.69
1973	41,572	3,184	14,099	316,122	3,381	3,510,840	84.45
1974	42,987	3,636	47,214	119,078	1	3,802,291	88.45
1975	44,437	3,636	74,797	59,980	18	3,770,759	84.86

Sources: Population and production statistics are drawn from the FAO *Production Yearbook* (1970 through 1976). Total trade statistics are from the FAO *Trade Yearbook* (1970 through 1976) and the statistics on trade with Thailand are from the Bank of Thailand *Monthly Bulletin* 18, no. 1 (January 1978), and 20, no. 1 (January 1980).

[a]Domestic disappearance is here defined as the sum of production and net imports.

Table 13–4
Population, Imports and Distribution, Exports Total, and per Capita Domestic Disappearance of Rice in Singapore[a]

Year	Population (1,000s)	Distribution of Imports: From Thailand (tons)	Distribution of Imports: From Other Countries (tons)	Exports (tons)	Domestic Disappearance: Total (tons)	Domestic Disappearance: Per Capita (kg)
1961	1,687	195,401	140,098	142,511	192,988	114.40
1962	1,773	172,787	176,743	187,807	161,723	92.21
1963	1,775	176,865	263,002	223,399	216,468	121.95
1964	1,842	227,762	42,504	108,722	161,544	87.70
1965	1,880	172,273	118,761	99,127	191,907	102.08
1966	1,934	143,256	118,253	106,539	154,970	80.13
1967	1,978	118,672	137,533	79,465	176,740	89.35
1968	2,012	130,901	156,603	73,367	214,137	106.43
1969	2,043	133,828	103,619	48,302	189,145	92.58
1970	2,075	139,417	154,123	46,684	246,856	118.97
1971	2,110	202,388	103,197	47,204	258,381	122.46
1972	2,147	342,192	34,428	71,191	305,429	142.26
1973	2,185	84,617	154,068	43,939	194,746	89.13
1974	2,219	86,539	77,817	15,089	149,267	67.27
1975	2,248	103,568	43,012	19,042	127,538	56.73

Sources: Population and production statistics are drawn from the FAO *Production Yearbook* (1970 through 1976). Total trade statistics are from the FAO *Trade Yearbook* (1970 through 1976) and the statistics on trade with Thailand are from the Bank of Thailand *Monthly Bulletin* 18, no. 1 (January 1978), and 20, no. 1 (January 1980).

[a]Domestic disappearance is here defined as the sum of production and net imports.

Table 13–5
Population, Exports Total, and per Capita Domestic Disappearance of Rice in Thailand[a]

			Exports		*Domestic Disappearance*	
Year	*Population (1,000s)*	*Production (1,000 tons)*	*To ASEAN (tons)*	*To Other Countries (tons)*	*Total (tons)*	*Per Capita (kg)*
1961	27,181	5,063	960,448	613,248	3,489,304	28.37
1962	27,995	6,598	638,186	633,077	5,326,737	90.27
1963	28,884	7,312	836,610	581,063	5,894,327	204.07
1964	29,733	7,911	1,082,961	813,327	6,014,712	202.29
1965	30,641	7,598	681,865	1,213,358	5,702,777	186.12
1966	31,581	7,257	513,276	994,274	5,749,450	180.05
1967	32,555	8,775	599,526	882,746	7,292,728	224.01
1968	33,569	7,279	366,419	711,522	6,201,059	184.73
1969	34,631	7,891	366,602	656,462	6,867,936	198.32
1970	35,745	10,667	411,428	652,178	9,603,384	268.66
1971	36,915	8,625	637,863	953,521	7,033,616	190.54
1972	38,140	8,934	929,577	1,193,236	6,811,187	178.58
1973	39,414	8,068	403,903	444,814	7,219,283	183.17
1974	40,734	9,684	337,138	708,881	8,637,981	212.06
1975	42,093	8,564	208,828	737,877	7,617,295	180.96

Sources: Population and production statistics are drawn from the FAO *Production Yearbook* (1970 through 1976). Total trade statistics are from the FAO *Trade Yearbook* (1970 through 1976) and the statistics on trade with other ASEAN countries are from the Bank of Thailand *Monthly Bulletin* 18, no. 1 (January 1978), and 20, no. 1 (January 1980).

[a]Domestic disappearance is here defined as the sum of production and net imports.

trated by Soegeng Amat in his review of Indonesia's Rice Stabilization Program in chapter 7. This intervention has led to the transfer of some food risk from consumers in these countries to governments, which must be prepared to pay almost any price for the rice imports needed to stabilize domestic supply.

Since relatively little rice is traded internationally, the simultaneous occurrence of poor rice crops in a few large producing or consuming countries can result in a destructive shortage in the rice available for export. Furthermore, the ASEAN importers—Indonesia, Malaysia, and Singapore—have periodically absorbed a large share of world rice exports. Their degree of dependence on the international rice trade therefore warrants the investigation of mechanisms whereby the risks to which those governments responsible for the regulation of domestic rice supplies are exposed might be shared throughout the ASEAN region.

In the remainder of this chapter, food security is measured in terms of the risk ASEAN governments face that adequate rice supplies will be unavailable from outside their borders. Given the relatively minor role that international market prices have played in determining the level of imports in countries such as Indonesia (Falcon and Monke 1980), food security is defined strictly on the basis of the probability with which the ASEAN importers are able to purchase sufficient quantities of rice abroad to meet their domestic requirements. Since extreme scarcities that would deny these governments access to imports are commonly short-lived, any scheme to insure against the resulting domestic-supply shortfalls might require a relatively modest joint investment, since it would usually be invoked as a stopgap measure only.

In the model discussed in the following sections, food security is defined as the probability that the ASEAN importers are able to purchase abroad 90 percent of the quantity of rice needed to keep domestic supplies stable. The scheme for sharing rice-import risk is the ASEAN Emergency Rice Reserve, which is a regionally coordinated reserve composed of shares of the national stocks of each ASEAN country. The effectiveness with which such a reserve would secure ASEAN against food import risk is examined by the model under a range of alternative conditions, including the maximum size of the reserve, its beginning level, rules for the release of rice from the reserve, and the firmness of Thailand's export commitments to countries outside the ASEAN region.

The Model

In order to properly reflect the influence of random disturbances in the domestic and international rice markets on ASEAN food-import risk, a stochastic simulation model is used. The model is based on the econometric analysis of time series data for the interval 1961–1975, listed in tables 13–1 through 13–5. The behavior of the rice trade within ASEAN is simulated over the six years from 1978 to 1984. The model does not incorporate the roles of international market prices and national per capita income in influencing imports or domestic requirements. Instead, the average level of rice consumption per capita in each country is derived for the period 1962–1975.[2] Consumption per capita in subsequent years is then assumed to remain constant at that level: 100.5 kg in Indonesia, 127.2 kg in Malaysia, 81.9 kg in the Philippines, 98.4 kg in Singapore, and 195.1 kg in Thailand.

Growth in rice consumption, production, and trade during the simulation period is then assumed to be driven by population growth alone. The population growth paths on which this more general growth is based are also estimated from the time series in tables 13–1 through 13–5. The resulting growth functions are as follows:

$$\text{Indonesia: } \ln(\text{Pop}_1) = 9.92 + 0.0253 \text{ Time} \tag{13.1}$$

$$\text{Malaysia: } \ln(\text{Pop}_2) = 7.24 + 0.0287 \text{ Time} \tag{13.2}$$

$$\text{Philippines: } \ln(\text{Pop}_3) = 8.32 + 0.0317 \text{ Time} \tag{13.3}$$

$$\text{Singapore } \ln(\text{Pop}_4) = 6.25 + 0.0197 \text{ Time} \tag{13.4}$$

$$\text{Thailand } \ln(\text{Pop}_5) = 8.30 + 0.0312 \text{ Time} \tag{13.5}$$

These results imply annual population growth rates of 2.5 percent in Indonesia, 2.9 percent in Malaysia, 3.2 percent in the Philippines, 2.0 percent in Singapore, and 3.1 percent in Thailand.

The levels of production in Indonesia, Malaysia, the Philippines, and Thailand are assumed to be dependent on both time and population in such a way that production per capita changes linearly with time.

$$\text{Indonesia: } Q_1/\text{Pop}_1 = -0.0381 + 0.00185 \text{ Time} + U_1 \text{ Time} \tag{13.6}$$

$$\text{Malaysia: } Q_2/\text{Pop}_2 = 0.0559 + 0.00218 \text{ Time} + U_2 \text{ Time} \tag{13.7}$$

$$\text{Philippines: } Q_3/\text{Pop}_3 = 0.0664 + 0.000231 \text{ Time} + U_3 \text{ Time} \tag{13.8}$$

$$\text{Thailand: } Q_4/\text{Pop}_4 = 0.281 - 0.000658 \text{ Time} + U_4 \text{ Time} \tag{13.9}$$

In this formulation, the coefficients, $U_1, \ldots, U_4$ are random variables based on the error terms to regression equations fitted using Ordinary Least Squares. In carrying out the simulation, random numbers from the joint distribution of these terms are generated, corresponding to random production fluctuations due to weather.

Similarly, the levels of imports to Indonesia, Malaysia, the Philippines, and Singapore from outside the ASEAN region, $M_1, \ldots, M_4$, respectively, and the level of exports from Thailand to destinations outside ASEAN, X_5, are also assumed to be dependent on population and time.[3]

$$\text{Indonesia: } M_1/\text{Pop}_1 = 0.000243 - 0.000076 \text{ Time} + U_5 \text{ Time} \quad (13.10)$$

$$\text{Malaysia: } M_2/\text{Pop}_2 = 0.0373 - 0.000293 \text{ Time} + U_6 \text{ Time} \quad (13.11)$$

$$\text{Philippines: } M_3/\text{Pop}_3 = 0.0284 - 0.000354 \text{ Time} + U_7 \text{ Time} \quad (13.12)$$

$$\text{Singapore: } M_4/\text{Pop}_4 = 0.140 + 0.00230 \text{ Time} + U_8 \text{ Time} \quad (13.13)$$

$$\text{Thailand: } X_5/\text{Pop}_5 = 669 + 1.71 \text{ Time} + U_9 \text{ Time} \quad (13.14)$$

In the case of the net import equations, the disturbance terms reflect fluctuations in the availability of rice from non-ASEAN exporters to individual ASEAN importing countries. In the importing producing countries—Indonesia, Malaysia, and the Philippines—these disturbance terms are negatively correlated with the disturbance terms affecting domestic rice output: U_1, U_2, and U_3. In the case of Thailand's exports outside ASEAN, the disturbance term reflects annual fluctuations in Thailand's commitments to importers in Hong Kong and the Middle East. The export disturbance term, U_9, is positively correlated with Thailand's production disturbance term, U_4.

If, in addition to the equations 13.1 through 13.14, a set of rules is included for the disposal within ASEAN of any rice surplus in Thailand after domestic consumption needs, and commitments to non-ASEAN importers are accounted for, the result is a simple model of ASEAN rice trade in the absence of international cooperation. To close the model, a private stock is introduced in Thailand, with a capacity of 1.5 million metric tons.[4] It is assumed that first priority in the allocation of any Thai surplus is given to this stock and that any remainder is distributed among ASEAN importers in proportion to their deficits relative to target consumption requirements.[5] The level of consumption in each importing country is then equal to domestic production combined with imports from Thailand and the rest of the world. The measure of food security adopted is then the probability that the quantity of rice imported from Thailand by Indonesia, Malaysia, the Philippines, and Singapore is at least 90 percent of the amount required to keep their combined domestic consumption from falling below the fixed target per capita consumption levels detailed earlier.

This probability is derived by generating random values of the disturbance terms, $U_1, \ldots, U_9$, on the assumption that they have a multivariate normal distribution (Naylor et al. 1966). For each set of random numbers, the model evaluates net trade and consumption for each ASEAN country. By repeating this process two-hundred times, the probability that at least 90 percent of the ASEAN importers' requirements of Thai rice are met can be estimated.

Incorporating ASEAN Cooperation

Intra-ASEAN cooperation on rice not only includes the establishment of the Emergency Rice Reserve (see Appendix 13A) but also a provision whereby ASEAN importers have first right of refusal to buy Thai rice in years when other exporters are unable to meet their requirements. To incorporate this provision, lower boundaries are set on the quantity of rice exported to non-ASEAN buyers. In the event that all sources available to the ASEAN importers are insufficient to meet their domestic requirements, the level of Thai exports outside ASEAN can be reduced below that set by equation 13.14 until these requirements are met or until the lower boundary is reached. The lower boundary is maintained to permit Thailand to retain needed good will with customers outside the region.

The second and more important area of intra-ASEAN cooperation in rice is in the establishment of the Emergency Rice Reserve. This reserve is included in the model with a relatively simple set of operating rules. In years of widespread bumper crop—after domestic consumption needs and Thailand's commitments to non-Asean importers have been met, after its private stock has been replenished, and after ASEAN import requirements are fulfilled—it is assumed that the surplus of Thai rice would be used to augment the regional reserve up to a specified capacity limit. Any additional rice would be returned for domestic consumption in Thailand, as before. In less bountiful years, when Thai rice remains insufficient to meet ASEAN import requirements, the reserve is drawn down. However, the amount by which it can be drawn down cannot exceed a specified "limiting release share" of the preexisting reserve. The limiting release share is set between 70 and 90 percent, leaving the remainder as a hedge against the possibility of consecutive subnormal regional rice crops in later years.

In the event that the amount of rice available to the Emergency Rice Reserve is inadequate to meet the requirements of ASEAN importers, the Thai private stock is drawn down by as much as is needed. Where this is still not adequate, the last line of defense is assumed to be the preference given ASEAN importers over non-ASEAN importers. Thai exports outside the region can thus be reduced by the amount needed, but not beyond the predesignated lower limit discussed earlier. Frequently, even this is not sufficient to permit ASEAN importers access to 90 percent of the rice needed from abroad in order that their levels of per capita consumption should remain constant at the average for the period 1961–1975 (tables 13–1 through 13–5). In those realizations of the stochastic process in which this occurs in particular years, the model records that ASEAN importer requirements are not met before moving to the next year. After two-hundred repetitions over the six-year simulation interval, in each year the number of repetitions in which these requirements are met is divided by 200 to yield the probability that the rice trading system, with ASEAN cooperation, would meet 90 percent of the import demand of ASEAN importers. This is then the index of food security on the basis of which alternative combinations of the reserve stock ceiling and its limiting release share are evaluated by the model.

The number of contingencies actually covered by the assumed operating rules of the Emergency Rice Reserve and the ASEAN preference system is more extensive than this summary reveals. A more detailed description of the model and the assumed operating rules is given by Hanpongpandh (1979).

To use the model for the evaluation of ASEAN cooperation in the rice market, five important parameters must be prescribed as follows:

1. The beginning level of Thai private stocks: Based on records indicating a carry-over stock of 1.32 million metric tons in 1977[6] and a pipeline level of approximately 1 million tons,[7] the beginning Thai private stock was set at 320,000 tons.
2. The capacity of the ASEAN Emergency Rice Reserve: A range of possible upper limits on the capacity of the reserve is considered, from 0 to 250,000 tons. The upper limit of 250,000 tons derives from an early proposal by the government of Indonesia that each ASEAN country set aside 50,000 tons to contribute to the reserve.
3. The beginning level of the ASEAN Emergency Rice Reserve: Most experiments with the model assume that the beginning level of the regional reserve is 0. However, one simulation is based on a beginning level of 250,000 tons.
4. The limiting release share of the Emergency Rice Reserve: In most results presented in this chapter, this is set at 90 percent. Experiments have also been conducted with this share set at 70 and 80 percent.
5. Lower boundary on Thai exports to non-ASEAN countries: Lower boundary levels of 0, 100,000, and 200,000 tons are set in the experiments presented in this chapter.

Results from Model Simulations

The results presented in this chapter are derived from a total of sixty-three separate simulations, each composed of two-hundred repetitions. The capacity of the Emergency Rice Reserve is set at six different levels, beginning with 0 and increasing at intervals of 50,000 tons. For each level, simulations are conducted in which the limiting release share is set at 70, 80, and 90 percent. This results in eighteen combinations of the reserve capacity and the limiting release share. For each of these, the lower boundary on Thai exports outside the region is set at 0, 100,000, and 200,000 tons, increasing the total number of simulations to fifty-four. In all these cases, the Emergency Rice Reserve is assumed to be empty in the base year. To examine the impact of the initial size of the reserve, nine simulations are added in which both the capacity and the beginning level of the reserve are set at 250,000 tons, and the limiting release share and export lower boundary are set at the range of alternative values specified previously. The results presented are for the third simulation year, 1980, and the sixth simulation year, 1983. They are listed in tables 13–6 through 13–8.

Capacity of the Emergency Reserve

The results listed in table 13–6 indicate that while a significant improvement in ASEAN rice-import security is realized as the capacity of the

Table 13–6
Probability that at Least 90 Percent of ASEAN Import Requirements Would Be Met when the Beginning Level of the Emergency Reserve Is Zero and the Limiting Release Share Is 90 Percent

	Emergency Reserve capacity (thousand tons)						
Minimum Thai Exports to Non-ASEAN Countries (thousand tons)	*0*	*50*	*100*	*150*	*200*	*250*	*Averages*
1980[a]							
0	.82	.90	.88	.88	.88	.89	.875
100	.78	.88	.90	.87	.86	.85	.857
200	.78	.83	.84	.86	.88	.90	.848
Averages	.793	.870	.873	.870	.873	.880	.860
1983							
0	.84	.88	.92	.93	.95	.92	.907
100	.79	.91	.92	.92	.88	.88	.883
200	.80	.91	.91	.89	.92	.90	.888
Averages	.810	.900	.917	.913	.917	.900	.893

Source: The result of eighteen model simulations, each with two-hundred repetitions.
[a]1980 is assumed to be the third year of operation of the ASEAN Emergency Rice Reserve.

Table 13–7
Effects of Limiting Release Shares and Lower Bounds on Thai Exports to Non-ASEAN Countries when the Beginning Level of the Emergency Reserve is Zero

	Probability that 90 Percent of ASEAN Import Requirements Will Be Met When the Limiting Release Share Is			
Minimum Thai Exports to Non-ASEAN Countries (thousand tons)	*70 Percent*	*80 Percent*	*90 Percent*	*Averages*
1980[a]				
0	.868	.865	.875	.869
100	.858	.863	.857	.859
200	.830	.832	.848	.837
Averages	.852	.853	.860	.855
1983				
0	.898	.902	.907	.902
100	.895	.895	.883	.891
200	.882	.878	.888	.883
Averages	.892	.892	.892	.892

Source: The result of fifty-four model simulations, each with two-hundred repetitions. Each listing in the table is an average of the results from six simulations, corresponding to the six alternative levels of ASEAN Emergency Rice Reserve capacity.

[a]1980 is assumed to be the third year of Emergency Rice Reserve operation.

Table 13–8
Effects of Limiting Release Shares and Lower Bounds on Thai Exports to Non-ASEAN Countries when the Beginning Level of the Emergency Reserve Is Set at 250,000 Tons

	Probability that 90 Percent of ASEAN Import Requirements Will Be Met When the Limiting Release Share Is			
Minimum Thai Exports to Non-ASEAN Countries (thousand tons)	*70 Percent*	*80 Percent*	*90 Percent*	*Averages*
1980[a]				
0	.94	.94	.93	.937
100	.93	.91	.92	.920
200	.90	.89	.91	.900
Averages	.923	.913	.920	.919
1983				
0	.93	.95	.94	.940
100	.91	.92	.93	.920
200	.91	.88	.90	.897
Averages	.917	.917	.923	.919

Source: The result of nine model simulations, each with two-hundred repetitions. The capacity of the Emergency Rice Reserve is set at 250,000 tons in all cases.

[a]1980 is assumed to be the third year of Emergency Rice Reserve operation.

regional reserve is raised from 0 to 50,000 tons, the further improvement to be derived from still higher capacity levels is relatively small. If the probabilities associated with the three minimal levels of Thai rice exports shown in table 13–6 are averaged, the probability that ASEAN importers would have access to at least 90 percent of their import needs in 1980 (after three years of reserve operation) increases from 79.3 to 87.0 percent with the introduction of a regional reserve of 50,000 metric tons capacity. The further enlargement of the capacity of this reserve to 250,000 tons results in the improvement of this probability to 88 percent.

A regional reserve capacity of 50,000 tons is small compared with annual rice consumption in the ASEAN countries. ASEAN rice consumption in 1978 totalled approximately 32.6 million tons, of which 50,000 tons is only 0.15 percent. The reserve would need to have a capacity of 90,000 tons to meet a single day's consumption. But the establishment of the reserve is to provide rice-import security to ASEAN countries, rather than consumption security to the entire region. Even the largest importer —Indonesia—only imports 10 percent of its annual consumption requirements. In addition, ASEAN importers are assumed to have access to a Thai private stock with a capacity of 1.5 million tons and first right of refusal in deficit years over non-ASEAN importers. With agreement formed on these particularly favorable terms, and given that rice-import requirements to the ASEAN countries do not fluctuate in phase,[8] a large regionally coordinated reserve is unnecessary.

The Limiting Release Share of the ASEAN Emergency Rice Reserve

It is assumed in the model that rice can be released from the regional reserve if the excess of Thai rice production, combined with the Thai private stock, over Thai consumption requirements and non-ASEAN excess demand is too small to meet ASEAN import requirements. The release would take place only if rice is available in the reserve and then only the "limiting release share" of this rice would be made available. The effect on ASEAN import security of permitting this release share to vary between 70 and 90 percent is detailed in table 13–7.

Since the adoption of a large limiting release share implies a high priority on food security in the short run and relatively little preparedness to set aside stocks for protection in future years, an increase in the release share should improve food security more in the early years of the simulations than in later years. Such a trend is observed in the results in table 13–7, although the effect is very slight. Averaging out the influence of the minimum Thai exports to non-ASEAN countries, the increase in release share from 70 to 90 percent improves the probability that ASEAN import requirements will be met from 0.85 to 0.86 after three years of operation. After six years of operation, no such improvement is observed in these average probabilities.

Lower Boundary on Thai Rice Exports to Non-ASEAN Countries

The establishment of this lower boundary in the model recognizes the need for the maintenance of Thailand's firm trading relationship with non-ASEAN importers. The larger the quantity of Thailand's supply set aside for non-ASEAN buyers, however, the weaker is the agreement giving first right of refusal to ASEAN importers in deficit years. When the minimum quantity set aside for non-ASEAN importers is increased from 0 to 100,000 tons, the results detailed in table 13–7 indicate that the average probability with which 90 percent of ASEAN import requirements will be met declines by about 1 percent, from 0.902 to 0.891. A further increase in the lower boundary results in an additional decline of about 1 percent, to 0.883.

Beginning Level of the ASEAN Emergency Rice Reserve

With the early commitment of 250,000 metric tons to the regional reserve, a marked improvement in ASEAN rice-import security would result (see table 13–8). After three years of operation, the average probability that ASEAN importers would receive at least 90 percent of their requirements increases from 0.855 (see table 13–7) to 0.919. After six years of operation, there is a more moderate improvement, from 0.892 to 0.919. As expected, the impact of a "windfall" supply of rice of 250,000 tons in the base year would be greatest in the early years of the reserve's operation. In the long run (when the model reaches asymptotic conditions), this initial condition would not be expected to have any effect on the food-security index used.

Conclusion

The governments of the ASEAN countries have identified the stability of domestic rice supplies and prices as an important condition for economic and political stability and economic development. To maintain stable domestic supplies, the rice-deficit members of ASEAN must resort primarily to imports that are dictated solely on the basis of the size of the domestic-supply deficit in each year. Less than 5 percent of the rice produced in the world is usually available for export, and, consequently, the international rice market is relatively volatile. The governments of the ASEAN rice importers, with their rigid supply-stabilization policies, are thus vulnerable to the incidence of international supply shortfalls that would reduce their access to rice from abroad. In this chapter, the ASEAN Emergency Rice Reserve has been examined as a means of improving the rice-import security of ASEAN governments, using a stochastic simulation model.

Although the 50,000 tons set aside for the Emergency Reserve (see Appendix 13A) seems small, results from the simulation model indicate that the incidence of a shortfall by more than 10 percent in the imports needed by ASEAN rice-deficit countries would fall with its implementation from once in five years to about once in ten years.[9] Access to private stocks held in Thailand and the first right of refusal accorded ASEAN importers of Thai rice in deficit years are also found to be major factors in improving the rice-import security of ASEAN governments.

In evaluating the results from the model, attention should be drawn to some caveats. The model represents a considerable simplification of the rice-trading system. Although the role of international trading prices is limited as a determinant of quantities traded in the rice market, the consumers and producers in each ASEAN country are responsive to price, and government stabilization policies are imperfect. In addition, subsistence producers tend to reduce their consumption slightly when their production falls. Consequently, a small amount of adjustment does take place in the domestic economies of the ASEAN countries which is ignored by the model. In addition, the introduction of prices in the model would provide a means of evaluating the financial burden that would be borne by ASEAN governments in association with their domestic stabilization policies, both with and without the Emergency Rice Reserve. The other major omission in the model is the lack of any allowance for annual changes in the national stocks of ASEAN rice-deficit countries. These are now relatively large fractions of their annual consumption, and they play a role in supply stabilization policies. Steps are taken to address these weaknesses in the methodology adopted for modeling the international grain trade by Rodney Tyers and Anthony Chisholm in chapter 14.

Despite these caveats, the results obtained through the simulation studies described in this chapter represent an important contribution to the formulation of mechanisms whereby ASEAN members are able to mutually benefit from increased regional cooperation. The ASEAN Food Security Reserve Agreement is the only international agreement of its type, and it paves the way toward the identification and implementation of still more constructive policies, which can result in increased welfare within the ASEAN region.

Notes

1. The prototype model was constructed by Leroy Blakeslee of the Iowa State team during his three-week service trip to Thailand's Division of Agricultural Economics in August 1977. The model has since been revised to include the following: constraints on Thailand's private stock, revisions to the estimates of each country's per capita consumption, and constraints on the quantity of Indonesian concessional rice imports available through the U.S. Public Law 480.

2. Note that the Philippines is considered as a net importer in the model, since the time series on which the parameters are based extend over a period during which the Philippine islands consistently imported more rice than they exported (see table 13–3).

3. Consumption is estimated based on domestic disappearance, as indicated in tables 13–1 to 13–5.

4. Taking the maximum carryover of rice in Thailand during 1968–1975, which was 2.36 million metric tons in 1972, and subtracting the pipeline level of 1.0 million tons, the size of Thailand's private stock is rounded at 1.5 million tons.

5. In the event that any remaining surplus is larger than the requirements of ASEAN importers for Thai exports, it is assumed that the residual is added to domestic consumption in Thailand. Changes in the independent components of the national stocks of ASEAN importers are not accounted for by the model.

6. See Ministry of Agriculture and Cooperatives, Government of Thailand (1975b).

7. See Ministry of Agriculture and Cooperatives, Government of Thailand (1975a).

8. Within the ASEAN region, not all member countries have been affected by adverse climate to the same degree at the same time. In 1977, for example, the rice crops of Indonesia, Malaysia, and Thailand were seriously affected by drought, but the rice production of the Philippines was at its peak, and the Philippines exported rice for the first time after long years of being a rice importer.

9. These rates of incidence correspond to the average probabilities listed in table 13–6.

Bibliography

Falcon, W.P., and Monke, E.A. 1980. "International Trade in Rice." *Food Research Institute Studies* 17, no. 3: 279–305.

Hanpongpandh, S. 1979. "The ASEAN Food Security Reserve Model." Paper presented at the Workshop on Food Security in Asia and the Pacific, East-West Resource Systems Institute, East-West Center, Honolulu, Hawaii, June 18–30.

Ministry of Agriculture and Cooperatives, Government of Thailand. 1975a. "Rice Trade Policy Guidelines." A bulletin of the Division of Agricultural Economics, Office of the Under-Secretary of State, Bangkok, Thailand.

———. 1975b. "Statistics on Rice Carryovers in Thailand." An unpublished working paper of the Division of Agricultural Economics, Office of the Under-Secretary of State, Bangkok, Thailand.

Naylor, T.H., Balinfy, J.L., Burdick, D.S. and Chu, K. 1966. *Computer Simulation Techniques.* New York: John Wiley & Sons, Inc.

Appendix 13A: Agreement on the ASEAN Food-Security Reserve

The Governments of the Republic of Indonesia, Malaysia, the Republic of the Philippines, the Republic of Singapore and the Kingdom of Thailand, being members of the Association of South East Asian Nations, which Association shall hereinafter be referred to as ASEAN:

Recalling the Declaration of ASEAN Concord signed in Bali, Indonesia, on 24 February 1976, which provides that ASEAN Member Countries shall take cooperative action in their national and regional development programmes;

Noting the high vulnerability of the region to wide fluctuations in the production of basic foodstuffs and hence to instability of the region's food supply;

Noting further that the assurance of food security in the ASEAN region is the common responsibility of the ASEAN Member Countries;

Emphasizing that the establishment of a food security reserve among ASEAN Member Countries based on the principle of collective self-reliance will contribute to the strengthening of the respective national economic resilience as well as to ASEAN economic resilience and ASEAN solidarity;

Affirming the need for effective and concerted action by ASEAN Member Countries aimed at strengthening food security in the region;

Have agreed on the following Provisions:

Article I
General Provisions

The ASEAN Member Countries hereby agree that food security needs

Source: Reprinted from ASEAN Documentation Series, 1981. Published with the permission of the ASEAN Secretariat, Jakarta, Indonesia.

to be dealt with from several aspects, especially, where appropriate, through:

(i) the strengthening of the food production base of the ASEAN Member Countries;
(ii) the prevention of post harvest losses of food grains;
(iii) the establishment of a food information and early warning system;
(iv) the adoption of effective national stock holding policies and improved arrangements for meeting requirements of emergency food supplies;
(v) the promotion of stability of food prices;
(vi) the adoption of policies and programmes for improving consumption and nutrition, particularly of the vulnerable groups within each ASEAN Member Country;
(vii) the promotion of labour opportunities especially in the rural areas and increasing the income particularly of the small farmers; and
(viii) other measures, including possible long-term trade arrangements.

Article II
Establishment of the ASEAN Food Security Reserve

1. The Governments of the ASEAN Member Countries hereby agree to establish the ASEAN Food Security Reserve.
2. The term "ASEAN Food Security Reserve" shall mean the sum total of the basic food stocks, particularly rice, maintained by each ASEAN Member Country within its national borders as a matter of national policy which includes commitment to the ASEAN Emergency Rice Reserve.

Article III
Coordination of National Food Stock Policies and of National Food Reserve

1. The Governments of the ASEAN Member Countries shall coordinate in conformity with their institutional and constitutional requirements, national food stock policies which take into account the policies of other ASEAN Member Countries and which together will result in maintaining a minimum safe level for the ASEAN Food Security Reserve.
2. It is hereby understood that the establishment of the ASEAN Food Security Reserve is not intended to fill continuing food deficits of

individual ASEAN Member Countries, which normally are met through imports, commercial as well as concessional. The elimination of such deficits should, where appropriate, be attempted through increased production at an accelerated rate.

3. The ASEAN Member Countries shall further take measures aimed at assuring that their national food reserves are replenished as soon as feasible whenever they have fallen below such minimum levels as may be specified.

Article IV
The ASEAN Emergency Rice Reserve

1. The Governments of the ASEAN Member Countries do hereby agree to the establishment of the ASEAN Emergency Rice Reserve for the purpose of meeting emergency requirements.
2. Each ASEAN Member Country shall earmark within or over and above its national reserve, a certain quantity of rice. Such earmarked quantities of rice shall constitute the ASEAN Emergency Rice Reserve, the total amount of which shall initially be 50,000 metric tons of rice.
3. For the first year of operation ASEAN Member Countries agree that the earmarked quantity of each ASEAN Member Country for the ASEAN Emergency Rice Reserve shall be as follows:

Indonesia	: 12,000 metric tons
Malaysia	: 6,000 metric tons
Philippines	: 12,000 metric tons
Singapore	: 5,000 metric tons
Thailand	: 15,000 metric tons

4. Both the total amount of the ASEAN Emergency Rice Reserve, as well as the amount earmarked by each ASEAN Member Country in such Reserve, shall be periodically reviewed by the Governments of the ASEAN Member Countries taking into account the general food situation in the ASEAN region and in the world.
5. An emergency as referred to in Paragraph 1 of this Article shall be understood to mean the state or condition in which an ASEAN Member Country, having suffered extreme and unexpected natural or man-induced calamity, is unable to cope with such state or condition through its national reserve and is unable to procure the needed supply through normal trade.

Article V
Release of Rice from the ASEAN Emergency Rice Reserve for Emergency Requirements

With regard to the release of rice from the ASEAN Emergency Rice Reserve to meet the emergency requirement of any ASEAN Member Country, the following procedure shall be adopted.

(i) The ASEAN Member Country in need shall directly notify the other ASEAN Member Country or Countries of the emergency it is facing and the amount of rice required.

(ii) The other ASEAN Member Country or Countries on being requested shall take immediate steps to make the necessary arrangements to ensure immediate and speedy release of the required rice.

(iii) The prices, terms and conditions of payments in kind or otherwise, in respect of rice so released, shall be the subject of direct negotiations between the ASEAN Member Countries concerned.

(iv) The requesting ASEAN Member Country shall at the same time inform the ASEAN Food Security Reserve Board of its request to the other ASEAN Member Country or Countries.

Article VI
Replenishment of the ASEAN Emergency Rice Reserve

1. The ASEAN Member Countries which have released rice under Article V either to meet their own emergency requirements or the emergency requirements of other ASEAN Member Countries shall take steps to replenish the rice so released so that the earmarked quantity of the countries concerned shall be restored to the level indicated in Article IV.
2. Fulfillment of the responsibility under Paragraph 1 of this Article shall be subject to the constraints on the availability of supply as well as other limitations.

Article VII
Food Information and Early Warning System

1. For the effective functioning of the undertakings contained in Articles III and IV, the Government of ASEAN Member Countries agree to furnish to the ASEAN Food Security Reserve Board, referred to in Article VIII, on a regular basis information on government stockhold-

ing policies and programmes, as well as other aspects of the food supply and demand situation, in particular rice. The ASEAN Food Security Reserve Board shall circulate the said information to the Member Countries.

2. On the basis of such data collected, concise factual appraisals of the situation and outlook shall be prepared periodically and circulated to ASEAN Member Countries.
3. The information or data made available pursuant to this Article shall be treated as confidential.

Article VIII
ASEAN Food Security Reserve Board

1. For the purpose of providing supervision and coordination in the implementation of the ASEAN Food Security Reserve, the Governments of ASEAN Member Countries hereby agree to establish an ASEAN Food Security Reserve Board, hereinafter referred to as "the Board".
2. The Board shall be composed of one representative from each ASEAN Member Country.
3. The Board's terms of reference shall be as in the Annex to this Agreement.

Article IX
Final Provisions

1. This Agreement is subject to ratification by the ASEAN Member Countries.
2. The Instruments of Ratification shall be deposited with the Secretary General of the ASEAN Secretariat who shall promptly inform each ASEAN Member Country of such deposit.
3. This Agreement shall enter into force on the thirtieth day after the deposit of the fifth Instrument of Ratification.
4. This Agreement may not be signed with reservation nor shall reservations be admitted at the time of ratification.
5. Any amendment to the provisions of this Agreement shall be effected by consent of all ASEAN Member Countries.
6. This Agreement shall be deposited with the Secretary General of the ASEAN Secretariat who shall promptly furnish a certified copy thereof to each ASEAN Member Country.

Terms of Reference of the ASEAN Food Security Reserve Board

1. To coordinate periodic exchanges of information on national food policies, and stocking policies as well as production, consumption and storage programmes pertaining to basic food commodities, particularly rice, among the ASEAN Member Countries.
2. To undertake a periodic evaluation of the food situation and prospects in the ASEAN region as well as worldwide, including production, consumption, trade, prices, quality and stocks of basic food commodities, particularly rice. These periodic evaluation reports shall be disseminated to the ASEAN Member Countries.
3. To examine immediate, short term and long term policy actions as may be considered necessary to assure adequate supplies of basic food commodities, particularly rice, and to submit on the basis of such examination recommendations for appropriate action to the Governments concerned.
4. To review periodically the size of the ASEAN Emergency Rice Reserves and to work out acceptable criteria for determining the contributions of each ASEAN Member Country to such Emergency Rice Reserve and recommend appropriate action to the ASEAN Member Countries concerned.
5. To work out immediately procedures for the payments of rice released under emergency situations taking into consideration Article V(iii) of the Agreement and prevailing market practices whenever deemed necessary.
6. To review the implementation of the provisions of the Agreement on the ASEAN Food Security Reserve.
7. To be responsible to the ASEAN Committee on Food, Agriculture and Forestry (COFAF) and to submit thereto reports on its activities.

14 Agricultural Policies in Industrialized and Developing Countries and International Food Security

Rodney Tyers and
Anthony H. Chisholm

This chapter introduces a stochastic simulation model of international grain and meat markets and then applies it to examine two hypotheses about agricultural and food-security policies in industrialized and developing countries. These hypotheses are as follows:

1. That the protectionist and stabilizing agricultural policies adopted by industrialized importing countries impose a net welfare cost, since the resulting burden on their governments and consumers outweighs the benefits to their producers.
2. That the policies adopted by Asian developing countries, while they act to improve the food security of poor consumers, frequently result in average domestic producer prices significantly below world price levels and hence act to suppress domestic food production.

The evidence in support of these hypotheses—as provided by the model—then leads to the conclusion that widely distributed benefits would accrue internationally from reduced government intervention in food production, distribution, and storage in the industrialized importing countries and that the transfer of some of the resources thus saved would provide additional incentives (deficiency payments[1]) to producers in developing countries. This is not to imply, however, that all modes of government intervention in industrialized importing countries are in conflict with more dispersed international food-security interests. Some agricultural policies in industrialized countries are probably in concordance with the food-security concerns of developing countries. However, the improved

Valuable comments on earlier drafts of this chapter have been received from John Freebairn, Peter Lloyd, James Roumasset, Ammar Siamwalla, and Kym Anderson.

international-market efficiency derived from some abatement of the stabilizing and protectionist policies of the industrialized importers would release resources for expenditure on food production where it is most needed, and at the same time, reduce food prices for domestic consumers.

Three Dimensions of Food and Agricultural Policy

International staple-food markets are influenced by national food and agricultural policies that have three principal dimensions. First, the general bias of economic policies serves either to protect or tax the agricultural sector. This is usually achieved through trade and domestic-price policies, resulting in sustained market distortions that have the net effect of either rewarding or taxing domestic agricultural output. Second is the stabilization dimension, which serves to maintain relatively stable domestic prices through the use of nontariff barriers that are adjusted year to year depending on domestic production performance in relation to target levels of supply and price. Finally, some governments intervene to promote or suppress the holdings of carry-over stocks. Although this intervention is frequently an instrument associated with the first two dimensions, it has independent effects on the international market and thereby on the international distribution of costs and benefits from government intervention.

Protection and Provision

The bias for or against food production in any country that results from government policies is usually the net result of intervention in all the factor markets, including the capital and land markets, and intervention in other sectors of the economy that affects the prices of these factors. In most cases, however, the important forms of intervention in commodity markets are trade and pricing policies, which directly affect the product price. When these policies lead to producer food prices that exceed those at the border (ignoring for now domestic infrastructural costs), the policies are classified as *protectionist*. Such policies are most common in industrialized countries, especially in industrialized food-importing countries such as Japan and the European Economic Community (EEC), all of which presently hold a comparative disadvantage in food agriculture.[2] All other things being equal, the application of these policies in a few large importing countries stimulates their domestic supply and reduces domestic demand. The effect of this protectionism is to reduce international trading prices.

When trade and pricing policies lead to average domestic food prices below those prevailing at the border, these policies are classified, after Heckscher (1935), as *provisionist*. Such food and agricultural policies are common in developing countries (Peterson 1979), where food prices tend to be kept low by price and trade controls, overvalued exchange rates, or food aid from abroad. Poor consumers—especially urban consumers—in these countries are an important political constituency and such policies are consistent with development strategies emphasizing growth in the nonfood sector, where labor productivity is relatively high.[3] Indonesia and Thailand are both examples of countries adopting provisionist agricultural policies, despite their respective food-deficit and food-surplus status.[4] Since these policies act to suppress domestic supply and increase domestic demand, they tend to place upward pressure on international trading prices.

Although it is not clear, a priori, whether the combined effect of protectionism in the industrialized countries and provisionism in the developing countries results in higher or lower international prices, the effect of the protectionism alone serves to reduce the marginal social cost of food in developing countries. And thus some concordance exists between the results of protectionist policy and the consumer-oriented short-run policy objectives of the developing countries.[5] In the long run, however, this distortion of the international terms of trade away from staple-food production will tend to retard production growth in developing countries (either directly through reduced producer incentives or indirectly through the effect on overall economic growth of high-cost producer subsidies), possibly leading to increased dependency on imports from the industrialized countries.[6] The prevalence of protectionism and provisionism and the magnitudes of the resulting distortions in domestic prices are illustrated for fifteen industrialized and developing countries and country groups in Appendix 14–A.

Stabilization

Agriculture is an inherently risky industry. The vagaries of weather, pest infestations, and other unpredictable events render the size of the product uncertain until the time of harvesting. Even though large unforeseen disturbances to the level of world food production are becoming more rare as technological improvements that reduce production risk are introduced, adjustments to unforeseen fluctuations in production must still be shared among the world's consumers and stockholders. But unanticipated production disturbances in all countries do not occur in phase. Thus if most of the world's countries were to adopt free trade policies in cereals and were stocks to be held in each country so that the expected marginal returns were equated with marginal costs, then the amount of adjustment consumers would need to make would be relatively small (Johnson 1981). However, when large trading countries adopt policies to relieve consumers of their burden of adjustment (through the management of imports so as to stabilize domestic supply and price), they remove incentives for domestic stockholding by the private sector and place the entire burden of adjustment on other countries active in the world market.[7] Stabilization policies are particularly common in the rice market, which is concentrated in Asia and the Pacific and where government control over trade is endemic (Siamwalla 1979). Variable nontariff barriers affect 93 percent of world rice imports and 76 percent of exports (Falcon and Monke 1980).

Such policies to protect domestic consumers from the need to adjust their consumption from year to year are not adopted only by the more "notorious" large importing countries (China, the EEC, Japan, and the USSR). In fact, policies to stabilize domestic markets prevail in almost all countries trading in staple foods. Important exceptions appear to have been the North American cereal exporters, whose stabilization policies have focused on producer incomes. Meanwhile, food-processing industries consuming cereals at the wholesale level appear to have borne a considerable burden of adjustment (table 14–1).

The increased international price volatility that results from widespread stabilization policies (Shei and Thompson 1977; and Zwart and Meilke 1979) increases the foreign-exchange risk carried by the governments of those countries seeking to protect their more vulnerable consumers from the burden of adjustment. Thus a conflict exists between the prevalence of stabilizing trade policies and the food-security interests of developing countries dependent on the international market.

Storage Policies

National cereal stocks can be an important instrument of domestic-stabilization policy. By carrying stocks that are permitted to respond positively to the difference between expected future and current spot prices on the international market, large importers can share the burden imposed by their domestic price stabilization policies while reducing their own exposure to foreign-exchange risk. In the analytical model of Feder et al. (1977), stocks held by relatively risk-averse importers should exceed those held by exporters, whose demand for stocks is purely speculative. Until recently, however, this behavior has not been characteristic of the international distribution of cereal stocks. Changes in the agricultural policies of the major exporters in the early 1970s ended an era in which large exporter-held stocks, in combination with concessional grain sales,

Table 14–1
Coefficients of Variation of Deflated Domestic and International Food Prices

	1960–1970					*1971–1977*				
	Rice	*Wheat*	*Coarse Grains*	*Ruminant Meat*	*Nonruminant Meat*	*Rice*	*Wheat*	*Coarse Grains*	*Ruminant Meat*	*Nonruminant Meat*
Major food exporters										
United States of America	15.7	19.2	16.7	8.2	22.3	52.6	53.3	38.9	12.9	23.6
Canada	14.5	14.5	13.9	5.7	7.5	48.5	28.7	26.4	17.6	17.7
Australia	5.8	3.1	—	6.4	19.9	4.4	15.8	—	18.2	1.4
Thailand	17.0	8.5	9.0	5.4	8.6	12.1	41.0	16.2	9.7	4.2
Major food importers										
European Economic Community	6.7	4.4	3.0	7.8	12.2	9.2	2.3	3.5	7.4	7.2
Japan	8.1	2.9	2.2	16.8	9.3	10.5	13.1	14.5	7.7	5.4
India	4.5	11.2	26.5	5.8	6.6	8.0	5.2	23.1	7.2	13.9
Indonesia	22.7[a]	51.8[a]	13.8[a]	16.9[a]	—	26.0	9.8	9.8	10.7	—
South Korea	3.8	5.1	8.6	14.0	—	8.1	14.8	8.6	12.0	9.3
Minor food importers										
Bangladesh	25.8	19.2	—	8.5	9.1	38.4	41.2	—	26.7	22.3
Malaysia	10.7	3.6	3.1	2.8	—	4.0	8.8	19.4	3.2	—
Pakistan	9.7	17.1	18.9	4.9	—	24.1	8.7	21.6	16.2	—
Philippines	—	—	—	—	3.7	8.5	10.1	10.3	5.8	7.1
Singapore	12.2	2.0	9.1	4.0	3.0	34.9	21.7	12.3	11.2	16.0
Sri Lanka	7.8	—	—	—	—	20.8	—	—	—	—
International prices[b]	19.6	7.7	8.1	17.1	15.9	42.9	31.5	21.9	59.0	10.6

Source: The data in this table are based on time series of domestic retail or wholesale prices for each country made available by the International Economics Division, ESCA, USDA. Where domestic prices show a consistent tendency to grow or decline between 1960 and 1977, the standard deviation is measured about fitted (OLS) linear trends.

[a]The unusually high variability in domestic prices in Indonesia during the 1960s was associated with extreme economic and political instability not typical of modern Indonesia or any of the other countries represented.

[b]The international prices are as follows: rice—FOB Bangkok 5 percent broken; wheat—Canadian no. 1 western red spring in store, Thunder Bay; coarse grains—U.S. no. 2 yellow corn, FOB Gulf ports; ruminant meats—Australian beef, export quality, 650–700 lb. dressed weight, wholesale, Brisbane; nonruminant meats—U.S. export unit value, slaughtered poultry.

were an instrument of protectionist policy (farm-price and income supports).

During the late 1970s an apparent increase occurred in the proportion of grain held in storage by major importers (especially Europe, Japan, the Middle East, and India), consistent with a trend toward the results of the Feder et al. model (Morrow 1980). The average marginal return from stocks held by major exporters has probably been less than the average marginal costs, however, even through the 1970s. Johnson (1977) reasons that exporters still appear to need substantial reserves in order to enhance their reliability as suppliers to countries that might otherwise seek to increase their degree of self-sufficiency through protectionist policies. As Morrow also notes, the holding of larger carry-over stocks than would be justified on purely speculative grounds is probably a valuable asset in the competition for market share where production is oligopolistic. Thus the cereal-storage policies adopted by the major exporters (and increasingly also by a few of the major importers) have probably served to improve the access of developing countries to supplies on the international market. In the short run at least, these policies appear to provide another example of concordance between the agricultural policies of the industrialized countries and food security in the developing world.

A Stochastic Simulation Model of Domestic and International Staple-Food Markets

In order to measure the international distribution of costs and benefits from the pure protection, pure stabilization, and storage components of agricultural and food-security policies, an empirical model has been developed that is capable of simulating both domestic and international-market responses to national-policy behavior. The model is more advanced than those previously developed to study market stability issues in several respects:

1. It incorporates the cross effects on both the demand and supply side between the markets for five staple-food commodities.
2. It distinguishes domestic and international markets through the use of equations that quantify the net effect on domestic prices of trade and pricing policies.
3. It distinguishes private speculative components from policy-induced components of storage behavior.
4. It calculates the forecast means and variances of a variety of welfare measures, including aggregate consumer and producer surplus, stock profits, domestic policy costs, net foreign-exchange requirements, staple-food budget shares, and food-energy consumption.

5. It is global in coverage, distinguishing eighteen Asian and Pacific Rim countries and dividing the rest of the world into five country aggregates (table 14–2). (The basic model is detailed mathematically in table 14–3.)

Consumption behavior in each country and country group is assumed to be characterized by constant income, own-price and cross-price elasticities of demand, as demonstrated by equations 14.1 and 14.2.[8] Production behavior is represented by a Nerlovian "partial adjustment" model which is linear in the logs of production and producer prices, as shown in equations 14.3 to 14.7. Short- and long-run own-price and cross-price supply elasticities are thus permitted to differ considerably in accordance with empirical evidence. No attempt is made, however, to incorporate the markets for factors of production. The effect of possible changes to input subsidies can be approximated by equivalent changes in relative producer prices.

The behavior of stocks in rice, wheat, and coarse grains is based on an empirical adaption by Tyers and Chisholm (1980) of the model for risk-neutral competitive speculators, first developed by Muth (1961) and later expanded by Turnovsky (1979) and Aiyagari et al. (1980).[9] The adaption here incorporates a term in quantities only, to explain stock changes in countries where government-held stocks dominate and where closing stocks do not depend significantly on either stabilized domestic prices or international trading prices. Depending on the commodity and the country, the model permits stocks to respond to either domestic or international

Table 14–2
Countries, Country Aggregates, and Commodity Groups Studied in the Model

Countries and Country Aggregates in Which Domestic Markets and Policies Are Studied	*Country Aggregates Studied as Net Trading Entities Only*	*Commodity Groups*
Australasia	Africa	Rice
Bangladesh	Burma and Indochina	Wheat
Canada	China	Coarse grains
India	Central and South America	Ruminant meats
Indonesia	USSR	Nonruminant meats
Japan	Middle East and other Asian Countries	
South Korea	Other European Countries	
Malaysia	Other Oceanic Countries	
Pakistan		
Philippines		
Singapore		
Sri Lanka		
Thailand		
United States		
European Economic Community (EEC)		

Table 14–3
The Model

Consumption:

$$c_{ilt} = c^{T}_{ilt}\, k_{il} \prod_{j}^{m} p_{jlt}^{a_{ijl}} , \qquad \forall i,l \quad (14.1)$$

Consumption shifter: $$c^{T}_{ilt} = c^{T}_{ilo} \left(\frac{N_{lt}}{N_{lo}}\right) \left(\frac{y_{lt}}{y_{lo}}\right)^{\eta_{il}} , \qquad \forall i,l \quad (14.2)$$

Production:

Producer target: $$q^{*}_{ilt} = q^{T}_{ilt}\, f_{il} \prod_{j}^{m} \left\{ \left(p_{jlt}\, \lambda_{jl}\right)^{b_{1ijl}} \left(p_{jlt-1}\, \lambda_{jl}\right)^{b_{2ijl}} \left(p_{jlt-2}\, \lambda_{jl}\right)^{b_{3ijl}} \right\} , \qquad \forall i,l \quad (14.3)$$

Partial adjustment: $$q_{ilt} = q^{T}_{ilt} \left(\frac{q_{ilt-1}}{q^{T}_{ilt-1}}\right) \left(\frac{q^{*}_{ilt}}{q^{T}_{ilt}} \Big/ \frac{q_{ilt-1}}{q^{T}_{ilt-1}}\right)^{\delta_{il}} e^{\epsilon_{ilt}} , \qquad \forall i,l \quad (14.4)$$

Production shifter: $$q^{T}_{ilt} = q^{T}_{ilo}\, e^{g_{il}t} , \qquad \forall i,l \quad (14.5)$$

Producer price/wholesale price ratio: $$\lambda_{il} = 1 - \tau_{il} , \qquad \forall i,l \quad (14.6)$$

Random disturbances: $$\epsilon_{lt} \sim N\left(o\,,\, U_l\right) , \qquad \forall l \quad (14.7)$$

Closing stocks:

$$s_{ilt} \big/ z_{ilt} = \alpha_{il} \left[p^{s}_{ilt+1} - \left(1 + r_l\right) p^{s}_{ilt} - \theta_l \left(s_{ilt} \big/ \bar{s}_{ilt-1}\right)\right]$$
$$+ \beta_{il} \left[\bar{q}_{ilt} + \bar{s}_{ilt-1} - \bar{q}_{ilt} - \bar{s}_{ilt}\right] \big/ z_{ilt} + \gamma_{il} , \qquad \forall i,l \quad (14.8)$$

Price transmission:

$$p_{ilt} = \begin{cases} u_{il} + \left(1 + w_{il}\right) \rho_{lt}\, h_{il}\, P_{it} + v_{ilt} \\ w_{il} \left(\rho_{lt}\, h_{il}\, P_{it}\right)^{\phi_{il}} e^{v_{il}t} \end{cases} \qquad \forall i,l \quad (14.9)$$

International market clearing:

$$\sum_{l}^{n} \left(c_{ilt} + s_{ilt} - q_{ilt} - s_{ilt-1}\right) = 0 , \qquad \forall i \quad (14.10)$$

Variables:

Quantities:

- c_{ilt} = consumption (domestic disappearance of commodity i in country l, year t.
- c^{T}_{ilt} = trend consumption of i in country l if real consumer prices remain constant beyond the base year.
- q_{ilt} = production of commodity i in country l, year t.
- q^{T}_{ilt} = trend production of i in country l if producer prices remain constant beyond the base year.
- $\bar{q}_{ilt}$ = equally weighted moving average of production in the three years prior to and including t.
- z_{ilt} = denominator in stock equations; equal to $\bar{q}_{it}$ where commodity i is not imported, and to an equally weighted three-year moving average of consumption where it is imported.
- ϵ_{ilt} = random disturbance to production of i in country l, year t.
- U_l = variance-covariance matrix of random disturbances to production of all commodities in country l.

s_{ilt}	= closing stock of i in country l, year t.
$\bar{s}_{ilt-1}$	= equally weighted moving average of closing stocks in the three years prior to t.
Prices:	
p_{ilt}	= domestic wholesale price of i in country l, year t.
p^s_{ilt}	= stock trading price for commodity i in country l, year t. Depending on the commodity and country, this may be either the international trading price or the domestic wholesale price.
p^s_{ilt+1}	= expected stock trading price in year $t + 1$. In the version presented here, expected price is set equal to a four-year equally weighted moving average of stock trading prices, including the price in year t.
P_{it}	= standard international trading price of commodity i in year t, based on f.o.b. prices at major ports in Thailand (rice), Canada (wheat), United States of America (maize), Australia (beef) and United States of America (pork and poultry).
Parameters:	
η_{il}	= income elasticity of demand for i in country l.
a_{ijl}	= the elasticity of the demand for i with respect to the price of j in country l.
g_{il}	= growth rate in the trend of production of commodity i in country l that would be sustained with constant real producer prices.
b_{ijl}	= elasticities of the target-level output of i with respect to the producer price of j in country l.
	b_{1ijl} = very short-run supply elasticity, nonzero only for ruminant meats.
	b_{2ijl} = one-year supply elasticity, nonzero for all commodities except ruminant meats.
	b_{3ijl} = two-year supply elasticity, nonzero only for ruminant meats.
δ_{il}	= partial adjustment elasticity in the production of commodity i in country l.
θ_l	= average cost of cereal storage in country l at stock level $\bar{s}_{it-1}$.
τ_{il}	= net sales tax (+ve) or producer subsidy (−ve) on commodity i in country l.
h_{il}	= ratio of the import or export unit value of commodity i in country l to the standard international price, P_{it}, reflecting shipment costs and access to concessional sales.
u_{il}	= specific tariff on commodity i in country l.
w_{il}	= advalorem tariff rate on commodity i in country l.
v_{il}	= linear trend in the difference of domestic and border prices of commodity i in country l.
ϕ_{il}	= elasticity of price transmission permitted by the government of country l between the domestic and international trading prices of commodity i.
ν_{il}	= rate of growth of the ratio of domestic and border prices of commodity i in country l.
Exogenous economic variables:	
N_{lt}	= population of country l in year t.
y_{lt}	= per capita income of country l in year t.
ρ_{lt}	= exchange rate in domestic currency of country l per U.S. $ in year t.
r_l	= real rate of interest in country l.

trading prices, whichever provided the best results in our econometric analysis of stock time series, based on equation 14.8. Two alternative forms are tested for the way in which stockholders formulate expected future price, p^s_{t+1}. The first is based on the geometric extrapolation of the trend between the average stockholder price for the period 1975–1977 and a three-year, equally weighted moving average of prices, including p_t. The second alternative form is simply an equally weighted, four-year moving average of past prices, including p^s_t. Although both expectational formulae were found to be generally positively correlated with closing stock levels, the adoption of the former led to divergence in the solution procedure, indicating asymptotic instability. All solutions presented in this chapter are based on the second formula.

Policies affecting trade are incorporated in the model through the specification of price-transmission equations for each commodity, as shown in equation 14.9. Following Bredahl (1979), Cronin (1979), and Tyers and Chisholm (1980), it is posited that the net result of the prevailing variable nontariff trade-policy instruments is most frequently the maintenance of constant elasticities of transmission between domestic and international prices. However, linear-transmission equations are used in countries for which this econometric analysis has indicated that the combination of fixed advalorem tariffs (with gradually changing specific tariffs) better fits the data. The price-transmission elasticities, ϕ, are zero where net trade in a particular commodity is completely unresponsive to trading prices. They are unity under free trade or where pure protection is maintained, but proportional fluctuations in trading prices are freely transmitted to the domestic market. Similarly, in the cases for which the linear variant is used, the advalorem tariff, w, is negative unity where net trade is unresponsive to trading prices and zero under free trade or pure protection.

The excess-demand behavior of country aggregates and the centrally planned countries are incorporated through the adoption of a linear version of the "partial adjustment" model, assuming that aggregate net imports adjust only partially to international price movements in a single year and that they are disturbed annually by additive random errors. The base year trend in net imports by some country aggregates is dwarfed by the standard deviation of the error term and projected growth in the net trade trends is not likely to be accompanied by proportional growth in the magnitude of random disturbances. Therefore, a linear formulation is used to maintain an appropriate balance in net trade forecasts between the determinate and the stochastic components of net imports in any year.

All parameters in the model have been derived using time-series analysis based on production, trade, and closing stocks data drawn selectively from Food and Agriculture Organisation (FAO) and U.S. Department of Agriculture (USDA) files. Data on domestic prices have been provided by colleagues and cooperating institutions in developing countries, published government documents, and by the USDA. In the case of elasticities of demand and supply, estimates from prior studies have been incorporated where these are the result of a more comprehensive analysis. Further details pertaining to the formulation of the model, the econometric analysis, and the parameters adopted are available in Tyers and Chisholm (1981).

The model is solved iteratively by beginning each new year with the initial assumption that all prices are equal to those in the preceding year, generating random disturbances in production and net trade, as well as calculating the production, consumption, and closing stock levels in each country. The resulting excess demands are then totaled and international prices adjusted to move world markets toward clearance. The procedure is then repeated until a satisfactory degree of market clearance has been achieved for each commodity, as given in equation 14.10. Thus the model selects that series of international and domestic prices, production, consumption, and closing stock levels that clear all markets in each successive year, from 1978 to 1990. Once fifty simulations of this type have been completed—each using a different set of generated random disturbances from the distributions of each error term—forecast means and standard deviations are calculated for all key variables in the model for each year of the simulation period.

To evaluate the international distribution of welfare impacts from government intervention in the staple-food markets considered by the model, the variety of welfare measures listed in table 14–4 are calculated for each country. Aggregate consumer surplus is estimated by first linearizing the multi-commodity demand functions (14.1) about the point $(c^T{}_{ilo}, \bar{p}_{lo})$ in each year and deriving the line integral, equation 14.11.[10] Aggregate producer surplus is estimated in a similar manner, by subtracting from actual producer revenues a cost function based on the level of output the producers expect to achieve in year t, linearized about the point $(q^T_{lt}, \bar{p}_{lo}\lambda_l)$. A complete derivation of both these economic surplus approximations is given in Appendix 14–B.

Net government revenues are calculated for each country as a composite of net revenue from all taxes and subsidies imposed on the import, export, consumption, and production of each commodity. To take steps toward quantifying any positive externalities resulting from the consumer-oriented food-price policies in developing countries, the model also evaluates the share of the staple-food budget in the gross domestic product (GDP) and food-energy consumption per capita from staples in each country.[11] Although the commodities included in the model (grains and meat) are not the main staple foods in many developing countries, they are the principal staples that are traded internationally in readily substitutable forms.[12]

Other welfare measures calculated include net profits from stockholding and the wealth in closing stocks held in each country. These are evaluated at international prices converted to domestic currency at the prevailing exchange rate to reflect their true social opportunity cost. This is appropriate since the quantity of stocks held in most countries reflects both government intervention in grain markets and policies directed specifically at stock levels. When the free-trade case is simulated, the constant and the quantity trigger terms are dropped from equation 14.8 and the competitive private speculator profit coefficient introduced, based on the derivation by Aiyagari et al. (1980). In this case, border prices are the appropriate public and private measure of the opportunity cost of stocks.

Table 14–4
Welfare Measures

Consumers' surplus:[a]

$$S^c_{lt} = -\tfrac{1}{2}\, c'_{lt}\, A_l^{-1}\, c_{lt}\ , \qquad Vl \quad (14.11)$$

Linearized Slutsky Matrix: $$A_l = \left[a_{ijl}\, c^{T}_{ilt} \,/\, \bar{p}_{ilo} \right]\ , \qquad Vl \quad (14.12)$$

Producers' surplus:[a]

$$S_{lt} = q'_{lt}\, p_{lt} - \tfrac{1}{2}\, q_{lt}\, b^{-1}\, \hat{q}'_{lt} - \tfrac{1}{2} f'_l\, B^{-1} f_l + \hat{q}'_{lt}\, B^{-1} f_l\ , \qquad Vl \quad (14.13)$$

Expected deviation from trend production: $$\hat{q}_t = q_t - q^{T}_l - \epsilon_t\ , \qquad Vl \quad (14.14)$$

Linearized supply response matrix:

$$B_l = [(b_{1ijl} + b_{2ijl} + b_{3ijl})\, q^{T}_{ilt} \,/\, \bar{p}_{ilo}\, \lambda_{il}]\ , \qquad Vl \quad (14.15)$$

Linearized production intercept:

$$f_{il} = q^{T}_{ilt} \left[- \sum_{j}^{m} \left(b_{1ijl} + b_{2ijl} + b_{3ijl} \right) \right], \qquad Vi,l \quad (14.16)$$

Government revenue:

$$G_{lt} = \sum_{iX} G_{Xilt} + \sum_{iM} G_{Milt}\ , \qquad Vl \quad (14.17)$$

$$G_{Xilt} = \chi_{ilt} \left(\rho_{ilt}\, h_{il}\, P_{it} - p_{ilt}\, \lambda_{il} \right) + c_{ilt}\, p_{ilt}\, \tau_{il}\ , \qquad Vi,l \quad (14.18)$$

$$G_{Milt} = -\chi_{ilt}\, (p_{ilt} - \rho_{ilt}\, h_{il}\, P_{it}) + q_{ilt}\, p_{ilt}\, \tau_{il}\ , \qquad Vi,l \quad (14.19)$$

Net exports of i: $$\chi_{ilt} = q_{ilt} + s_{ilt-1} - c_{ilt} - s_{ilt}\ , \qquad Vi, \quad (14.20)$$

Intrayear profits from stock:

$$R_{lt} = \sum_{i}^{m} \left[\rho_{ilt}\, h_{il}\, P_{it} \left(s_{it-1} - s_{it} \right) - \theta_l \left(s_{ilt} \,/\, \bar{s}_{ilt-1} \right) s_{ilt} \right], \qquad Vl \quad (14.21)$$

Wealth in stocks:

$$W_{lt} = \sum_{i}^{m} \rho_{ilt}\, h_{il}\, P_{it}\, s_{ilt}\ , \qquad Vl \quad (14.22)$$

Share of staple food budget in GDP:

$$S_{lt} = \left(\sum_{i}^{m} c_{ilt}\, \mu_{il}\, p_{ilt} \right) \Big/\ N_{lt}\, y_{lt} \qquad Vl \quad (14.23)$$

Food-energy consumption per capita:

$$F_{lt} = \left(\sum_{i}^{m} c_{ilt}\, \kappa_i \right) \Big/\ N_{lt} \qquad Vl \quad (14.24)$$

Variables not previously defined:

c_{lt}	=	m-component vector of consumption levels in country l, year t.
q_{lt}	=	m-component vector of production levels in country l, year t.
$\bar{p}_{ilo}$	=	the average wholesale price of commodity i in country l over the three years (1975–1977) prior to the simulation period.
p_{lt}	=	m-component vector of wholesale prices in country l, year t.
G_{Xilt}	=	net government revenue from taxes and subsidies on exported commodity i in country l.
G_{Milt}	=	net government revenue from tariffs, taxes, and subsidies on imported commodity i in country l.
μ_{il}	=	average retail/wholesale price ratio for commodity i in country l.
κ_i	=	average food-energy content of commodity i.

[a]Consumers' and producers' surplus are estimated by first deriving linear approximations to the demand and production relationships listed. In estimating consumers' surplus, the consumption vector is modified so that only the quantity of coarse grains directly consumed is incorporated. In addition, the terms linking coarse-grain consumption to meat prices are dropped from the Slutsky matrix, A_l. The complete linear approximations to producers' and consumers' surplus are derived in Appendix 14–B.

Testing Two Hypotheses about International Food and Agricultural Policy

The purpose of this chapter is to use the international-market model, as described in the previous section, to test the following two hypotheses:

1. That the protectionist and stabilizing agricultural policies adopted by the industrialized importing countries impose a net welfare cost in these countries.
2. That the removal of the provisionist and stabilizing agricultural and food policies of most Asian developing countries would increase consumer food risk in these countries though it would at the same time increase production incentives.

In order to accomplish these tests, the model has been applied to the simulation of four different international policy scenarios for the interval 1978–1985.[13] The first is simply a reference projection—a basis against which to measure the impacts of policy changes. Then to test hypothesis 1, a second simulation treats the case in which all government intervention in cereal and meat markets in the Organization for Economic Cooperation and Development (OECD) countries represented by the model terminates as of 1978. A third simulation examines hypothesis 2 by removing all government intervention in all fifteen countries for which domestic markets are identified, including the Asian developing countries. Finally, a fourth simulation examines the impact of deficiency payments to eliminate the distortions against agriculture in provisionist countries, applied concurrently with the adoption of free trade policies in the OECD countries.

Reference Projection

The effects of government policies on prices and on storage levels are reflected in the price-transmission equations (14.10) and the storage equations (14.8) of the model, which have been estimated using time-series analysis for the interval 1960–1977. In cases in which the descriptive power of the equations was found to be poor in the latter years of the series, the parameters have been tuned so as to maintain a uniform standard of goodness of fit during the interval 1975–1977. Consequently, the equations used in the reference projection reflect the behavior of policy institutions over the length of the time series, with some correction in cases in which significant changes occurred in the mid- to-late 1970s. In the reference case, these behavioral parameters are projected to be applicable through 1985.

With the continuance of existing policies, the model projects real increases to 1985 in the expected international trading prices of all the commodities studied. The price of rice shows the most rapid growth, increasing 69 percent by 1983, although it declines slightly thereafter. The coefficient of variation of the 1985 rice price forecast is 29 percent. The wheat price shows uniform growth through 1985. A period increase of 44 percent is projected with a coefficient of variation of 38 percent. Relatively large elasticities of demand and supply lead the coarse grain price projection to be the most stable among the grains, with a period increase of 25 percent and a coefficient of variation of 23 percent. Of the meats, the market for ruminant meats is most volatile, with a period increase of 67 percent in the expected indicator price (the Australian export price of beef) and a coefficient of variation of 21 percent. Although this projected price increase is large, it represents only a partial return to the relatively high beef prices that prevailed in the early 1970s.[14] The market for nonruminant meats is projected to be relatively stable, with an expected increase in the indicator price (based on the export unit value of poultry meat from the United States) of 12 percent by 1985 and a coefficient of variation of 6 percent.

The prevalence of price-transmission elasticities less than unity results in relatively sluggish adjustment by domestic markets as international prices increase.[15] Consequently, there is a trend toward reduced protectionism in the industrialized importing countries and increased provisionism in the developing countries. This is most dramatic in the case of rice, where state trading is prevalent and where movements in the international price have been a consequence of, rather than a major causal factor in, state decisions regarding quantities traded (Falcon and Monke 1980). In a recently revised version of the model, account has been taken of slower forecast economic growth during the 1980s.[16] This leads to more moderate commodity price projections and considerably less change over time in the average rates of protection adopted by each country. The resulting welfare impacts of government policies differ in magnitude from, but are consistent in direction with, those presented in subsequent sections of this chapter.

Policies of the OECD Countries

To examine the international impact of OECD agricultural policies, the second simulation differs from the reference projection in that the price-transmission equations for all commodities in Australasia, Canada, the EEC, Japan, and the United States are reconstituted so that domestic producer and consumer prices are always equal to border prices. This eliminates all protectionist and stabilizing policy impacts. In addition, the cereal-storage equations for these countries are reconstituted so that stockholding behavior is restricted to that of competitive private speculators. Storage parameters then depend only on physical storage costs and the market rate of interest in each country. The projected international prices are listed in table 14–5, while the impacts of the changes in OECD policies on each country's expected net trade in 1985 are detailed in table 14–6.

In the rice market, the major policy changes are the removal of pure protection in Japan and the United States and of pure stabilization in Australasia, the EEC, Japan, and the United States. Japan becomes a major importer of rice, while exports from the United States decline. In accordance with pure theory, the removal of protection in these countries results in higher international trading prices, while the removal of widespread national stabilization policies leads to reduced forecast uncertainty, implying a decline in the volatility of the international market.[17]

In the case of wheat, the important policy changes are the removal of protection in Japan and the EEC and of stabilization in Australasia, Canada, Japan, and the EEC. In the short run, Japan's wheat imports increase, as do those of the EEC. However, in the reference case, the 24 percent nominal protection rate prevailing in the EEC in 1975–1977 had not been sustained. By 1985, international trading prices in wheat had risen more rapidly than domestic prices, resulting in a nominal provision rate of 1.3 percent. With the removal of this policy, there is an increase in excess wheat supply in the EEC. Thus, by 1985, the reference OECD wheat policies had comprised protectionism counterbalanced with provisionism.

Consequently, liberalization brings about no significant change in the expected international trading price for that year.

Table 14–5
Projected International Trading Prices
(U.S. $ 1970/ton)

Simulation Year	*1977 Base*	*1978 1*	*1980 3*	*1983 6*	*1985 8*
Rice					
Reference	117	124	169	209	202
		(30)	(45)	(49)	(58)
Free trade (OECD)		122	225	249	237
		(8)	(57)	(39)	(47)
Free trade (fifteen countries)[a]		110	99	133	129
		(8)	(9)	(11)	(10)
Wheat					
Reference	50	62	82	86	89
		(18)	(32)	(32)	(34)
Free trade (OECD)		53	89	98	89
		(2)	(52)	(19)	(23)
Free trade (fifteen countries)		53	71	85	80
		(2)	(35)	(14)	(20)
Coarse Grains					
Reference	41	52	56	62	65
		(8)	(14)	(10)	(15)
Free trade (OECD)		44	51	63	69
		(3)	(8)	(8)	(12)
Free trade (fifteen countries)		42	51	60	66
		(2)	(8)	(7)	(11)
Ruminant meat[b]					
Reference	460	488	516	676	817
		(48)	(93)	(140)	(175)
Free trade (OECD)		903	819	882	945
		(27)	(35)	(53)	(51)
Free trade (fifteen countries)		878	800	851	907
		(26)	(31)	(47)	(43)
Nonruminant meat[b]					
Reference	570	675	653	713	755
		(32)	(42)	(54)	(47)
Free trade (OECD)		789	712	793	837
		(29)	(40)	(54)	(45)
Free trade (fifteen countries)		774	705	780	813
		(27)	(37)	(50)	(40)

Note: Forecast means are shown with standard deviations in parentheses (based on fifty simulations).

[a]The international price is underestimated by the model in the free-trade case. See note "e" to table 14–6.

[b]For the indicator prices used for meats, see note "b" to table 14–1.

Table 14–6
Expected Net Imports in 1985

Country/Group[a]	*Rice*	*Wheat*	*Coarse Grain*	*Ruminant Meat*	*Nonruminant Meat*
Australasia					
Reference	−.4	−12.6	−5.6	−3.2	.3
FT(OECD)[c]	−.4	−13.6	−5.7	−4.2	.03
FT(15)[d]	−.3	−12.4	−5.8	−4.1	−.02
Bangladesh					
Reference	−.1	1.0	.1	−.1	—[d]
FT(OECD)[b]	−1.6	1.1	.1	−.15	—
FT(15)[c]	2.5	.8	.1	−.15	—
Canada					
Reference	.1	−14.6	−10.5	—	—
FT(OECD)	.1	−15.0	−6.8	−.6	—
FT(15)	.1	−14.9	7.5	−.5	—
India					
Reference	1.5	.9	−1.2	—	—
FT(OECD)	.5	1.5	−1.6	—	—
FT(15)	−4.8	−1.9	.8	−.1	—
Indonesia					
Reference	1.9	1.3	.2	.1	—
FT(OECD)	1.6	1.4	−.2	.1	—
FT(15)	−8.0[e]	1.9	1.0	−.2	—
Japan					
Reference	−.2	6.3	24.5	.3	.1
FT(OECD)	3.7	7.7	10.9	3.1	1.0
FT(15)	6.7	6.8	10.2	3.3	1.0
South Korea					
Reference	—	2.7	2.1	—	—
FT(OECD)	−.2	2.7	2.1	—	—
FT(15)	1.6	2.5	.8	.2	.1
Malaysia					
Reference	.2	.6	.5	—	.1
FT(OECD)	.2	.6	.5	—	—
FT(15)	.5	.6	.5	—	—
Pakistan					
Reference	−1.0	.6	—	—	—
FT(OECD)	−1.1	.7	—	−.1	—
FT(15)	−1.1	−1.9	−.1	−.5	—
Philippines					
Reference	.2	.8	.8	—	−.1
FT(OECD)	.2	.8	.8	—	−.1
FT(15)	.5	.8	.7	−.1	.1
Singapore					
Reference	.2	.1	.5	—	—
FT(OECD)	.2	.1	.5	—	—
FT(15)	.2	.1	.4	—	—
Sri Lanka					
Reference	.2	1.1	—	—	—
FT(OECD)	.2	1.1	—	—	—
FT(15)	.2	1.1	—	—	—

Table 14–6 continued

Country/Group[a]	*Rice*	*Wheat*	*Coarse Grain*	*Ruminant Meat*	*Nonruminant Meat*
Thailand					
Reference	−1.0	.2	−3.6	—	—
FT(OECD)	−1.0	.2	−3.6	—	—
FT(15)	−.8	.2	−3.6	−.3	—
United States					
Reference	−3.8	−39.4	−71.9	1.2	−.9
FT(OECD)	−3.1	−34.7	−78.9	2.1	−3.0
FT(15)	−1.5	−34.0	−77.7	2.5	−3.1
European Economic Community					
Reference	.2	−2.5	14.6	−.2	−1.8
FT(OECD)	−.1	−7.6	32.0	−1.9	−.2
FT(15)	.3	−3.7	30.0	−1.7	−.3
Africa					
Reference	2.0	16.7	2.1	.2	.5
FT(OECD)	1.8	16.8	2.1	.2	.5
FT(15)	2.3	16.8	2.1	.2	.5
Burma/Indochina					
Reference	—	1.0	.2	—	−.1
FT(OECD)	−.3	1.0	.2	—	−.1
FT(15)	.4	1.1	.2	—	−.1
China					
Reference	−3.2	9.8	3.1	—	—
FT(OECD)	−3.4	9.8	3.0	—	—
FT(15)	−2.7	9.9	3.1	—	—
Central and South America					
Reference	.2	9.0	−.8	.1	.1
FT(OECD)	.2	9.0	−1.0	—	.1
FT(15)	.2	9.1	−.8	—	.1
USSR					
Reference	.5	8.7	25.1	.5	.6
FT(OECD)	.4	8.6	25.0	.4	.6
FT(15)	.6	9.0	25.1	.4	.6
Middle East and other Asian countries					
Reference	2.3	7.8	6.0	.4	2.2
FT(OECD)	2.2	7.8	5.9	.3	2.2
FT(15)	2.4	7.9	6.0	.3	2.2
Other European countries					
Reference	—	.3	15.4	.7	−1.0
FT(OECD)	−.4	.3	15.4	.6	−1.0
FT(15)	.6	.5	15.4	.6	−1.0

Note: Units are millions of metric tons. Negative numbers indicate net exports.

[a]The category "other Oceania" has been omitted from this table, since its net imports are small (of the order of 200,000 tons of wheat, 200,000 tons of rice, and less than 50,000 tons each of coarse grains, ruminant and nonruminant meats).

[b]The case of free-trade policies in OECD countries.

[c]The case of free-trade policies in all fifteen countries for which domestic markets are simulated (table 14–2).

[d]Indicates less than 50,000 tons.

[e]The expected value of rice exports from Indonesia in 1985 is overestimated by the model, resulting in some underestimating of the free-trade international price of rice. Full account has not been taken of the difference in quality between the rice domestically produced and that imported. The base year relationship between the domestic producer and consumer prices of rice and the import unit value is detailed in Appendix 14–A. The domestic price in the period 1975–1977 is based on the BULOG Retail Ceiling Price for rice in 1977 [125 Rp(1977)/kg or 38.4 Rp(1970)/kg], while the border price is set at the average of the import unit value for 1975–1977 [361 $(1977)/ton or 182 $(1970)/ton]. Between the reference and free-trade projections for 1985, the domestic price rises from 39.5 to 72.2 Rp(1970)/kg, rice production increases from 21.2 to 25.1 million tons, and rice consumption falls from 23.0 to 17.0 million tons.

The most important change in international wheat prices, however, is in their volatility. A rundown of stocks between 1977 and 1979 reduces average prices in the short run. This is followed by an upward spurt in prices and an increase in forecast uncertainty as the market adjusts to private speculative stockholding. Under the asymptotic conditions prevailing beyond 1982, forecast uncertainty is reduced relative to the reference case, reflecting the influence of increased risk-bearing by OECD consumers and producers. As for the coarse-grain market, although OECD government intervention is slight relative to that in the markets for rice and wheat, similar patterns are observed with the adoption of free trade policies.

In the case of ruminant meats, the removal of protection in the EEC and the United States, and of stabilization in all the OECD countries leads to dramatic changes in the structure of the international market. Ruminant-meat imports to Japan and the United States increase markedly, driving up the international trading price by almost a factor of two in the first year. The market slumps again through the early 1980s as producers respond to this sudden increase in price before the forces of scarcity evident in the reference projection again take effect, pushing the expected price in 1985 above the reference level. Again, in the case of ruminant meats, increased risk-sharing by OECD producers and consumers results in a significant reduction in forecast uncertainty and hence a decline in the volatility of the market. The market for nonruminant meats shows similar, though more muted, effects as a result of the OECD policy change, reflecting the lower level of government intervention affecting this market in the reference case.

To examine the hypothesis that the existing OECD agricultural policies result in a net welfare loss, we have adopted an aggregate economic surplus measure comprising the sum of consumers' surplus, producers' surplus, net government revenues, and intrayear profits from stockholding (the sum of equations 14.11, 14.13, 14.17, and 14.21). For the year 1985, the changes in the expected value of this aggregate welfare measure that result from deregulation of food markets in the OECD are listed in table 14–7. The results clearly support the hypothesis that the OECD countries incur a substantial net welfare cost as a consequence of their own agricultural policies. In 1985 alone, liberalization would reap a net welfare gain exceeding U.S. $ (1970) 18 billion. Principal among the net gainers is Japan, where the potential gain to consumers from liberalization exceeds the corresponding loss to producers and the government by over U.S. $ (1970) 12 billion.

Other net gainers from liberalization are the EEC and the industrialized food exporters. In the case of the EEC, by 1985 the principal distortions effective in the reference case are protection in the coarse-grain and ruminant-meat markets, at rates of 16 and 2 percent, respectively. Liberalization in the coarse-grain market results in a lower domestic price and a doubling of imports to 32 million metric tons. The consumer gain from this change dominates producer and government losses and is the principal factor in the overall welfare gain to the EEC from OECD free trade. In the EEC ruminant-meat market, the increase in the international-market price that results from liberalization exceeds the reference rate of protection, and the domestic price grows by 13 percent. Since the EEC is a net exporter of meats in 1985, this change reinforces the welfare gain from liberalization. Gains to the industrialized exporters as a consequence of OECD liberalization are principally the result of an improvement in their terms of trade as international food prices rise. In the United States, small gains in the coarse-grain and nonruminant-meat markets are augmented by net gains from reduced protection of domestic ruminant-meat producers. These are counterbalanced, however, by small declines in the domestic prices of the other major export commodities: rice and wheat. As a consequence, aggregate economic surplus in the United States in 1985 changes by less than one-half a percent.[18]

Losers from the liberalization of OECD agricultural policies are the net food-importing developing countries that face higher food-import prices than those prevailing in the reference case. These countries include Bangladesh, Indonesia, South Korea, Malaysia, and Singapore. Their expected net loss—estimated by the model at U.S. $ (1970) 219 million—is small by comparison with the gains made by the OECD countries.[19] Developing countries that lose as a consequence of the OECD policies include those that are net exporters of agricultural commodities in 1985. The expected net loss incurred by India, Pakistan, the Philippines, and Thailand combined is U.S. $ (1970) 180 million.

Table 14–7
Expected Welfare Impacts of Liberalization

	Expected Net Gain in Aggregate Economic Surplus in 1985			
	Free Trade (OECD)		*Free Trade (Fifteen Countries)*	
Country	*Percent*	*10^6 $US(1970)*	*Percent*	*10^6 $US(1970)*
Australasia	7	396	5	251
Bangladesh	−1	−53	6	388
Canada	9	1,019	7	812
India	—	29	—	160
Indonesia	−1	−70	8	477
Japan	18	12,451	63	43,376
South Korea	−1	−65	13	1,322
Malaysia	—	−18	3	206
Pakistan	2	74	—	−14
Philippines	—	8	7	236
Singapore	−8	−13	14	24
Thailand	—	69	1	269
United States of America	—	236	−2	−1,565
European Economic Community	4	4,146	4	3,926
Net gain to these countries		18,209		49,888
Net gain to OECD		18,248		46,820
Net gain to Asian developing countries		−39		3,068

Note: *Economic surplus* here signifies the sum of consumers' surplus, producers' suplus, net government revenues, and stock profits. *Net gains* are expressed relative to the reference projection in both cases. To evaluate the effect of the developing countries' policies, taken alone, subtract column two from column four.

Policies of the Developing Countries

To examine the international impact of the food and agricultural policies of Asian developing countries, the third simulation eliminates government intervention not only in the OECD countries but also in the developing market economies represented in the model. Relative to the second simulation, depicting the OECD free-trade case, the principal changes of policy to be observed in this case are the elimination of the provisionism and stabilization characterizing the policies of the developing countries, particularly in the market for rice. As theory indicates, this change results in lower expected international cereal prices with uniformly lower forecast uncertainty and hence less volatile international food markets. These changes are detailed in tables 14–5 and 14–6.

The most dramatic change occurs in the international rice market, in which liberalization in developing countries alone results in a drop in the expected trading price by 46 percent in 1985. The principal factors behind this change are large increases in excess supply in India and Indonesia, resulting from the increases in their domestic prices that accompany liberalization.[20] Also significant is the large reduction in international market volatility that occurs as rice price risk is increasingly shared by consumers and producers in the developing countries. The standard deviation of the international trading price of rice in 1985 falls by 79 percent. Changes in other commodity markets that result from liberalization in the developing countries are similar in direction but smaller in magnitude than those in the rice market.

Relative to the welfare impacts of food policies in developing countries, for 1985 the expected net changes in aggregate economic surplus are detailed in table 14–7. From these it is apparent that the policies adopted by all the Asian developing countries impose a net welfare cost of U.S. $ (1970) 3.1 billion, in expected value terms. In fact, the only countries appearing to lose significantly as a consequence of liberalization in the developing countries (comparing columns 2 and 4 of table 14–7) are the cereal exporters: Australia, Canada, Pakistan, and the United States. A minor net loss is also recorded by the EEC, which by 1985 in the OECD free-trade case, is an exporter of rice and wheat, the prices of which fall in the absence of provisionist policies in the developing countries. The EEC's net loss through the rice and wheat markets is not quite balanced by its welfare gain associated with reduced coarse-grain import prices.

In a comparison now of the case in which all fifteen countries discard all forms of government intervention, with the reference projection, we can see that the expected net welfare gain from free trade is about U.S. $ (1970) 50.0 billion. The OECD countries would be by far the largest beneficiaries, with U.S. $ (1970) 46.9 billion or 94 percent of the total net gain. Only two countries appear to be net losers from the change to free trade, and they lose by only small amounts when compared with the economic surplus generated by their individual cereal and meat sectors. In both Pakistan and the United States, these losses occur as a consequence of an adverse shift in the international terms of trade. Both countries are exporters of rice, the price of which falls significantly with the adoption of free-trade policies. The United States is also an importer of ruminant meat, the price of which rises significantly. For the United States, both of these factors—in combination with a slight decline in the international wheat price—outweigh the benefits accruing from a small increase in the price of its major export item: coarse grains.

Thus, far, this discussion has focused on the expected values of projected changes in welfare measures. The level of risk to which consumers, producers, and governments are exposed under free trade is incompletely accounted for when expected economic surplus is the welfare measure used in the multicommodity case (Turnovsky et al., 1980). In the absence of a convenient means of incorporating risk preferences into empirically based welfare criteria, other measures have been included in the model (table 14–4), which will now be examined.

To test our hypothesis that food risk in developing countries would increase without government intervention, evidence from the three model simulations discussed so far is detailed in table 14–8 for the year 1985. The

Table 14–8
Trade Liberalization and Consumer, Producer, and Foreign-Exchange Risk for Selected Developing Countries: Forecasts for 1985

	Reference	*Free Trade (OECD)*	*Free Trade (Fifteen countries including those listed)*
Bangladesh			
Consumer surplus (10^6 Taka)	83,965	74,487	92,846
	(6,881)	(4,220)	(3,688)
Food-energy consumption (kcal/capita/day)	1,686	1,647	1,758
	(61)	(39)	(33)
Retail staple-food cost as percent of GDP	67.5	71.4	59.0
	(7.0)	(5.0)	(3.2)
Producer surplus	17,119	19,641	14,063
	(6,714)	(6,267)	(3,640)
Net foreign-exchange requirement (10^6 U.S. $)	−3	−337	190
	(360)	(437)	(244)
India			
Consumer surplus (10^6 rupees)	246,710	244,070	226,780
	(4,169)	(2,619)	(8,210)
Food-energy consumption (kcal/capita/day)	1,683	1,673	1,622
	(20)	(14)	(33)
Retail staple-food cost as percent of GDP	22.6	23.1	27.0
	(.8)	(.5)	(2.1)
Producer surplus	87,226	89,888	106,680
	(7,565)	(6,410)	(15,236)
Net foreign-exchange requirement (10^6 U.S. $)	340	180	−981
	(956)	(1,018)	(790)
Indonesia			
Consumer surplus (10^9 rupia)	1,751	1,725	1,076
	(33)	(21)	(64)
Food-energy consumption (kcal/capita/day)	1,746	1,736	1,076
	(15)	(10)	(48)
Retail staple-food cost as percent of GDP	16.8	16.9	21.1
	(.1)	(.1)	(.7)
Producer surplus	839	853	1,511
	(80)	(78)	(223)

Table 14–8 continued

	Reference	*Free Trade (OECD)*	*Free Trade (Fifteen countries including those listed)*
Net foreign-exchange requirement (10^6 U.S. $)	925	908	−1,504[a]
	(522)	(567)	(352)
Malaysia			
Consumer surplus (10^6 ringgit)	18,740	18,709	18,956
	(53)	(35)	(125)
Food-energy consumption (kcal/capita/day)	1,840	1,838	1,830
	(1.7)	(1.1)	(8)
Retail staple-food cost as percent of GDP	6.5	6.6	6.1
	(.2)	(.2)	(.4)
Producer surplus	810	846	651
	(414)	(419)	(149)
Net foreign-exchange requirement (10^6 U.S. $)	207	214	142
	(108)	(118)	(59)
Pakistan			
Consumer surplus (10^6 rupees)	33,270	33,072	26,046
	(645)	(442)	(2,459)
Food-energy consumption (kcal/capita/day)	1,855	1,851	1,640
	(18)	(13)	(85)
Retail staple-food cost as percent of GDP	30.0	30.0	36.5
	(.7)	(.5)	(3.7)
Producer surplus	13,251	13,586	21,523
	(1,613)	(1,541)	(4,043)
Net foreign-exchange requirement (10^6 U.S. $)	−211	−303	−786
	(164)	(157)	(190)
Philippines			
Consumer surplus (10^6 pesos)	18,829	18,559	18,811
	(390)	(301)	(649)
Food-energy consumption (kcal/capita/day)	1,754	1,745	1,776
	(21)	(16)	(31)
Retail staple-food cost as percent of GDP	15.1	15.4	16.4
	(.6)	(.4)	(.9)
Producer surplus	8,896	9,288	9,626
	(595)	(495)	(678)
Net foreign-exchange requirement (10^6 U.S. $)	152	131	157
	(110)	(117)	(75)
Sri Lanka			
Consumer surplus[b] (10^6 rupees)	185,090	185,030	184,750
	(94)	(61)	(140)
Food-energy consumption (kcal/capita/day)	1,587	1,576	1,596
	(17)	(11)	(21)
Retail staple-food cost as percent of GDP	18.2	18.6	26.8
	(.7)	(.5)	(2.8)
Producer surplus	1,140	1,200	1,055
	(379)	(371)	(378)
Net foreign-exchange requirement (10^6 U.S. $)	159	157	148
	(71)	(64)	(39)
Thailand			
Consumer surplus (10^6 baht)	328,470	326,430	328,930
	(2,996)	(2,022)	(2,442)

Table 14–8 continued

	Reference	Free Trade (OECD)	Free Trade (Fifteen countries including those listed)
Food-energy consumption (kcal/capita/day)	2,049	2,041	2,024
	(10)	(6.7)	(11)
Retail staple-food cost as percent of GDP	12.0	12.4	11.3
	(.7)	(.5)	(.5)
Producer surplus	44,037	46,380	50,309
	(3,734)	(3,034)	(3,743)
Net foreign-exchange requirement (10^6 U.S. $)	−419	−530	−875
	(263)	(271)	(194)

Note: Forecast means of selected welfare measures are shown with standard deviations in parentheses (based on fifty simulations).

[a]Indonesian export earnings under free trade are overestimated. See note "e", table 14–6.

[b]The magnitude of the consumer surplus depends not only on the level of consumption but also on the elasticities of demand. Since demand elasticities are assumed very small in Sri Lanka, the value of the surplus is inflated.

consumer-welfare measures included are consumers' surplus, food energy consumption per capita per day, and the retail cost of the five staple foods studied, as a fraction of each country's national income. Producer interests are represented by producers' surplus and those of governments by the net foreign-exchange requirement associated with trade in all five commodities (rice, wheat, coarse grains, and ruminant and nonruminant meats).

Despite the considerable decrease in international-market volatility brought about by liberalization in all fifteen countries studied, for most developing countries liberalization brings with it an increase in consumer food risk. Large increases in the forecast uncertainty of consumers' surplus, in food-energy consumption, and in the retail cost of staple foods occur in all countries except Bangladesh and Thailand. In most countries, the degree to which governments stabilized prices in the reference case exceeds the improvement in international price stability brought about by the transition to widespread free trade. The exceptions are cases in which rice is the principal consumption item and in which the reference price-transmission elasticities were closer to unity than in other cases. The relatively dramatic decline in the volatility of international rice prices (table 14–5) is then sufficient to exceed in effect the prior stabilization policy.

In India, Indonesia, and Pakistan, free trade not only results in a large increase in the forecast uncertainty of consumer-welfare measures, it also causes a deterioration in consumer welfare in expected value terms. Expected food-energy consumption, for example, falls by 4 percent in India, 18 percent in Indonesia, and 12 percent in Pakistan. In these countries, the provisionist policies of the reference case were so effective as to reduce domestic cereal prices below the level to which border prices would fall under widespread free-trade conditions. Thus, in all but two cases, the exposure of consumers to food risk increases markedly with the cessation of all government intervention. The change is most significant in countries that had most actively pursued cheap-food policies in the reference case.

Accompanying the increase in consumer risk as governments adopt food-trade liberalization is a decline in most countries' exposure to foreign-exchange risk; free trade would thus shift the burden of risk from governments in developing countries to consumers. No single standard exists by which to judge whether this transfer of food risk to consumers in developing countries would be tolerable—either in terms of hardship to vulnerable groups or political costs. The increase in consumer food risk predicted in these results, however, is a lower-bound estimate on what governments might expect from food-trade liberalization. Unilateral liberalization by any individual developing country—particularly one depending heavily on the international rice market—would place a much larger burden of adjustment on that country's consumers.

With respect to the welfare impacts on producers in developing countries, the results in table 14–8 indicate that the forecast uncertainty of producers' surplus in most countries increases with trade liberalization, as does its expected value. Despite the lower international prices that prevail under free trade, producers could be better off in India, Indonesia, Pakistan, the Philippines, and Thailand. Suppressed producer incentives are an inevitable consequence of provisionist policies wherever governments do not have access to the resources to ensure parity of producer with border prices or equivalent transfers in the form of investments in irrigation, flood control, or input subsidies.

Deficiency Payments for Developing Countries as a Step toward Increasing International Market Efficiency and Food Production

Government intervention in the developed market economies serves to increase their food self-sufficiency and to support agricultural income. The policy can be justified on neither efficiency nor humanitarian grounds since few OECD farmers can be considered truly needy by international standards. There probably do exist, in at least some of these countries, positive externalities associated with food self-sufficiency and in keeping rural lands in agriculture—born partly out of the fear of some international conflict that would interrupt the supply of imports and partly out of social sentiments favoring the maintenance of traditional rural life-styles. The cost of intervention in industrialized importing countries is met relatively easily because agriculture has a relatively small share of national income. In developing countries, on the other hand, consumers are in general relatively poor, access to efficient capital markets is limited, and governments typically face foreign-exchange constraints that limit their ability to withstand fluctuating food-import costs. All these factors together more clearly justify government intervention to reduce consumer food risk.[21]

Table 14–7 shows that a considerable welfare improvement resulted from reduced government intervention in all countries represented in the model and that most of the benefits accrued in the OECD countries. If developing countries were to adopt provisionist policies, but if some liberalization were to be achieved in the OECD, resources would be released that could be used to counteract the depressing effect of provisionist policies on producer incentives in the developing countries. In order to evaluate this possibility, the advalorem producer subsidies were estimated that would be required in developing countries in order to achieve parity between producer and border grain prices in 1985 if the OECD countries were to have adopted free-trade policies as of 1978 (table 14–9). A fourth projection was then made, based on the second projection (free trade, OECD), in which government policies toward consumer prices in developing countries remain unchanged, but in which producer prices are maintained at proportionally higher levels by these advalorem

Table 14–9
Deficiency Payments to Provide Producer Price Parity in Developing Countries under OECD Free Trade in 1985

	Advalorem Producer Subsidy (Percent)		
Country	*Rice*	*Wheat*	*Coarse Grain*
Bangladesh	35	8	21
India	120	39	9
Indonesia	230	—	30
South Korea	16	10	28
Malaysia	55	—	31
Pakistan	50	74	21
Philippines	76	—	15
Thailand	61	—	13

Advalorem subsidies would raise producer prices to the border price levels that would prevail in 1985 if OECD countries had adopted free-trade policies in grain and meat as of 1978. In this scenario, as can be seen from table 14–6, rice prices rise more rapidly than in the reference projection. Sluggish transmission of the price growth to domestic markets in some countries results in large gaps between domestic and border prices by 1985, hence the large subsidies required for parity.

subsidies.[22] The changes in international prices and trading patterns that result are detailed in table 14–10.

Given the very large deficiency payments to rice producers in India and Indonesia, it is not surprising that excess supplies develop in these countries and that international prices fall. In a few countries adopting the deficiency payments, rice supplies do not increase since the decline in international prices places downward pressure on producer prices sufficient to outweigh the effect of the subsidy. Despite the declines in the

Table 14–10
Effect on Prices and Trade of Free Trade in the OECD with Deficiency Payments in Developing Countries

	Rice	*Wheat*	*Coarse Grain*	*Ruminant Meat*	*Nonruminant Meat*
International trading prices, U.S. $(1970)/ton					
1980					
FT(OECD)[a]	225	89	51	819	712
FT(OECD)/DP[b]	101	77	51	820	715
1985					
FT(OECD)	237	89	69	945	837
FT(OECD)/DP	111	86	69	943	836
Net imports in 1985, million tons					
Bangladesh					
FT(OECD)	−1.6	1.1	.1	−.1	—
FT(OECD)/DP	1.6	.8	.1	−.1	—
India					
FT(OECD)	.5	1.5	−1.6	—	—
FT(OECD)/DP	−5.4	−.6	2.5	—	—
Indonesia					
FT(OECD)	1.6	1.4	.2	.1	.1
FT(OECD)/DP	−5.6	1.3	.4	.1	.1
South Korea					
FT(OECD)	−.2	2.7	2.1	—	—
FT(OECD)/DP	.3	2.6	1.9	—	—
Malaysia					
FT(OECD)	.2	.6	.5	—	.1
FT(OECD)/DP	.3	.6	.4	—	.1
Pakistan					
FT(OECD)	−1.1	.7	—	−.1	—
FT(OECD)/DP	−1.0	−.2	−.2	−.1	—
Philippines					
FT(OECD)	.2	.8	.8	—	−.1
FT(OECD)/DP	−.1	.8	.8	—	−.1
Thailand					
FT(OECD)	−1.0	.2	−3.6	—	—
FT(OECD)/DP	−1.0	.2	−3.8	—	—

Note: Table lists forecast means only.
[a]The case of free trade in the OECD with reference policies in the developing countries.
[b]Free trade in the OECD with deficiency payments to producers in developing countries.

expected international prices of all the cereals to levels near those resulting from complete liberalization in all developing countries, no increase occurs in this case in the exposure to risk of consumers or producers in these countries. In comparing the reference projection with the deficiency payment case, an important difference is that food risk has been redistributed internationally. Market fluctuations are absorbed to a greater extent by OECD consumers, although the average cereal prices paid in these countries are lower than in the reference case. The expected welfare impacts of deficiency payments, including the effects on government revenues, are detailed in table 14–11.

In all countries except the United States, the net impact on expected consumer and producer welfare is positive, with a net total over all countries represented of U.S. $ (1970) 47 billion. Of this, U.S. $ (1970) 32 billion derives from the excess of consumer-welfare improvement over producer

Table 14–11
Welfare Impact of Deficiency Payments in Asian Developing Countries, 1985

	Expected Net Change in Consumers' and Producers' Surplus Plus Stock Profits	*Expected Net Change in Government Revenues*	*Expected Net Change in Aggregate Economic Surplus*[a]	
Country	*10⁶ U.S. $(1970)*	*10⁶ U.S. $(1970)*	*Percent*	*10⁶ U.S. $(1970)*
Australasia	982	−569	8	413
Bangladesh	1,023	−535	7	488
Canada	1,113	−160	9	953
India	6,437	−9,103	−7	−2,666
Indonesia	4,085	−5,531	−25	−1,446
Japan	28,129	−7,405	30	20,724
South Korea	211	35	2	246
Malaysia	33	10	1	43
Pakistan	1,370	−1,199	4	171
Philippines	583	−549	1	34
Singapore	13	2	9	15
Thailand	690	−653	—	37
United States	−1,831	438	−2	−1,393
European Economic Community	3,787	219	4	4,006
Total	46,625	−25,000		21,625
OECD Total	32,180	−7,477		24,703
Developing country total	14,445	−17,523		−3,078

Note: Net gains and losses listed are relative to the reference projection.

[a]Aggregate economic surplus includes net government revenues from grain- and meat-market intervention.

losses as a result of free-trade policies in the OECD. A further U.S. $ (1970) 14 billion results from a combination of consumer- and producer-welfare improvements in developing countries. Gains in developing countries are caused by increased producer subsidies and a decline in consumer prices with the transmission of the changes in international trading prices. These net welfare gains come at considerable cost to governments, however, and not only to governments in developing countries. In Japan, net profits from importing at low international prices and selling domestically at higher prices are lost to the government with the introduction of free trade in grains and meat. In Australasia and Canada, government revenues that accrued in the reference case as a result of the sluggish response of domestic prices to the tightening of the international market are also lost with the change to free trade.[23]

In the developing countries, the cost of the large deficiency payments must be borne from revenues generated elsewhere in their economies. The sum of government revenues in the OECD foregone with the increases in net costs to governments in developing countries amounts to U.S. $ (1970) 25 billion, of which U.S. $ (1970) 17.5 billion would be borne in the developing countries. Given that the net welfare gain for all the countries represented is about twice this increased cost to governments and that three-quarters of this net gain accrues to the industrialized countries, a share of the cost of the deficiency payments should appropriately be borne by consumers in the OECD.

Conclusion

Food and agricultural policies are usually evaluated on the basis of their domestic impacts, with the measurement of affects on international markets restricted to the assessment of market power and the design of optimal trade policies to enhance it. In this chapter, the behavior of food markets in countries engaging in trade are seen as interdependent and it is shown that accounting for this interdependence in the design of policy can result in nonzero-sum improvements in the net welfare of large groups of countries. In order to measure this interdependence and to experiment with policy alternatives in cereal markets, it is necessary to account simultaneously for the effects of policies on both the average level and the volatility of international trading prices. Furthermore, since 40 percent of the cereals produced worldwide are fed to animals, it is not sufficient to study cereal markets alone. Thus, an innovative model is required that incorporates the stochastic behavior of both cereal and meat markets, their cross-commodity interactions, and the policies of governments as they seek to protect or stabilize their respective domestic markets. Our model represents several steps toward meeting these challenges, while focusing especially on interdependence among Asian and Pacific countries.

To examine the proportions of any "North-South" polarity in the international impacts of food and agricultural policies, the model is first used to separate the consequences of the protectionist and stabilizing policies widely adopted in the OECD countries of the North and the provisionist and stabilizing policies most common in the developing countries of the South. The theoretical premise that the cost to consumers of protectionist policies in the OECD importing countries exceeds the corresponding gains to producers and the government is borne out by results from the model. Continuation of the existing policies in all the OECD countries studied would impose by the mid-1980s an expected annual net cost of U.S. $ (1970) 18 billion, two-thirds of which would be incurred by Japan alone. Although these policies significantly affect the level and stability of international trading prices, their impact on Asian developing countries is mixed. They are beneficial to Asian net importers, who would gain about U.S. $ (1970) 220 million annually, but costly to Asian net exporters, who would lose about U.S. $ (1970) 180 million annually. Thus, as measured in terms of expected economic surplus, the welfare impacts of the policies of the North are adverse from the North's own viewpoint and mixed in the South, where the most important factor is the direction of the resulting shift in the international terms of trade in relation to the net trade position in each developing country.

The hypothesis that the policies of the developing countries—while imposing a net welfare cost in expected value terms—protect relatively poor consumers from food risk is also borne out by results from the model. These policies would, by the mid-1980s, impose an expected net cost across all the developing countries studied of U.S. $ (1970) 3.1 billion annually. By raising international cereal prices, they would also add U.S. $ (1970) 33.9 billion to the expected cost borne by OECD importers, 90 percent of which would be carried by Japan alone. The resulting improvement in the terms of trade of net food exporters—especially Australia, Canada, and the United States—would offset the total cost to the OECD by U.S. $ (1970) 2.2 billion. Considerable welfare costs, as measured in expected value terms, are associated with the continuance of the existing policies in developing countries. However, their elimination would increase the exposure of consumers in many developing countries to food risk. This would occur as a consequence of increases in expected domestic food prices—especially in India, Indonesia, and Pakistan—and because of increased domestic price volatility in the absence of government supply regulation.

In evaluating food security only in terms of expected economic surplus, in combination with measures of food risk, it is simpler to justify the provisionist and stabilizing policies of the developing countries than to rationalize the protectionism of the industrialized importers. Although the form of intervention needed to smooth the consumption of food by the relatively poor need not involve direct participation in commodity markets by public agencies, trade policy and public-supply management have been the most common means of intervention in developing countries, and it is these policies that are best evaluated in using the model. Consider a world in which the only government intervention in food markets is that which limits the exposure of poor consumers to food risk. In such a world, the most efficient intervention would be restricted only to the consumer side of markets in developing countries, and hence producers in those countries would be compensated at international parity levels, through deficiency payments or their equivalent.

Results from the model indicate that—had such policies been adopted as of 1978—there would be no increase in consumer food risk in developing countries, but by 1985, there would be an annual total net welfare gain to all participating producers, consumers, and stockholders amounting to U.S. $ (1970) 46.6 billion, two-thirds of which would accrue in the OECD countries. Net costs to governments would, however, increase by U.S. $ (1970) 25 billion, of which 70 percent would need to be borne by those of developing countries. Thus, based on the narrow welfare criteria adopted,there is a clear case for international cooperation to bring about the necessary liberalization in the OECD and in assisting governments in developing countries to support increased incentives to food producers.

Throughout the analysis, an important role has been played by Japan. Consumers in Japan presently bear the cost of the highest rates of protection to agricultural producers in all the countries studied (see table 14–2). Furthermore, unlike most other countries in which the degree of protection or provision differs markedly across food commodities, Japan's policies are uniformly highly protectionist. Consequently, liberalization has a dramatic effect on the welfare of Japanese consumers, as measured by the model. It is this potential welfare gain that must be compared by Japanese policymakers with the less measurable benefits of agricultural protection. Another important country is the United States. Despite its dominance as a cereal exporter, the welfare impacts in the United States of the policy changes considered are relatively small. This is largely because the markets for America's largest export items—wheat and coarse grain—are relatively unaffected by trade liberalization in other countries. The adoption of free-trade policies by all the countries studied does, however, appear to have a slight negative impact on the United States, since such widespread liberalization would result in an adverse shift in the international terms of trade.

In an assessment of the results presented in this chapter, two caveats should be borne in mind. First, the welfare impacts have been evaluated only for 1985, the eighth year simulated. This year was chosen since the relationship between different policy scenarios stabilizes late in each simulation following the period of relative turbulence brought forth as a consequence of sudden changes in policies, particularly cereal stock policies. A more proper evaluation of the international impacts of these changes might, however, have been based on accumulated welfare impacts over a period of years, including those during which adjustment takes place. Second, the welfare impacts measured late in the simulation period are dependent on the levels of protection and provision projected by the model to apply during the mid-1980s. This gives special importance to the reliability of the model's price projections, not to mention the assumption that price-transmission parameters would continue to remain constant in the face of relatively large and sustained increases in the international trading prices of some commodities.

Because of these caveats, which apply in the interpretation of results from most empirical models, the conclusions reached with respect to specific welfare impacts cannot be relied on as accurate to the last billion dollars. However, certain relatively robust conclusions emerge from this exercise. The most important of these is that improved international food security can be achieved—from the viewpoints of poor consumers, poor producers, and the governments of developing countries—while at the same time providing an increase in welfare that is widely and internationally distributed. The welfare improvement from liberalization in the OECD, combined with deficiency payments in developing countries, would be so great that the principal net gainers could finance net losses in other countries with only 20 percent of their net gain. This would include transfers to the governments of large developing countries, such as India and Indonesia, to cover all financing of producer deficiency payments, as well as compensation for a small welfare loss in the United States. The result would be a Pareto superior reconstitution of the international food economy.

Notes

1. The use in this chapter of the term *deficiency payment* refers to the payment required to raise producer prices in developing countries above average consumer prices to world parity.

2. One incentive for large importing countries to adopt protectionist policies is so that they can improve overall domestic welfare through the

imposition of an "optimum tariff" on imports. With respect to Japan and the EEC, this position is argued by Carter and Schmitz (1979) for the case of wheat.

3. An additional incentive for some countries, whose exports are large in relation to world demand, to reduce domestic prices is to exploit their market power and achieve a net welfare gain domestically from the curtailment of exports. Although the potential to achieve this is recognized in the literature (Carter et al. 1980; and Schmitz and McCalla 1981), the extent to which large exporters or groups of exporters have actually implemented such policies over extended periods is a matter of debate (Alaouze et al. 1978; and Carter and Schmitz 1979).

4. In the case of Thailand, its role as a large exporter of rice leads to the possibility that a net welfare gain to the country as a whole might be achieved through the imposition of an export tax. In his examination of Thailand's current "rice premium," Setboonsarng (1982) concludes that the level of taxation is presently too high to meet this criterion and that it principally serves as a transfer between producers and urban consumers.

5. As shown by Valdes and Zietz (1980), OECD protection to the producers of agricultural commodities exported by developing countries is in conflict with developing-country interests.

6. The argument that increased dependency will result depends on the assumption that, despite the somewhat lower real trading prices that occur, the capital-intensive agriculture of the major grain exporters will continue to adjust through technological advance at a rate greater on the average than that which might be achieved in the developing countries—an assumption not borne out by the patterns of agricultural productivity growth observed in the latter half of the 1970s (O'Brien 1981).

7. It is worth noting here that by giving first priority to stabilization of domestic supplies through trade, governments reduce the capacity of their countries to adjust their level of imports in accordance with short-run changes in the international terms of trade. As shown by Sarris (1980), the potential advantage held by large trading countries is lost in the short run when they adopt supply-stabilization policies. The more these countries need to import to satisfy their short-run domestic requirements, the higher will be the import price. This behavior increases the short-run market power of trading countries able to adjust their excess supply in accordance with changes in international trading prices (Shei and Thompson 1978).

8. In their analysis of excess demand functions in the international wheat market, Sarris and Taylor (1978) propose a nonlinear form with variable price elasticity. Other nonlinear forms are also analyzed for their welfare implications by Turnovsky (1978). To ensure that both demand and

supply elasticities remain constant as consumption and production grow over the forecast interval, nonlinear constant-elasticity demand and supply functions have been adopted in our study.

9. As in the treatment by Aiyagari et al. (1980), negative stocks are prohibited.

10. Although the debated quality of economic surplus is recognized as being a measure of utility (Currie et al. 1971; and Willig 1976), no readily available alternative is seen for applied analysis. A further qualifier is required, however, in the multicommodity case. As Turnovsky et al. (1980) have shown, consumers' surplus is based on a line integral, the value of which is only independent of the path of integration if the Slutsky matrix (of price coefficients in the equations for consumption) is symmetrical. This requires that the implied income elasticities of demand for all commodities studied be equal to the Arrow-Pratt coefficient of relative risk aversion. This condition cannot be met exactly in most countries.

11. The social value of increased food consumption in poor households appears to exceed its private counterpart (Pinstrup-Anderson 1981). These other measures are also needed because the consumer surplus measure does not adequately account for food risk.

12. Important omissions from the commodities covered by the model are soybeans and cassava, both of which are staple foods in many developing countries and both of which are extensively traded internationally.

13. The model is designed to simulate market movements for the interval 1978–1990. Since stochastic simulations involving at least fifty repetitions are expensive, these experiments were terminated at 1985 after it became clear that the relationship between alternative scenarios would stabilize by that year.

14. The export beef price from Brisbane, Australia did increase from U.S. $567/ton in 1977 to U.S. $1,665/ton in 1979, in current terms. If the World Bank International Price Index is used to deflate this price change, the real price increase is 124 percent.

15. Price-transmission elasticities are documented, along with the other parameters of the model, in Tyers and Chisholm (1981).

16. Since 1978, the rates of economic growth achieved in both industrialized and developing countries have been lower than were forecast. This has been attributed, in part, to the sharp rise in world oil prices in 1979–1980 and the subsequent global recession.

17. Note that the forecast standard deviation increases in 1980, relative to the reference case, then declines in later years. This is due to a ripple effect introduced as a consequence of the sudden change in storage policies between 1977 and 1978 in the OECD countries. The same effect is observed

in the forecast price of wheat when the very large stocks held by the major exporters are suddenly dumped on the market in 1978 and 1979. The projections approach asymptotic conditions from 1982 onward.

18. In 1985, the reference projection has the domestic prices of rice, wheat, coarse grains, ruminant meats, and nonruminant meats at 321, 88, 72, 1,133, and 748 U.S. $ (1970)/ton, respectively. With liberalization in OECD countries, including the United States, the new domestic prices in that year are 277, 83, 76, 1,124, and 837 U.S. $ (1970)/ton. Note that the international wheat price is unchanged by this liberalization in 1985, but a small decline occurred in the domestic wheat price due to the loss of protection in the United States. Note also that border prices differ from the international indicator prices listed in table 14–5 by the shipment cost and quality factors, h_{il}.

19. Were it possible to evaluate it, the net welfare gain from OECD agricultural policies that accrues to other large importers such as China and the USSR would be comparatively large.

20. In 1985, the domestic price of rice in India is Rupees (1970) 959/ton in the reference case. In Indonesia the price is Rupia (1970) 39,500/ton. After liberalization these prices rise to Rupees (1970) 1,195/ton and Rupia (1970) 72,200/ton, respectively. In the case of Indonesia, this price increase is an overestimate, as explained in note "e" to table 14–6. In terms of U.S. $ (1970), at the 1977 exchange rates used in the model (Appendix 14A), the price of rice in India increases from $109 to $136, while the increase in Indonesia is from $95.2 to $174.

21. Such intervention might focus on the efficiency of capital or foreign-exchange markets rather than engage government as a participant in domestic or international food markets. These alternatives have been reviewed in earlier chapters.

22. Since it is not possible to calculate, a priori, the level to which international cereal prices would fall with the imposition of a fixed ad-valorem, producer price subsidy, the subsidies applied are based on the assumption that no decline would take place from the levels prevailing in the OECD free-trade case. This assumption is not borne out by the results from the fourth simulation, especially in the case of rice, with the result that some developing countries oversubsidize rice producers. Ideally, additional simulations might be made until the producer subsidies adopted just remove the distortion against producers associated with the provisionist policies of the reference case.

23. In the case of Australia, the reference projection depicts a government taxing rents in the international market for ruminant meats as prices rise rapidly. By 1985, the domestic ruminant-meat price rises from

A.$(1970)404/ton in 1975–1977 to A.$(1970)596, but the expected export price is still higher, at A.$(1970)710. In terms of U.S. $ (1970), at the 1977 exchange rate used in the model, these prices are $465, $685, and $817, respectively.

Bibliography

Aiyagari, S.R., Eckstein, Z., and Eichenbaum, M. 1980. "Rational Expectations, Inventories and Price Fluctuations." Economic Growth Center Discussion Paper No. 363, Yale University, October.

Alaouze, C.M., Watson, A.S., and Sturgess, N.H. 1978. "Oligopoly Pricing in the World Wheat Market." *American Journal of Agricultural Economics* 60, no. 1:22–31.

Bigman, D., and Reutlinger, S. 1979. "National and International Policies Toward Food Security and Price Stabilization." *American Economic Review* 69, no. 2:159–163.

Bredahl, M.E., Meyers, W.H., and Collins, K.J. 1979. "The Elasticity of Foreign Demand for U.S. Agricultural Products: The Importance of the Price Transmission Elasticity." *American Journal of Agricultural Economics* 61:58–63.

Carter, C., and Schmitz, A. 1979. "Import Tariffs and Price Formation in the World Wheat Market." *American Journal of Agricultural Economics* 62:517–522.

Carter, C., Gallini, N., and Schmitz, A. 1980. "Producer-Consumer Trade-Offs in Export Cartels: The Wheat Cartel Case." *American Journal of Agricultural Economics* 62:812–818.

Cronin, M.R. 1979. "Export Demand Elasticities with Less Than Perfect Markets." *Australian Journal of Agricultural Economics* 23:69–72.

Currie, J.M., Murphy, J.A., and Schmitz, A. 1971. "The Concept of Economic Surplus and Its Use in Economic Analysis." *Economic Journal* 81 (324):741–799.

Duloy, J.H., and Norton, R.D. 1975. "Prices and Incomes in Linear Programming Models." *American Journal of Agricultural Economics* 57:591–600.

Falcon, W.P., and Monke, E.A. 1980. "International Trade in Rice." *Food Research Institute Studies* 17, no. 3:279–305.

Feder, G., Just, R., and Schmitz, A. 1977. "Storage with Price Uncertainty in International Trade." *International Economic Review* 18, no. 3:553–568.

Heckscher, E. 1935. *Mercantilism,* Vols. 1 and 2, Second Edition, London: Allen and Unwin.

Johnson, D.G. 1977. "Estimating Appropriate Levels of Grain Reserves for the United States: A Research Report." Paper No. 77:2b, University of Chicago, Office of Agricultural Economic Research, November.

———. 1981. "Grain Insurance, Reserves and Trade: Contributions to Food Security for LDC's." In *Food Security for Developing Countries* Ed. A. Valdes. Boulder, Colo. Westview Press.

Morrow, D.T. 1980. "The Economics of International Stockholding of Wheat." Research Report 18, International Food Policy Research Institute (IFPRI), September.

Muth, S.F. 1961. "Rational Expectations and the Theory of Price Movements." *Econometrica* 29, no. 3:315–335.

O'Brien, P.M. 1981. "Global Prospects for Agriculture." In U.S. Department of Agriculture, *Agricultural-Food Policy Review: Perspectives for the 1980's,* Economics and Statistics Service AFPR-4, April.

O'Mara, P., Knopke, P., and Roberts, I. 1981. "Costs of Japanese Agricultural Support Policies: Some Concepts and Estimates." *Quarterly Review of the Rural Economy* 3, no. 2:141–148.

Peterson, W.L. 1979. "International Farm Prices and the Social Cost of Cheap Food Policies." *American Journal of Agricultural Economics* 61:12–21.

Pinstrup-Anderson, P. 1981. "Food Policy, Household Behavior and Nutrition." Paper presented at the Fourth Biennial Meeting of the Agricultural Economics Society of Southeast Asia, Singapore, November 3–7.

Reutlinger, S., and Knapp, K. 1979. "Food Security in Food Deficit Countries: A Brief Historical Review and Probabilistic Simulations of the Effect of Trade and Stock Policies." Paper presented at the International Conference on Operations Research in Agriculture and Water Resources, Jerusalem, November 26–29.

Sampson, G.P., and Snape, R.H. 1980. "Effects of the EEC's Variable Import Levies." *Journal of Political Economy* 88, no. 5:1026–1039.

Sarris, A.H. 1980. "Grain Imports and Food Security in an Unstable International Market." *Journal of Development Economics* 7, no. 4:489–504.

Sarris, A.H., and Taylor, L. 1978. "Buffer Stock Analysis for Agricultural Products: Theoretical Murk or Empirical Resolution?" In *Stabilizing World Commodity Markets* ed. F.G. Adams and S.A. Klein. Lexington, Mass.: Lexington Books, D.C. Heath and Company.

Schmitz, A., and McCalla, A.F. 1981. "Analysis of Imperfections in International Trade: The Case of Grain Export Cartels." In *Imperfect Markets in Agricultural Trade* ed. A.F. McCalla and T.E. Josling. Montclair, N.J.: Allanheld, Osmun.

Setboonsarng, S. 1982. "Pricing Agricultural Commodities under Policy Constraints: Rice and Corn in Thailand." Ph.D. dissertation, University of Hawaii, Department of Economics, forthcoming.

Shei, S.Y., and Thompson, R.L. 1977. "The Impact of Trade Restrictions on Price Stability in the World Wheat Market." *American Journal of Agricultural Economics* 59, no. 4:628–638.

———. 1978. "The Short Run Welfare Effects of Export Controls." *Canadian Journal of Agricultural Economics* 26, no. 1:29–34.

Siamwalla, A. 1979. "Government Policies and Price Formation in the International Rice Market." *Kajian Ekonomi Malaysia* (Malaysian Economic Studies). 16, nos. 1, 2 (June/December).

Turnovsky, S.J. 1978. "The Distribution of Welfare Gains from Price Stabilization: A Survey of Some Theoretical Issues." In *Stabilizing World Commodity Markets* ed. F.G. Adams and S.A. Klein. Lexington, Mass.: Lexington Books. D.C. Heath and Company.

———. 1979. "Futures Markets, Private Storage and Price Stabilization." *Journal of Public Economics* 12:301–327.

Turnovsky, S.J., Shalit, H., and Schmitz, A. 1980. "Consumers' Surplus, Price Instability, and Consumer Welfare." *Econometrica* 48, no. 1:135–152.

Tyers, R., and Chisholm, A.H. 1980. "World Trade and Food Security in Asia and the Pacific Rim—A Multi-Commodity Stochastic Simulation Model." East-West Resource Systems Institute Working Paper WP-80-4, Honolulu, August.

———. 1981. "Food Security and Agricultural Policy in Asia and the Pacific: Applications of a Multi-Commodity Stochastic Simulation Model of World Trade in Staple Foods." Working Paper No. WP-81-19, Honolulu, Hawaii: East-West Resource Systems Institute, December.

Tyers, R., and Rachman, A. 1981. "Food Security and Consumption Diversification in Indonesia: Results from a Multi-Commodity Stochastic Simulation Model." East-West Resource Systems Institute Working Paper WP-81-1, Honolulu, June.

Valdes, A., and Zietz, J. 1980. "Agricultural Protection in OECD Countries: Its Cost to Less Developed Countries." Research Report No. 21, International Food Policy Research Institute, Washington, D.C., December.

Willig, R.D. 1976. "Consumers' Surplus Without Apology." *American Economic Review* 66, no. 4:589–597.

Zwart, A.C., and Meilke, K.D. 1979. "The Influence of Domestic Pricing Policies and Buffer Stocks on Price Stability in the World Wheat Industry." *American Journal of Agricultural Economics* 61:434–447.

Appendix 14A: Domestic and Border Prices

Table 14A–1
Domestic and Border Prices Indicating Base Year Pure Protection Levels

			Rice		Wheat		Coarse Grain		Ruminant Meat		Nonruminant Meat	
Country	*Exchange Rate, U.S. $/Local Currency*	*Price*	*Local*	*U.S. $(1970)*	*Local*	*U.S. $(1970)*	*Local*	*U.S. $(1970)*	*Local*	*U.S. $(1970)*	*Local*	*U.S. $(1970)*
Australasia	1.15/A$	International	118	136	59.8	68.9	43.4	50.0	404	465	562	647
		Border	121	139	62.4	71.9	50.5	58.2	404	465	578	666
		Wholesale	121	—	62.4	—	50.5	—	404	—	578	—
		Producer	121	—	62.4	—	50.5	—	404	—	578	—
Bangladesh	0.65/Taka	International	2092	136	1060	68.9	769	50.0	7154	465	9954	647
		Border	1831	119	1217	79.1	769	50.0	8738	568	7000	455
		Wholesale	1750	—	1217	—	769	—	8738	—	7000	—
		Producer	1750	—	1217	—	769	—	8738	—	7000	—
Canada	.941/C$	International	145	136	73.2	68.9	53.1	50.0	494	465	688	647
		Border	177	167	73.2	68.9	68.1	64.1	663	624	817	769
		Wholesale	180	—	76.0	—	68.1	—	663	—	817	—
		Producer	180	—	76.0	—	68.1	—	663	—	817	—
India	.114/rupee	International	1193	136	605	68.9	438	50.0	4079	465	5675	647
		Border	1254	143	782	89.2	327	37.3	5868	669	3110	354
		Wholesale	900	—	700	—	327	—	5868	—	3110	—
		Producer	900	—	700	—	327	—	5868	—	3110	—
Indonesia	2.41/10³ rupia	International	56.4	136	28.6	68.9	20.7	50.0	193	465	268	647
		Border	75.5	182	31.5	75.9	20.7	50.0	481	1158	330	795
		Wholesale	38.4	—	34.7	—	21.0	—	481	—	330	—
		Producer	38.4	—	34.7	—	21.0	—	481	—	330	—
Japan	3.74/10³ yen	International	36.4	136	18.4	68.9	13.4	50.0	124	465	173	647
		Border	42.2	158	21.3	79.8	16.9	63.1	184	689	329	1229
		Wholesale	142	—	67.0	—	67.0	—	1280	—	690	—
		Producer	142	—	67.0	—	67.0	—	1280	—	690	—

South Korea	2.07/10³ won	International	65.8	136	33.4	68.9	24.2	50.0	225	465	313	647
		Border	67.8	140	36.4	75.2	40.2	83.1	163	336	380	785
		Wholesale	92.5	—	40.0	—	40.2	—	650	—	536	—
		Producer	110.0	—	48.0	—	48.2	—	975	—	536	—
Malaysia	.406/ringgit	International	335	136	170	68.9	123	50.0	1145	465	1594	647
		Border	362	147	180	73.2	163	66.2	1434	582	1660	674
		Wholesale	362	—	234	—	163	—	1577	—	1660	—
		Producer	579	—	234	—	163	—	1735	—	1660	—
Pakistan	.101/rupee	International	1347	136	682	68.9	495	50.0	4604	465	6406	647
		Border	1663	168	796	80.4	495	50.0	3861	390	3651	369
		Wholesale	1003	—	580	—	495	—	3861	—	3651	—
		Producer	1003	—	580	—	495	—	3861	—	3651	—
Philippines	.135/Peso	International	1007	136	511	68.9	370	50.0	3444	465	4793	647
		Border	933	126	570	77.0	452	61.0	3667	495	2570	347
		Wholesale	840	—	570	—	452	—	3850	—	2700	—
		Producer	840	—	570	—	452	—	4235	—	3780	—
Singapore	.403/S$	International	337	136	171	68.9	124	50.0	1154	465	1605	647
		Border	320	129	177	71.3	154	62.1	1643	662	1355	546
		Wholesale	336	—	177	—	154	—	1643	—	1400	—
		Producer	—	—	—	—	—	—	—	—	1470	—
Sri Lanka	.116/rupee	International	1173	136	594	68.9	431	50.0	4009	465	5578	647
		Border	1035	120	764	88.6	431	—	3187	370	2200	255
		Wholesale	932	—	189	—	431	—	3187	—	2200	—
		Producer	1062	—	—	—	431	—	3187	—	2200	—
Thailand	.049/bhat	International	2776	136	1407	68.9	1020	50.0	9490	465	13200	647
		Border	2776	136	2265	111.0	1284	62.9	16060	787	15740	771
		Wholesale	2164	—	2265	—	1284	—	16060	—	15740	—
		Producer	2164	—	2265	—	1284	—	16060	—	15740	—
United States	1.0	International	136	136	68.9	68.9	50.0	50.0	465	465	647	647

Table 14A–1 continued

			Rice		*Wheat*		*Coarse Grain*		*Ruminant Meat*		*Nonruminant Meat*	
Country	*Exchange Rate, U.S. $/Local Currency*	*Price*	*Local*	*U.S. $(1970)*	*Local*	*U.S. $(1970)*	*Local*	*U.S. $(1970)*	*Local*	*U.S. $(1970)*	*Local*	*U.S. $(1970)*
		Border	159	159	64.4	64.4	50.0	50.0	553	553	647	647
		Wholesale	256	—	68.0	—	55.2	55.2	1078	—	647	—
		Producer	256	—	68.0	—	55.2	55.2	1078	—	647	—
European Economic Community	.204/French franc	International	667	136	338	68.9	245	50.0	2279	465	3172	647
		Border	877	179	405	82.6	308	62.8	4583	935	3804	776
		Wholesale	877	—	504	—	461	—	7712	—	4775	—
		Producer	877	—	504	—	461	—	7712	—	4775	—

Note: Domestic and international prices for the years 1975–1977 are used in the model's production and storage equations. The prices in this table are arithmetic means over these three years. International prices are based on annual average f.o.b. prices of each commodity at principal exporters: rice, Thailand; wheat, Canada; coarse grain (maize), U.S.; ruminant meat (beef), Australia; nonruminant meat (average of poultry and pork), U.S. Border prices are based on trading unit values, calculated from FAO quantity and value data. Domestic prices are estimated to deviate from border prices only to the extent of government tariffs, taxes, and subsidies.

Appendix 14B: Derivation of Linear Expressions for Economic Surplus

Consumers' Surplus

Absorbing the demand shifter, c_t, into the intercept term, k, the linearized multicommodity demand curve is given by the vector equation:

$$c = k + A\,p, \tag{A.1}$$

the inverse of which is:

$$p = A^{-1}c - A^{-1}k.$$

An expression for consumers' surplus is then obtained by integrating this expression and subtracting consumer payments.

$$S_c = \int_o^{c_t} p\,dc - c_t'\,p. \tag{A.2}$$

The first term in equation A.2 is a line integral that, as noted by Turnovsky et al. (1979), is not in general independent of the path of integration. The expression used here assumes a linear path of integration through the consumption space from the origin to c_t. Substituting A.1 and integrating:

$$S_c = \left(1/2\,c'A^{-1}c - c'A^{-1}k\right)_o^{c_t}$$

$$- \left(c_t'A^{-1}c_t - c_t'A^{-1}k\right) = -1/2\,c_t'A^{-1}c_t \tag{A.3}$$

Producers' Surplus

The *producers' surplus* is defined as the difference of total revenues and production cost. To first derive an expression for cost, it is convenient to redefine q_t so that the supply equations 14.3 and 14.4 refer to deviations from the supply shifters, $q_t{}^T$. The linearized production equations are then:

$$q_t^* = f + B\,p_{t-1} \tag{A.4}$$

$$q_t = q_{t-1} + \delta'\left(q_t^* - q_{t-1}\right) + \epsilon_t \tag{A.5}$$

We assume here that the costs incurred by producers prior to harvest are dependent on their expected production level, q_t,

where

$$\hat{q}_t = q_t - \epsilon_t$$

Production costs are then determined, based on equation A.4, as

$$C_p = \int_f^{\hat{q}_t} p\,(q^*)\,d\,q^* \tag{A.6}$$

where

$$p\,(q^*) = B^{-1}q^* - B^{-1}f$$

Thus

$$C_p = \int_f^{\hat{q}_t} \left(B^{-1}q^* - B^{-1}f\right) = d\,q^* \tag{A.7}$$

As in the case of consumers' surplus, this is a line integral not generally independent of the path of integration. Again, the expression used here assumes a linear path of integration through the production space from f to q_t.

$$C_p = \left(1/2\; q^*B^{-1}q^* - q^*B^{-1}f\right)\Big|_f^{\hat{q}_t}$$

$$= 1/2\; \hat{q}_t'B^{-1}\hat{q}_t + 1/2\, f'B^{-1}f - \hat{q}'B^{-1}f \tag{A.8}$$

Producers' surplus is then the difference of producer revenue and production cost. Note that producer revenue is based on sales of total output, including the vector of supply shifters. Hence, q_t is returned to its earlier role as total production. Since cost in this model includes only variable costs and is thus independent of supply shifters, q continues to be defined as the expected deviation of production from the supply shifters, or price-independent trends. Thus where

$$\hat{q}_t = q_t - q_t^T - \epsilon_t,$$

$$S_p = q_t'\,p_t - 1/2\; \hat{q}_t'\,B^{-1}\hat{q}_t - 1/2\, f'B^{-1}f + q'B^{-1}f \tag{A.9}$$

Index

About the Contributors

Soegeng Amat is a member of the expert staff, National Logistics Agency (BULOG), Jakarta, Indonesia.

Howarth Bouis is a postdoctoral Fellow at the International Food Policy Research Institute (IFPRI), Washington.

John A. Dixon is an economist and research associate at the East-West Environment and Policy Institute, East-West Center, Honolulu.

Neville Edirisinghe is the former general manager of the Paddy Marketing Board of Sri Lanka and is currently a doctoral candidate in the Department of Agricultural Economics, Cornell University.

Somporn Hanpongpandh is director of the ASEAN Agricultural Development Planning Center (ADPC), Bangkok.

Robert W. Herdt is an agricultural economist with the International Rice Research Institute (IRRI), Los Baños, Philippines.

Ralph G. Lattimore is a senior analyst with the International Trade Policy Division, Agriculture Canada, Ottawa.

Shlomo Reutlinger is a senior economist at the World Bank, Washington.

James Roumasset is an associate professor of economics, University of Hawaii, and a research associate, East-West Resource Systems Institute, East-West Center, Honolulu.

Alexander H. Sarris is an assistant professor of agricultural and resource economics at the University of California, Berkeley.

Saburo Yamada is professor of agricultural economics at the Institute of Oriental Culture, University of Tokyo.

About the Editors

Anthony H. Chisholm is currently acting chairman of the Department of Economics, The Faculties, Australian National University. He participated in the Working Group Meeting on Food Security held at the East-West Resource Systems Institute, East-West Center in 1979 and was a visiting Fellow at the institute during 1980. He received the Ph.D. in economics from the Australian National University in 1976.

Rodney Tyers is a research Fellow, Research School of Pacific Studies, Australian National University, and adjunct research associate, East-West Resource Systems Institute, Honolulu. He was a research associate at the East-West Resource Systems Institute from 1978 through 1981 where he coordinated the research program on food security within the institute's Food Systems Project. He received the Ph.D. in systems engineering from the Division of Applied Science at Harvard University in 1978.